THE NEW C

(NEW

General Editor: THE REVD. H. F. D. SPARKS, D.D., F.B.A.

THE GOSPEL ACCORDING TO LUKE

THE GOSPEL ACCORDING TO
LUKE

IN THE
REVISED STANDARD VERSION

With introduction and commentary

by

G. H. P. THOMPSON
FORMERLY VICE-PRINCIPAL
SALISBURY THEOLOGICAL COLLEGE

OXFORD
AT THE CLARENDON PRESS
1972

Oxford University Press, Ely House, London W.1
GLASGOW NEW YORK TORONTO MELBOURNE WELLINGTON
CAPE TOWN IBADAN NAIROBI DAR ES SALAAM LUSAKA ADDIS ABABA
DELHI BOMBAY CALCUTTA MADRAS KARACHI LAHORE DACCA
KUALA LUMPUR SINGAPORE HONG KONG TOKYO

PRINTED IN GREAT BRITAIN
AT THE UNIVERSITY PRESS, OXFORD
BY VIVIAN RIDLER
PRINTER TO THE UNIVERSITY

OXFORD UNIVERSITY PRESS

EDUCATION DEPARTMENT

Please mark
all correspondence
'Education Department'

Walton Street
Oxford OX2 6DP
Telephone: OXFORD 57457/8

We should like to emphasise that the enclosed is/are being sent with our compliments.

We would however greatly appreciate any comments on the post-paid card.

OXFORD UNIVERSITY PRESS

GENERAL EDITOR'S PREFACE

LIKE its predecessor, the New Clarendon Bible (New Testament) sets out to provide concise but scholarly commentaries on individual books of the New Testament in English suitable for candidates taking G.C.E. 'A' level, students in universities and colleges of education, and others who need something less ambitious than the full-scale 'academic' commentary.

In the old series the English text used as the basis of the commentaries was the Revised Version. At the time the old series was projected the choice could hardly have been otherwise. But now, when there are so many newer English versions available, the problem is more difficult. After taking what seemed the best advice the publishers have chosen the American Revised Standard Version for the new series, believing that this is the version which in the foreseeable future is most likely to be found suitable for examination purposes in schools and colleges; they hope also that the publication of a Catholic edition of RSV, which differs only slightly from the original, will enable commentaries based on the RSV to be more generally useful. And they wish to express their gratitude to the National Council of Churches of Christ in the United States of America for the permission, so readily given, to make use of the RSV in this way.

The design of the new series follows that of the old, except that it has been thought more practical to print both text and notes on the same page. Subjects requiring more comprehensive treatment than the scope of the notes allows will be found as before in the Introductions and in appendices at the end of the volumes.

GENERAL EDITOR'S PREFACE

CONTENTS

AUTHOR'S NOTE

STUDIES in Luke, especially in recent years, have been extensive, and in writing a book of this kind I am indebted to the stimulus provided by the thought of many scholars. A word may be said about the use of the book. It will be helpful to read the Commentary on the text in the light of the Introduction, where many of Luke's themes, interests, and terminology are discussed. The use of a synopsis, setting out the parallels between the Four Gospels, will be found useful. Reference back, to the original place where a particular term has been explained and discussed, has not usually been made, but a careful use of the Index is assumed. It will be appreciated that detailed argument of every point made has not been possible, but an attempt has been made to clarify this Gospel in its original setting, in the course of which it is hoped that its message for today may also become clear.

I have benefited from the most helpful advice of the Reverend Dr. H. F. D. Sparks, the General Editor of the Series, to whom my very grateful thanks are due for the time that he has spared me.

G. H. P. T.

ABBREVIATIONS

AV	The Authorized Version
LXX	Septuagint: the Greek Version of the Old Testament
NEB	New English Bible
N.T.	New Testament
O.T.	Old Testament
RSV	Revised Standard Version

LITERATURE ON THE GOSPEL OF LUKE

(A) COMMENTARIES

On the Greek Text:

A. PLUMMER, *St. Luke* (1896)

J. M. CREED, *The Gospel according to St. Luke* (1930)

On the English Text:

W. MANSON, *The Gospel of Luke* (1930)

N. GELDENHUYS, *Commentary on the Gospel of Luke* (1951)

A. R. C. LEANEY, *St. Luke* (1958)

G. B. CAIRD, *Saint Luke* (1963)

E. J. TINSLEY, *The Gospel according to Luke* (1965)

E. EARLE ELLIS, *The Gospel of Luke* (1966)

Also, in French or German:

A. SCHLATTER, *Das Evangelium des Lukas* (1931)

K. H. RENGSTORF, *Das Evangelium nach Lukas* (1949)

M. J. LAGRANGE, *L'Évangile selon S. Luc* (1947)

(B) OTHER STUDIES IN LUKE

VINCENT TAYLOR, *Behind the Third Gospel* (1926)

H. CONZELMANN, *The Theology of Saint Luke* (1960)

C. K. BARRETT, *Luke the Historian in Recent Study* (1961)

C. S. C. WILLIAMS, 'Luke–Acts in Recent Study', in *The Expository Times*, lxiii (1961–2), pp. 133–6

H. FLENDER, *St. Luke: Theologian of Redemptive History* (1967)

L. E. KECK and J. L. MARTYN (Eds.), *Studies in Luke–Acts* (1968)

V. WILKINSON, *The Centre of History* (1967)

I. H. MARSHALL, 'St. Luke in Recent Study', in *The Expository Times*, lxxx (1968–9), pp. 4–8

Also, in German:

R. Morgenthaler, *Die lukanische Geschichtsschreibung als Zeugnis* (1949)

Synopses of the Gospels:

The following, giving the text of the Gospels in parallel columns, are suggested:

K. Aland, *Synopsis Quattuor Evangeliorum* (1964)

A. Huck, *Synopsis of the First Three Gospels*, ed. F. L. Cross (1936)

H. F. D. Sparks, *A Synopsis of the Gospels* (1964)

B. H. Throckmorton, *Gospel Parallels* (1961)

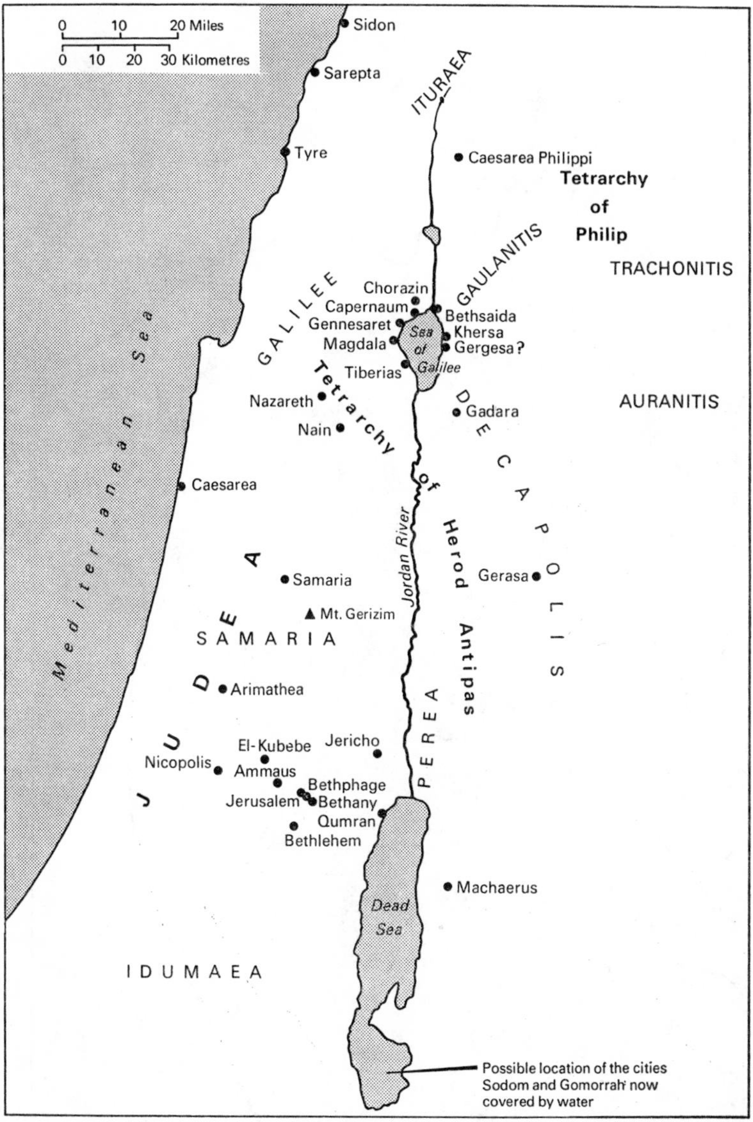
0 10 20 Miles
0 10 20 30 Kilometres
Sidon
Sarepta
Tyre
ITURAEA
Caesarea Philippi
Tetrarchy of Philip
TRACHONITIS
GAULANITIS
Chorazin
Capernaum
Gennesaret
Magdala
Bethsaida
Khersa
Gergesa?
Sea of Galilee
Tiberias
GALILEE
Tetrarchy of Herod Antipas
Nazareth
Nain
Gadara
AURANITIS
DECAPOLIS
Mediterranean Sea
Caesarea
Jordan River
Samaria
Gerasa
Mt. Gerizim
SAMARIA
JUDEA
Arimathea
PEREA
El-Kubebe
Jericho
Nicopolis
Ammaus
Bethphage
Jerusalem
Bethany
Qumran
Bethlehem
Machaerus
Dead Sea
IDUMAEA
Possible location of the cities Sodom and Gomorrah now covered by water

MAP OF PALESTINE

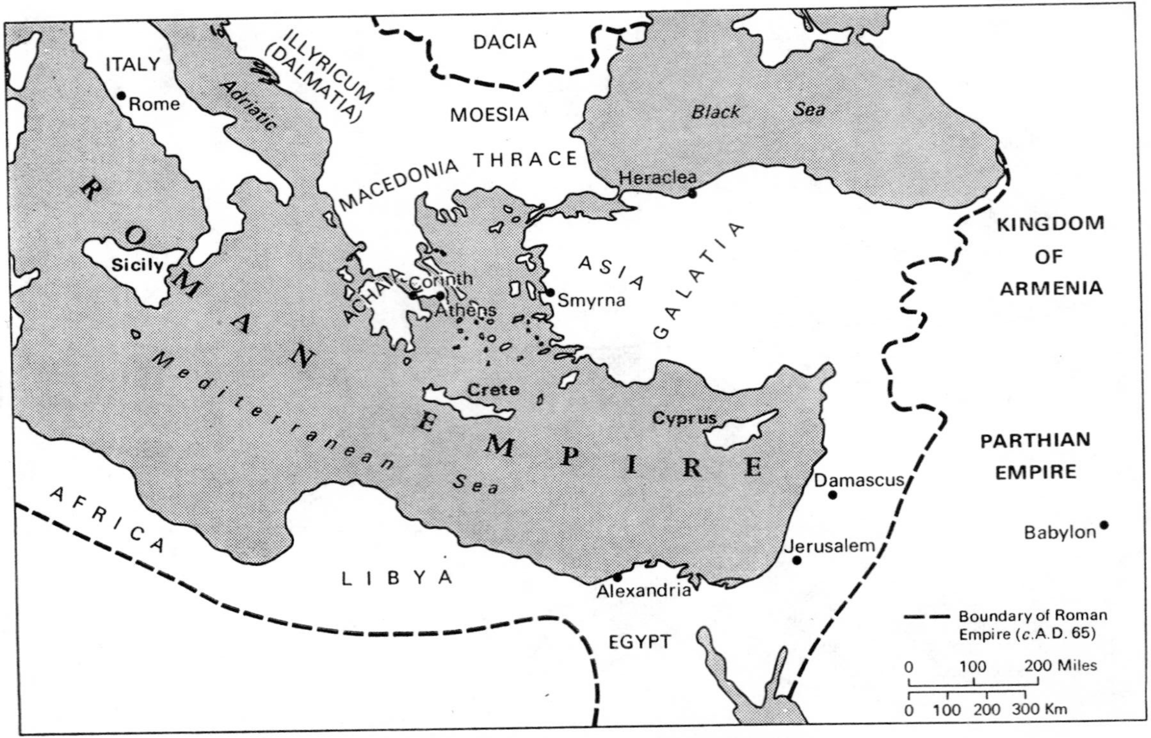

MAP OF THE ROMAN WORLD

DIVISIONS OF HEROD'S TEMPLE

(*reconstruction according to the data of Josephus and the Mishnah*)

1 Holy of Holies
2 Sacrificial Altar
3 Nicanor's Gate
4 Womens Court
5 Corinthian Gate
6 Treasury
7 Separation wall between Jews and Gentiles
8 Court of the Gentiles
9 Royal porch
10 Solomon's portico
11 Golden Gate
12 Underground entrances from the south
13 Antonia Fortress

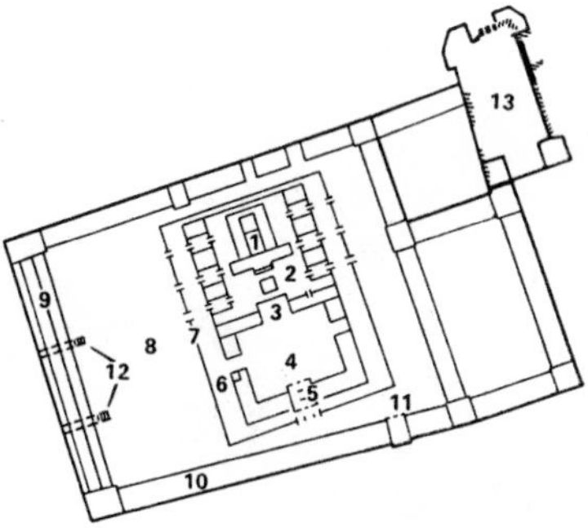

PLAN OF THE TEMPLE OF JERUSALEM

INTRODUCTION

THE GOSPEL OF LUKE AND THE ACTS OF THE APOSTLES

IN the Canon of Scripture as we have it today the Gospel of Luke and the Acts of the Apostles are separated from each other, and this arrangement goes back to an early date. It arose from a desire to associate this Gospel with those of Matthew, Mark, and John to form the four books, giving a statement of the true Gospel or 'good news' brought to men in Jesus. The Muratorian Canon (an early short commentary on the books of the New Testament, written about A.D. 180) speaks of 'the third book of the Gospel, according to Luke'. Its similarities with Matthew and Mark ensured that it was placed in close proximity to them. Luke's Gospel and Acts were, however, planned originally as two parts of a single work:

(*a*) The opening sections of each link them closely together. Luke 1^{1-4} and Acts 1^{1-5} are 'prefaces', and each mentions Theophilus, to whom the whole work is dedicated. In his use of prefaces the author is following the convention of his day. Writers of this period divided their works into volumes or parts (called λόγοι or 'books', cp. Acts 1^{1}, 'In the first book . . .'). At the beginning a main preface (προοίμιον) would cover the whole work and explain its scope and range, while each succeeding volume might begin with a 'subsidiary' preface, consisting of a summary of the preceding book and giving a short account of the volume to follow. Such a 'subsidiary' preface would often consist of two clauses, the first, introduced by 'on the one hand' (μέν) and looking back to the previous volume, the second introduced by 'on the other hand' (δέ) and looking forward to what was to follow. The Preface to Luke's Gospel is therefore a general one covering the whole work, while that in Acts 1^{1} is a subsidiary one looking back to the previous volume. The extraordinary features of this 'subsidiary preface' are: (i) the 'on the one hand' clause (present in the Greek but not brought out in the RSV) is not balanced by another clause beginning with 'on the other hand', i.e. there is no summary of the contents of the book that follows; and (ii) the concluding part of the Gospel is summarized and elaborated to prepare for what follows. A certain elasticity about prefaces was expected from authors (Lucian, second century A.D., *How to Write History*, 52–5), and the subject-matter of the succeeding volume can be easily inferred from Acts $1^{5, 8}$. In any case, the use of the 'preface' and the 'subsidiary preface' links the Gospel and Acts together.

(*b*) The two volumes appear to be constructed on parallel lines. Each opens with a section that centres on Jerusalem and the temple, with prominence given to the Holy Spirit (Luke 1^{5}–4^{13}; Acts 1^{1}–7^{60}). Similarly, the final section of the Gospel (19^{28}–24^{53}), with its themes of Jerusalem, the temple, the activity of Jesus there, and the hearing of his case by Pilate and Herod, has its counterpart in Acts 21^{15}–26^{32}, where Paul's visit to Jerusalem is described, together with its consequences, and where the city, the temple, and the various hearings of Paul's case before Roman governors and Herod Agrippa are prominent. These and other parallels suggest that the two works were planned to form a unity from the start.

THE AUTHOR

1. *The use of Luke–Acts as an authoritative document in the second century* A.D.

Ignatius (Bishop of Antioch, whose letters are dated A.D. 97–117) may have known both volumes, the casual way in which the allusions occur being all the more impressive. In *Smyrnaeans*, iii. 1–3, he quotes words of the risen Jesus, 'Take, handle me and see that I am not a phantom without a body', and records that 'he ate and drank with them as a being of flesh', probably reminiscent of Luke 24^{39} and Acts 10^{40-41}. The unusual expression 'each is to go to his own place' (*Magnesians*, v. 1) can be traced to Acts 1^{25} ('place' qualified by 'his own' is highly unusual). *2 Clement* (about A.D. 130) seems to use the Gospel as a source for Jesus' teaching. In vi. 1, 'No servant can serve two masters' approximates to Luke 16^{13} (Matthew 6^{24} omits 'servant'), and in viii. 5 '. . . he who is faithful in that which is least is faithful also in that which is much' is identical with

Luke 16^{10}. The teaching on love (xiii. 4) is probably influenced by Luke 6^{27-36}, and here and in the previous example the author may well be paraphrasing sayings of Jesus that he knows from Luke.

Polycarp's only surviving work, the letter to the Philippians, is composite, Chapters xiii and xiv dating from the period of Bishop Ignatius' death (perhaps A.D. 108), and Chapters i–xii from a later time (about A.D. 135). He knows 'the scriptures', which include authoritative Christian writings (xii. 1), and almost certainly Luke–Acts. The unusual 'having loosed the pangs of Hades' (i. 2) is probably derived from Acts 2^{24}; it is characteristic of Polycarp to make quotations from documents familiar to him. 'The judge of the living and of the dead' (ii. 1) could be taken from Acts 10^{42}, but the dependence of ii. 3 ('with what measure you mete it shall be measured to you again') on Luke 6^{38} is even more certain, in each the rare compound verb *ἀντιμετρηθήσεται* being used (contrast Matt. 7^{2}).

Justin, the Apologist (A.D. 150–60), quotes from the Gospel of Luke. For example, he cites 10^{19} and 23^{46} (*Dialogue with Trypho*, 302A and 333B), and quite clearly includes the Gospel among writings authoritative for the Christian faith. This writing, which the evidence suggests had had an influential position in the Church's life for many years, is now becoming one of the Four Gospels, accepted as definitive for Jesus' teaching and work.

2. *The lack of mention of Luke the physician as the author of Luke–Acts in the period A.D. 100–50*

Nowhere in the above writings is Luke, the physician (Col. 4^{14}; 2 Tim. 4^{11}), connected with quotation from the Gospel or allusion to it, which might suggest that it was not attributed to him in this period. But a feature of these authors is that they make hardly any direct reference to the written sources on which they are dependent. For example, citations of Jesus' sayings are introduced by such expressions as 'And the Lord says' (*2 Clement*, vi. 11), 'God says' (*2 Clement*, xiii. 4), 'Jesus said' (Justin, *Dialogue with Trypho*, 333B), and 'It is written' (Justin, *Dial.*, 49A). Justin quotes Gospel passages, without naming the particular Gospel, and similarly Polycarp is influenced by 1 Peter and incorporates parts of it into his text (e.g. i. 3; ii. 1–2; viii. 1; x. 2) without any acknowledgement. The same applies to the author of *1 Clement* (A.D. 96), who quotes Hebrews (xxxvi. 2–3), and to Ignatius, who uses Matthew (e.g. *Smyrnaeans*, i. 1). Quotations occur from Paul's letters, too, without the source being mentioned. The lack of reference, therefore, to Luke as the author in the period A.D. 100–50 is not significant, as these early Christian writers are only interested in their quotations as containing the words of God, or Jesus, or the Gospel, and so keep the human author in the background (similarly in citing the O.T. the particular book is not normally mentioned).

3. *The tradition that Luke is the author of Luke–Acts is firmly established by the time of Irenaeus, Bishop of Lyons (about A.D. 178 onwards), and Tertullian of Carthage (writing about A.D. 200), and becomes important in the controversies with Gnostics and Marcion*

Irenaeus (*Against Heresies*, III. xiv) argues that Luke, just as much as Paul, knew the truth, as he was 'inseparable' from Paul, and he demonstrates this last statement by reference to the passages in Acts where 'we' is used, to Col. 4^{14}, and to 2 Tim. 4^{11}: it is not legitimate to accept as true some of the things said by Luke, but to reject certain others, as if he had not known the truth. The Lucan authorship of the Gospel and Acts is firmly established: both sides in the argument accept it, and Irenaeus can start from this common ground. Tertullian (*Against Marcion*, IV. ii) attacks Marcion for basing his gospel on Luke alone, and on a mutilated version of it: Luke was 'not an apostle but a follower of the apostles, not a master but a disciple'; his Gospel therefore needs the support of others with 'our faith . . . based on John and Matthew', and 'built up on Luke and Mark, followers of the apostles'. Again, Lucan authorship is accepted by both Tertullian and his opponents, with the important implication that Marcion strongly held this view; hence Tertullian's attempt to reduce the Lucan writings to their proper perspective.

4. *Marcion and Lucan authorship*

The dividing line in the career of Marcion of Sinope was his separation from the Church Catholic in A.D. 144 and the founding of his own fraternity. But before this he had been a centre of controversy, and many of his views, about which we learn from Tertullian, Irenaeus, and others, had probably been propagated and held well before A.D. 144. For his restoration of 'the genuine and true gospel' he used the Gospel of Luke in addition to the Pauline letters. Marcion's aim is to reconstruct the Christian message as preached by Paul; hence his preference for our Gospel, to which he almost certainly attaches importance as coming from Luke, a companion of Paul. The implication is that the tradition of Lucan authorship is well established before Marcion's formulation of his theories, going back to the early part of the second century A.D.

5. *The tradition of Lucan authorship arose at a time when the authority of the Gospels was not linked with the identity and status of the particular author*

Only in the later part of the second century, when the Church's theologians, such as Irenaeus and Tertullian, had to reply to Marcion and the Gnostics, was the authority of the Gospels traced to their being written by 'apostolic men' or by those connected with apostles. Luke–Acts in the period A.D. 100–50 was regarded as the work of Luke, the physician, more probably because of a firm tradition to this effect than because of a desire to attribute the writing to him as a known companion of the Apostle, Paul. If the two books were originally anonymous, or the author's name was lost, why was a comparatively little-known person like Luke chosen to supply the deficiency? The use of 'we' in certain passages of Acts (e.g. 16^{10}) would suggest that the writer had been an associate of Paul, but there were other trusted companions available and yet overlooked, e.g. Titus, who is never mentioned in Acts, and might have been a better choice. There are also the following considerations:

(*a*) Much of the information about Luke given in Christian writers from the second century onwards is certainly deduced from Luke–Acts. But this does not lead to the conclusion that he was originally chosen as the author by a similar deduction assisted by evidence from the Pauline Letters. The idea that such deductions would have reached an identical conclusion is fanciful.

(*b*) Luke is sometimes thought to have been singled out as the author by a process of elimination from other companions of Paul, one of the presuppositions being that the writer must have been present at all that he describes (cp. the Muratorian Canon: 'Luke compiled what things were done in detail in his presence'), including the imprisonment of Paul described at the end of Acts. Of all the possible candidates, i.e. Mark, Luke, Aristarchus, Epaphras, Jesus Justus, and Titus, only Luke was thought to fulfil the requirement, in view of 2 Tim. 4^{11} ('Luke alone is with me'), which may have been interpreted to refer to the imprisonment of Acts 28. But in the first place the question arises: who worked out the process of elimination? Presumably it would be some of the leading thinkers of the Church, and it is surprising that they all arrived at the same result. Secondly, would the assumption that the author must have been present all through Paul's imprisonment have been so strong that the whole two-year imprisonment had to be included in what was done 'in his presence'? Thirdly, is it so clear that the statement in 2 Timothy would have been taken as a reference to this imprisonment of Paul? The Muratorian Canon speaks of his departure from the city of Rome after his imprisonment there (Acts 28), and mentions his journey to Spain, with the implication that a second imprisonment was known. Fourthly, would the supposition or obsession that the author must have been present with Paul during his imprisonment have outweighed the desire or temptation to attribute the work to someone more prominent than Luke? It is also worth noting that this interest in the writer's being present at what he describes is closely related to a wish to connect the Gospels with apostles or their associates, and, as already seen, pp. 4–5, the tradition of Lucan authorship predates this interest.

(*c*) The supposed serious discrepancies between Luke–Acts and the letters of Paul have also been raised as objections against the author's being a companion of Paul. But, in the face of a strong tradition in favour of Lucan authorship, the question may not be: How can a companion of Paul possibly have written an account so divergent from that of Paul?, but rather: What may have led a companion of Paul to present us with a divergent viewpoint (if in fact he has done so)? The supposed contradictions between the Pauline letters and Luke–

Acts cannot be discussed fully here. But in the present writer's view they are not so real as is sometimes imagined, and have been exaggerated (see also C. S. C. Williams, *A Commentary on the Acts of the Apostles*, pp. 22–30). Most of the apparent differences are due to the fact that Paul and Luke are writing from different perspectives and viewpoints, from different situations within the Church, and at different dates.

6. *The supposed medical interests of Luke–Acts as a pointer to its author's being a physician*

(i) Language. The use of medical terms has been seen to suggest the writer's medical background. The effectiveness of such an argument would depend on showing that the terminology could *only* be used by a professional medical man, and the evidence falls far short of this. Some of the supposed medical terms turn out not to be so, and some that have medical connections would not be confined to medical men: e.g., 'was ill' (*σονέχομαι*, 4^{38}) is not a technical term; 'freed' (*ἀπολύω*, 13^{12}) is used of release from illness in non-medical writers; and the same applies to such terms as 'who had dropsy' (*ὑδρωπικός*, 14^{2}), and 'half-dead' (*ἡμιθανής*, 10^{30}). (ii) The interest in Jesus' works of healing. The attention given in the Gospel to the healing of disease has been urged in favour of the author's being a doctor. But the preference for such incidents is no greater than in the other Gospels, and the interest in them is the same, i.e. to show the presence of God's new era and kingdom.

7. *Conclusion*

While the arguments under 6 are inconclusive, the points made under 3, 4, and 5 must be given due weight, and the tradition of Lucan authorship of the Gospel and Acts is not lightly to be set aside.

THE DATE OF LUKE–ACTS

1. *The evidence for a date after* A.D. *93*

While a date about A.D. 150 is discounted by the evidence already considered, Luke is sometimes thought to be dependent on the Jewish historian, Josephus, whose *Antiquities of the Jews* was published in A.D. 93. At certain points he is supposed to have misread this work of Josephus, and so to have been guilty of certain errors (e.g. at Acts 5^{35-37}). But it should not be too readily assumed that Luke would have used Josephus in so careless and naïve a way as to make blunders of this kind. The dependence on Josephus is by no means proved, nor is it accepte by many scholars.

2. *The evidence for a date after* A.D. *70 (the date of Jerusalem's capture by the Romans)*

(*a*) The argument from passages predicting this event: see Luke 19^{42-43} (only found in Luke); 21^{20} (cp. and contrast Mark 13^{14}: instead of 'the desolating sacrilege set up where it ought not to be', Luke has the more explicit 'Jerusalem surrounded by armies'); 23^{28} (found only in Luke). The vividness and definiteness of the language in these passages are supposed to betray that the siege and capture of Jerusalem are events of the past; Luke, it is argued, has made Mark's language more explicit in the light of experience. But, in the first place, Luke could well have altered Mark 13^{14} to clarify it for some of his readers (but see below, p. 249). Secondly, the language is not necessarily coloured by the events of A.D. 70, but rather reflects O.T. descriptions of God's coming judgement on Jerusalem (see the Commentary). Thirdly, such predictions of the city's downfall may very well come from Jesus himself. Fourthly, if Luke knew that these predictions had been fulfilled, he might be expected to have pointed it out (cp. Acts 11^{28}).

(*b*) In Acts 20^{18} Paul expresses his conviction of never seeing the Ephesian elders again. If this speech is the author's free composition, as is sometimes supposed, it may reflect his awareness that Paul has been dead for some time, and that he never did return to Ephesus. Then a date after A.D. 70 would appear plausible. On the other hand, the speech may reflect premonitions of Paul himself.

(*c*) Appeal might also be made to the impression that Luke–Acts gives of being the work of one who has had time to sit back and review the broad sweep of the development of the early Church, and assess its significance; for example, the journey of Paul to Jerusalem (Acts 20–21) and its sequel to Rome (Acts 27–28) are seen as part of God's purpose, by which Paul is able to preach the Gospel in Rome and cement the Church there.

But this vision of a Church spreading over the world and of the invincibility of the Gospel against all obstacles is already reflected in Col. 1^{6}, and almost certainly in Rom. 10^{18}, passages that date to A.D. 55–61. Again, the providential nature of Paul's journey to Rome (A.D. 59–61) may have been discerned very shortly after the event, and such a viewpoint may be traced to Paul's own attitude expressed in Phil. 1^{12-14} (probably referring to his Roman imprisonment of Acts 28).

(*d*) As will be seen later (below, pp. 20–1), Luke is interested in interpreting the person of Jesus as the new temple of God. At first sight this might appear to be a very relevant theme after A.D. 70, when the Jewish temple had been destroyed: even if this shattering event has taken place, yet the true and vital temple, Jesus, remains. On the other hand, this interpretation of Jesus' person was almost certainly part of early Christian apologetic before A.D. 70, as is reflected in the view of the Church as the temple of God (e.g. 1 Cor. 3^{17}; Eph. 2^{21}).

3. *The evidence for a date in the period A.D. 60–5*

The ending of Acts would suggest that Luke takes his account of the early progress of the Church up to the time that he is writing, and that he knows of no event after the two years of Paul's imprisonment in Rome. There is no evidence that Luke planned or wrote a third volume containing an account of subsequent events. A date in this period raises the problem of Luke's dependence on Mark, since he incorporates sections of this Gospel into his general scheme. Mark would then have to be placed before A.D. 64–5 (the date commonly attributed to it), which could well be the case. It is generally thought likely that Mark is using material about Jesus that had been in use in the Roman Church, before it was finally given shape in his Gospel about A.D. 65, and this material could have come to Luke's notice during his stay with Paul in Rome. The theory that Luke–Acts was published, or perhaps planned, without its Marcan sections is neither probable nor demanded by the evidence (see below, p. 19). On the other hand, the conclusion of Acts may not be determined by the time at which Luke is writing, but by another motive, namely the presentation of his theme—'nothing prevents the onward march of the Church': the Church is at first a small impotent group in Jerusalem, but is finally rooted firmly in the Roman capital itself. If, however, part of Luke's aim is to demonstrate that the Christian Church presents no threat to Roman law and order, then it would be strange that he could write after the Neronian persecution, in which Paul was probably put to death, and yet not refer to these events. One would expect him to vindicate the position of Paul and the other Christians in the face of Nero's action, just as in his account of Jesus' condemnation to death the injustice of this act is underlined. If Acts dates from later than A.D. 65, it is very odd that Luke leaves Paul in prison without recording subsequent events. It is not sufficient to say that his readers or hearers would know the rest of the story, especially if the audience consisted of non-committed Christians.

4. *Summary*

While it is very difficult to reach a definite conclusion about dating, there is a firm consensus of opinion amongst scholars that Luke–Acts belongs to the first century A.D. and not the second. If the reasons for a date after A.D. 70 are not considered entirely convincing, then serious consideration may have to be given to a date before the death of Paul (*c.* A.D. 65).

THE PURPOSE OF LUKE–ACTS

'Purpose' is a vague term and can be applied to Luke–Acts in various ways. Luke's *general* purpose is made clear in his opening Preface (Luke 1^{1-4}): 'to write an orderly account' concerning 'the things that have been accomplished among us', which probably refers to the fulfilment of God's plans in the mission of Jesus, and in the preaching and spread of the 'good news' of that mission in the wider world. In Volume 1, therefore, Luke shows how through the coming of John the Baptist, and particularly of Jesus, a further stage is reached in God's dealings with Israel, with its sequel in the emergence of the Christian Church; while in Volume 2 the growth of that Church is described. Like Mark (e.g. 1^{1}), Luke, views the coming of Jesus as 'the good news of God's salvation' (εὐαγγέλιον), and for this purpose he, again like Mark, uses material from the life and teaching of Jesus, which illuminates this theme. But within this wider framework he wishes to present Jesus (see below, pp. 20–33) more specifically as the expected Messiah or King of the Jews (which must have been an important part of Christian apologetics from the start), as the new temple, and as the author of a new and vital rescue operation with significance for the whole world. Similarly in Acts, while Luke's theme is the proclamation of the good news by the Church, and the Church's progress further afield outside Palestine, he obviously does not record *all* the missionary activity that took place, but pinpoints some of the highlights, centring mainly on the careers of Peter and Paul, and taking a broad sweep over events, to show how after its small beginnings in Jerusalem the gospel is finally being proclaimed by Paul in the heart and capital of the Roman Empire. A careful selection of events and episodes is made to play on the theme: against all the odds, the Church in the power of the Holy Ghost makes headway, a sign of its God-given origin (see Acts 5^{38-39}).

Both volumes display their special interests, and one to be traced in both is Luke's desire to show that neither in origin nor subsequent history is Christianity a movement guilty of insurrection against Rome or of disturbing the Roman peace. In the eyes of the outside observer the early Christians were followers of a condemned criminal, sentenced on a charge of treason by a Roman governor, Pontius Pilate. For this reason Luke lays emphasis on Jesus' innocence of the charge against him (e.g. in $23^{4, 14, 22}$ Pilate's three-times-expressed belief in Jesus' innocence; in 23^{15} the similar judgement of Herod Antipas; in 23^{20} Pilate's desire to release Jesus; and in 23^{47} the centurion's declaration). Luke's careful clarification of Jesus' kingship and its nature may also partly be connected with this same apologetical interest. The theme that Christianity is no menace to Roman law and order is also prominent in Acts (e.g. 18^{12-17}, 23^{29}, 25^{25}, 26^{31-32}, 28^{31}). On the other hand, the responsibility both for the execution of Jesus and for the disturbances that occur in Acts is attributed to the Jews and their obtuseness towards God's plans. These emphases do not mean that Luke–Acts is the brief for Paul's defence before the Imperial court, as has sometimes been suggested, yet Luke can plausibly be said to be writing a defence of Christianity. This includes not only a defence against the charge of being an insurrectory force, but also the broader aim of presenting the Christian faith as soundly based on good evidence, and as showing an inherent power that is God-given.

But 'purpose' also raises the question: to what audience and in what situation was Luke's work written? The following points need to be borne in mind:

(*a*) The name 'Theophilus', to whom the work is dedicated, could be held by a Jew or a Gentile, and so gives no clue as to the audience that Luke has in mind.

(*b*) The internal evidence would suggest that the book is intended for those who are full members of the Jewish religion, or for those, such as the so-called 'God-fearers' (e.g. Acts 13^{43}, RSV, 'devout converts to Judaism'), who are conversant with Jewish ideas and thought, and have adopted some Jewish beliefs and practices, including attendance at the synagogue. First, Luke assumes the knowledge of O.T. terminology and theological ways of thinking, and expects that his readers will be instructed in them, so that an appeal to 'the scriptures' will be understood. Second, the categories that he uses to present Jesus are those familiar to Jews, e.g. 'the Messiah', 'the temple', a 'salvation' or 'rescue operation' in history, 'Exodus'. Third, a familiarity with more recent Jewish history is taken for granted (e.g. some knowledge of the various kings of the line of Herod).

(*c*) Perhaps the background to Luke–Acts also receives illumination from the comment of the Jewish elders in Rome (Acts 28^{22}): 'But we desire to hear from you what your views are; for with regard to this sect we know that everywhere it is spoken against.' It is a plausible claim that Luke wrote for an audience of this kind to supply information about this new 'sect', to sweeten the evil odour in which it was held and correct misunderstandings about its teachings, and to make the Jews, especially those of the Dispersion, think again: Had not God given clear signs that in Jesus he was making a more perfect revelation of himself and his plans? Did not the victorious advance of the Church indicate the truth of its message and fulfil the criterion of Gamaliel, the Jewish Rabbi (Acts 5^{38-39}: '. . . for if this plan or this undertaking is of men, it will fail; but if it is of God, you will not be able to overthrow them. You might even be found opposing God')? Was not the attraction of the Gentiles to the Christian Church (a prominent theme in Acts) a sign that it was fulfilling Israel's role of being a 'light to the Gentiles', and satisfying the hope of winning them to the one true and living God—a hope dear to many of the Jews of the Dispersion? In addition to these challenges, the picture of Jesus as a king, but one who does not conform to the pattern of a nationalist and political revolutionary, would appeal to Jews of the Dispersion, who were probably not too sympathetic towards the nationalist ambitions of some of their fellow Jews of Palestine. The Jews outside Palestine, living in the great centres of the Roman world, appreciated the law and order created by the Roman peace; hence Luke's assurance that the Church and her leaders are not political incendiaries, and that breaches of the peace can often be laid at the door not of the Christians, but of certain misguided Jews.

(*d*) Luke–Acts may therefore be a contribution to the dialogue between Jews and Christians in which Luke had seen Paul so often engaged; it asks the Jews to consider whether they are in danger of fulfilling the prophecy of Isa. 6^{9-10} and proving obdurate to God's will (Luke 8^{10}; Acts 28^{26-27}). Luke also has an eye on Jewish sympathizers, brought up in a Gentile background where religious and philosophical thought was at this time very much concerned with the desire to be free from the shackles of the various fears that fettered human life; hence the relevance of Luke's theme of 'deliverance' and of his picture of Jesus as the 'free' man, dominated only by his trust in God. Luke hopes to include cultured people among his readers, as his literary presentation of his work makes clear, and may have intended that his writing should find its way into the libraries of the well-to-do, or that it should be read to interested audiences and should form the basis of discussion (cp. the practice of ancient historians, who read their works aloud to an invited audience; see Lucian, *How to Write History*, 5). Luke is not in the first instance writing for those who are committed to, and have been initiated into, the Christian faith, but for those who are interested in it or have received information about it (see note on 1^4); Luke is going to fan that interest and supplement that information.

LUKE AND LUCIAN'S CRITERIA FOR WRITING HISTORY

In his essay, *How to Write History*, Lucian criticizes contemporary historians and lays down certain rules for good history-writing. He is writing (*c.* A.D. 170) later than Luke, but supplies criteria which enable us to judge the kind of tests that Luke would have had to face, as a historian, from educated people of his day; and even if in part he has an eye on a Jewish audience, this is not incompatible with Luke's further desire to produce a work that satisfies the man of culture.

First, Lucian stresses that history is not a bare catalogue or diary of events, and that due weight should be given to what is important and interesting, and contributes to the main theme. Luke lives up to this criterion by giving no complete biography of Jesus, but by selecting events from the life of Jesus, and relevant parts of his teaching, to bring out his significance in God's plans; similarly in Acts he does not give a complete account of the early Church, but chooses material that illustrates the progress of the Church. Further, Lucian's main yardstick for historians is that of truth and an impartiality that avoids a bias due to fear, hatred, or attempt at gratification. Luke's attitude is similar (he records, for example, what will give offence to Jews). He aims at truth (1^4), which for him does not mean standing completely aloof and refusing to interpret what he describes; rather it means giving the interpretation that seems to be demanded by the evidence of eyewitnesses and the extraordinary nature of the events. In line with Lucian's demand for painstaking investigation and for first-hand knowledge of his subject, Luke is clearly writing as an involved member of the Church, who claims to 'have followed all things closely' and to have been a companion of the Apostle Paul. Lucian also gives an importance to the arrangement of material, for by it events are illuminated. Luke's fulfilment of this criterion is seen in his careful arrangement and construction of his Gospel, by which he lays stress on the final events in Jerusalem, and in his interweaving of events of a similar kind and ordering of sections according to topics and theme. Lucian's attack on long pretentious 'prefaces' does not apply to Luke, who states his aim in one well-constructed sentence (1^{1-4}). He also cannot be said to fall into the danger, mentioned by Lucian, of neglecting events to indulge in panegyric of leaders, and in flattery. Luke's concentration on Jesus is very much related to the fact that it is he who controls the events and makes the history, and while Jesus is the centre of praise and thanksgiving to God, and of his own devotion, Luke would feel that panegyric was quite out of place, as Jesus' grandeur stands out sufficiently in the recital of his ministry, death, and resurrection. Again, the attention given in Acts to the leaders of the Church and their qualities of endurance, bravery, and insight is not aimed at flattering them, but at showing that they are inspired by God's Holy Spirit. Luke's accuracy about geography and customs, stressed by Lucian, has been generally vindicated in modern studies (see especially A. N. Sherwin-White, *Roman Society and Roman Law in the New Testament*, pp. 48 ff.); and in his descriptions he avoids tasteless word display, attacked by Lucian, his only extended powerful piece of descriptive writing being that of the sea voyage and wreck (Acts 27–28). With regard to the general purpose of historical writing, Lucian stresses that the aim should be at eternity, and the production of a work valuable for posterity and looking to the future. Luke fulfils this criterion because he is recording events in which God, the power behind the whole world, is summoning human beings to face his love and his demands; he is therefore dealing with the things that ultimately matter. Further, discipleship of Jesus enables death and the future to be faced with confidence.

Two further points made by Lucian remain to be mentioned —chronology and language. A chronological arrangement is recommended as far as possible, though the advice seems to be related particularly to the narration of battles. But very little stress is laid on exact chronology, and Luke's attempts at dating, while not extensive, would probably be thought adequate by ancient standards. On language the need to avoid clever rhetoric is stressed; diction is to resemble the subject-matter and match it. Luke lives up to this latter advice, particularly in Chapters 1 and 2, where the Jewish background to the birth and mission of Jesus is underlined by use of a Jewish literary style and language. Lucian's general maxim is: the language should illuminate the theme in the clearest fashion, and should be such as ordinary folk may understand and the educated commend. By the first century A.D. Greek had become one of the leading languages of the Mediterranean world. Out of the older classical Greek with its various dialects there had developed the so-called Koine, 'the common language' created for colloquial purposes and used by authors with varying degrees of polish. Luke uses this Greek with refinement and effect and is obviously at ease in this medium of expression. Like some of his contemporaries, he introduces touches and characteristics of the old classical Greek, such as the period construction (e.g. 1^{1-4}), the genitive absolute to construct a longer sentence (e.g. 3^{15}), and the optative mood in indirect questions (e.g. 8^{9}, 9^{46}). His style is also influenced by the language and idioms of the Greek Old Testament (LXX), seen in his vocabulary and in, for example, the frequent use of 'and it came to pass that' (e.g. 3^{21}), normally not present in the English translation, and the marked preference for 'and behold' in the sense of 'there was' or 'there came' (e.g. 5^{18}). Luke does not show the wealth of particles, for connecting sentences, found in some authors, and is often content with 'and' (*καί*) for this purpose (under the influence of the Greek O.T.), but his sentences are well constructed and show the following characteristics:

(*a*) the use of prepositions with the verbal noun to express temporal, purpose, and causal clauses (e.g. 9^{18}, 18^{1}, 19^{11});

(*b*) the frequent use of participles leading up to the main verb (22^{55-56});

(*c*) the occurrence of the abstract noun as the subject of the verb (e.g. 5^{9}, 22^{24});

(*d*) the verb 'begin' in the sense of 'proceed' or 'go on' (e.g. 4^{21}, 20^{9});

(*e*) the variety of conjunctions (*ὡς* in the sense of 'when', e.g. 11^{1}; *ὅτε* meaning 'when', e.g. 22^{1}; *ἐπειδή* in the sense of 'when' or 'since', e.g. 7^{1}, 11^{6}; *ὅπως* instead of *ἵνα* after verbs of command, 7^{4}; *ὥστε* expressing result with accusative and infinitive, 5^{7}).

Luke can be said, therefore, to write with dignity and clarity, and so fulfils Lucian's criteria.

Judged by the criteria for historical writing that Lucian lays down, Luke would in his contemporary world be thought to attain a high standard as a historian, and would compare favourably with other literary men of his day.

LUKE'S SOURCES AND HIS USE OF THEM

1. *His sources*

It is generally agreed that Luke used the Gospel of Mark as one of his sources, or was at least familiar with the tradition later incorporated into that Gospel. The question of Luke's other sources is raised by the following classes of passage:

(i) Passages where (with no parallel in Mark) the material overlaps with Matthew not only in theme, but also in language (e.g. 6^{42-42}/Matt. 7^{3-5}; 10^{13-16}/Matt. 11^{21-23}; 10^{21-22}/Matt. 11^{25-27}; 11^{24-26}/Matt. 12^{43-45}; 13^{34-35}/Matt. 23^{37-39}).

(ii) Passages where (with no parallel in Mark) there is agreement between Matthew and Luke in theme and subject, without exact identity of language (e.g. 6^{20-23}/Matt. 5^{3-12}; 6^{32-35}/Matt. 5^{45-48}; 7^{1-10}/Matt. 8^{5-13}; 11^{37}–12^{1}/Matt. 23^{4-36}; 14^{15-24}/Matt. 22^{1-10}; 17^{26-30}/Matt. 24^{37-41}).

(iii) Passages where in a Marcan context, though not in the Marcan order, Luke appears to follow a source other than Mark, but having the same theme, while Matthew shows signs of having used Luke's source, and of having at the same time combined it with Mark (e.g. 11^{14-23}).

The usual conclusion drawn from these features is that Luke and Matthew drew on a common source (Q, as it has been called for convenience), though the idea that Luke is dependent on Matthew has found favour with some scholars. One difficulty about the latter suggestion is that Luke and Matthew use the material in such differing contexts, which would presuppose that Luke switched it about in a very radical fashion. Another problem would be that Luke's dependence on Matthew might demand a date for Luke–Acts later than was thought likely above (pp. 7–10). The hypothesis of a common source Q is plausible in the case of Class i and Class iii passages, but whether such a document comprised any of the Class ii material would be difficult to establish. Much more probably both writers are here drawing on different sources, where the material has strong resemblances, but with differences in details of language, due to several factors: (*a*) the use by Jesus of similar sayings and themes, which varied from occasion to occasion; (*b*) the variations in the translations of the original Aramaic of Jesus' sayings into Greek; (*c*) certain changes in Jesus' sayings that took place in the Church's use of them, while the original spirit and theme were retained. Nor is it clear that in the case of the Class i and Class iii passages only one document is involved. The material may have occurred in several written documents, perhaps Gospels, shaped like Mark, but containing more saying-material. Such a probability increases, if we take Luke's 'many' (1^{1}) in a literal and not just rhetorical way. The three classes of passage were almost certainly found by Luke in written form, and some of them may have been translations from Aramaic documents (see below, pp. 179–80, and 190).

Luke also had at his disposal a quantity of material, not found in Matthew and Mark, consisting of narrative and sayings. For convenience, this material is called L, but the designation should not be taken to imply that Luke drew it from a single document.

2. *Luke's use of his sources*

Luke's presentation of his material reveals some clear features:

(*a*) Large sections of the Gospel are composed of Q and L material alone: 1^{1}–4^{30} (with possible exception of 3^{3-6}, 3^{21-22}); 6^{12}–8^{3}; 9^{51}–18^{14}.

(*b*) The passages from Mark tend to stand separately: 4^{31-44}; 5^{12}–6^{11}; 8^{4}–9^{50}; 18^{15-43}; 19^{28-38}; 19^{45}–21^{4}. The exceptions are 21^{5-38} (the discourse on the future), which seems to be woven together from Mark and L, and 22^{1}–24^{53}, in which again Mark and L have been used to form a continuous narrative.

(*c*) If one considers the space given to the different sources, then it becomes clear that, while Mark is an important source for Luke, Q and L play an equally prominent place in the formation of his Gospel, and could, indeed, appear to provide its framework.

From these features of the Gospel B. H. Streeter (*The Four Gospels*, pp. 201–22) developed a theory that underlying this Gospel was a document, which he called 'Proto-Luke', composed of Q and L material, written perhaps by Luke himself, into which Luke inserted extracts from Mark. 'Proto-Luke' started with the chronological note of 3^{1}, and was not at this time combined with Acts. Later in the period (A.D. 70 onwards) Luke came across Mark and made a limited number of insertions from it into Proto-Luke, mainly in blocks. But in 21^{5}–24^{53} the Marcan material had to be interwoven with the rest. At this stage the section 1^{5}–2^{52} was added, Acts was composed, and the two works combined into a two-volume book with suitable prefaces. Several criticisms of this theory can be offered:

(*a*) The idea that Luke–Acts came into its present form by

gradual stages is not convincing, and perhaps reflects the time in the history of criticism when it was popular to see documents coming into being by various pieces of editing. It is just as plausible to believe that Luke was working to a definite pattern for the construction of the whole work from the outset.

(*b*) It can be claimed that the Marcan sections are an intrinsic part of the Gospel and were not added to an already existing document: (i) 4^{31-44} and 5^{12}–6^{11} (dependent on Mark) are required as a necessary follow-up to 4^{18-19}, to show the sense in which Jesus releases the prisoners, lets the broken victims go free, and proclaims the year of the Lord's favour; they also demonstrate the nature of Jesus' kingship. Indeed, if the Marcan portions are removed, one is left with an amorphous mass of material. (ii) As discussed below, pp. 23–4, the first 'journey-narrative' appears by conscious design of the author to be divided into three sections, the first two of which have very close parallels; the material mentioned in (i), and the Marcan material of 8^{1-56}, are essential to these parallels. The third section, 9^{1-50}, is also Marcan, and is the necessary preliminary to the second 'journey-narrative'. (iii) 18^{15-34} (from Mark) helps us to understand once more the destination of Jesus. In 18^{31-32} there is Jesus' prediction of coming events in Jerusalem, while 'Jericho' (18^{35}) prepares for Jesus' entry into that town (19^{1}). (iv) 19^{45}–21^{4} (from Mark) helps to form a section with the theme of Jesus' occupying the temple, i.e. 19^{45}–21^{38}, an inherent part of Luke's final Jerusalem-temple scene which balances 1^{5}–4^{13} (see below, pp. 21–2).

(*c*) The suggestion that 1^{5}–2^{52} is a later addition is arbitrary. The section plays an important part in introducing Jesus as the expected Messiah or King of the Jews. It is true that in style it does stand apart from the rest of the Gospel, being akin to that of the Greek Old Testament, but this may well be Luke's way of stressing that it is out of the midst of Jewish life that Jesus comes.

But Streeter did important service in drawing attention to the fact that Luke had at his disposal a lot of non-Marcan material about Jesus' acts and words, which he was able to use in addition to Mark. Some of it he perhaps found already woven together, and some of it he was able to weave together himself, to form the backbone of his work. In drawing attention to the subordinate place played by Mark as a source, Streeter has also made us face the possibility that Luke had some outline or plan other than that provided by Mark, which he wished to develop and which he was able to construct by utilizing his non-Marcan material.

The less frequent use of Mark raises in particular the problem of Luke's omission of Mark 6^{45}–8^{26}. For this various reasons have been suggested: (*a*) The section may not have been in Luke's text of Mark. (*b*) It contains doublets of other Marcan incidents already recorded by Luke—e.g. Luke did not wish to include two 'feedings' of a crowd. (*c*) The story of Jesus' dealing with the woman of Syro-Phoenicia might have been misunderstood. (*d*) Jesus here makes a big journey and detour to the north to the region of Tyre and Sidon, and perhaps for Luke this would take something away from the journey on which he wishes to lay emphasis, that to Jerusalem, beginning at 9^{51}. (*e*) Much of this Marcan material is concerned with Jesus' contact with Gentiles, and is meant by Mark to emphasize that Jesus has relevance to non-Jews as well as to Jews. Luke perhaps sees that this was Mark's purpose, and so intentionally omits this material, as he is going to make this point in a different way (see below, p. 23).

THE PATTERN OF LUKE'S GOSPEL AND ITS THEOLOGY

1. *The Jerusalem-temple scenes*

The Gospel is balanced at its beginning and its end by two sections (1^{5}–4^{13}: 19^{28}–24^{53}), each of which itself begins and ends with a reference to the temple in Jerusalem (1^{5}, 4^{9}: 19^{45}, 24^{53}). We may call these sections I and II. In each not only is Jerusalem prominent, but attention is also focused on the temple, and Jesus' connection with it. There the birth of John, the forerunner of Jesus, is foretold, and Jesus is greeted as the expected Saviour (1^{8-23}, 2^{22-38}). He has a special right to the temple (2^{49}), to occupy it and use it for his teaching (19^{47}–20^{1}, 21^{37}), thus giving it its proper function. The temple is not for the satisfaction of selfish purposes (4^{9-12}), but for the proclamation of God's word. Only Jesus can make the temple significant (indeed, once the Jews reject Jesus, it ceases to symbolize the presence of God and is 'forsaken', 13^{35}). At Jesus' death 'the curtain of the temple' is torn in two (23^{45}), an event which would make the Day of Atonement ritual impossible (cp. Lev. 16), and so suggest that the temple is no longer the meeting-place between God and man. It can, indeed, be an obstacle to God's plans (cp. Acts 7, where Stephen asserts that obsession with the temple can blind the Jews to God's further revelation, and prevent them from seeing his world-wide sovereignty; and 21^{27-35}, where the temple is the scene of controversy, involving Jewish exclusiveness, and of an attempt to murder Paul, God's Apostle). But the temple's destruction (21^{6}) does not hamper God's plans, which are now centred on Jesus, who, as Luke implies, is the new temple, an idea which seems to have been prominent in Stephen's preaching (Acts 6^{13-14}), and is deep-rooted in the tradition used by the Gospel of John (2^{18-22}, 4^{21-24}). The Qumran community, the Jewish sect contemporary with Jesus and the early Church, was also dissatisfied with the temple worship, and looked forward to its reorganization and purification (*Damascus Rule*, vi; *The War Rule*, ii; Vermes, *The Dead Sea Scrolls in English*, pp. 45–6, 102–3, 125–6), but Christian thought was more radical in seeing the replacement of the old temple by an entirely new one, Jesus.

Other important themes hold sections I and II together:

(*a*) '*Testing*'. I ends with the devil waiting for an opportunity to turn Jesus from his purpose and undermine his loyalty to God (4^{13}), and forms a link with II, where at 22^{3} the devil plays his final card of putting Jesus to the supreme test by engineering his betrayal into the hands of his enemies. Between the temptation narrative (4^{1-13}) and the final section of the Gospel there are other parallels. In contrast with 4^{3}, Jesus now uses bread to symbolize his coming death (22^{19}); in contrast with 4^{9}, Jesus now receives strength from an angel after he has committed himself to God's purposes (22^{43}).

(*b*) '*Kingship*'. The messiahship and kingship of Jesus are prominent in I and II. In I he is seen as the expected King of the Jews, of the line of David (e.g. 1^{32-33}), while in II Jesus' kingship and its nature are also to the fore (e.g. 19^{38-40}, 20^{41-44}, 22^{66-71}, $23^{2, 35-39}$, $24^{26, 46}$). But whereas in I Jesus is set against the background of a king who satisfies Jewish nationalist hopes, liberates them from their enemies, and sets up an earthly kingdom, in II Jesus' kingship takes a corrected form: he proves to be a heavenly king, sharing in God's glory, after suffering and death—a king claiming the whole world and offering a liberation consisting in the forgiveness of sins.

(*c*) '*The Holy Spirit*'. In I the activity of the Holy Spirit is seen in the revival of prophetic activity (e.g. 1^{67}, etc.), and in the conception and mission of Jesus (1^{35}, 3^{22}, 4^{1}), while the Holy Spirit's future role is foretold (3^{16}), made possible through the work of Jesus. In II Jesus holds out to his disciples a share in his kingship (22^{29-30}) and with it a 'mouth and wisdom' (21^{15}), and offers to them 'the promise of my Father' and 'power from on high', in each case the reference being to the Holy Spirit.

Other smaller links also exist between sections I and II. The Passover festival figures in each (2^{41}, 22^{1}), and Jesus is in discussion in the temple with the Jewish experts on the Law (2^{41-51}, 20^{1-34}). Important characters of I recur in II (the Emperor Tiberius, 3^{1}, 20^{21-25}; Pontius Pilate, 3^{1}, 20^{20}, 23^{1-2}; Herod Antipas, $3^{1, 19}$, 23^{6-12}; John the Baptist, 1^{57}, etc., 20^{3-8}; the high priests, 3^{2}, 22^{66}, 23^{13}). Angelic activity is found in I (1^{26}, etc.) and in II (22^{43}; 24^{23}); cp. too 2^{13-14} with 19^{38}. The acknowledgement of Jesus as 'Son of God' at his baptism (3^{22}) is paralleled by Jesus' confession of his Sonship (22^{70}, best taken as an admission), while Jesus, 'wrapped in swaddling cloths', as a baby, and 'laid in a manger' (2^{7}), is at the end of his earthly life 'wrapped in a linen shroud' and laid in 'a rock-hewn tomb' (23^{53}). There is also a contrast between Elizabeth's greeting of Mary, who is 'blessed among women', and Jesus' words to the women on his road to crucifixion (1^{42}, 23^{29}).

2. *The 'journey' narratives*

The remainder of the Gospel may be divided into two further sections (4^{14}–9^{50}: 9^{51}–19^{27}), each of which is concerned with journeys. To distinguish them we shall call these sections *A* and *B*. *A* mentions a number of localities as the scene of Jesus' work, e.g. Nazareth, Capernaum, and stresses the extent of his activity (4^{43}, 8^{1}) and that of his disciples (9^{6}). *B* is concerned with a *single* journey of Jesus—to Jerusalem. The parallelism between *A* and *B* is stressed by Luke, because he has made each open and end on the note of rejection (4^{16-30}, 9^{44-45}: 9^{52}, 19^{11-27}). The opening of each section also shows an interest in non-Jews. The parallelism is increased by the fact that each 'journey' narrative contains material with similar themes.

A and *B*, besides presenting the acts and teaching of Jesus, also underline two other important points:

(*a*) The all-embracingness of Jesus' mission. (i) In *A* the centre of Jesus' activity is mainly Jewish (particularly Galilean), while *B* gives an important place to Samaria, with the impression of Jesus making a kingly progress to Jerusalem through Samaria (9^{52}, 17^{11}). Samaritans, representing for Luke non-Jews, figure in 10^{29-37} and 17^{12-19}. *A* and *B*, set side by side, stress that Jesus' 'good news' concerns Jew and non-Jew alike. (ii) The mission of 'the twelve' in *A* (9^{1-6}) is balanced by that of 'the seventy' (or 'the seventy-two') in *B* (10^{1-20}), 'twelve' probably symbolizing the Jewish nation, and 'seventy' (or 'seventy-two') representing the number of nations supposed to inhabit the earth. Thus the world-wide relevance of Jesus is implied—a theme expanded in the Acts of the Apostles. (iii) In both *A* and *B* Jesus has dealings with people who in the eyes of Jewish society are not respectable, e.g. the tax-collectors and other outcasts (5^{27-32}, 7^{36-50}: 15^{1}, 19^{1-10}). *A* and *B* therefore stress Jesus' love and concern for non-Jew and Jew, for bad as well as good, for those who are frowned upon by society as well as those who stand well with it, for both women and men (an important place is given by Luke to women, both as characters in his story and in Jesus' parables): cp. Col. 3^{10-11}.

(*b*) The decisiveness of Jesus' death. *A* and *B* also focus attention on this event, as a closer analysis of *A* will show. *A* falls into three parts: *A1*, 4^{14}–7^{17}; *A2*, 7^{18}–8^{56}; *A3*, 8^{57}–9^{50}. Each opens with reference to Jesus' work and mission and contains the note of rejection: *A1* and *A2* end with sections where Jesus cures someone approaching death and then restores to life someone who has died (7^{1-17}, 8^{40-56}), while *A3* culminates in a reference to the death of Jesus himself (9^{44}). All centre on the nature of Jesus' kingship (4^{16-21}, the programme of the king; 7^{18-23}, Jesus' reply to John reveals the nature of his kingship; 9^{18-22}, Jesus' kingship will involve death). All three have other features in common: (i) Jesus is acknowledged as 'the Son of God' (4^{41}, 8^{28}, 9^{35}); (ii) the title 'the Son of man' occurs in all with varying connections (5^{24}, forgiveness; 6^{5}, sovereignty over the Sabbath; 7^{34}, sharing in human life; 9^{22}, suffering; 9^{44}, betrayal; 9^{26}, triumph); (iii) references are made to 'the twelve' (6^{13}, 8^{2}, 9^{1}), with Peter, John, and James figuring in an incident in each (5^{1-11}, 8^{49-56}, 9^{28-36}). But between *A1* and *A2* the connections are even closer; to the ones already mentioned the following may be added:

A1	*A2*
the poor (4^{18})	the poor (7^{23})
Jesus and the forgiveness of sins (4^{17-26})	Jesus and the forgiveness of sins (7^{36-50})
doubts about Jesus in Nazareth (4^{22-23})	John the Baptist's doubts about Jesus (7^{19-20})
exorcisms of Jesus (4^{31-41})	exorcisms of Jesus (8^{22-39})
the question asked by a demon-possessed man (4^{34})	the question asked by a demon-possessed man (8^{28})
comment on Jesus' mixing with the 'scum' of society (5^{30})	comment on Jesus' accepting the action of the immoral woman (7^{39}: cp. 7^{34})
the fasting of John's disciples (5^{33})	the asceticism of John the Baptist (7^{33})
a long discourse ends with the note of action (6^{48-49})	a long discourse ends on a practical note (8^{19-21})
healing of a leper (5^{12-14})	Jesus refers to his healing of lepers (7^{22})

In *A1* and *A2* the kingship of Jesus is related to his demonstration of power over the forces of evil, including death, to his bringing the assurance of God's forgiveness, to his love and concern for the least respectable. But in *A3*, while the theme of Jesus' power over demons is still there (9^{1-2}, 9^{37-43}), the note of Jesus' coming death becomes prominent ($9^{22, 44}$), a theme foreshadowed by 9^{9} (John the Baptist's death) and underlined by 9^{23-25} (the need for Jesus' followers to die to 'self'). *A1* and *A2* reveal something of Jesus' kingship, but *A3* introduces the further important factor: Jesus' fullest claim to kingship will be made through his death in Jerusalem.

In relating *A* and *B* together, to show how they pinpoint the importance of Jesus' death, it will be helpful to summarize some characteristics of *B*: (*a*) Its dominant theme, in addition to its connections with Samaria, is 'To Jerusalem' (shown by its opening, 9^{51}, and its close, 19^{11}; see also 13^{22}, 13^{31-35}, 17^{11}, 18^{31}). (*b*) Frequent references are made to the death of Jesus (12^{49}, 13^{31-33}, 17^{25}, 18^{31-33}). (*c*) The theme of kingship is present as in *A* (9^{52}, the king's preparation for his reception; 19^{11-27}, the parable of the king, who receives his kingdom despite opposition and disloyalty).

B is therefore an important sequel to *A* in two senses: (*a*) In *A* Jesus journeys far and wide, especially in Galilee, but in *B* there is only the decisive journey to Jerusalem. (*b*) Of the sections comprising *A*, only *A3* is devoted to the coming death of Jesus in Jerusalem, but now this crucial theme is pinpointed by concentration in *B* on Jesus' regal progress to Jerusalem, and on the constant reminder of his coming death. Luke's arrangement of *A* and *B* thus draws attention to the vital nature of Jesus' death on the cross, followed by his resurrection, a viewpoint central in early Christian belief (e.g. 1 Cor. 15^{3}; for the connection between Jesus' kingship and his death see Phil. 2^{5-9}), but also firmly rooted (as Luke wishes to stress) in Jesus' own words and in his action of going to Jerusalem.

Summary

Luke's arrangement of his material therefore serves the following purposes: (*a*) To suggest that Jesus is the new temple of God, the meeting-place between God and man. (*b*) To underline the importance of Jesus' death. (*c*) To stress the concern of Jesus and his message with *all* human beings. (*d*) To draw out the nature of Jesus' kingship (to be discussed further in the next section). (*e*) To show that the new faith stems from Jerusalem, the centre of the Jewish religion, and so is its true development and fulfilment.

LUKE'S INTEREST IN 'KINGSHIP' AND 'DELIVERANCE'

I. *The Kingship of Jesus and Luke's Development of this Theme*

In Chapters 1 and 2 Jesus is aligned with the Messiah, the Davidic king who was to be the liberator of the Jews from their earthly enemies, and whose special relationship to God could be expressed by the title 'the Son of God' ($1^{32-33, 35}$), a status connected in the O.T. with kingship (2 Sam. 7^{14}; Ps. 2^{7}). This view of Jesus' royalty later receives radical correction in 24^{1-53}, where the sense in which Jesus views his kingship becomes clear. Further, in these opening chapters Jesus' kingship is restricted to the Jews (2^{31-32} probably being no exception), a limited view which will also be corrected (24^{47}). The appearance of John the Baptist raises speculation about his being the Messiah, but John points away from himself to the coming of the mightier one (3^{15-16}), who turns out to be Jesus. Jesus at his baptism is commissioned with the words: 'Thou art my beloved Son' (3^{22}), which in the light of Chapters 1 and 2 are intended by Luke to identify Jesus with the Messiah. John is obviously expecting a king who will bring Israel to judgement and will sort out the worthy from the unworthy (3^{17}), another viewpoint which will also later receive correction and clarification (24^{47}). Significantly, Jesus' baptism is followed by the genealogy going back to Adam (3^{23-38}), and by the 'temptation' narrative (4^{1-13}), with its stress on the loyalty and obedience of Jesus to God, and his selflessness—the qualities of the new Adam in contrast with the first Adam's self-centredness and disobedience. Luke is, therefore, anticipating that Jesus' kingship will be seen in his obedience to God and his will, even when it means complete self-effacement and a readiness to be put to death in apparent defeat: this will be the supreme test (cp. 4^{13} with 22^{3}; 4^{5-8} makes it clear that Jesus is not seeking the splendours of an earthly kingdom). At 4^{14} 'full of the Holy Spirit' looks back to 3^{22}, and so links Jesus with kingship. The reading from Isaiah can be regarded as the King's programme (4^{18-19}), 'the Spirit of the Lord' and 'anointed' having connections with kingship in Jewish thought (e.g. 1 Sam. $10^{1, 10}$; Isa. 11^{1-2}). The sense in which this programme of 'deliverance' is to be interpreted becomes clear in the sequel ($4^{31\,ff.}$), and in contrast with Jewish nationalist expectations of deliverance from earthly enemies—accompanied sometimes by bitterness and hatred—Jesus teaches the need for loving your enemies and showing generosity without hope of return (6^{27-36}). Jesus' demand for love to 'those who hate you' (6^{27}) vividly contrasts with 1^{71}, where the hope is expressed of being 'saved from our enemies, and from the hand of all who hate us'. Jesus is a king who teaches and lives out the way of love, a point also stressed in 7^{18-23}, where in answer to John's question Jesus suggests that his kingship is to be discovered in his works of mercy, which reveal God's love; such a view may not suit those whose idea of the Messiah takes other forms.

Up to this point in the Gospel Jesus' kingship has only been acknowledged by the demon world (5^{41}), but Herod's question about Jesus' identity (9^{7-9}) leads to the disciple's assessment of him as 'the Messiah' (9^{20}). But Luke guards against misunderstanding of the term. (i) The preceding incident is 'the feeding of the crowd' (9^{10-17}), and, like the healing works with which it is introduced, this incident is to be interpreted as a sign of loving care, the expression of Jesus' kingship (9^{11}). (ii) The immediate sequel is the prophecy of Jesus' rejection and death (9^{22}). (iii) The language of 'the Messiah' is replaced by that of 'the Son of Man', a term already associated with Jesus' loving concern (5^{24}, 6^{5}, 7^{34}). (iv) Jesus' command to silence (9^{21}) suggests that the title 'Messiah' is not wholly adequate.

The Gospel now begins to suggest that Jesus will prove to be a heavenly king and not an earthly ruler. The mention of 'the Son of Man' in connection with heavenly glory (9^{26}) is followed by the appearance of Jesus in heavenly splendour (9^{28-36}). The title 'Son of God' is now used in this context (9^{35}) and the splendour is linked with Jesus' death in Jerusalem. 9^{51} points forward to Jesus' exaltation to heaven, while 9^{51}–19^{27} gives warning of the necessary prelude to it.

In 19^{28} Jesus enters Jerusalem in kingly state, but he is not the king of Jewish popular expectations. For he deplores the consequences of nationalist passions (19^{41-44}), gives a place to the Roman Emperor (20^{25}), reinterprets 'the Messiah' to mean a heavenly figure (20^{41-44}), and, though confident of his kingship and able to assure his disciples of places at his court (22^{28-31}), yet sees it in terms of being a servant (22^{24-27}). Before the Sanhedrin (22^{66-71}) Jesus appears to admit that he is the Messiah (the Jews cannot believe that in his present helpless state he is claiming to be a king of a militant type!), but here also looks forward to being exalted to heaven as the Son of Man. Yet, despite all, Jesus is ironically charged with being a political revolutionary, and condemned to death (23^{1-25}). In the crucifixion scene 'save yourself' ($23^{35, 36, 39}$) is made the criterion of the rightness of Jesus' claim to be king, but, again ironically, it is his refusal to 'save himself' and his commitment of himself to God that leads to his enthronement. The inscription over the cross (23^{28}) is an ironic reminder of Jesus' kingship; the criminal recognizes it and receives a royal promise (23^{42-43}).

In 24^{1-53} the resurrection sets the seal on Jesus' kingship, which is the theme of discussion between the Risen Jesus and his disciples. In it the following important points emerge: (*a*) so far from suffering and death being alien to the Messiah, it is an essential feature of his mission, as a right understanding of the O.T. shows; (*b*) so far from Jesus proving to be a Messiah who establishes himself as an earthly ruler, he is one who performs a mission on earth, but is raised through death to a heavenly splendour. The title 'Messiah' bestowed on Jesus in 1 and 2 is now definitely claimed by him, but in the process is given a new content and meaning, and loses its nationalist associations (24^{47}). Similarly, John's expectation that the Messiah would be the bearer of God's judgement (3^{16}) receives similar redirection: the teaching, death, and resurrection of Jesus face men with God's demands, and so with judgement, as they are summoned to repent (24^{47}).

Luke's aim in presenting Jesus as the Messiah, and in showing the reasonable sense in which the term can be applied to him, is closely connected with early Christian apologetics, and the attempt to demonstrate that in Jesus Jewish hopes for the future, centring on this figure, are fulfilled (see also Acts 2^{22-36}). Thus the title 'Messiah', which Jesus himself in his earthly teaching was hesitant to use, becomes vital for the early presentation of the Gospel; so much so that, in its Greek form, it soon became part of his name 'Jesus Christ'.

II. *Jesus' Work of 'Deliverance'*

In Jewish thought kingship was closely connected with deliverance from enemies and oppressors, and therefore in depicting Jesus as a king Luke also presents him as the leader of a rescue operation.

1. *Luke's 'deliverance' vocabulary*

He gives prominence to terms that in the O.T. describe God's rescue of his people.

(*a*) 'Saviour' (*σωτήρ*). The term is applied to God (e.g. Isa. 43^{3}), but also to human deliverers who are agents of God (e.g. Judg. $3^{9, 15}$). Luke uses the title of God (1^{47}), and also of Jesus (2^{11}; Acts 5^{31}, 13^{24}, where 'the deliverance' is related to the chance of 'repentance' and 'forgiveness of sins').

(*b*) 'salvation' (*σωτηρία* or *σωτήριον*). This terminology commonly describes God's acts of deliverance (e.g. Exod. 14^{13}; Ps. 37^{39}; Isa. 26^{1}), and Luke begins and ends his work on this note ($1^{69, 71, 77}$, 2^{30}; Acts 28^{28}). The quotation from Isa. 40^{3-5} is extended by Luke to include 'and all flesh shall see the salvation of God' (3^{4-6}). Zacchaeus' change of heart is described as 'salvation', a pointer to the kind of deliverance that Jesus brings (19^{9}). The same theme is found in Acts 4^{12}, 13^{26} (cp. 2^{40}), and it may be that Luke has taken up a key term in the early presentation of the Gospel to present an important aspect of Jesus' work (see also 2 Cor. 6^{2}; Gal. 1^{4}).

(*c*) 'redemption' (*λύτρωσις*), 'redeem' (*λυτροῦμαι*). These terms, though used in the O.T. sometimes in the general sense of 'ransoming', also denote God's ransoming of his people from their enemies, with the emphasis on 'deliverance' rather than on the payment of a ransom (e.g. Exod. 15^{13}; Ps. 111^{9}). In Luke the noun occurs in 1^{68} and 2^{38}, and the verb in 24^{21}, all in close connection with Jesus.

(*d*) 'visit' (*ἐπισκέπτομαι*), 'visitation' (*ἐπισκόπη*). God 'visits' both in the sense of bringing deliverance (e.g. Exod. 4^{31}; Ps. 106^{4}), and of bringing judgement (e.g. Job 7^{18}), and the same twofold meaning attaches to 'visitation' (e.g. Exod. 13^{19}; Jer. 10^{15}). Luke uses 'visit' with the meaning of 'deliver' (1^{68}, 7^{16}, and perhaps 1^{78}), and 'visitation' with the same sense (19^{44}: Jerusalem does not recognize the real hour of her deliverance in Jesus' mission, with fatal results).

(*e*) 'peace' (*εἰρήνη*). The word presents the picture of God's people delivered from their enemies and restored to prosperity (Isa. 55^{12}, 66^{12}), and enjoying a positive harmony with God. Luke connects Jesus with the creation of such 'peace' (1^{79}, 2^{14}, 19^{38}; and cp. 19^{42}, where the implication is that Jesus is the bringer of the true peace). We note too that Jesus' deliverance of people from the grip of evil is marked by his reassurance: 'go in peace' (e.g. 7^{50}, 8^{48}).

(*f*) 'bring good news' (*εὐαγγελίζομαι*). The term, from its use in the O.T., has close connections with God's rescue of his people (Ps. 40^{9}, 'I have told the glad news of deliverance'; Isa. 52^{7}—note here the association with 'peace,' 'salvation', and God's 'reign'). While the noun, 'good news' or 'gospel', is the norm in Matthew and Mark, Luke never uses the noun; but he does use the verb frequently, in connection with the birth of John and Jesus (1^{19}, 2^{10}), and particularly of the good news that Jesus brings, partly expressed in his healing miracles (4^{18}, 4^{43}, 9^{6}, 20^{1}). For the message of the early Church as 'good news', see, e.g., Acts 5^{42}.

2. *Jesus' sermon at Nazareth* (4^{16-21})

Luke's interest in Jesus as the bringer of 'deliverance' is shown by the way in which his ministry is introduced. Jesus in the synagogue claims to be fulfilling a passage from Isa. 61^{1-2}, where the prophet announces 'release to the captives', 'sight to the blind', and 'liberty to the oppressed', all of which is 'good news to the poor', closely related in Isaiah 40–66 to God's deliverance of his people. Luke wishes to set Jesus' whole ministry against this background of 'liberation', and to see it as 'the acceptable year of the Lord', the time when God's favour and care are being demonstrated.

3. *The liberating work of Jesus*

(*a*) *The liberation of the 'captives' and the 'oppressed'.* This language had originally been applied to the rescue of the Jews from captivity in a foreign land; it is now reapplied to those who are suffering from disruptive forces in life.

(i) Disruption caused by the devil's activity, including demon possession, i.e. mental disorder (4^{33-36}, 8^{26-39}), and physical disease, seen as the devil's work (e.g. 4^{38-39}, 5^{12-15}, etc.). Luke intends us to see something of the 'release of the captives' and 'the liberation of the oppressed' in Jesus' acts of healing (cp. $13^{10, 17}$, especially vv. 12 and 16). These acts of healing proclaim God's breaking of the power of evil (11^{20-21}; cp. 10^{18}), and the assertion of his kingly power, and so speak of 'liberation' to those who feel in the grip of an inexorable fate or evil.

(ii) Disruption caused by sin and guilt. Jesus brings release here by his assurance of God's forgiveness, which he claims special authority to pronounce (5^{20-24}, 7^{47-49}); the word for 'release', ἄφεσις (4^{18}), is the same as for 'forgiveness'. This aspect of Jesus' liberating work is also seen in his bringing the sense of being wanted to the outcasts of society (5^{29}, 19^{1-10}, 23^{39-43}).

(iii) Disruption caused by the fear and tragedy of death. Jesus' acts of raising the dead (7^{11-17}, 8^{49-56}) symbolize the release offered by Jesus from the dread and fear of death, and the purposelessness that they introduce into life. Similarly, Jesus' own resurrection (24^{1-53}) takes the sting out of death and shows that it is not something irrevocable, no final disaster.

(*b*) *Jesus the Liberator in his own person.* 4^{14}–21^{38} presents Jesus as triumphant over the disruptive forces of evil, and has sometimes been described as giving an account of the 'Satan-free period'. But the 'opportune time' (4^{13}) comes when Satan once more takes the offensive (22^{3}), and engineers that Jesus should be put into the hands of his enemies: Jesus is faced with the supreme test of allowing himself to be reduced to nothingness and outward defeat (22^{39-46}). But while Satan and the forces of disruption outwardly have Jesus in their control, there are senses in which they never control Jesus, and so he becomes the liberator defeating the evil powers. First, Jesus' loyalty to God, and his assurance about the triumph of God in his own personal mission, remain firm ($22^{15-20, 29, 69}$, $23^{28, 43, 46}$: despite the taunts of the rulers (23^{35}), the soldiers (23^{36}), and of one of his fellow victims (23^{39}), Jesus is content to leave his 'safety' to God. Jesus is 'liberator', because he is completely emancipated from the control and influences of the forces of evil. Secondly, Jesus' love and concern for others are undefeated. He had stressed that the big quality of the God-centred life was a generous love not governed by expectation of return or the attitudes and reactions of others (6^{27-36}), and Luke stresses how Jesus remained true to this love in his worst hour ($22^{51, 61}$, $23^{28-31, 34, 43}$). Jesus is again the liberator, because he is himself 'liberated', in the sense that his love and concern for people are unaffected by the selfish and degrading attitudes around him. Thirdly, the resurrection of Jesus (24^{1-53}), his coming back to be a real force in the life of the disciples and of the world, demonstrate that the evil powers had not had the last say, and that the principles of life for which he stood were vindicated.

(*c*) *The mission of Jesus as 'the acceptable year of the Lord'*. Luke wishes the ministry of Jesus to be seen as a new era of God's favour and loving intervention to win human beings to himself. It is marked by two important features. The first of these is the call to repentance, i.e. to a willingness to face God's demands. The urgency is brought out in 5^{32} (Luke adds 'to repentance' to clarify Mark), in 10^{13-14} (the mighty works of Jesus are demonstrations of God's activity and call for human response), in 11^{32} (the situation is more pressing than in the time of Jonah), and in 13^{1-9} (the opportunity is now being given to come to terms with God). In $23^{39-43, 48}$ the hint is given that it is the cross and the love that Jesus displays that will draw out human repentance. Such a summons to repentance becomes an important feature of the Church's message (24^{47}: cp. Acts 2^{38}). The second feature of this new era is the search for the lost. This vital aspect of Jesus' mission is underlined by 19^{10}, and particularly in the three parables about the lost (15), and is outwardly demonstrated in Jesus' dealings with the outcasts of Jewish society (5^{29-32}, 7^{36-50}, 15^{1}, 19^{1-9}).

(*d*) *The work of Jesus as a new Exodus.* In the O.T. God's work of deliverance is exemplified in the Exodus, the rescue of the Jews from Egypt, and it is not surprising that the prophet of the Exile is influenced by that event in his description of the coming deliverance from Babylon (Isa. 43^{16-21}, 48^{21}). Similarly the Rabbis pictured God's future deliverance in terms of the original Exodus. The description of Jesus' achievement against this same background would therefore be natural, and Luke shows signs of being influenced in this way. The key passage is 9^{31}, where Luke alone gives the subject of conversation between Jesus and the two figures of Moses and Elijah ('And behold, two men talked with him, Moses and Elijah, who appeared in glory and spoke of his departure, which he was to accomplish at Jerusalem'). The word translated 'departure' here is ἔξοδος, which can mean 'death', and so partly points forward to Jesus' death in Jerusalem; but it is also the technical term for God's deliverance of Israel from Egypt (Exodus). Luke's 'accomplish' (πληροῦν) suggests that he has the latter sense in mind. The implication is that Jesus is to bring about an Exodus and deliverance in Jerusalem that will rival the one from Egypt under Moses, and a further link with later events in Jerusalem is supplied by 'and behold, two men', a phrase which occurs also in 24^{4} and Acts 1^{10}. The first is the 'empty tomb' scene (contrast Mark 'a young man'), and the second is the occasion of Jesus' 'ascension'. In view of the earlier reference to Moses and Elijah under this designation, the allusion in the later passages is probably also to them: Moses and Elijah, the mediator and the upholder of the first covenant, made at the time of the Exodus from Egypt, both look forward to the new Exodus (9^{31}), and are present to witness to its accomplishment (24^{4}; Acts 1^{10}). 11^{20} may also reveal an Exodus-background where Jesus contends: 'but if I by the finger of God cast out demons, then the kingdom of God has come upon you'. The imagery of 'the finger of God' as a description of his powerful activity is rare and only found in the O.T. in two contexts: at Exod. 8^{19} the plagues of Egypt are attributed to God's 'finger', and at Exod. 31^{18} and Deut. 9^{10} the tablets of stone are written with God's 'finger'. The term in Luke was probably part of the original saying of Jesus, being later clarified by the more usual 'the Spirit of God' (Matt. 12^{28}). It has a definite Exodus-ring about it, and Luke (and Jesus) may be suggesting that, just as the plagues of Egypt were the preliminary to the Exodus from Egypt, so Jesus' mighty works of healing are the opening stage in a new and greater Exodus, achieved through the death and resurrection of Jesus in Jerusalem.

4. *Summary*

The mission of Jesus was so decisive for the early Christians, and so rich in meaning, that it could be viewed from different angles and could be presented in different ways. The above discussion shows that Luke was particularly concentrating his attention on the sense in which Jesus could be described as king, and on the kind of deliverance that he, as king, had brought.

JESUS OF NAZARETH—HIS TEACHING AND PERSON

1. *The importance of Jesus*

Luke wishes to present Jesus of Nazareth as the central figure in God's dealings with both the Jews and the rest of the human race. The decisive place given to him can be traced to the pressure of several factors, all of which Luke probably includes in 'that which has been accomplished' (1^1). These factors are:

(*a*) The impact made on the disciples of Jesus by his resurrection from the dead, and their consequent conviction that death had not ended the living relationship between Jesus and themselves. The consciousness of a surviving living contact with someone who had been a historical character of the past would seem to be a unique feature of early Christianity, unexampled elsewhere in Jewish thinking. This experience acted as a vindication of Jesus' claims and mission, and drove his followers to offer him a loyalty normally given to God alone, and expressed in the title 'Lord'. Luke is very familiar with this title of the Risen Jesus, and sometimes refers to the historical Jesus by it (e.g. 10^1). The title, while it could in general describe someone in a position of superiority to someone else, had close connections with 'the divine', being used of God in the O.T., and also of various deities, including the Roman emperor, in the wider world (cp. 1 Cor. 8^{5}).

(*b*) The teaching of Jesus in word and act, with his claims to have a crucial part to play in God's plans, and to be the focal point where Jewish hopes for the future meet.

(*c*) The impression made on his followers by Jesus' claim to exercise a special authority on behalf of God.

(*d*) The experience of the power of God's Holy Spirit in the life of the post-resurrection Christian community, in accordance with the promise of Jesus.

In the light of (*a*), which set God's seal on the mission of Jesus, his words and acts assumed a God-given importance, and needed to be preserved and studied as part of God's revelation of himself, leading to the preservation of important sayings and actions of Jesus now contained in our Gospels. The formulation of such a tradition may, however, predate the resurrection of Jesus, because his disciples may already have learnt some of his sayings by heart, and he had already drawn their attention to the decisiveness of some of his actions. Luke (1^{1}) suggests that this tradition goes back to 'eyewitnesses', and his statement must be taken seriously, as suggesting that the record of Jesus' teaching and actions was carefully preserved.

2. *Important elements in the teaching of Jesus*

(*a*) *God's final kingdom and new age.* Jewish thought in the time of Jesus, and for centuries before, was 'eschatological', looking to 'the end', which was the full establishment of God's sovereignty over his creation and the coming of a new age, in which God would be supreme and in which his faithful people would be vindicated. Such a hope took various forms and shapes. Jesus' teaching falls into this pattern of thought, and starts from the standpoint that God and his purposes are the ultimate things that matter and have a future (like the O.T. prophets, he sometimes stresses this point by presenting God's final reign as imminent). For example, Jesus talks of the future coming of the Son of man (see below, pp. 38–40), warns his hearers of the danger of failing to face the demands of God's kingdom (13^{25-30}), teaches the certainty of God's vindication of his cause and of those who are loyal to him ($18^{1-7,\ 28-30}$), and underlines the danger of allowing material things to obscure the really important factor, God's sovereignty (12^{31-32}).

(*b*) *God's kingdom and the present.* A unique feature of Jesus' message is his claim that God's kingdom and new era are no longer future but with his own mission have broken in upon the present order, and that God's final assault on evil is already under way. This is reflected in Jesus' verbal teaching (4^{18-21}, 16^{16}, 17^{20-21}), especially in the parables on 'the decisiveness of the present time' (5^{33-39}, 7^{31-35}, 11^{33-36}, 12^{54-57}, 13^{6-9}, 14^{15-24}), and is also demonstrated in Jesus' mighty acts (10^{23-24}, 11^{20-22}, 13^{16}).

(*c*) *Jesus' death and resurrection.* There is a strong tradition that Jesus attached importance to his coming sufferings and death, as part of God's plan and purpose (e.g. 9^{22}, 13^{32-33}, 18^{31-33}): they would have important results in which his disciples would share ($22^{15-20,\ 28-30}$). There is also in these sayings the belief, either explicit or implicit, that Jesus will be vindicated after death.

The relation between (*a*), (*b*), and (*c*) is left vague in the Gospel tradition, and there is no attempt to make Jesus systematize them; this carries the implication (i) that his teaching has been accurately preserved and has not been moulded to fit the Church's post-resurrection experience, and (ii) that Jesus himself, while convinced of the importance of his ministry, death, and future vindication, only saw vaguely how these would fit into the exact pattern of God's future plans and final sovereignty.

(*d*) *Jesus' founding of a community.* Jesus' consciousness of his mission's importance is shown by his formation of a special group, 'the twelve', who are to be special witnesses of his mission and to receive his special teaching (8^{9}): they are given a share in his proclamation (9^{1-6}), are left behind to await the decisive events that will follow his death ($22^{28-30,\ 32}$), and are to be ready for what the future holds (12^{35-48}). The number 'twelve' would suggest the twelve tribes of Israel, and the implication is that Jesus is creating within the old Israel a new and true community of God, which is to wait for the completion of God's plans and purposes, partially realized in the teaching and mighty acts of Jesus, and taking a further step forward with his death and resurrection. The creation of this community may be compared with the Qumran sect of the Dead Sea

Scrolls, founded likewise to be 'a house of truth in Israel' (*Community Rule*, viii; Vermes, *The Dead Sea Scrolls in English*, p. 38), and to be ready for 'the end'. Jesus perhaps regarded himself as the one in whom the mission of Israel was embodied, and so could envisage his followers as the true people of God, the recipients of his deeper revelation, and responsible for witnessing to it (24^{46-49}). The designation of 'the twelve' as 'apostles' (6^{13}), which in accordance with Luke's view almost certainly goes back to Jesus, also shows the importance that Jesus attached to his disciples. 'Apostle', literally 'one sent', probably meant 'plenipotentiary' or 'representative', and in the light of 9^{48} and 10^{16} suggests that, just as Jesus is the plenipotentiary of God, so in turn they become his plenipotentiaries, with the implication that his mission has a future. The revolutionary kind of behaviour expected from Jesus' community is recorded, e.g., at 6^{20-49}.

3. *The person and status of Jesus*

The claims made by Jesus and their vindication at his resurrection bring to the fore the question of his person and identity. Luke, as we have seen, presents him as king and as the central figure in a new Exodus that involves not only the Jews but the whole of mankind. Other features about the status of Jesus may be noted.

(*a*) *Jesus the Rabbi*. In the first century A.D. the Rabbis, called 'scribes' (e.g. 5^{30}), and 'lawyers' (e.g. 11^{45}), formed a Jewish professional class, authorized and ordained to interpret the Law and apply it to contemporary conditions. Resemblances between Jesus and the Rabbis are seen: (i) in his concern with interpretation of the Law, and pronouncement on such matters as Sabbath observance (6^{1-11}), divorce (16^{18}), and the resurrection of the dead (20^{27-40}); (ii) in his inner band of disciples or pupils, who are given tasks to perform, and to whom, as happened with a Rabbi's pupils, he may have committed some of his sayings to be learnt by heart (hence their poetical form); (iii) in his synagogue teaching, the kind of task that a Rabbi would perform (e.g. 4^{31}), and in his informal instruction, given in the open air and on social occasions (e.g. 5^{1}). It is unlikely that Jesus was authorized as a Rabbi (cp. Luke 4^{22}; John 7^{15}), but his similarity to them is shown when he is addressed as 'Teacher' (e.g. 7^{40}) or 'Master' (e.g. 5^{5}), titles of respect appropriate to a Rabbi (see also John 1³⁸). But 'Rabbi' is not a sufficient description of Jesus. When he was put to death, it was not because he differed from other Rabbis over points in the Jewish Law and their interpretation.

(*b*) *Jesus the Prophet.* Jesus has much more in common with the Old Testament prophet than with the Rabbi. The latter was an interpreter of a law, but the former claimed to have an authority direct from God, as one who had been caught up in the heavenly council of God and was his mouthpiece, and so could say: 'Thus says the Lord.' Jesus' authority is closer to that of the prophet, and impressed his contemporaries as such (e.g. 7^{16}, 9^{8}; cp. 13^{33} for Jesus' similar estimate of himself). The prophetic line, after several hundred years, had revived with John the Baptist, and was also represented by Jesus himself. There are various similarities between Jesus and the prophets. First, his authoritative style of speech, 'I tell you' (e.g. 11^{9}), resembles the prophetic 'Thus says the Lord', and his style of teaching similarly is oracular, and given in startling and paradoxical terms to challenge faith. Secondly, Jesus, like the prophets, is concerned with the contemporary situation (e.g. 11^{37-52}), and also makes predictions about the immediate future, e.g., about the fall of Jerusalem (19^{41-44}) and his own suffering and death (9^{22}). Further, just as the prophets traced their call to a great experience (e.g. Isa. 6), so in the life of Jesus his baptism and its attendant circumstances can be regarded as the commissioning of Jesus for his work (Luke 3^{21-22}); and, like the prophets, Jesus is very conscious of his God-given mission (e.g. 4^{43}). Again, the use of symbolical acts is another prophetic feature that Jesus shares (for these see, e.g., 1 Kgs. 11^{29}; Jer. 19^{10} and 27^{1-11}): the mighty acts of Jesus, e.g. his acts of healing (demonstrations of God's sovereignty over evil), the setting of the child before the disciples as an example (9^{47}), the state entry into Jerusalem (19^{28-38}), and the actions at the last supper (22^{17-20}), expressive of Jesus' confidence in the future and in the meaningfulness of his death—all come in this category.

Finally, the teaching of Jesus, like that of the prophets, is closely connected with the coming of the last days and the judgement of God. But the claims of Jesus (as discussed in 2 above) go beyond those of a prophet.

(*c*) *Jesus' consciousness of his special relationship with God.* While the Gospels are not psychological treatises, yet the teaching of Jesus recorded there reveals a person who claims to speak with a special authority from God and to stand at a decisive point in God's dealings with his people Israel. This sense of Jesus' unique relation to God is brought out by his reference to God as 'Father'. In the first place, Jesus addresses God directly as 'Father' (10^{21}, 22^{42}, 23^{46}); such a mode of address was not customary among contemporary Jews. In the second, with a striking consistency, Jesus refers to God either as 'my Father' (2^{49}, 22^{29}, 24^{49}) or as 'your Father' (6^{36}, 12^{30}, etc.), with the implication that his own relationship to God is different from that of others (see too 10^{21-22}). Jesus' consciousness of a divine authority is also shown in his claim to exercise the prerogative of God: in pronouncing God's forgiveness of human sin (5^{20}, 7^{48}); in demanding an undivided allegiance to himself that would normally be due only to God (9^{57-62}, 14^{25-26}); in claiming that a man's attitude to him had a decisive influence on God's judgement ($12^{8,9}$); and in his promise of 'eternal life' to his followers (18^{29-30}).

On the reverse side, this unique position of Jesus is brought out in passages where the claims of Jesus are acknowledged by divine authority and his special sonship recognized (3^{22}, 9^{35}). On the implications of the title 'Son of God' see below, p. 83.

(*d*) *Jesus, the Son of man.* With a telling consistency in all four Gospels, which suggests a usage going back to Jesus himself, the term is found only on the lips of Jesus (in John 12^{34} it is, by implication, taken up by the crowd from Jesus' own words). It is not used as a description of him in narrative, nor as a way of referring to him by others. Outside the Gospels, it is found in the N.T. only at Acts 7^{56}, where it refers to the exalted Jesus. 'The Son of man' is used impersonally by Jesus: he does not say that he is the Son of man, though this is strongly implied. Such a circumlocution or impersonal way of speaking has been thought either to denote the official and authoritative capacity in which Jesus speaks, or else to express the reluctance of Jesus to equate himself with 'the Son of man' until he has completed his mission of suffering and death. Another suggestion has been that the term is a corporate one, including Jesus and his followers, as the loyal remnant of Israel. The term occurs in three main contexts: Jesus' earthly ministry (e.g. 5^{24}); his death and resurrection (e.g. 9^{22}); a final advent in glory (e.g. 9^{26}). The discussion of the term's meaning has been extensive, and only some of the main points will be made here.

(i) *The linguistic background.* In Greek *ὁ υἱος τοῦ ἀνθρώπου* is a strange expression, being a literal translation of the Hebrew *ben 'adam*, meaning 'the man' or 'humanity'. Hence 'the Son of man' could mean 'the one of human stock' or 'those who belong to human stock'. The equivalent in Aramaic, apart from the above meaning, could mean 'one' (the collective pronoun), or 'I' (used in an authoritative pronouncement). The term in the Gospels has sometimes been taken in the latter sense, but it appears to carry far deeper implications (it is striking that the term was not just translated into Greek as an authoritative 'I').

(ii) *The background in Ezekiel.* Ezekiel is often addressed by God as 'Son of man' (e.g. 2^{1}), and this suggests not only his smallness as a human being, but also the greatness of the mission to which God calls him. 'The Son of man' has therefore been interpreted to mean 'one who is a special messenger of God', with overtones, perhaps, of 'one who is God's sign to his particular generation', and 'one who through his prophetic words sets God's purposes in motion' (both of which are functions of Ezekiel). From being such a mode of address in Ezekiel the term has become a title with all these implications. But it is doubtful whether the term in Ezekiel carries all these overtones: it may serve only the purpose of bringing out the transcendence of God in relation to humanity.

(iii) *The connection between 'the Son of man' and God's sovereignty.* The evidence of the so-called Similitudes of Enoch (an apocryphal work), with its references to a figure called 'the Son of man', has led to the view that in the time of Jesus the Jews, or at least a section of them, believed in a heavenly Son of man, a being who would in the last days exercise God's sovereignty and judgement. This would then supply a possible background to the use of the phrase in the Gospels. However, the value of the evidence of Enoch is disputed. But quite apart from this possibility, 'the Son of man' has associations with God's sovereignty and kingship through its use in the Gospels in connection with quotation of or allusion to Dan. 7^{13-14} (see Matt. 24^{30}, 26^{64}; Mark 13^{26}, 14^{62}; Luke 21^{27}). The passage in Daniel runs as follows: 'Behold, with the clouds of heaven there came one like a son of man, and he came to the Ancient of

Days and was presented before him. And to him was given dominion and glory and kingdom. . . .' Here the 'one like a son of man' probably refers to the redeemed community of Israel, who forms the real humanity, in contrast to the world-kingdoms, who are represented as beasts. 'The Son of man' in the Gospels has been thought to be a development of this expression, perhaps originating with Jesus himself, and, while against the background of Daniel it could denote him as the real representative of Israel and humanity, the root connection would seem to be with God's sovereignty and kingship exercised by the 'one like a son of man'. The title might, therefore, mean 'the representative and agent of God's sovereignty'.

(iv) *The importance of the expression as used by Jesus.* Jesus' use of the term and application of it to himself are deeply rooted in the tradition of his sayings, and this fact needs to be given due weight. Luke 9^{26} does not conclusively show that Jesus distinguished himself from the Son of man, as some have asserted. The important feature in the teaching of Jesus is that, while he uses 'the Son of man' in connection with God's final reign and sovereignty (e.g. Luke 9^{26}, 17^{26}, 21^{36}), the same term is also related to his earthly life and his death. God's sovereignty is, therefore, what we might call 'humanized', and seen in, e.g., forgiveness (5^{24}), the search for the lost (7^{34}, 19^{10}), in self-givingness (9^{22}, 9^{44}, 18^{31}), in the sharing of human hardship (9^{58}), and in the emphasis on the fact that the care and relief of human beings must come before the over-scrupulous observance of the Sabbath (6^{5}). In this way God's sovereignty and his claim to be king are not something remote but made in the midst of human life; hence it is not surprising that the early Church thought of God's kingship in terms of love (e.g. Rom. 5^{6-8}: similarly in the Gospel of John the glory of God and the glory of the Son of man are seen in terms of love and self-givingness). The important feature about the teaching of Jesus is not that he did or did not equate himself with a figure, the Son of man, of the future, who would assert God's final sovereignty and judgement, but that he saw this function and role already being played out in his own ministry. The impersonal use of the term may be due to Jesus' self-effacingness, to concentrate attention on God's activity, in and through him, rather than on himself.

4. *The birth of Jesus*

The belief that the child Jesus was conceived in the womb of Mary, not through ordinary human intercourse, but by the special activity of God's Holy Spirit, is well established in the teaching of the Church by the end of the first century A.D. Bishop Ignatius of Antioch in the period A.D. 98–117 includes it in his summaries of the Christian creed (*Ephesians*, viii. 2, 'For . . . Jesus the Christ was conceived by Mary according to God's plan, of the seed of David and of the Holy Spirit'; *Smyrnaeans*, i. 1, '. . . Son of God by the will and power of God, truly born of a [or "the"] virgin'). The earliest record of this tradition is found in Luke 1^{26-35} and Matt. 1^{18-25}, two separate accounts, which are thought to be independent of each other, and which appear to be written from the standpoint of Mary and Joseph respectively. The manner of Jesus' conception and birth is not described in the rest of the New Testament. Gal. 4^{4} ('God sent forth his Son, born of a woman'), is not concerned with the peculiarity of Jesus' conception but with his birth into a human situation. The description of Jesus as 'son of Mary' (Mark 6^{4}) is derogatory—a person not usually being named with reference to his mother—and is sometimes thought to be recorded by Mark for ironic effect (i.e. what the people of Nazareth said was true in a way that *they* did not realize, but the Church understood full well!). Such evidence is, however, indirect. On the other hand, the absence of direct mention must be carefully interpreted. For example, the silence of the speeches of Acts points only to the conclusion that the early preaching of the Gospel concentrated on the end of Jesus' life rather than the beginning (it is in favour of Luke's faithful presentation of early Christian teaching that, despite his knowledge of the special circumstances of Jesus' birth, he does not insert it into the speeches of Acts). The manner of Jesus' birth may have become a matter of interest only when deeper definition of his person was explored and an explanation sought how 'the Word became flesh'. Perhaps Mary herself revealed the matter only later, so that at first the belief may have been that Jesus was the son of Joseph and Mary.

In support of a 'virgin conception' the following points may be made:

(*a*) There is no precedent for it in Jewish thought. Examples occur where God blessed human intercourse and made possible a child's conception where parents were barren or past child-bearing (Gen. 18^{9-15}, 21^{1-7}; Judg. $13^{1-7, 24}$: cp. Luke 1^{7-25}). But there is no suggestion that a person important for God's purposes should be conceived by the conjunction of the creative activity of the Holy Spirit and a woman, without the part played by the father. Further, in the above examples God's miraculous intervention is aimed at overcoming barrenness, which cannot thwart God's purposes, but this does not apply in the case of Mary.

(*b*) Was the 'virgin conception' created out of the O.T. text, Isa. 7^{14}, quoted at Matt. 1^{22-23}, and perhaps underlying Luke 1^{30-31}? Such a procedure would be unprecedented, and a careful distinction needs to be made: on the one hand, it was an important part of Christian apologetic to justify beliefs about Jesus by recourse to proof texts from the O.T.; on the other hand, there is no evidence that events and doctrines were constructed wholesale out of the O.T. We should have to imagine that some thinker constructed the belief in this way, and on this flimsy basis that it was then accepted by the whole Church. In any case, the Isaiah passage would not necessarily suggest a 'virgin'.

(*c*) Stories are common in ancient mythology in which children are born as the result of intercourse between gods, who come to earth, and human women. A story of this kind is found in Gen. 6^{1-4}, where 'the sons of God', i.e. angels, come to earth and have intercourse with 'the daughters of men'; see also the expansion of the story of Noah, found in the *Genesis Apocryphon* of the Dead Sea Scrolls (Vermes, *The Dead Sea Scrolls in English*, pp. 214–16), where Lamech suspects that the miraculous birth of Noah is the result of his wife's consorting with the angels who descended from heaven. In Jewish mythology such a story is an illustration that God's world has become marred and tarnished with wickedness. It is sometimes suggested that the story of Jesus' conception developed under the influence of these stories. But there is a certain naïvety in seeing the early Church developing doctrines from pagan models, which were frowned upon by people in the pagan world itself. Further, the language and terminology in which Matthew and Luke describe the event is Jewish throughout (see below, p. 46). The leaders of the early Church came from a Jewish background, and were not likely to favour the creation of traditions based on a pagan background! It has even been surmised that Paul was averse from mentioning 'the virgin conception' for fear that it should be confused with some of these disreputable pagan myths! The only possible motive for the creation of this belief out of these myths would be the attempt to create an anti-type: just as intercourse between heavenly and earthly beings brought wickedness into the world, so now the conjunction of God's Holy Spirit and Mary brings the opportunity for reconciliation with God.

(*d*) The question of Jesus' birth was a matter of controversy between Jews and Christians at least by the end of the first century A.D. This is reflected probably in John 8^{41}, as well as in the Jewish Rabbinical writings, where the accusation is made that Jesus was illegitimate. The doctrine of the virgin conception would counteract such polemic, a fact which does not, however, presuppose its invention for this purpose. The greater probability is that Jewish thinkers, refusing to accept the special manner of Jesus' conception, took the other alternative conclusion—that Jesus was born out of wedlock.

(*e*) The full humanity of Jesus in his earthly life was an important feature of the Gospel (cp. Rom. 5^{12-21}). His unusual conception might have suggested that he was not fully human, and this would have told against accepting such a doctrine, unless the evidence pointed to it.

(*f*) The N.T. suggests that beliefs about Jesus were based on empirical evidence and human experience (e.g. Luke 1^{1-2}; 1 John 1^{1-4}), which again raises the question: Would this belief about Jesus' conception have been created without the pressure of such evidence?

(*g*) From the point of view of scientific probability such a phenomenon cannot be ruled out. God does work normally according to fairly well-defined laws, or else scientific investigation would be impossible. But the event by which 'the Word becomes flesh' is unique and abnormal, and so goes outside God's normal working in his universe.

THE GOSPEL ACCORDING TO

LUKE

1: INASMUCH as many have undertaken to compile a narrative
of the things which have been accomplished among us, just
2 as they were delivered to us by those who from the beginning

---

I. PREFACE AND THE FIRST JERUSALEM-TEMPLE SCENE— THE PRELUDE (CHAPTERS 1: 1–4: 13)

1: 1–4. *The Preface*

A preface distinguishes Luke from the other Gospel writers and puts him in line with the literary men of his contemporary world. Dioscorides (first century A.D.) begins his treatise *On Medicine* with a similar Preface: 'Although many writers, both ancient and modern, have compiled treatises concerning the preparation, action, and testing of drugs, my dearest Areius, I will endeavour to show you that it was no vain or unreasonable impulse which moved me to the present undertaking.'

1 *Inasmuch as*, or 'since'. *many*: Dioscorides seems to use the word literally, and Gospels other than Mark may well have existed at an early stage. *undertaken*: as a literary task. *the things that have been accomplished among us* refers to the achievement of God's purposes in the mission of Jesus, and to the progress of the Church and the Gospel. There is another less likely translation: 'the things on which there is full conviction among us'. *us*: the collective experience of the early Christians.

2 *delivered*: used of the passing on of a tradition. The Jews were familiar with tradition as something carefully formulated, accurately preserved and transmitted to others. It is this kind of tradition to which Luke probably refers. It is reasonable to suppose that the early disciples of Jesus took measures to see that the records of his deeds and sayings were carefully preserved and transmitted. *the word*, God's revelation of

3 were eyewitnesses and ministers of the word, it seemed good
to me also, having followed all things closely[a] for some time
past, to write an orderly account for you, most excellent
Theophilus, that you may know the truth concerning the
4 things of which you have been informed.

[a] Or *accurately*

---

himself through the person and mission of Jesus, qualifies both the other terms, *eyewitnesses and ministers*, which probably refer to the twelve apostles. Just as God's *word* had been contained in the Jewish Law, so now it was found for the Christian in a person, Jesus of Nazareth. Hence Jesus came to be described as God's Word or Wisdom, through whom God made the world, keeps it in being, and makes himself known. Ancient historians commonly appealed to *eyewitnesses*, or claimed themselves to have been eyewitnesses of the events described. The Christian faith is based on the empirical evidence of the early disciples of Jesus, who through their living contact with him were forced to believe that he was the all-decisive figure in God's dealings with men, and so were able to testify to the truth of what they had seen. *ministers of the word*: under the direction of *the word*, and responsible for its transmission to others. *from the beginning*: perhaps from the beginning of John the Baptist's ministry.

3 *it seemed good to me also*: Earlier Christian writings have given Luke a precedent, and he feels that he has a contribution of his own to make. His particular claim is that he has *followed all things*, probably in the sense of having witnessed the origins and development of the Christian movement. *closely*, or, better, 'accurately'. *for some time past* could also mean 'from the beginning': Luke is going to testify to the truth of the official tradition from his own experience. *an orderly account* refers not to chronological order (in which the Gospel writers do not seem interested), but to a neat arrangement of material. *Theophilus*, to whom the book is dedicated, was probably well known to Luke, perhaps his literary patron. *most excellent* is a courteous form of address and does not reveal the social standing of the person so addressed. It is likely, however, that Theophilus and the circle for whom the book is intended belonged to the cultured classes.

4 *informed*: or 'taught', in the sense of receiving official instruction. The first is the more likely meaning, as the verb normally has this meaning when followed by 'about'. Luke is supplementing Theophilus' and others' (perhaps inadequate) knowledge of Christianity.

5 **In the days of Herod, king of Judea, there was a priest named Zechariah, of the division of Abijah; and he had a**

[b] Greek *Zacharias*

1: 5–2: 52 *John and Jesus are introduced*

(1) The setting for the work of John and Jesus is now given. John is seen as the forerunner of Jesus, fulfilling the function of Elijah, who in Jewish expectation prepares the way for God's decisive intervention. Jesus is viewed as the king or Messiah of the line of David, who comes to rescue the Jews from their enemies and reign over them in a restored Jewish kingdom. Luke will show later that Jesus does not fit exactly the pattern of these Jewish hopes.

(2) God's Holy Spirit is prominent in Jesus' conception, but particularly in connection with prophecy ($1^{15, 41, 67}$, $2^{26, 36}$). In Jewish thought the Spirit is connected with God's creative activity and with prophecy. By the time of Jesus the belief was held that the line of God's prophets had ended in the period after the Jewish exile in Babylon (cp. 1 Macc. 4^{46}, 11^{27}, 14^{41}). In God's new age, however, the Spirit would again inspire men to prophesy (Joel 2^{28}; cp. Acts 2^{17-21}). In the Dead Sea Scrolls the Holy Spirit is thought to be at work in the Qumran community, but only because the latter is vitally connected with the triumph of God over evil and the coming of his new age. Luke's emphasis on the outburst of prophecy suggests that God's expected new era has dawned.

(3) There is constant reference to joy expressed in various terms: 'joy and gladness' (1^{14}), 'rejoice' (1^{14}), 'praise' (2^{13}), 'glorify' (2^{20}), 'give thanks' (2^{38}). In the O.T. this language has close links with God's new order and his rescue of his people (Isa. 21^{1}, 35^{10}; Ps. 50^{15}). This note of joy is a characteristic of the whole Gospel.

(4) The language and background are very Jewish: it is out of the midst of the Jewish religion that Christianity, the true development of Judaism, springs (cp. John 4^{22}).

(5) In the early presentation of the Christian faith it was thought important to demonstrate that Jesus was the Messiah or Saviour descended from David (e.g. Acts 2^{22-36}; Rom. 1^{3}). These stories and reminiscences (some from Mary herself)

wife of the daughters of Aaron, and her name was Elizabeth.
6 And they were both righteous before God, walking in all the
7 commandments and ordinances of the Lord blameless. But
they had no child, because Elizabeth was barren, and both
were advanced in years.

---

about the birth of John and Jesus and their childhood may well have been collected together at an early date, as part of this apologetic.

(6) The construction of 1^{5-80} falls into four divisions:

$$A\text{: } 1^{5-25}\text{; } B\text{: } 1^{26-38}\text{; } C\text{: } 1^{39-56}\text{; } D\text{: } 1^{57-80}.$$

Between *A* and *B* the parallels of language and theme stand out clearly, thus stressing the importance of both John and Jesus for God's purposes. But John's role is preparatory, while Jesus will prove to be a king whose reign never ends. Again, while John is to be filled with the Holy Spirit 'from his mother's womb' (1^{15}), Jesus is conceived through the Holy Spirit (1^{35}). Similarly *C* and *D* are constructed on parallel lines (cp. $1^{41, 44}$ with $1^{57, 59}$; 1^{41} with 1^{67}; $1^{48\,ff.}$ with $1^{68\,ff.}$).

A: 5–25 John's birth and future status are foretold

5 Herod 'the Great' was King of Judea, 40–4 B.C., his territory covering a wider geographical area than Judea proper, and including Samaria and Galilee. He ingratiated himself with successive Roman leaders, and is correctly described as *king*, a title conferred on him by Rome. For their duties in the temple the priests of the line of *Aaron* were divided into different groups or orders, named after the twenty-four grandsons of Aaron, one of whom was *Abijah* (cp. 1 Chr. 24^{1-19}).

6 God uses for his purpose those who are devoted to him. *righteous before God* (cp. Gen. 7^{1}, 17^{1}): either righteous and accepted as such by God, or righteous as living their lives in the sight of God. Such righteousness is due to their *walking in*, or 'living in accordance with' *the commandments and ordinances* (cp. Deut. 28^{45}) contained in the Jewish Law, found in the first five books of the O.T. *blameless* denotes the meticulous observance of God's demands.

7 Cp. Gen. 18^{1}; Judg. 13^{2}; 1 Sam. 1^{2}. Childlessness was regarded as a stigma and was sometimes miraculously remedied by God for his special purposes (cp. Ps. 113^{9}).

8 Now while he was serving as priest before God when his
9 division was on duty, according to the custom of the priest-
hood, it fell to him by lot to enter the temple of the Lord and
10 burn incense. And the whole multitude of the people were
11 praying outside at the hour of incense. And there appeared
to him an angel of the Lord standing on the right side of the
12 altar of incense. And Zechariah was troubled when he saw him,
13 and fear fell upon him. But the angel said to him, 'Do not
be afraid, Zechariah, for your prayer is heard, and your wife
Elizabeth will bear you a son, and you shall call his name John.
14 And you will have joy and gladness,
and many will rejoice at his birth;

8–9 The various duties were assigned by the casting of lots. One of these functions was to make the incense offering morning and evening in the temple (Exod. 30^{7-8}; 2 Chr. 13^{11}) on a special altar in front of the Holy of Holies, the inner of the two temple sanctuaries.

10 The assembly of the people outside the temple is similar to the O.T. picture of the 'tent of meeting' where God promises to meet with the congregation of Israel (Exod. 29^{42-43}). Incense, an offering in honour of God, also symbolized the offering of prayers (Ps. 141^{2}): the hour of incense was, therefore, naturally an hour of prayer.

11 *there appeared to him an angel of the Lord*: cp. Exod. 3^{2}; Judg. 13^{3}. *the right side* may denote favour and protection. From the sixth century B.C. angels become prominent in the Jewish religion as intermediaries between God and his world. This interest can be traced (*a*) to the contact with the Iranian religion, in which such powers were prominent, and (*b*) to a desire to stress the transcendence of God. One angelic function was to convey messages from God to man.

12 *troubled* and *fear* describe awe in the presence of the supernatural.

13 *do not be afraid*: a word of reassurance from God (cp. Gen. 15^{1}). Like Hannah (1 Sam. 1^{10-17}), Zechariah and Elizabeth had prayed to God to end their childlessness. Names were given to children to describe either the circumstances in which they were born or their future destiny (cp. Matt. 1^{21}): the Hebrew *Johanan* means 'God has been gracious', and so may be a reminder that John's conception has been due to the special favour of God.

14 This verse, with vv. 15–18, shows signs of the structure and pattern of Hebrew poetry; hence the arrangement in the RSV.

15 for he will be great before the Lord,
and he shall drink no wine nor strong drink,
and he will be filled with the Holy Spirit,
even from his mother's womb.
16 And he will turn many of the sons of Israel to the Lord their God,
17 and he will go before him in the spirit and power of Elijah,
to turn the hearts of the fathers to the children,
and the disobedient to the wisdom of the just,
to make ready for the Lord a people prepared.'

---

15 *before*: 'in the judgement of' or 'in the opinion of'. John's status is one that depends on God's choice of him. Abstention from wine and strong drink was part of a rule laid on Samson's mother (Judg. 13^{4-14}), on those who undertook a Nazirite vow (Num. 6^{3}), and on the Rechabites (Jer. 35^{1-11}). This regulation may not merely be an attempt to uphold the ideals of the nomadic way of life, but probably symbolizes the condition of the man of God who is set apart from the ordinary pleasures of life in complete dedication to God. Such asceticism (cp. 7^{33}) is not necessarily connected with John's future life away from the settled village or town (1^{80}); for the Qumran community, although it saw itself as called to live in the wilderness of Judaea, nevertheless drank wine at ritual meals. *even from his mother's womb* (cp. Judg. 13^{5}) perhaps means not 'from his very birth' (so NEB), but 'even before birth', a vivid way of stating that a nation's or person's status, here John's prophetic office, is deeply rooted in the purposes of God. *filled with the Holy Spirit* and the similar 'full of the (Holy) Spirit', both common in Luke–Acts, denote the possession of people by God, so that they become the vehicle of his words and deeds. The exhilaration from wine is contrasted with the inspiration from God's Holy Spirit (cp. Eph. 5^{18}).

16 *turn*: restore to allegiance with God (cp. Zech. 1^{3}). God may himself have to initiate such a change of heart (Ps. 85^{4}), as here by the sending of John. *sons of Israel*: those who belong to Israel, the special name for the Jews viewed as God's chosen people.

17 Cp. Mal. 4^{5-6}; Ecclus. 48^{10}. *before*: (*a*) 'in advance of', 'preparing the way for', or (*b*) 'in the sight of', i.e. having God's approval. There had arisen a firm Jewish expectation that Elijah or some other great prophet would appear to warn the nation of God's impending intervention;

18 And Zechariah said to the angel, 'How shall I know this? For
19 I am an old man, and my wife is advanced in years.' And the
angel answered him, 'I am Gabriel, who stand in the presence
of God; and I was sent to speak to you, and to bring you this
20 good news. And behold, you will be silent and unable to

---

hence probably the importance of 'the prophet' in the expectations of the Qumran community (*The Community Rule*, ix; see Vermes, *The Dead Sea Scrolls in English*, p. 87). *in the spirit and power of Elijah*: the authority and status of Elijah are now vested in John (cp. 2 Kgs. 2^{15}). Elijah's main task was to bring the Israelites back to the worship of the true God. John's connection with Elijah is firmly rooted in the Gospel tradition (Matt. $11^{10, 14}$; Mark 1^{2}, 9^{13}; Luke 7^{27}). The vivid language sometimes suggests that John is Elijah himself, but it is unlikely that any more is meant than what Luke states here—that John fulfils the function assigned to Elijah. Any idea of Elijah's being reincarnated in John would be alien to Jewish thinking. In John 1^{21} John the Baptist denies that he is Elijah, which links up with the fact that he nowhere himself makes a claim to have the status of Elijah, which is always attributed to him by others. *turn the hearts*: heal the dissensions in the nation of Israel. God's wisdom is the way of life laid down by him for those who are *just*—in a right relationship to him. *to turn . . . the disobedient to the wisdom*: the parallelism of this section has strange features, obscured in the translation. Two different prepositions for 'to' are used (ἐπί and ἐν), and the personal word 'children' is paralleled by the abstract term 'wisdom'. Another translation might be: 'to turn the hearts of the fathers to the children and to turn the disobedient (to the Lord) by the wisdom of the just'. The strangeness of the whole construction may suggest a Hebrew or Aramaic original. *prepared*: for God's coming judgement. John is portrayed as the forerunner of God himself, and not of God's agent, Jesus: this may suggest the pre-Christian origin of this description.

18 A request for a sign, or the provision of one, to authenticate a divine promise, is common in the O.T. (e.g. Exod. 4^{1}). For the incredulity of Zechariah cp. Gen. 17^{17}, 18^{11-14}.

19 For *Gabriel* ('God is mighty') see Dan. 8^{16}, 9^{21}, and *The War Rule* of the Qumran community, ix (Vermes, *The Dead Sea Scrolls in English*, p. 136), where Gabriel with other angels fights on the side of the sons of light in their battle with evil. The growing importance of angels is seen in their being given personal names. God is pictured as a king surrounded by his court (cp. 1 Kgs. 22^{19}).

20 Zechariah, like Ezekiel (3^{26}), is to have his tongue unloosed to attest

speak until the day that these things come to pass, because
you did not believe my words, which will be fulfilled in their
21 time.' And the people were waiting for Zechariah, and they
22 wondered at his delay in the temple. And when he came out,
he could not speak to them, and they perceived that he had
seen a vision in the temple; and he made signs to them and
23 remained dumb. And when his time of service was ended, he
went to his home.

24 After these days his wife Elizabeth conceived, and for five
25 months she hid herself, saying, 'Thus the Lord has done to
me in the days when he looked on me, to take away my reproach among men.'

26 In the sixth month the angel Gabriel was sent from God to

---

the fulfilment of God's promise (see 1^{64}). Zechariah's loss of speech is both a punishment for his lack of faith and a token of the genuineness of the angel's promise. *in their time*: at the decisive moment chosen by God (cp. Gen. 18^{14}).

21 Were they *waiting* for Zechariah to come out to tell them that the incense offering had been made, or was the time of prayer concluded by the priest's giving the blessing?

22 *vision*: a regular term for seeing something supernatural from which a prophet receives a message (cp. Dan. 10^{1}).

23 Presumably Zechariah stayed in Jerusalem for the whole period of his duty: thus he would keep the rules of ritual purity binding on the priests.

25 Perhaps Elizabeth *hid herself* or remained secluded at home, because she did not wish to risk any harm to the child in the early days of pregnancy. Or was this act of self-denial and renunciation an acknowledgement of God's blessing shown to her? *looked on*: has shown favour to. *her reproach*: her childless state (cp. Gen. 30^{23}). *men*, or, better, 'people', 'society'.

1: 26–38 Mary receives God's message about the birth of her child

26 *In the sixth month*: of Elizabeth's pregnancy (cp. 1^{36}). According to Luke (2^{3}) Joseph and Mary are already settled in Nazareth before the birth of Jesus, while Matthew mentions it for the first time on their settlement there after their return from Egypt (1^{23}); there is no

27 a city of Galilee named Nazareth, to a virgin betrothed to a
man whose name was Joseph, of the house of David; and the
28 virgin's name was Mary. And he came to her and said, 'Hail,
29 O favoured one, the Lord is with you!'[c] But she was greatly
troubled at the saying, and considered in her mind what sort
30 of greeting this might be. And the angel said to her, 'Do not
31 be afraid, Mary, for you have found favour with God. And
behold, you will conceive in your womb and bear a son, and
you shall call his name Jesus.

[c] Other ancient authorities add '*Blessed are you among women!*'

---

necessary contradiction between the two accounts. *Galilee*, part of the kingdom of Herod the Great, passed into the hands of his son, Antipas (cp. 3^1). The association of Jesus with Galilee is strong in the Gospel tradition, and is emphasized here by Luke from the outset. Nazareth lay on the slopes of the mountain called Tabor.

27 *virgin*, or, better, 'a young woman', or 'a woman eligible for marriage'. For the betrothal cp. Matt. 1^{18}. This giving of the man and woman to each other was a contract binding in such a way that the relationship could only be broken by divorce (cp. Matt. 1^{19}), though the marriage proper and its consummation might only take place months or even a year later. The ceremony of betrothal was performed in the presence of witnesses, and the pledges were made either by word of mouth or in writing; a dowry would be given. The occasion probably concluded with the blessing over a cup of wine which the betrothed tasted in turn. *of the house of David* probably refers to *Mary*, who, like Joseph (2^4) belongs to the royal family—a connection important because of Jesus' presentation as the King of Davidic descent.

28 *Hail*: a common greeting. Mary is *favoured*, or singled out by God for a special purpose. *The Lord is with you* brings the reassurance that God is favourably disposed towards her (cp. Josh. 14^{12}). Some MSS. add 'Blessed are you among women!' (RSV margin), which has been introduced here from 1^{42}.

30 Cp. 1^{13}. *you have found favour*: commonly used of gaining the approval or goodwill of God or man.

31 Cp. 1^{13}; Judg. 13^3; Isa. 7^{14}. Jesus, the leading character, is now mentioned for the first time. The name probably means 'great in salvation' (Ecclus. 41^1), and is another form of 'Joshua' (cp. Matt. 1^{21}).

He will be great, and will be called the Son of the Most
High;
and the Lord God will give to him the throne of his father
David,
and he will reign over the house of Jacob for ever;
and of his kingdom there will be no end.'

And Mary said to the angel, 'How can this be, since I have no

---

As in 1^{14-17}, the angel's message has the form and structure of Hebrew poetry. *will be called*: will have the status of. *the Most High* here describes the transcendence and power of the one true God (cp. Dan. 4^{17}). 'Son of God', used of the Israelite king, is now transferred to the expected ideal Davidic king of the future. This picture of Jesus, ruling, like David, over an earthly Jewish kingdom is very different from the kingship associated with Jesus after his resurrection; it is unlikely to have originated in the early Church, but probably reflects hopes centred on Jesus before the course of his mission became clear. For vv. 32–33 see also Isa. 9^{7}.

The Jews were sometimes called the *house* or family of *Jacob*, in whose sons the twelve tribes of Israel were thought to originate (Gen. 49^{1-27}). In contrast with the temporary splendour of David's kingdom, the future Davidic kingdom would have endless prosperity. 'whose kingdom shall have no end', based on our present text, was added to the Nicene Creed and some of the other creeds in order to combat theologians who, on the basis of 1 Cor. 15^{28}, postulated that the lordship of Jesus would come to an end.

Cp. 1^{18}. The question has been thought strange. If Mary was betrothed to Joseph, then she could expect to be married in the next year, and so could look forward to having a child. One solution is that Luke or the tradition he followed has combined two sources. One described the conception and birth of Jesus from the natural union between Mary and Joseph; the other described how Mary, unbetrothed and unmarried, was to conceive and give birth to the child through the activity of the Holy Spirit. In favour of this two-source theory is also urged the fact that, while in 1^{32} the title 'Son of God' seems to be related to the possession of kingship, in 1^{35} it is connected with the miraculous conception. But perhaps Mary felt that the angel's prediction, applying seemingly to the near future, was premature, as she is not yet fully married to Joseph or having intercourse with him. *since I have no husband* can be translated 'since I am not having intercourse with a man'. Hence Mary's shock: it is strange to

35 husband?' And the angel said to her,

'The Holy Spirit will come upon you,
and the power of the Most High will overshadow you;
therefore the child to be born[d] will be called holy,
the Son of God.

36 And behold, your kinswoman Elizabeth in her old age has
also conceived a son; and this is the sixth month with her who
37 was called barren. For with God nothing will be impossible.'

[d] Other ancient authorities add *of you.*

---

be talking of children when I am not yet fully wed. The further explanation of the 'Sonship' (v. 35) could be merely an amplification of the title, giving an additional reason why the child will hold it. If the difficulty of Mary's question is pressed, the answer may not lie in two sources: it may be better to view the phrase 'betrothed to a man whose name was Joseph' (1^{27}) as a later addition to the original story, in which Mary was not yet betrothed to Joseph when she had the vision. Then 'of the house of David' would also fit better into the sentence.

35 In the O.T. *the Holy Spirit* only occurs in Isa. 63^{10-11}, while 'thy Holy Spirit' is found in, e.g., Ps. 51^{11}. The term is also found in the *Hymns* of the Qumran community (e.g. *Hymn* xi; Vermes, *The Dead Sea Scrolls in English*, p. 173). It is the equivalent of the common expression 'the Spirit of the Lord', since 'Holy' means 'belonging to God'. *the Holy Spirit* and *the power of the Most High* are synonyms. The imagery of 'overshadow' suggests God's protection (cp. Ps. 17^{8}). *the child to be born*, or 'the child that is being conceived'. The additional 'of you' (RSV margin), found in some MSS., is probably a later clarification. Another possible translation is: 'the holy child to be born will be called "Son of God" ' (NEB). For the conception of Jesus cp. Matt. 1^{18-20}.

36 *And behold* introduces an important statement. Elizabeth's conception authenticates the reliability of the promise now made to Mary. Elizabeth *is called* or 'reputed to be' *barren* in the opinion of human beings, in contrast with what she is enabled to do by the power of God. *kinswoman*: the exact relationship is not known. *the sixth month*: of the pregnancy.

37 Cp. Gen. 18^{14}.

38 And Mary said, 'Behold, I am the handmaid of the Lord; let
it be to me according to your word.' And the angel departed
from her.

39 In those days Mary arose and went with haste into the hill
40 country, to a city of Judah, and she entered the house of
41 Zechariah and greeted Elizabeth. And when Elizabeth heard
the greeting of Mary, the babe leaped in her womb; and
42 Elizabeth was filled with the Holy Spirit and she exclaimed
with a loud cry, 'Blessed are you among women, and blessed
43 is the fruit of your womb! And why is this granted me, that
44 the mother of my Lord should come to me? For behold, when
the voice of your greeting came to my ears, the babe in my
45 womb leaped for joy. And blessed is she who believed that
there would be[e] a fulfilment of what was spoken to her from
the Lord.'

[e] Or *believed, for there will be*

---

38 *Behold, I am the handmaid* expresses Mary's act of submission to the will of God (cp. 2 Sam. 9^{6}). *word*: the commandment or declared intention of God.

: 39–56 Mary's visit to Elizabeth. The Song of Mary.

39 *the hill country*: the mountain range that lies between the Mediterranean coast and the line of the Jordan valley and the Dead Sea.

41 *leaped*, or 'stirred': used in Gen. 25^{22} of babies stirring in the womb, which is usual at this advanced stage of pregnancy. Even the unborn child recognized the importance of Mary and her child. 'leap' can also mean 'leap for joy' (cp. 6^{23}), and so the stirring of the child suggests the joy of the unborn child (cp. 1^{44}).

43 Elizabeth feels privileged that Mary the mother of the expected king has paid her a visit. *my Lord*: the title of a king and so appropriate to describe Jesus.

45 *she who believed*: Mary had shown her belief that God would carry out his promise, however strange and unusual it seemed. For *a fulfilment . . . spoken* cp. Judith 10^{9}. *from*: 'at the hands of', or 'by command of'.

46 And Mary said,
'My soul magnifies the Lord,
47 and my spirit rejoices in God my Saviour,
48 for he has regarded the low estate of his handmaiden.
For behold, henceforth all generations will call me blessed;

---

46 *Mary* is the most common reading. 'Elizabeth' is an early alternative, which is sometimes favoured, for several reasons. The song is reminiscent of the song of Hannah (2 Sam. 2^{1-10}), a thanksgiving by a woman who thought that she would be childless. Elizabeth fits this situation rather than Mary. 1^{56} suggests that Elizabeth has been speaking. The preference for 'Mary' rather than 'Elizabeth' may have been due to the greater interest in the mother of Jesus. In 1^{67} the description of Zechariah being 'filled with the Holy Spirit' is followed by a song of praise, and if Elizabeth, 'filled with the Holy Spirit' (v. 41), uttered the song in 1^{46-56}, it would form a striking parallel. But 'Mary' is strongly attested and has overwhelming MSS. support. A scribe may have made the alteration because he appreciated the above arguments for the reading 'Elizabeth', although he obviously had very little influence on the general MSS. tradition. The importance attached to the Virgin Mary is unlikely to have been so prominent in the first centuries of the Church as to effect so thoroughgoing a change in the MSS. Further, apart from the theme of God's exaltation of the unassuming, common in Jewish literature, the connections between this Psalm and the song of Hannah are slender (see also the commentary). Originally 1^{56} may have followed on 1^{45} in continuous prose narrative, before the song was added by either Luke or his source. The reading 'Mary' is, therefore, preferable. Later Jewish Psalms were, like this one, based on the structure and language of the O.T. Psalms (cp. the Psalms of Solomon (first century B.C.), and the *Hymns* of the Qumran community, Vermes, *The Dead Sea Scrolls in English*, pp. 149–201). The precedent for prose narrative interspersed by poetical songs of praise is found, e.g., in Exod. 14–15; 1 Sam. 1^{1}–2^{11}. For *My soul* and 'my spirit' (v. 47), referring to the speaker, cp. Pss. 35^{9}, 42^{2}. *magnifies the Lord*: acknowledges the Lord as powerful to achieve his purposes.

48 God's deliverance is now explained further. *regarded the low estate* is an idiom with the sense of 'coming to the aid of someone who is in distress', God being normally the subject (cp. 1 Sam. 1^{11}). It is doubtful whether *low estate* can mean 'humble station', especially when combined with 'regard'. The term could, therefore, apply more easily to Elizabeth than to Mary. But the song perhaps related originally to

for he who is mighty has done great things for me,
and holy is his name.
And his mercy is on those who fear him
from generation to generation.
He has shown strength with his arm,
he has scattered the proud in the imagination of their
hearts,
he has put down the mighty from their thrones,
and exalted those of low degree;

Mary's joy when Joseph was convinced that her pregnancy was no disgrace but part of the plan of God (Matt. 1^{18-21}). *generations* could also be 'nations', but in view of 1^{50} it most likely refers to future generations of people. The phrase vividly expresses the decisiveness of the role that Mary is to play and it has also been literally fulfilled.

For *he who is mighty* cp. Ps. 24^{8}. The poem now changes to a general act of praise to God. God's *name* stood for his being, character, and all that he is. *and holy is his name* is, therefore, the acknowledgement that God is powerful to achieve his purpose (Ps. 111^{9}).

Cp. Ps. 103^{17}, where *mercy* or 'love', as here, is a characteristic of God. *from generation to generation* expresses the sureness and certainty of God's mercy, which is experienced by *those who fear him*, i.e. treat him with awe and reverence as the one to whom their loyalty is due.

He has shown strength: lit. 'he has done mighty deeds' (cp. Ps. 117^{15}). *arm*, or 'right arm'. God was revealed in his mighty acts especially in the Exodus from Egypt and the deliverance from captivity in Babylon. *in the imagination of their hearts* goes closely with the word *proud* (cp. Ps. 89^{11}): those who are self-assertive in outlook and intention. The *proud*, those who ignore the will and demand of God and pursue their own selfish aims, are often contrasted with the 'poor' or 'humble' (cp. v. 52), who are ready to submit themselves to God. It is a common theme that such arrogance will come to nothing, having no value at all in God's sight (cp. Ps. 18^{27}).

Cp. Ecclus. 10^{14}. God is no respecter of the normal worldly estimates of power; he introduces the unpredictable into human situations. *put down . . . from their thrones*: perhaps reminiscent of the history of Israel, when God removed kings and replaced them with others. *those of low degree*: people with no worldly position, but content to rely on God and suffer for their faith in him. *exalted*: raised to a high position and vindicated the rightness of their cause. In the present instance God has chosen the obscure and unknown Mary for his great purposes.

53 he has filled the hungry with good things,
and the rich he has sent empty away.
54 He has helped his servant Israel,
in remembrance of his mercy,
55 as he spoke to our fathers,
to Abraham and to his posterity for ever.'
56 And Mary remained with her about three months, and returned to her home.
57 Now the time came for Elizabeth to be delivered, and she
58 gave birth to a son. And her neighbours and kinsfolk heard

---

53 Cp. Pss. 34^{10}, 107^{9}. *hungry* also contains the idea of a desire and need of God, while *rich* suggests those who are self-satisfied. God is not influenced by people's outward circumstances.

54 *Israel* is often described as God's servant (e.g. Isa. 41^{8}): God has chosen her for his purposes and she only has significance as serving those purposes. *in remembrance of*, lit. 'to remember': God's help is an expression of his *mercy* or 'love', seen in his covenant with Israel. When God remembers his love, he makes it effective in the present (cp. Ps. 98^{3}).

55 Cp. Mic. 7^{20}. *as he spoke to our fathers* is best taken as a parenthesis, and then *to Abraham* goes closely with 'mercy' (v. 54). *our fathers*, or 'ancestors': the patriarchs, Abraham, Isaac, and Jacob, to whom God had made special promises about the future of their descendants. *posterity*: lit. 'seed'. *for ever*: the covenant had no time limit, unlike human covenants and agreements (cp. Ps. 105^{10}). The thought is of God's help given to Israel down the ages, but it includes the new rescue operation that will come through the birth of Jesus. Some readers would also see in 'seed' a reference to Jesus himself, the one in whom God's promises to Abraham are fulfilled (cp. Gal. 3).

56 Mary perhaps remained to see the child safely born. Luke in that case finishes his description of Mary's visit and then goes back a little in time to record the birth of John and its attendant circumstances in more detail. *her home*: Nazareth.

1: 57–66 The Birth of John

57 *the time came*, or 'the time was fulfilled' (cp. Gen. 25^{24}).

58 *shown great mercy*: lit. 'made great his mercy' (cp. Ps. 57^{10}). The joy is that Elizabeth, contrary to all expectations, had given birth to a male child to carry on the family name. The closely knit village society sharing joys and sorrows is depicted.

that the Lord had shown great mercy to her, and they re-
59 joiced with her. And on the eighth day they came to circum-
cise the child; and they would have named him Zechariah
60 after his father, but his mother said, 'Not so; he shall be
61 called John.' And they said to her, 'None of your kindred is
62 called by this name.' And they made signs to his father,
63 inquiring what he would have him called. And he asked for
a writing tablet, and wrote, 'His name is John.' And they all
64 marvelled. And immediately his mouth was opened and his
65 tongue loosed, and he spoke, blessing God. And fear came on
all their neighbours. And all these things were talked about
66 through all the hill country of Judea; and all who heard them

---

59 For the regulations about circumcision see Gen. 17^{10}, 21^{4}; Lev. 12^{3}. It became the hallmark of the Jewish nation as established by the reforms of Ezra and Nehemiah, and was a sign of the special place that the Jews had in God's plan; hence they were sometimes called 'the circumcision' (cp. Eph. 2^{11}; Phil. 3^{3}). Probably a benediction or act of praise was spoken before the circumcision, and the ceremony closed with the usual grace over the cup of wine when the child received his name. *they*: the neighbours and kinsfolk. The ceremony would take place in the parents' house with a family gathering. A Jewish son was sometimes named after his father. *Zechariah* means 'the Lord remembered', and so may have been thought especially appropriate for a child who was the answer to human prayer.

60 For *John* see 1^{13}. Zechariah had somehow communicated the angel's message to his wife, presumably either by 'sign' language (as in 1^{22}) or by writing (as in 1^{63}).

62 Zechariah was temporarily deaf as well as dumb.

63 Such a *writing tablet* consisted of thin pieces of wood fastened or strung together: the wood might be covered with papyrus or with wax. The latter type was probably the one used here and the writing would be done by an iron stylus. *is*: the name has already been determined by God (1^{13}). *marvelled*: probably at the assurance of Zechariah's answer, which was recognized as divinely inspired.

64 Now that God's promises are fulfilled, Zechariah's speech is restored, so that he can add his contribution to the benediction, or act of praise, in which he had been unable to join during the first part of the ceremony.

laid them up in their hearts, saying, 'What then will this child be?' For the hand of the Lord was with him.

67 **And his father Zechariah was filled with the Holy Spirit, and prophesied, saying,**

---

66 *laid them up in their hearts*: cp. 1 Sam. 21^{12}, and below, $2^{19, 51}$. The hearers took careful note of the news and remembered it. Perhaps Luke means that the birth of John and its attendant circumstances made such a deep impression on the neighbourhood that, when John turned out to be a prophet, the earlier events were vividly remembered and related. *the hand of the Lord*: God's power to help or punish. Here *with* makes it clear that God's activity is favourable. The expression is used of God's control of the prophets (e.g. Ezek. 3^{14}; cp. Acts 11^{21}, 13^{11}). If *was* is omitted (the evidence is weak) the words would be part of the people's comment.

1: 67–80 The Song of Zechariah; John in the wilderness

The song is almost certainly pre-Christian. First the picture is that of God's deliverance of Israel by a Davidic king (who deals with the nation's earthly enemies) and by a prophet (who brings the nation to repentance), the object being the creation of an Israel free from fear of outside enemies and restored to a new harmony with God, so as to offer him a new and perfect worship. This picture of the victorious Davidic ruler does not fit the figure of the crucified and risen Jesus, the centre of the early Church's belief. Similarly, the picture here of the limited hope of the Jewish nation, secure in its worship of God, does not accord very well with the Church's interest in the Gentiles, evident at an early date. Further, equal status is assigned to the Davidic king and the prophet. In Jewish expectation several figures are given important roles in the coming of God's new age (the Qumran community looked for the coming of 'the anointed one of Aaron', 'the anointed one of Israel', and also 'the prophet'). But such a picture does not accord with the belief of the early Christians, for whom the only decisive figure was Jesus, and who studiously subordinated John the Baptist to him, the functions of priest, prophet, and king being concentrated in Jesus alone. The psalm here, therefore, predates the crucifixion of Jesus, and very probably reflects the much earlier speculation about the possible status and future roles of John and Jesus. For Luke it gives one of the lines that Jewish hopes took, and provides a background to the work of Jesus. A priest, like Zechariah, may well have composed such a psalm: it was the function of the priest in the Qumran community to offer acts of praise for the favours of God. The psalm may originally have been in Aramaic, and can be

68 'Blessed be the Lord God of Israel,
for he has visited and redeemed his people,
69 and has raised up a horn of salvation for us
in the house of his servant David,
70 as he spoke by the mouth of his holy prophets from of old,

---

analysed as follows. If one works back and forward, starting from 'covenant' and 'oath' (vv. 72, 73), which elsewhere are found in close proximity to each other (cp. Ps. 105^{8-9}), there are parallels of language:

68	visited	H
	his people	G
69	salvation	F
70	prophets	E
71	saved from our enemies	D
	from the hand	C
72	our fathers	B
	covenant	A
73	oath	A
	our father Abraham	B
74	from the hand of our enemies	C
	delivered	D
76	prophet	E
77	salvation	F
	his people	G
78	will visit (RSV margin)	H

The important theme is that God is faithful and will fulfil his word and promise.

68 *Blessed be*: introducing an act of praise to God. *God of Israel*: the one who has made himself known in a special way to the Jewish nation. The title links up with the national character of the deliverance envisaged.

69 *raised up*: in the sense of sending to meet a crisis (cp. Judg. 3^{9}). *horn*: strength or source of strength. *of salvation*: bringing deliverance.

70 The construction of this and the following verses is difficult and irregular: (*a*) vv. 71–75 may be loosely connected with *spoke* of our

71 that we should be saved from our enemies,
and from the hand of all who hate us;
72 to perform the mercy promised to our fathers,
and to remember his holy covenant,
73, 74 the oath which he swore to our father Abraham, to grant
us

---

present verse (so NEB), or (*b*) v. 71 alone qualifies *spoke* and vv. 72–75 explain further vv. 68–69 (the implication of the RSV). Perhaps it is best to regard v. 70 as a parenthesis, with the whole of vv. 71–75 expanding the thought of vv. 68–69. *as he spoke by the mouth*: the prophets of the O.T. regarded themselves as the mouthpieces of God himself, and could say 'Thus says the Lord'. *from of old*: the line of prophets goes well back into history (cp. Jer. 28^{8}; Heb. 1^{1}) with the thought that God's promise is sure. The prophets are *holy* as dedicated to God's purposes.

71 Cp. Pss. 18^{17}, 106^{10}. Jewish hopes centred on deliverance from oppression by outside nations, resulting in their being left free to worship their God. *the hand*, or 'the control'. The Jews incurred hatred by their exclusiveness in religious belief and practice and by their refusal to compromise with other religions and philosophies. Perhaps the Roman authorities are in mind; although in Roman law the Jews enjoyed special rights to practise their religion, yet the Roman representatives did not always show understanding of Jewish susceptibilities.

72 *perform the mercy promised to*: an idiom meaning 'deal lovingly with'. In coming to the rescue of the present generation of Jews God is showing love to, and keeping faith with, the Jewish patriarchs, not only because the Jews were descended from the patriarchs, but also because the Jewish nation is part of them, considered as corporate beings. *remember his holy covenant*: come to the rescue of Israel in faithfulness to the covenant (cp. Ps. 105^{8}). The relationship between God and the Jews was based on a covenant or series of covenants, the most important of which was that made at the time of the Exodus (Exod. 24): God promised his protection and guidance to Israel, who in turn promised obedience and faithfulness to God.

73 The *oath* of God: his solemn assurance that he will prosper Abraham's descendants, the nation Israel (Gen. 15^{18-21}, 17^{2}). The covenant of v. 72 is probably, therefore, that made with Abraham.

74 This clause could explain the 'oath', but is probably parallel to v. 72. The Jewish ideal of the future is often pictured in terms of God's

that we, being delivered from the hand of our enemies,
might serve him without fear,
75 in holiness and righteousness before him all the days of our life.
76 And you, child, will be called the prophet of the Most High;
for you will go before the Lord to prepare his ways,
77 to give knowledge of salvation to his people
in the forgiveness of their sins,
78 through the tender mercy of our God,
when the day shall dawn upon[f] us from on high

[f] Or *whereby the dayspring will visit*. Other ancient authorities read *since the dayspring has visited*

---

being worshipped by his faithful people. *without fear*: unhampered by outside enemies. Man achieves his true purpose in a life of full harmony with God.

75 *holiness* means giving God his due and putting him first, while *righteousness* probably refers to right dealing between human beings, an inescapable part of the worship of God. *before him*, or 'in his presence': perhaps the picture of a restored Jerusalem, with a new temple symbolizing the presence of God. *all the days of our life* might mean that the hope is limited to the speaker and his contemporaries, but more likely refers to Israel's living for evermore on earth in this perfect harmony with God (cp. Ps. 90^{14}).

76 *child*: John the Baptist. *will be called*: shall receive the status of. John is to be the special prophet who will prepare the way for the new age of God.

77 The prophet will reveal the imminence of God's deliverance, part of which will be the assurance of God's forgiveness for the nation's sins, an important part of John's proclamation (cp. Jer. 31^{33-34}).

78 *the day*: another translation would be 'the branch' (cp. Jer. 23^{5}), denoting the king of the line of David, who rules over a restored kingdom of Israel. This is the most probable meaning, with a reference back to 'the horn of salvation' (v. 69). *day* or 'dayspring' (RSV margin) would suggest a picture of the rising sun, i.e. the light of God, coming to break the darkness of evil. The alternative reading 'will visit' (RSV margin) is preferable.

79 to give light to those who sit in darkness and in the shadow
of death,
to guide our feet into the way of peace.'
80 And the child grew and became strong in spirit, and he was
in the wilderness till the day of his manifestation to Israel.

2: IN those days a decree went out from Caesar Augustus
2 that all the world should be enrolled. This was the first enrol-

---

79 *darkness* and the *shadow* (or 'cloud') *of death* describe the oppression and captivity of God's people (cp. Ps. 107^{10}; Isa. 9^{2}). *peace*: full and unhampered fellowship with God.

80 Cp. $2^{40, 52}$; 1 Sam. 2^{21}. *strong in spirit* could describe John's powerful and purposeful personality, but *spirit* could mean the Holy Spirit at work in John. *in the wilderness*: John may have been a member of the Qumran community which had its headquarters in the desert of Judaea, but this is highly speculative. A contrast is made between the early years of John, lived in seclusion in the wilderness, and his public ministry, *his manifestation to Israel*. The description is meant to suggest a connection with Elijah, who had associations with the desert (1 Kgs. 19^{4}), and lived an ascetical life away from civilization (2 Kgs. 1^{8}).

2: 1–7 The Birth of Jesus. See also Matt. 1^{18-25}

1 *in those days* refers probably to the period of John's conception and birth. There is no evidence of a census held for the whole Roman Empire simultaneously, but an imperial decree for the registration of a particular population was sometimes prefaced by reference to the Emperor's wish that a census should be made of the whole Empire. The first Emperor, Octavian (31 B.C.–A.D. 14), became known as *Augustus*, originally a title conferred on him, meaning 'one who is revered'. *Caesar*, originally part of his name, after that of his adoptive father, Julius Caesar, became equivalent to 'Emperor' (cp. Acts 23^{8}). Luke connects the birth of Jesus with the whole Roman world, to mark it as a world-shaking event, a theme elaborated in Acts.

2 *Syria*, an important Roman province on the eastern frontier, was governed by a representative of the Emperor, called a *legatus pro praetore*, with four legions under his command; he would have general oversight of the Palestinian area. *Quirinius* held various posts in the Syrian area in the period before A.D. 6, when he became governor of

3 ment, when Quirinius was governor of Syria. And all went to
4 be enrolled, each to his own city. And Joseph also went up
from Galilee, from the city of Nazareth, to Judea, to the city
of David, which is called Bethlehem, because he was of the
5 house and lineage of David, to be enrolled with Mary, his
6 betrothed, who was with child. And while they were there,
7 the time came for her to be delivered. And she gave birth to
her first-born son and wrapped him in swaddling cloths, and

Syria. The RSV translation is ambiguous: the meaning is that it was the first enrolment or census of its kind in the area, and that it happened in Quirinius' governorship. The enrolment that Luke has in mind is almost certainly that which was held when Judaea became a province of the Roman Empire, after the deposition of King Archelaus in A.D. 6 (cp. Acts 5³⁷). Luke may intentionally have dated the birth of Jesus in this year rather than in the closing years of Herod the Great (a tradition found in Matt. 1¹⁸–2¹², and implied in 1⁵⁻⁸⁰ above, where the births of John and Jesus are synchronized). The possibility that Quirinius had an earlier period as governor of Syria in the closing days of Herod, and conducted an earlier enrolment, cannot be absolutely ruled out, but is not supported by any clear evidence. Another suggested solution is that Jesus was born at the time of an enrolment conducted by Herod, and that this was later confused with the famous census of A.D. 6.

3 This method is not attested elsewhere. Luke or his source probably had good historical reason for recording it.

4 For *the city of David* cp. 1 Sam. 16¹. Jesus is viewed as the expected king of David's family.

5 *his betrothed* implies that the marriage between Joseph and Mary had not yet been consummated, and that the child had some origin other than intercourse between them.

6 Cp. 1⁵⁷.

7 *the inn*, or 'lodging house', probably a house accommodating people during the census. Owing to overcrowding, accommodation usually kept for animals had to be brought into use for visitors, and the *manger*, or 'eating trough', filled with straw, formed a makeshift cot for the baby. This story illustrates the important theme that Jesus, the Son of God, shared human frustrations and difficulties right from the beginning of his earthly life (cp. 2 Cor. 8⁹), and may foreshadow for Luke his later humiliation on the cross.

laid him in a manger, because there was no place for them in
the inn.
8 And in that region there were shepherds out in the field,
9 keeping watch over their flock by night. And an angel of the
Lord appeared to them, and the glory of the Lord shone
10 around them, and they were filled with fear. And the angel
said to them, 'Be not afraid; for behold, I bring you good
11 news of a great joy which will come to all the people; for to
you is born this day in the city of David a Saviour, who is
12 Christ the Lord. And this will be a sign for you: you will find

---

2: 8–20 The visit of the shepherds; the angels' witness

A group of people (cp. Matt. 2[1–12]) are brought by a God-given sign to visit the child, Jesus, who is revealed to them as the expected king and saviour of the Jews; hence Luke's interest in the story (note especially v. 11). Stories of unusual events attending the birth of great men have always been popular, and, whatever their origin and historical credibility, reflect the importance and stature of the persons concerned. Our present story is told in a restrained manner and without embellishment. Its early origin is perhaps shown by v. 10, 'great joy which will come to all the people'—the Jews, which does not seem to presuppose the Gentile mission and the rejection of Jesus by the majority of the Jewish nation.

8 David himself was a shepherd (1 Sam. 16[11]), and so, perhaps significantly, his great successor is made known to shepherds. They may typify the 'babes' (10[21]), or ordinary people, to whom God reveals his wisdom.

9 God's *glory*, his being, presence, and character in all its majesty, was seen in his mighty acts, and was also sometimes visible to men as a bright light (e.g. Exod. 13[21]; Ezek. 43[2]).

11 *Christ the Lord*: an unusual way of describing the expected king, occurring, however, in Ps. of Sol. 17[32]; the alternative, 'the Lord's Christ', is a later attempt to alter a difficult phrase. *Christ*, or 'the anointed one' (Heb. 'Messiah'), was by now a technical term to describe the future king and deliverer of Jewish expectations (cp. Mark 8[29]). *Lord*: an appropriate title for a king (cp. 2 Sam. 3[31]). Luke also uses it to refer to the earthly Jesus.

12 For the giving of a *sign* or 'proof' of the truth of God's words cp. 2 Kings 19[29]. Here the *sign* would also be a guide to the shepherds in

a babe wrapped in swaddling cloths and lying in a manger.'
13 And suddenly there was with the angel a multitude of the
heavenly host praising God and saying,
14 'Glory to God in the highest,
and on earth peace among men with whom he is pleased!'[g]
15 When the angels went away from them into heaven, the
shepherds said to one another, 'Let us go over to Bethlehem
and see this thing that has happened, which the Lord has
16 made known to us.' And they went with haste, and found
17 Mary and Joseph, and the babe lying in a manger. And when
they saw it they made known the saying which had been told
18 them concerning this child; and all who heard it wondered
19 at what the shepherds told them. But Mary kept all these
20 things, pondering them in her heart. And the shepherds

[g] Other ancient authorities read, *peace, goodwill among men*

---

their search: the cradling of a baby in a cattle manger would be a rare occurrence.

13 One of the functions of *angels* is the praise of God (cp. Rev. 5). *Glory to*: a way of acknowledging God's greatness (cp. 19^{38}). *in the highest* brings out the transcendence of God, in contrast with *on earth* in the next clause, which gives the reason for such praise: God is bringing *peace*, a restoration of harmony between himself and human beings. *men with whom he is pleased*: lit. 'men of goodwill', a noun usually describing God's favourable attitude rather than that of men; hence the translation in the RSV, which makes men the recipients of the goodwill. 'peace, goodwill among men' (RSV margin) is a less likely reading.

17 For *the saying* cp. v. 11.

18 The element of wonder is again stressed.

19 The story may thus go back to Mary herself, who vividly remembered what happened. These strange events imprinted themselves on her mind, and after the resurrection of Jesus she saw their real significance.

20 The human praises are now joined to the praises of angels (vv. 13–14).

returned, glorifying and praising God for all they had heard
and seen, as it had been told them.
21 And at the end of eight days, when he was circumcised, he
was called Jesus, the name given by the angel before he was
conceived in the womb.
22 And when the time came for their purification according
to the law of Moses, they brought him up to Jerusalem to
23 present him to the Lord (as it is written in the law of the
Lord, 'Every male that opens the womb shall be called holy
24 to the Lord') and to offer a sacrifice according to what is
said in the law of the Lord, 'a pair of turtledoves, or two
young pigeons.'

2: 21–24 The circumcision of Jesus and his presentation in the temple

21 Jesus' circumcision illustrates the fact that he entered fully into the human situation (cp. Gal. 4^{4}).

22–24 For a mother's *purification* after childbirth see Lev. 12. The purificatory rites were concerned with the restoration of the woman to normal society after her confinement. *their* implies that the child and perhaps Joseph as well were involved in the 'purification', though nothing in the Law demands this. There are laws in the O.T. stating that all male firstborn, whether human beings or animals, belong to God. In the case of animals this meant the offering of them to God in sacrifice, and the same had applied at one time to human beings. Under the regulations, however, of Exod. $13^{12-13, 15}$, the male firstborn of human beings were to be redeemed, and so were exempt from the law of sacrifice. Such laws were a reminder that all life comes from God and belongs to him, as well as being a commemoration of God's redemption of Israel from Egypt. The presentation of children in the temple, though not required by the Jewish Law, may well have become the custom by this time, in order to dedicate them to the service of God. Such a presentation of the child Jesus may have symbolized for Luke his complete consecration to God's service during his whole life. The citation in v. 23 is a general summary of the Exodus law. The *sacrifice* or offering (v. 24) is the climax of the mother's purificatory ceremonies; it consisted of either a lamb with a young pigeon and turtledove, or a choice between *a pair of turtledoves* and *two young pigeons*. As the alternative is mentioned here, Joseph and Mary were not well-to-do.

25 Now there was a man in Jerusalem, whose name was
Simeon, and this man was righteous and devout, looking for
the consolation of Israel, and the Holy Spirit was upon
26 him. And it had been revealed to him by the Holy
Spirit that he should not see death before he had seen the
27 Lord's Christ. And inspired by the Spirit[h] he came into the
temple; and when the parents brought in the child Jesus,
28 to do for him according to the custom of the law, he took him
up in his arms and blessed God and said,

29 'Lord, now lettest thou thy servant depart in peace,
according to thy word;

[h] Or *in the Spirit*

25–35 The witness of Simeon to Jesus' future role

Simeon views Jesus as (*a*) 'the Lord's Christ' (v. 26), (*b*) the centre of God's coming deliverance (vv. 30–32), and (*c*) the all-decisive figure, who will show men up in their true light (vv. 34–35).

25 For *devout* see also Acts 2^5, 22^{12}. *consolation*: God's coming to rescue his people from captivity and oppression (cp. Isa. 49^{13}).

27 *inspired by the Spirit*: the Holy Spirit both inspires Simeon to come into the temple at the decisive moment, and also to utter the prophetic words of vv. 29–35. *the parents*, with its implication that Joseph was the real father of Jesus, might suggest that the story comes from a source unaware of the virginal conception. But the story probably goes back to Jewish circles and to people who witnessed the incident, who would naturally refer (without knowing the inner story) to the two persons present as the parents of Jesus. Joseph had accepted Jesus as part of his family and so could in that sense be regarded as his earthly father. *custom* suggests that the presentation of the child was a tradition that sprang up out of the Law's regulations.

29 This prophecy, like many prophetic oracles in the O.T., has a poetical structure. For the language cp. Isa. 40^5, 44^{13}, 49^6, 52^{10}. Simeon, well versed in the O.T., would naturally use its terminology. *Lord* (here δέσποτης) suggests absolute authority. *servant*, lit. 'slave', expresses Simeon's total allegiance to God. Simeon knows that God is letting him depart this life in peace, i.e. contentment in having seen the future king and saviour. *according to thy word*: the promise of v. 26.

30 for mine eyes have seen thy salvation
31 which thou hast prepared in the presence of all peoples,
32 a light for revelation to the Gentiles,
and for glory to thy people Israel.'

33 And his father and his mother marvelled at what was said
34 about him; and Simeon blessed them and said to Mary his
mother,

'Behold, this child is set for the fall and rising of many in Israel,
and for a sign that is spoken against

---

32 *revelation to the Gentiles*: God's acts will reveal to non-Jews the presence and power of the creator of the whole earth. Another translation is 'revelation of the Gentiles': God's powerful act of deliverance will show up the rest of the nations in their real light as ignorant of the true God. But God's action will bring *glory* to Israel: Israel will be vindicated as the special people of God and will enjoy full fellowship with him (cp. Isa. 60^{19-22}). The implication is that the Jews will reap the benefits of God's intervention, while the part of the Gentiles is to be astonished and impressed. The prophecy of Simeon is, therefore, nationalistic, like so much of the material in these chapters. Luke here refers for the first time to the *Gentiles*, or 'the nations'—non-Jews. In the sequel Gentiles will not only be impressed by God's rescue operation, but will also be received on equal terms with the Jews into the Christian Church—a major theme of Acts (cp. Acts 13^{47}, 26^{23}). The disparity between Jew and Gentile, reflected in Simeon's words, suggests that the prophecy is a Jewish composition and not an invention of the early Church.

34 Simeon underlines the cruciality of a right decision about Jesus. *set*: destined by God. Acceptance of Jesus as the appointed agent of God will mean *rising* or 'resurrection' to a new status with God; rejection of him will bring a *fall*, a rupture with God's plans and alienation from him (cp. Pss. 41^{10}, 113^{7}; Isa. 24^{20}; Amos 8^{14}). *sign*: one in whom God's decisive purposes are proclaimed and encountered (cp. Ezek. 12^{6}). But (as happened with Ezekiel) Jesus will be *spoken against*, rejected by many of the Jews—a prophecy fulfilled in the persecution, suffering, and death of Jesus. For the decisiveness of reaction to Jesus cp. 9^{26}, 12^{8-9}.

35 (and a sword will pierce through your own soul also),
that thoughts out of many hearts may be revealed.'

36 And there was a prophetess, Anna, the daughter of Phan-
uel, of the tribe of Asher; she was of a great age, having lived
37 with her husband seven years from her virginity, and as a
widow till she was eighty-four. She did not depart from the
temple, worshipping with fasting and prayer night and day.
38 And coming up at that very hour she gave thanks to God,

---

35 The first part is best regarded as a parenthesis, and the second, as a purpose clause qualifying 'Behold, . . . spoken against'. The parenthesis implies that Mary will be involved in the hostility to Jesus. The *sword* may symbolize Mary's anguish at the cruel treatment meted out to her son, or may be a metaphor of testing and trial—i.e. Mary's faith in Jesus will be sorely tested (cp. Heb. 4^{12}). Two further points may be noted: (i) Simeon with prophetic insight now also sees that Jesus will prove a centre of controversy, a sombre touch that contrasts with the general joyful tone of this section and prepares for Jesus' coming rejection; (ii) *that thoughts out of many hearts may be revealed*: the decision for or against Jesus (or the reaction of indifference) will show up human *thoughts* or attitudes in their true light, whether they are in step or out of step with God's purposes (cp. John 3^{17-21}). Luke will later underline the disparity between the Jewish insights and the purposes of God, shown for instance in the preference for Barabbas the brigand.

2: 36–40 The witness of Anna, the prophetess, to Jesus

The testimony of a woman now parallels that of the man Simeon. For the placing of a woman-centred incident side by side with a man-centred incident see also 1^{46-79}, 7^{1-17}, 8^{40-56}, 10^{29-42}, 15^{1-10}, 24^{1-35}.

37 *prophetess*: the gift of prophecy was not confined to men (cp. 2 Kgs. 22^{14}), and so Elizabeth and Anna prophesy the coming of God's new order (cp. Acts 21^{9}). Anna's great age, far greater than the customary 'three score years and ten' (Ps. 90^{10}), probably stresses God's special favour. Her devoted service in the *temple* depicts her as one in close touch with God and so one who can be the reliable mouthpiece of God. *night and day* suggests that Anna perhaps followed the pattern of prayer found in Ps. 119^{62}.

38 *at that very hour* implies that Anna's arrival was due to divine inspiration (cp. v. 26). *spoke of him*: as the expected Saviour king. Anna's estimate of Jesus agrees with that of Simeon.

and spoke of him to all who were looking for the redemption
of Jerusalem.
39 And when they had performed everything according to the
law of the Lord, they returned into Galilee, to their own city,
40 Nazareth. And the child grew and became strong, filled with
wisdom; and the favour of God was upon him.
41 Now his parents went to Jerusalem every year at the feast
42 of the Passover. And when he was twelve years old, they went
43 up according to custom; and when the feast was ended, as they
were returning, the boy Jesus stayed behind in Jerusalem.

39–40 Verse 39 completes the account of the visit to Jerusalem. *performed . . . the Lord*: Jesus was 'born under the law' (Gal. 4^{4}), and, like John, comes from a family loyal to it. The summary in v. 40 (cp. 1^{18}) bridges the years between Jesus' birth and the age of twelve, and prepares for the next incident, concluded by a similar summary (cp. the summaries in Acts on the progress of the Church, e.g. Acts 6^{7}). God's *favour* towards Jesus and Jesus' *wisdom* are stressed in the following incident, the only story in our Gospels of the boyhood of Jesus.

2: 41–52 Jesus as a boy in the temple

The stories of 'infant prodigies' have always been popular. The present one is very restrained in tone and lacking in any extravagant claims. The incident leads up to the significant words in v. 49, which brings out Jesus' consciousness of being in a special relationship with God. The dearth of information about Jesus' childhood in the Gospels may be due to the fact that what was known would have shed very little information on Jesus' future mission and his attitude to it.

41 *the Passover*: the chief of the Jewish religious festivals, which was held in April each year, and commemorated the Exodus or deliverance from Egypt (Exod. 12^{2}, 23^{14-17}; Deut. 16). The festival had to be held in Jerusalem. Probably Luke sees a parallel between this Passover, at which Jesus is present in his early life, and the later Passover, at which Jesus is put to death and raised from the dead, thus effecting a new and greater Exodus and Passover.

42 At the age of thirteen a Jewish boy became officially a 'son of the Law', under the obligation to attend Jewish festivals. This was sometimes, as here, anticipated by a year.

43 The whole festival lasted seven days.

44 His parents did not know it, but supposing him to be in the
company they went a day's journey, and they sought him
45 among their kinsfolk and acquaintances; and when they did
46 not find him, they returned to Jerusalem, seeking him. After
three days they found him in the temple, sitting among the
47 teachers, listening to them and asking them questions; and all
who heard him were amazed at his understanding and his
48 answers. And when they saw him they were astonished; and
his mother said to him, 'Son, why have you treated us so?
Behold, your father and I have been looking for you anxiously.'
49 And he said to them, 'How is it that you sought me? Did you
50 not know that I must be in my Father's house?' And they
did not understand the saying which he spoke to them.

---

45 Jesus stayed behind not out of wilful disobedience, but out of curiosity, and to take advantage of the novel opportunity of being able to hear the great Jewish teachers; like other boys he was perhaps forgetful of time, and the thrilling occupation of the moment made him forget that others might be wondering what had happened to him. He was also driven on by the higher compulsion (v. 49) of knowing that the temple and its activities were his special concern.

49 Jesus has felt an allegiance that transcends the obedience due to his earthly parents. *Did you not know . . . ?* could be a reference back to the unusual events surrounding his birth. *must*: in accordance with God's purpose (cp. 9^{22}). *in my Father's house*, lit. 'in the things of my Father', is sometimes translated as 'concerned with the business of my Father', but the RSV is preferable. There may be a play on the words 'your father' (v. 48) and 'my Father' in this present verse. Ultimately Jesus has only one father, God (cp. John 8^{28}); see also above, p. 38.

50 For this failure to understand Jesus cp. 9^{45}, 18^{34}. Luke is probably hinting that only after Jesus' death and resurrection would the meaning of his person and mission become clear (cp. John 2^{22}, 12^{16}).

obedient: Jesus is not defiant of parental authority (as the incident might at first suggest), but shared human life to the full, carrying out the Jewish commandment, 'Honour your father and your mother' (Exod. 20^{12}); cp. Eph. 6^{1}; Col. 3^{20}, inspired probably by Jesus' own obedience. The time has not yet come when obedience to the higher

51 And he went down with them and came to Nazareth, and was obedient to them; and his mother kept all these things in her heart.

52 And Jesus increased in wisdom and in stature,[i] and in favour with God and man.

3: IN the fifteenth year of the reign of Tiberius Caesar, Pontius

[i] Or *years*

---

authority of God will lead Jesus to go against the wishes of his family and to put into practice his own teaching, contained in such passages as 14^{26}.

52 Cp. 1 Sam. 2^{26}. *favour with . . . man*, that marked Jesus' early life, is in contrast with the antagonism that his public ministry will provoke, though Luke all through lays some stress on Jesus' popularity (cp. 4^{15}, 21^{38}).

3: **1–20** *The work of John the Baptist*

(1) Luke shows little dependence on Mark. 'preaching . . . forgiveness of sins' (v. 3) and 'but he . . . untie' (v. 16) could be from Mark 1^{4} and 1^{7}, but may be due to an identity of language between Mark and one of Luke's other sources.

(2) The view is sometimes held that Luke has stripped John of his role as Elijah who prepares the way for the final 'day' of God. The quotation from Mal. 3^{1} (Mark 1^{2}) is omitted. No reference is made to John's dress (Mark 1^{6}), which is reminiscent of that of Elijah (2 Kgs. 1^{8}). More emphasis is laid on John's ethical teaching (vv. 10–14). Luke may, therefore, be removing John's connection with the 'end' time, part of his restatement of the Gospel in view of the delay of the advent of Jesus and of the final completion of God's plans. But Luke has already presented John as a successor to Elijah. The just as relevant passage, Mal. 4^{5-6}, has already been cited in relation to John (1^{17}). In contrast with Mark 1^{1}, John is indeed no longer said to be 'the beginning of the Gospel of Jesus Christ', but the omission does not reduce John's status; for his vital role in relation to Jesus has already been stressed, and his part in the bringing of the Gospel or good news is brought out below, 3^{18}.

Pilate being governor of Judea, and Herod being tetrarch of Galilee, and his brother Philip tetrarch of the region of Ituraea and Trachonitis, and Lysanias tetrarch of Abilene,

---

(3) The prophecy of John (vv. 16–17) presents a picture of fiery judgement, different from the course of Jesus' mission, and so suggests that John's teaching has been correctly preserved and not made to approximate to the exact manner of its fulfilment.

1–6 The setting for John's ministry

The chronological note (the only attempt in the N.T. to give an absolute date) is based, in accordance with ancient custom, on the rulers of the period (cp. Jer. 1^{1-3}; and Thucydides, *Peloponnesian War*, ii. 2). Luke uses this date to mark the decisive moment in his history—the beginning of the ministry of John and Jesus, and to stress the world-wide importance of the historical events that follow.

Tiberius, the second Emperor of the Roman Empire (A.D. 14–37), was the stepson of Augustus. He had already been made co-Emperor with Augustus in A.D. 12, and so the *fifteenth year* could be either A.D. 27 or 29, probably the former. *Judea* became a Roman province in A.D. 6, under the control of a praefectus responsible to the Emperor. *Pontius Pilate* held the office A.D. 26–35, his long tenure being not unusual under Tiberius. *Herod*, a son of Herod the Great, and commonly known as Antipas, was tetrarch (the name for a small dependent ruler) from 4 B.C. to A.D. 41, when he was deposed and his kingdom incorporated in that of King Agrippa I (Acts 12^{1}). *Philip*, another son of Herod the Great, was tetrarch from 4 B.C. to his death in A.D. 33 or 34. *Lysanias, tetrarch of Abilene*: there was a king of Chalcis (in the same area as Abilene) with this name in the period 40–36 B.C.; he was the son of Ptolemais, ruler of the same area. Luke has sometimes been thought to be referring to this Lysanias, and so to be guilty of a serious chronological error. But such carelessness should not readily be attributed to Luke. Our knowledge of the period is limited and such a later Lysanias may well have existed. Josephus refers to 'Abila, the territory of Lysanias' (*Antiquities*, xix. 275) and to 'Abila, the tetrarchy of Lysanias' (*Antiquities*, xx. 138), a probable reference to this later Lysanias in the period A.D. 25–30. This later Lysanias is also probably mentioned in inscriptions (CIG 4521 and 4523). Luke's concern to mention this comparatively insignificant figure points to his conviction that Lysanias was a contemporary of the other rulers.

2 in the high-priesthood of Annas and Caiaphas, the word of
God came to John the son of Zechariah in the wilderness;
3 and he went into all the region about the Jordan, preaching a

---

2 The *high-priesthood of Annas and Caiaphas* might suggest a joint tenure of the office, but there could be only one high-priest at a time (cp. $22^{50, 54}$). Annas, high-priest A.D. 6–15, was deposed by the Romans and succeeded later by his son-in-law, Caiaphas, who held the office A.D. 18–36. In giving both names Luke may be reflecting the opinion of those who still considered Annas to be the rightful high-priest, or he may be suggesting that Annas was the real 'power behind the throne' (see also John 18^{13}; Acts 4^{10}). *the word of God came* (cp. e.g. Jer. 1^{2}) sets John in line with the great O.T. prophets.

3 *the region about the Jordan* or 'the Jordan plain' (Gen. 13^{10}) is more explicit than Mark 1^{4}. Luke is thought to be giving John a limited sphere, compared with that of Jesus, who exercises a wider ministry in Galilee, Samaria, and Judea. But Luke may have taken over the phrase from his special source or may be clarifying Mark's vagueness in the light of John's definite connection with the river Jordan (Mark 1^{6}). The O.T. prophets often dramatized their message in symbolical acts (e.g. Jer. 19^{1-12}), but John's symbolical act of *baptism* is the way in which his hearers are to seal their acceptance of his message. *of repentance*: the baptism is to portray a change of attitude and a re-dedication to God; such a call to repentance often marked the message of the O.T. prophets (e.g. Joel 2^{12}). The background to John's use of baptism is varied: (*a*) the metaphorical use of 'washing' to describe a change of heart (e.g. Isa. 1^{16}); (*b*) the use of washing to remove ritual defilement (e.g. Lev. 14^{8}); (*c*) the ritual bathings of the Qumran community, one of which was used on entry into the community and covenant (*The Community Rule*, iii, Vermes, *The Dead Sea Scrolls in English*, p. 75)—the outward act here having to be accompanied by the acceptance of the laws of God and a turning from wickedness, so representing a point of view in line with John's teaching; (*d*) 'proselyte' baptism, or 'the bath', part of the non-Jewish convert's initiation into the Jewish faith. But John's baptism had the unique feature of being an act of dedication to God in readiness for divine events. On the other hand, Christian baptism will prove to be a means of entering into these events when they have taken place. *for the forgiveness of sins*: (*a*) those who accept John's baptism receive with it the assurance of God's forgiveness; or (*b*) their baptism will lead to the forgiveness of God brought by Jesus himself. Probably (*a*) is meant. The call to repentance also becomes part of Jesus' message, all the more urgent both because of his superior status and because of the new stage he introduces in God's dealings with men.

4 baptism of repentance for the forgiveness of sins. As it is
written in the book of the words of Isaiah the prophet,

'The voice of one crying in the wilderness:
Prepare the way of the Lord,
make his paths straight.
5 Every valley shall be filled,
and every mountain and hill shall be brought low,
and the crooked shall be made straight,
and the rough ways shall be made smooth;
6 and all flesh shall see the salvation of God.'
7 He said therefore to the multitudes that came out to be

4–6 The quotation from Isa. 40^{3-5} grounds John's mission in the O.T. and so in God's purposes (see also Matt. 3^{3}; Mark 1^{3}; John 1^{23}). Luke, like the other Gospel writers, follows the LXX in taking 'in the wilderness' with 'a voice of one crying', as the place of John's activities (in the Hebrew it goes with 'prepare the way'; cp. *The Community Rule*, viii and ix, Vermes, *The Dead Sea Scrolls in English*, pp. 85–8), and he continues the quotation to include 'and all flesh shall see the salvation of God', showing his interest in the world-wide importance of Jesus' mission. 'And the glory of the Lord shall be revealed' (Isa. 40^{5}) is probably omitted because Luke regarded this clause as already fulfilled in 2^{8-14}. *Every valley . . . smooth* (Isa. 40^{4}), only included by Luke, may have represented for him the breaking down of all obstacles to the preaching of the gospel in the wider world—the theme of Acts. In v. 4 Luke, with Matthew and Mark, substitutes *his* for 'of our God', and so *the Lord* can denote Jesus.

3: 7–9 The coming of judgement

See also Matt. 3^{7-12}. Like the O.T. prophets, John seeks to disillusion the Jews from resting on their privileges.

7 For *multitudes* Matthew has 'many of the Pharisees and Sadducees', an expression which may reflect his antagonism to these sects. Luke's *multitudes* links up with 7^{29-30} (where 'the people' accept John's baptism) and with 3^{10}. For *brood of vipers* cp. Matt. 12^{34}, 23^{33}. *Who warned you . . . ?* is ironical: how could people so poisoned with evil have thought of coming to terms with the judgement of God? *wrath* describes the reaction of the righteous God to all that is evil and opposed to his will. Here the final judgement is in mind.

baptized by him, 'You brood of vipers! Who warned you to
8 flee from the wrath to come? Bear fruits that befit repentance,
and do not begin to say to yourselves, 'We have Abraham as
our father'; for I tell you, God is able from these stones to
9 raise up children to Abraham. Even now the axe is laid to the
root of the trees; every tree therefore that does not bear good
fruit is cut down and thrown into the fire.'
10 And the multitudes asked him, 'What then shall we do?'
11 And he answered them, 'He who has two coats, let him share
with him who has none; and he who has food, let him do like-
12 wise.' Tax collectors also came to be baptized, and said to

---

8 More is required than outward acknowledgement of *repentance*, symbolized in John's baptism, and perhaps wrung from people by the awe-inspiring thought of God's judgement (see also Acts 26^{20}). In face of Israel's default, God can end the special covenant-relationship with this people. Since it is purely a matter of God's will and choice (see Rom. 9), he can here and now create a new nation and give it the status of descent from Abraham. Similarly Paul argues that the Gentile Christians, though not descended physically from Abraham, are nevertheless 'sons of Abraham' because of their faith (Rom. 4; Gal. 3).

9 *trees* stands for the individual Jews, while *axe* is a symbol of God's impending judgement. The picture is of a tree found unfruitful and so only fit to be used for fuel. For *fire* and God's judgement cp. Jer. 4^{4}.

3: 10–14 John's teaching and advice to various classes of people

The passage is recorded only by Luke. Josephus (*Antiquities*, xviii. 116–19) records that John 'bade the Jews practise virtue' and 'behave righteously to one another', and Luke includes examples of this teaching, though the Gospel writers' main interest is in John's role of preparation for Jesus. Luke's purpose probably is to clarify 'bear fruits' (v. 8) and to draw a parallel between John's dealings with these people and Jesus' later contact with them. Verse 11 anticipates the deeper teaching of Jesus on 'generous love' (6^{27-38}).

11 The *coat* was the tunic or shirt worn next to the skin by both sexes. The wearing of two tunics was sometimes criticized as over-indulgence. By a concrete example John underlines the need for selflessness in the whole of life. Jesus makes an even more stringent demand for selfless love (6^{29}).

12 *Tax collectors*: both from the Roman province of Judaea, and from

13 him, 'Teacher, what shall we do?' And he said to them,
14 'Collect no more than is appointed you.' Soldiers also asked
him, 'And we, what shall we do?' And he said to them, 'Rob
no one by violence or by false accusation, and be content with
your wages.'
15 As the people were in expectation, and all men questioned
in their hearts concerning John, whether perhaps he were
16 the Christ, John answered them all, 'I baptize you with water;
but he who is mightier than I is coming, the thong of whose
sandals I am not worthy to untie; he will baptize you with the
17 Holy Spirit and with fire. His winnowing fork is in his hand,

---

the tetrarchies of the Herods, which almost certainly paid taxes to the Roman power. There were the general tax officials who collected taxes on property and income, and the custom-house officials who were responsible for the special taxes on, for example, imports, exports, and use of roads. Both were condemned by the Rabbis for their unjust and cruel exactions, their petty tyranny and avarice. The second class were considered to be under the ban of Lev. 20^{5}, and for both repentance was thought to be difficult. John does not refuse them baptism, but summons them to keep strictly to the tax scale laid down by the government. John's action anticipates the friendship and love shown by Jesus both to them and to other social and religious outcasts.

14 *Soldiers*: probably Jewish soldiers belonging to Herod's troop (23^{11}) or forming the temple guard (22^{52}), but perhaps also Roman soldiers, attracted to Judaism and to John the Baptist. *rob . . . by violence*: in the sense of extorting money by violence or bullying. *false accusation*, or 'blackmail'. *wages*, lit. 'rations', which came to describe a soldier's pay.

3: 15–20 John's prediction of the mightier one: his imprisonment. See also Matt. 3^{11-12}, 4^{12}; Mark $1^{7-8,\ 14}$

15 This is Luke's way of preparing for John's next statement about the mightier one, and his indication that in the sequel John is referring to the expected Jewish Messiah or *the Christ*.

16 *sandals* consisted of a leather sole secured to the foot by straps. In the case of important people the task of untying them would be that of a servant; so John is protesting his utter inferiority in relation to his successor. John's subordination to Jesus is underlined in the Gospel

to clear his threshing floor, and to gather the wheat into his
granary, but the chaff he will burn with unquenchable fire.'
18 So, with many other exhortations, he preached good news
19 to the people. But Herod the tetrarch, who had been reproved
by him for Herodias, his brother's wife, and for all the evil
20 things that Herod had done, added this to them all, that he
shut up John in prison.

---

tradition and especially in the Gospel of John (e.g. 1^{19-23}, 3^{27-30}). This emphasis probably reflects both John's own estimate of his status and the early Christians' desire to guard against any idea of Jesus being commissioned by John. Two features would have shocked John's contemporaries: (*a*) the contrast with the popular Jewish idea of the Messiah, who would free the Jews from foreign domination; and (*b*) John's grim portrayal of the judgement of God threatening the chosen people itself. John now uses 'baptize' metaphorically, in the sense of 'wash' or 'purify'. *Holy Spirit* could also be translated 'holy wind', and then the picture is of God using 'wind' and 'fire' (cp. Ps. 104^{4}) to clear from Israel undesirable elements, a metaphor which fits in with the 'threshing floor' analogy that follows. John may originally have spoken of a baptism 'with wind and fire'; then 'holy' was added to show that the prophecy of John was fulfilled in the coming of the Holy Spirit to inspire the Christian Church in its life and work (cp. Acts 2^{1-4}, where wind and fire become symbols, not of judgement, but of the power given by the Holy Spirit). On the other hand, in the thought of the Qumran community, the Holy Spirit is connected with purification, and so John may well have used the phrase as in the text (cp. *Hymn* xvi, Vermes, *The Dead Sea Scrolls in English*, p. 97).

17 Cp. Jer. 51^{33}. *threshing floor*, or better 'threshed corn': the latter was thrown into the wind with a shovel (the winnowing-fork) to remove the chaff, which was then available for fuel. *wheat*: those who are loyal to God. *chaff*: the wicked (cp. Ps. 1^{4}). For *unquenchable fire*, connected with God's hostility to those who oppose his will, cp. Jer. 4^{4}, 7^{20}. John sees that the decisive hour of God's vindication of his people and cause is near.

18 The grim prediction of John does not sound *good news*. Luke probably so regarded it because John is the prelude to Jesus, who brings the good news of God's new deliverance. *many other exhortations* show that Luke is only giving a summary of John's message.

19–20 Cp. Mark 6^{17}. *Herodias* was the granddaughter of Herod the Great being the daughter of his son Aristobulus. She was the mother-in-law

Now when all the people were baptized, and when Jesus
also had been baptized and was praying, the heaven was
opened, and the Holy Spirit descended upon him in bodily
form, as a dove, and a voice came from heaven, 'Thou art my
beloved Son;[j] with thee I am well pleased.'[k]

[j] Or *my Son, my* (or *the*) *Beloved*
[k] Other ancient authorities read *today I have begotten thee*

---

of Philip the tetrarch (3^{1}), who married her daughter Salome, and she was previously married to another Herod, a half-brother of Herod Antipas, who is referred to here as *his brother*, and who is, perhaps erroneously, given the name of Philip in Mark 6^{17}. Herodias was now, it seems, the wife of Herod Antipas, a relationship which John had condemned as being unlawful. It is not known whether Herodias had merely deserted her former husband, or had repudiated him by a process of divorce. John's firm stand against royalty is probably intended to be reminiscent of Elijah's protest against King Ahab and his queen Jezebel (1 Kgs. 1^{21}). Detailed information on the *evil things* is lacking, but Herod's character is said to have been marked by covetousness and the desire for luxurious living. His greater achievements lay in his building schemes, e.g. the city of Tiberias. According to Josephus, John's *prison* was the fortress of Machaerus, and the reason for Herod's treatment of John was fear of the latter's influence over the people, due, as the Gospel writers make clear, to the fact that he was regarded as a prophet.

: 21–4: 13 *The baptism, genealogy, and temptation of Jesus*

See also Matt. 3^{13}–4^{11}; Mark 1^{9-13}; cp. John 1^{32-34}. In the tradition about Jesus as Luke received it the baptism and temptation narratives were already closely associated, probably to reflect the pattern of the Exodus from Egypt, when the Israelites were 'baptized' in the water of the Red Sea and later were 'tested' in the wilderness (cp. 1 Cor. 10^{1-13}).

: 21–22 The baptism of Jesus

The incident is firmly rooted in the early tradition about Jesus' ministry (cp. Acts 10^{38}). Its invention is unlikely because of its embarrassing nature. It might suggest that Jesus was somehow commissioned by John or might be misinterpreted in this way. The acceptance of baptism at the hands of John might imply or be twisted to imply that Jesus was inferior to John. The awkward question arises: why did the sinless Jesus undergo a 'baptism for the remission of sins'? Matthew, alive to these problems, adds an explanatory dialogue (Matt. 3^{14-15}), and separates the experience of Jesus from the baptism (Matt. 3^{16}). Similarly, in Luke no reference is made to John as the one who administered the baptism, the actual baptism is passed over very quickly, and the divine revelation is linked with the prayer of Jesus subsequent to the baptism. Luke may be drawing on a source (other than Mark) in which the risks of misinterpretation have been lessened.

21 Only Luke has *all the people* (looking back to 3^{15}, and forward to 7^{29}), a description of the ordinary Jews in contrast with the Jewish hierarchy. Jesus associates himself with people's desire to repent and their hope of the renewal of Israel (cp. Heb. 2^{11}). It is also possible to translate 'when all the people had been baptized': Jesus' baptism followed the general baptism, and so, while identifying him with other human beings, is unique, as the occasion of a special commission from God. *praying*: Luke marks the decisive moments in Jesus' ministry in this way, and so underlines the readiness of Jesus to align himself with the will of God (6^{12}, $9^{18, 28}$, 11^{1}, 22^{41}). It is when Jesus has humbled himself to undergo John's baptism and is waiting upon God that his status is revealed to him. If the revelation was private to Jesus, then the details of it must have been passed on by him to his disciples, just as the vision of Isaiah (Isa. 6) was no doubt passed on by him to his disciples. As in Mark 1^{9}, Jesus appears abruptly, but Luke has already introduced us to him in Chapters 1 and 2. *the heaven was opened*: symbolical language for the receiving of a vision or revelation from God (cp. Ezek. 1^{1}). Like Matthew, Luke uses *open* for the more vivid 'cleft asunder' of Mark 1^{10} (RSV 'opened').

22 Possession of God's Spirit would be a mark of the future ideal king (Isa. 11^{2-3}). *descended* depicts how God from his exalted state gives his Spirit of power to human beings. The contrast in Mark between Jesus' ascent from the water and the Holy Spirit's descent upon him is lost, but we have what Luke may have seen as a parallel in Acts 1^{14}–2^{4}, where the disciples' attention to prayer likewise has its sequel in the coming of the Holy Spirit to equip them for their task. *in bodily form* might suggest that a dove was seen (not necessarily implied by Matthew and Mark), the outward sign of God's favour. Another translation would be 'in substantial form' or 'in full measure': in Jesus the Spirit has the fullest possible scope for working (cp. John 3^{34}). The Spirit's temporary inspiration of the prophets is perhaps being contrasted with the real and lasting union between Jesus and the Spirit (cp. John 1^{32}). The rabbis sometimes compared the Holy Spirit brooding on the face of the waters (Gen. 1^{2}) to a dove brooding over her young: so here God's protective power is over Jesus, and he is the centre of a new creative activity by the Holy Spirit. There

3 **Jesus, when he began his ministry, was about thirty years**

---

might also be a connection with Noah's dove (Gen. 8^{8-12}), regarded as a symbol of safety: the Spirit-anointed Jesus will bring God's salvation to the world. *a voice from heaven* describes a divine communication (e.g. Gen. 3^{8}). There is a variant reading which instead of 'with thee I am well pleased' has 'today I have begotten thee', thus making the sentence approximate to Ps. 2^{7}. Jesus is then addressed in words used of an Israelite king at his coronation, and now reinterpreted of the expected Messianic king of the future: the incident is thus seen as Jesus' coronation. In favour of this reading it is urged that it is unlikely that the reading as in RSV was changed to one which could suggest that Jesus only became Son of God at his baptism, whereas the change from the variant reading to the one in the text is easily explained as an assimilation to the text of Matthew and Mark. Even so, the variant may be merely an early attempt to bring the words of *the voice* into the form of a quotation from scripture. In Jewish usage 'Son of God' did not suggest divine status, but rather a special function to perform. Thus the nation Israel (Exod. 4^{22}; Hos. 11^{1}), the Israelite king (Ps. 2^{7}; 2 Sam. 2^{14}), and the faithful man of God (Wisd. 2^{18}) are designated in this way. The address to Jesus as 'Son of God' means that he is being commissioned for a special mission. The title in itself would not connect Jesus with the expected Messianic king, though Luke has already connected Jesus' 'sonship' with his being the Messianic king. When, after his resurrection, Jesus was given an allegiance usually reserved for God, his sonship was seen to imply divine status. *beloved*, which can mean 'only' or 'unique', is best taken as 'chosen' or 'specially favoured', a term applied to Israel (Isa. 5^{1}) and the faithful within Israel (Ps. 60^{5}). *with thee I am well pleased* (ἐφ' σοὶ ηὐδόκησα): this verb in the LXX describes God's special favour to Israel, the Israelite king, or the faithful within Israel (Isa. 62^{4}; 2 Sam. 22^{20}; Ps. 146^{11}), and his choice of them; the aorist tense suggests that the action is part of the predetermined will of God. A particular reference to Isa. 42^{1} is not necessarily intended. In 12^{50} Jesus sees his coming death as a baptism (cp. Mark 10^{38}), and so he perhaps viewed his original baptism, in which he was engulfed by the waters, as a foreshadowing of another baptism, in which he will be engulfed by death. Jesus' baptism, therefore, becomes the pattern of Christian baptism in which the believer dies with Jesus, receives the Holy Spirit, and is assured of his status as an adopted son of God.

23–38 The genealogy of Jesus traced through Joseph

Cp. Matt. 1^{1-17}.

(1) The use of a family tree to mark a man's or nation's importance was common.

of age, being the son (as was supposed) of Joseph, the son of
24 Heli, the son of Matthat, the son of Levi, the son of Melchi,
25 the son of Jannai, the son of Joseph, the son of Mattathias,
the son of Amos, the son of Nahum, the son of Esli, the son of
26 Naggai, the son of Maath, the son of Mattathias, the son of

---

(2) In view of 1^{26-38}, the derivation of Jesus' ancestry through Joseph seems strange, both here and in Matt. 1^{1-17}, but apparently the Gospel writers saw no inconsistency: Jesus, though not born in the usual way, was accepted by Joseph as one of his family and so as descended from David. Even if Mary was also of the line of David, the tracing of a family line through the mother would have been unusual.

(3) Luke traces the genealogy to Adam, who typifies humanity, in order to present Jesus as the new Adam, in whom the human race is to be reconciled to God and the effect of Adam's disobedience reversed (cp. Rom. 5^{15-19}); just as Adam's action was thought to have had universal significance, so will the mission of Jesus.

(4) The siting of the genealogy here might be merely because Luke found it at this point in a source, but it may have a theological purpose: at Jesus' baptism his unique sonship is attested, and then in the genealogy his connection with Adam is stressed, followed by the emphasis on Jesus' obedience in the temptation narrative. Thus Jesus' sonship means in part that he is the new Adam who is obedient to God's purpose.

23 *Jesus . . . of age*, lit. (*a*) 'Jesus was about 30 years old, when he began' (his ministry), or (*b*) 'Jesus began to be about 30 years old' (was coming up to 30). Both would be odd usages in Greek. Perhaps Luke is drawing on a source where 'began' referred back to a previous section which he has omitted. This is the only reference to Jesus' age (John 8^{57} is vague). In the O.T. a king's reign is commonly introduced by a note of his age on accession (e.g. 2 Kgs. 14^{2}). If Luke sees Jesus' baptism partly as his accession as king, then after the O.T. pattern he at once refers to his age. *as was supposed*: Joseph and Mary allowed it to be so; the child's unusual birth would be revealed in God's good time.

24–31 According to Eusebius, the bishop and historian of the fourth century A.D., Joseph was the real son of Jacob (Matt. 1^{16}), but the legal son of Heli (v. 24) in consequence of Levirate marriage. According to 1 Chr. 3^{19} (Hebrew), Shechaniah was Zerubbabel's uncle, but Luke may be following the tradition of the LXX (cp. Ezra 3^{2} and Hag. 1^{1}), where Zerubbabel is called 'son of Shealtiel' as in v. 27.

27 Semein, the son of Josech, the son of Joda, the son of Jo-
anan, the son of Rhesa, the son of Zerubbabel, the son of
28 Shealtiel,[l] the son of Neri, the son of Melchi, the son of Addi,
29 the son of Cosam, the son of Elmadam, the son of Er, the son
of Joshua, the son of Eliezer, the son of Jorim, the son of
30 Matthat, the son of Levi, the son of Simeon, the son of Judah,
31 the son of Joseph, the son of Jonam, the son of Eliakim, the
son of Melea, the son of Menna, the son of Mattatha, the
32 son of Nathan, the son of David, the son of Jesse, the son of
Obed, the son of Boaz, the son of Sala, the son of Nahshon,
33 the son of Amminadab, the son of Admin, the son of Arni,
34 the son of Hezron, the son of Perez, the son of Judah, the son of
Jacob, the son of Isaac, the son of Abraham, the son of Terah,
35 the son of Nahor, the son of Serug, the son of Reu, the son of
36 Peleg, the son of Eber, the son of Shelah, the son of Cainan,
the son of Arphaxad, the son of Shem, the son of Noah, the
37 son of Lamech, the son of Methuselah, the son of Enoch,
38 the son of Jared, the son of Mahalaleel, the son of Cainan, the
son of Enos, the son of Seth, the son of Adam, the son of God.

4: AND Jesus, full of the Holy Spirit, returned from the

[l] Greek *Salathiel*

---

38 For the names from Nathan to Adam see 1 Chr. 1^{1}–3^{5}, and especially 1^{1-34}, 2^{4-13}, 3^{5}; 1 Sam. 16^{1-13}; 2 Sam. 5^{14}; Ruth 4^{18-22}; Gen. 29^{35}, 25^{26}, 21^{2-3}, 11^{10-26}, 5^{3-32}, 4^{25}, 5^{1-3}. *Cainan* (v. 36) is only found in the LXX of Gen. 11^{12-13} between Arpaxshad and Shelah. *Adam, the son of God*: not in the sense of physical descent from God, but in the sense of having been created by him. Such a usage may be connected with the idea of Adam's being in God's image (Gen. 1^{26-27}).

: 1–13 The temptation or testing of Jesus

See also Matt. 4^{1-11}. Mark 1^{12-13} describes Jesus' testing by Satan, without recording the form that the testing took, or the triumph of Jesus. Matthew and Luke are probably drawing on a common source,

2 Jordan, and was led by the Spirit for forty days in the wilderness, tempted by the devil. And he ate nothing in those days;

---

in which reference to Jesus' being tested by Satan is combined with the account of three actual testings and of Jesus' refusal to accede to the suggestions of Satan. Thus Matthew and Luke wish to sound the note of Jesus' victory over evil before his public ministry begins. The three testings may not belong to one occasion but are here collected together for convenience. In Jewish thought the faithful servant of God has his loyalty tested by God himself, by the powers of evil, by his environment, and by impulses within himself. The three testings may be vivid representations of what was going on in the mind of Jesus, who is conscious that his faithfulness to God is being assailed by suggestions which he ascribes, as a Jew would, to the agency of Satan. This inner experience may well have been passed on by Jesus to his close circle of disciples. The answers of Jesus from Deuteronomy suggest that he is facing the same kind of testings as those of Israel during the desert wanderings and a contrast seems to be drawn between the disobedient Israel of the old covenant, and Jesus, the new and obedient embodiment of Israel, in whom God's purposes are achieved. Jesus may well have been conscious that Israel's role of representing God and of bringing the nations to him was now centred in himself. For the obedience of Jesus cp. Rom. 5^{12-21}; Phil. 2^{5-11}; Heb. 2^{17-18}.

1–2 *full of the Holy Spirit* looks back to Jesus' baptism. *led*: Jesus is both driven (cp. Mark 1^{12}) by the Holy Spirit into *the wilderness* to come to grips with his calling, and during his stay there is under the Spirit's guidance (cp. Deut. 8^{2}). *forty days* suggests preparation for a God-given mission (cp. Exod. 24^{18}; 1 Kgs. 19^{8}; see also Deut. 2^{7} for the 'forty years' of Israel's preparation in the wilderness of Sinai). This kind of language once applied to Israel and the heroes of the Jewish nation shows the impression made by Jesus on his followers. A parallel may also be intended between this *forty days* and that of the resurrection appearances (Acts 1^{3}), which were the prelude to the Church's ministry. *tempted*, or better 'put to the test'; the participle denotes that the whole period was marked by testing. *the devil*, 'the adversary' or 'the slanderer': originally an angel of God's heavenly court who acted as a kind of public prosecutor and tested human loyalty to God (Job 1–2; Zech. 3^{1-2}), but later an evil power (1 Chr. 21^{1}; Wisd. 2^{24}) actively opposed to God, and portraying the Jewish conviction that there are many forces in the world working against God's purposes. *hungry* recalls the Israelites' 'hunger' in the wilderness (Exod. 16^{1-3}), and the fast of Moses (Exod. 24^{28}).

3 and when they were ended, he was hungry. The devil said to
him, 'If you are the Son of God, command this stone to be-
4 come bread.' And Jesus answered him, 'It is written, "Man
5 shall not live by bread alone." ' And the devil took him up,
and showed him all the kingdoms of the world in a moment
6 of time, and said to him, 'To you I will give all this authority
and their glory; for it has been delivered to me, and I give it

---

4 The first testing. The devil plays on human weakness, here the physical hunger of Jesus, whose reply from Deut. 8³ probably supplies the background. God allowed Israel to go without food to test her reaction to privation and to teach the lesson of dependence and reliance on him. The result was a lack of trust and an outburst of doubt (Exod. 16²⁻²³), and only a miraculous provision of heavenly manna restored the nation's faith. In the same way the suggestion is put to Jesus that he should change *stones* (something absolutely uneatable) into *bread* by using his power as Son of God, and so prove for himself the dependability of God and his special status. Jesus, in contrast with Israel, did not need to prove his trust in God, nor were his thoughts centred on himself. Another less probable interpretation is that the provision of bread was not to be for himself, but to gain a popular following as king. Jesus in working out the course of his mission is presented with this method of procedure and rejects it.

8 The second testing. The devil tries to distract Jesus from his mission by presenting to him the attraction and glamour of earthly power. But the suggestion seems not that Jesus should compromise with evil, but that he should cease altogether to regard himself as an agent of God and should ally himself entirely with the devil and his methods. Jesus' reply (v. 8) not only resembles Deut. 6¹³, but is also a summary of the whole book, where 'serve' and 'worship' are commonly used in warnings to Israel not to offer service to any other gods but their own God (e.g. 6⁴). But while Israel did abandon the one true God and ally herself with other gods to achieve entry into Canaan (Exod. 32¹⁻⁶), Jesus himself refuses to accede to the devil ('the other gods' here) and remains true to God. Again there is the implicit contrast between the disloyalty of Israel and the loyalty of Jesus. *took him up*: Luke does not say where (contrast Matt. 4⁸, 'to a very high mountain'). The implication of this phrase (cp. Ezek. 11¹) and of *in a moment of time* is that Jesus is presented with a mental vision. *the world*: here the whole inhabited earth. *kingdoms* include the great Roman and Parthian empires. The bait dangled before Jesus is a highly extravagant one, the way in

7 to whom I will. If you, then, will worship me, it shall all be
8 yours.' And Jesus answered him, 'It is written,

"You shall worship the Lord your God, and him only shall you serve." '

9 And he took him to Jerusalem, and set him on the pinnacle
of the temple, and said to him, 'If you are the Son of God,
10 throw yourself down from here; for it is written,

"He will give his angels charge of you, to guard you,"

---

which the devil whets the appetite! Perhaps the possibility of such an extravagant suggestion being put to Jesus shows his deep consciousness of the key role he has to play in the world's history. The phrase *this authority and their glory* suggests the Roman 'imperium' exercised by the Emperor and provincial governors, and the pomp that goes with *the kingdoms*. A contrast is implied with the authority given by God and exercised by Jesus in his ministry (e.g. 5^{24}), and with the glory on which Jesus enters at his resurrection (24^{26}); cp. also 22^{24-27}. In Jewish thought the nations of the world are sometimes depicted as under the control of evil forces, which was only a temporary usurpation of God's power (cp. Jer. 27^{5}). Here, however, the devil's *delivered to me and I give it to whom I will* suggests that such authority is his by right.

9–12 The third testing. *tempt . . . God*, or 'put God to the test', is commonly used in the O.T. of questioning God's adequacy, and so comes to mean 'doubt God' (e.g. Num. 14^{22}). The classic example of putting God to the test is the incident in Deut. 6^{16} (described at greater length in Exod. 17^{2-7}), from which Jesus takes his reply. There, in face of water shortage, the Israelites doubt God and need a miraculous sign (the water out of the rock) to reassure them. Here Jesus is to throw himself down from the top of the temple, and he will then have clear proof of his calling, as no harm will befall him, according to Ps. 91. But in contrast with Israel's doubts, Jesus does not need a continual demonstration of God's choice of him. Another less likely interpretation suggests that Jesus should make such a demonstration in public to gain a popular following. Ironically, the devil quotes scripture (Ps. 91^{11-12}), part of his masquerade as an 'angel of light' (2 Cor. 11^{14}), with an unscrupulous disregard for the context; for the Psalm, while an expression of trust in God's protection, does not envisage setting a test case to see whether the confidence is justified.

11 and

"On their hands they will bear you up,
lest you strike your foot against a stone."'

12 And Jesus answered him, 'It is said, "You shall not tempt the
13 Lord your God."' And when the devil had ended every
temptation, he departed from him until an opportune time.
14 And Jesus returned in the power of the Spirit into Galilee,
and a report concerning him went out through all the sur-
15 rounding country. And he taught in their synagogues, being
glorified by all.

---

13 Apart from the reference to the devil's departure (so also Matthew) the verse is peculiar to Luke. *ended*, or 'completed'. *until an opportune time*, or 'for a while': the translation in RSV would look forward to Satan's final assault, of which Luke makes special mention in $22^{3, 31, 53}$; the alternative suggests Satan's return to test Jesus on various occasions in his ministry (cp. 22^{28}).

II. THE FIRST JOURNEY-NARRATIVE—JESUS' MINISTRY IN GALILEE (CHAPTERS 4:14–9:50)

4: 14–30 *Jesus' public ministry; in the synagogue at Nazareth*

Luke is almost certainly using a special source. In vv. 14–24 there are resemblances to Mark 6^{1-6}, e.g. the teaching in the synagogue, the amazement and speculation of the people, and the proverb about the prophet. But the main emphasis and features are very different. The occasion is probably the same (Luke having a fuller account of it at his disposal), but the setting is different for theological reasons. In Mark the incident forms part of the following pattern of events: the raising of Jairus' daughter (5^{35-43})—rejection of Jesus in Nazareth (6^{1-6})—mission of the twelve (6^{7-13}), a foreshadowing of Jesus' resurrection, his rejection by the Jewish nation as a whole, and the mission of the Church, the new Israel. Luke's siting of the incident serves a different purpose. The reading from Isaiah (vv. 17–21), which Jesus now claims to be fulfilled, summarizes his mission and its significance. The stories about Elijah and

16 And he came to Nazareth, where he had been brought up;
and he went to the synagogue, as his custom was, on the
17 sabbath day. And he stood up to read; and there was given
to him the book of the prophet Isaiah. He opened the book
and found the place where it was written,

Elisha (vv. 25–28) stress God's concern for non-Jews, and so introduce the important Lucan theme of the Gospel's universal significance. As in Mark, the tension between Jesus and his audience, culminating in the attempt on his life (v. 29), foreshadows Jesus' coming rejection by the Jews. Verses 25–30 may not originally have belonged to the first part of the incident. The illustrations do not strictly demonstrate a prophet's lack of recognition among his own people, but rather God's concern for Gentiles as well as Jews, and so this part of the incident, with its violent sequel, may belong to a different occasion in Jesus' life. Jesus' rejection has a parallel in 9^{51-56}.

14–15 This summary stands in place of Mark 1^{14-15} and may be Luke's own composition and a means of transition to the following incident (see also Matt. 4^{23}; Mark 1^{28}): Jesus, who has received the Holy Spirit for his mission, and in that Spirit's power has been tested and found true to God, now in the same power begins his public ministry, in which the attack on the powers of evil will be continued. *being glorified by all*: 'all sang his praises' (NEB); this general approval contrasts with the unfavourable reception in Jesus' home town which follows, and his later rejection in Jerusalem (for Galilee friendly to Jesus see John 4^{45}).

16 Synagogues were found both in Palestine and in the Jewish Dispersion. In the normal service there were two readings, one from the Law (the first five books of the O.T.) and one from the Prophets. The reader would be a member of the congregation appointed by 'the attendant' (v. 20).

17 *the book*, or 'the scroll'. The scriptures were written on rolls, which would be unwound to find the passage. The book of Isaiah would probably have a roll to itself. *found the place*: does this mean that Jesus found the passage set in the lectionary, or that what he read was one he chose himself to form the basis of the sermon? Our evidence for synagogue procedure at this time is incomplete, and so we cannot rule out the latter suggestion, which might fit the general picture far better.

'The Spirit of the Lord is upon me,
because he has anointed me to preach good news to the
poor.
He has sent me to proclaim release to the captives
and recovering of sight to the blind,
to set at liberty those who are oppressed,
to proclaim the acceptable year of the Lord.'
And he closed the book, and gave it back to the attendant,
and sat down; and the eyes of all in the synagogue were fixed on
him. And he began to say to them, 'Today this scripture has

The passage read is Isa. 61^{1-2}, but 'bind up the brokenhearted' is omitted from the original, and *to set at liberty those who are oppressed* is inserted from Isa. 58^{6}. *recovering of sight to the blind*, the version of the LXX, is followed closely. The question arises whether the passage was originally read in Greek from the LXX rather than in Hebrew with an Aramaic translation (as was usual in the Palestinian synagogues). The view is sometimes held that the Galileans were bilingual, and perhaps spoke Greek better than Aramaic, the ordinary Jewish language of the time in Palestine. Some of the Galilean synagogues may then have conducted their services in Greek, as happened in the Jewish Dispersion. The original context of the quotation is the prophet's announcement of a coming deliverance of Jerusalem and the restoration of the Jews from their captivity in Babylon (about 540 B.C.). Now Jesus applies the prophecy to the new and greater deliverance that he is bringing. *anointed*: set apart or given a special task. Jesus has been so anointed at his baptism. *the poor*: those who can only trust in the power of God (cp. Ps. 9^{18}). This programme of Jesus' mission (discussed above, pp. 30–32) stands in a position corresponding to Mark 1^{14-15}, where Jesus announces that 'the kingdom of God is at hand'. Luke is, therefore, focusing his readers' attention on the ministry of Jesus as the 'era of God's favour'—a special period of history in which that kingdom and sovereignty are revealed.

closed: 'rolled up'. The *attendant* or *chazzan*, an important synagogue official, usually conducted the services and might also be the local schoolmaster. The sermon followed the reading from the Prophets, and the preacher sat down to give his discourse; it could be given by either a rabbi or a distinguished stranger. The choice of Jesus suggests confidence in his power to explain the scriptures.

Jesus' treatment of the passage is simple and direct, asserting the

22 been fulfilled in your hearing.' And all spoke well of him,
and wondered at the gracious words which proceeded out
of his mouth; and they said, 'Is not this Joseph's son?'
23 And he said to them, 'Doubtless you will quote to me
this proverb, "Physician, heal yourself; what we have
heard you did at Capernaum, do here also in your own
24 country." ' And he said, 'Truly, I say to you, no prophet is
25 acceptable in his own country. But in truth, I tell you, there
were many widows in Israel in the days of Elijah, when the
heaven was shut up three years and six months, when there
26 came a great famine over all the land; and Elijah was sent to

---

relevance of it to the present. For *today*, stressing the decisiveness of the present, cp. 23^{43}; Heb. 4^{1-11}.

22 *spoke well of him*, 'or passed a favourable verdict on him'. *gracious words*, lit. 'words of grace', a term often used of God's favour, but here denoting something pleasing. *proceeded out of his mouth*: cp. Num. 30^{2}. For the question, contrast Mark 6^{3}, and cp. Matt. 13^{55}.

23 The sermon might be followed by objections and questions, and the audience obviously wants evidence for Jesus' claims. The meaning of the proverb is: 'do not only perform to strangers, but also among those who know you'. Luke has so far recorded no activity of Jesus in *Capernaum* (cp. 4^{31}). Reference has, however, been made to his teaching in Galilee (vv. 14–15). Perhaps in Luke's source an account of Jesus' ministry in Capernaum preceded the present incident. Luke reserves details of Jesus' acts, until they can be seen in the light of vv. 18–19.

24 Both this verse and v. 23 imply that Jesus knows the fickleness of his audience's enthusiasm. He quotes a proverbial expression to account for their indifference, and perhaps for his own inability to perform mighty works. Prophets (and Jesus is in their line) were notoriously badly treated by their countrymen; hence the content of the proverb.

25 For the incident see 1 Kgs. 17^{8-24}. Elijah was sent to the widow woman in non-Israelite territory at a time of drought, which according to 1 Kgs. 18^{1} lasted three years or less (for Luke's three years and six months, a period of time which sometimes symbolized evil, cp. Jas. 15^{17}).

26 *Zarephath* was on the Phoenician coast between Tyre and Sidon.

none of them but only to Zarephath, in the land of Sidon, to
27 a woman who was a widow. And there were many lepers in
Israel in the time of the prophet Elisha; and none of them
28 was cleansed, but only Naaman the Syrian.' When they heard
29 this, all in the synagogue were filled with wrath. And they
rose up and put him out of the city, and led him to the brow
of the hill on which their city was built, that they might
30 throw him down headlong. But passing through the midst of
them he went away.
31 And he went down to Capernaum, a city of Galilee. And

---

27 For this incident see 2 Kgs. 5. The life-stories of Elijah and Elisha have several incidents parallel to each other, among them their dealings with non-Jews.

28 The audience's national pride as Jews was hurt; they failed to see their privileges as part of God's purpose of making himself known to non-Jews and the whole world. For the equal importance of Jew and Gentile in God's sight cp. Isa. 2^{2-4}, 19^{24-25}.

-30 The Jewish sentence for a conviction of blasphemy was death by stoning (Deut. 13^{10}), the convicted being rolled over the side of a hill and then crushed by a boulder, a procedure which is attempted here. The description of Jesus' escape hints at divine protection (cp. John 8^{59}).

4: 31–44 *Jesus' Ministry in Capernaum*

See also Matt. 7^{28-29}, 8^{14-16}; Mark 1^{31-39}. Luke probably uses Mark for the first time. The cures that follow show Jesus' release of 'the captives' (4^{18-19}).

4: 31–37 The demon-possessed man in the synagogue

This is Luke's first exorcism. The man is suffering from some kind of madness, traced at that time to the man's personality being taken over by a demon or demons. This viewpoint underlines the conviction that such a state is contrary in God's plans. But to whatever source the derangement may be attributed today, Jesus' power is shown in restoring the man's balance of mind and in demonstrating the presence of God's sovereignty (cp. 11^{20}).

31 *Capernaum* was a town at the northern end of the Lake of Galilee and a centre of Jesus' ministry. The remains of a synagogue, built about A.D. 200 on the ruins of the synagogue in which Jesus taught, can still be seen.

32 he was teaching them on the sabbath; and they were aston-
33 ished at his teaching, for his word was with authority. And
in the synagogue there was a man who had the spirit of an
34 unclean demon; and he cried out with a loud voice, 'Ah![m]
What have you to do with us, Jesus of Nazareth? Have you
come to destroy us? I know who you are, the Holy One of
35 God.' But Jesus rebuked him, saying, 'Be silent, and come
out of him!' And when the demon had thrown him down in
the midst, he came out of him, having done him no harm.
36 And they were all amazed and said to one another 'What is

[m] Or *Let us alone*

---

32 Cp. Mark 1^{22}. *his word was with authority* suggests that Jesus spoke with the compelling force of the prophets, and that his words were seen to be effective in his deeds.

33 Perhaps this incident followed the sermon and became a proof of what Jesus taught. *the spirit of an unclean demon*: either 'a spirit [or 'evil influence'] sent by an unclean demon', or 'a spirit, consisting in an unclean demon' (cp. Rev. 16^{14}). In Jewish thought the demons were part of the kingdom of evil arrayed against the true God, who would ultimately triumph over them. The demonic force here is thought of as having supplanted the man's real personality and as speaking through him.

34 *Ah*, or 'let us alone'. *what have you to do with us . . . ?*, lit. 'what to us and to you?', conveys the idea that two persons have met and that the meeting and contact are in some way unwelcome (cp. Mark 5^{7}). Does the demonic force use the royal plural, or does it speak as the representative of the demon world? In this confrontation between the representative of God and that of evil the defeatism of the evil spirit is seen in the questions asked and in the acknowledgement of Jesus' status as *the Holy One of God*—the one set apart and chosen for God's purposes, here the defeat of evil (cp. Acts 3^{14}; see also Ps. 106^{16}).

35 *rebuked* (cp. Mark 4^{39}): condemned the demon to loss of power. *Be silent*: lit. 'be muzzled'. *Having done him no harm* stresses the competence of Jesus.

36 The reaction of the bystanders is often important in a story of healing. The power of Jesus made a deep impression on his contemporaries, and Luke underlined it (cp. 5^{17}, 6^{19}). This working of extraordinary cures by Jesus is also attested by the early Christians'

this word? For with authority and power he commands the
37 unclean spirits, and they come out.' And reports of him went
out into every place in the surrounding region.
38 And he arose and left the synagogue, and entered Simon's
house. Now Simon's mother-in-law was ill with a high fever,
39 and they besought him for her. And he stood over her and
rebuked the fever, and it left her; and immediately she rose
and served them.
40 Now when the sun was setting, all those who had any that
were sick with various diseases brought them to him; and he
41 laid his hands on every one of them and healed them. And
demons also came out of many, crying, 'You are the Son of

---

claims to do the same in his power (e.g. Acts 3^{1-12}; cp. John 14^{12}), and has a place in the early preaching of the Gospel (e.g. Acts 2^{22}).

37 Cp. 4^{14}.

4: 38–39 The healing of Simon's mother-in-law

38 *Simon* is introduced abruptly, as Mark 1^{16-20} has been omitted, and his call to be a disciple comes later (5^{1-11}). For Simon as a married man cp. 1 Cor. 9^{5}. *ill with*, or 'in the grip of'. *high*, lit. 'large' or 'great': it was medical practice to classify fevers into large and small; Luke alone uses this technical term. *besought him for her*: asked Jesus to help her.

39 *rebuked the fever*: showing that it is regarded as a demonic force. *immediately* underlines Jesus' power: the patient can resume at once her household duties.

4: 40–44 The healings at sunset, and the sequel

Luke may be combining Mark 1^{32-34} with another source.

40 *when the sun was setting* replaces Mark's 'that evening at sundown': the people waited for the sabbath to end and for the next day to begin at sunset. *every one of them* underlines the capacity of Jesus' healing power, and guards against any misunderstanding of Mark's 'many'. Luke alone adds the personal touch that Jesus laid his hands on them.

41 To clarify Mark 1^{34} Luke, by a transference here of part of Mark 3^{11-12}, explains what the demons are trying to say; he also amplifies Mark's 'knew him'. Jesus does not relish testimonials from such a source, though the early Christians saw the demons' reaction as important evidence that they recognized Jesus as their conqueror.

God!' But he rebuked them, and would not allow them to
speak, because they knew that he was the Christ.
42 And when it was day he departed and went into a lonely
place. And the people sought him and came to him, and would
43 have kept him from leaving them; but he said to them, 'I
must preach the good news of the kingdom of God to the
44 other cities also; for I was sent for this purpose.' And he was
preaching in the synagogues of Judea.[n]

5: WHILE the people pressed upon him to hear the word of

[n] Other ancient authorities read *Galilee*

---

42 *when it was day*: Mark has 'a great while before day': in Luke the suggestion is that all the night was taken up with service of others. The reference to *the people* underlines Jesus' popularity, as does the concluding part of the verse, peculiar to Luke.

43 This is the first mention of the *kingdom of God*. The preaching of *the good news* and the kingdom of God are closely connected in the teaching of Jesus, though only in Luke is 'the kingdom of God' made the object of 'preach the good news'. *I was sent* shows Jesus' consciousness of his divine mission: in the Gospel according to John he frequently speaks of being 'sent' (e.g. 7^{16}), and can also, therefore, be given the title of 'apostle', 'one sent' (Heb. 3^{1}).

44 *Judea*, in contrast with Mark's 'Galilee' (an alternative reading in Luke but not original). Luke normally uses the term of the area centred on Jerusalem, and so at an early stage he connects Jesus with the centre of the Jewish faith, as well as with Galilee (on which Matthew and Mark lay emphasis; contrast John, who stresses Jesus' activity in Judea, e.g. 4^{3}). Luke thus prepares us for 19^{28}–24^{53} and for Acts 1–7, centred on Jerusalem and the surrounding Judea.

5: 1–16 *Jesus' first disciples; the leper*

5: 1–11 The catch of fish

The incident from a special source takes the place of Mark 1^{16-20}. Perhaps Luke prefers this account, because (*a*) it gives prominence to Simon, who will be the leader among the apostles in the early Church (Acts 1^{15}), and (*b*) the catch of fish symbolizes the future work of the Church, 'the great shoal' standing for the gathering of the nations into the Church (cp. John 21^{1-8}).

2 God, he was standing by the lake of Gennesaret. And he saw
two boats by the lake; but the fishermen had gone out of them
3 and were washing their nets. Getting into one of the boats,
which was Simon's, he asked him to put out a little from the
land. And he sat down and taught the people from the boat.
4 And when he had ceased speaking, he said to Simon, 'Put out
5 into the deep and let down your nets for a catch.' And Simon
answered, 'Master, we toiled all night and took nothing! But
6 at your word I will let down the nets.' And when they had
done this, they enclosed a great shoal of fish; and as their nets
7 were breaking, they beckoned to their partners in the other
boat to come and help them. And they came and filled
8 both the boats, so that they began to sink. But when
Simon Peter saw it, he fell down at Jesus' knees, saying,
9 'Depart from me, for I am a sinful man, O Lord.' For he was

---

1 *Gennesaret*, more usually Gennesar, is the name for the fertile and thickly populated plain south of Capernaum. It gave its name to the large lake, also called 'the Sea of Galilee' (Mark 1^{16}) or 'the Sea of Tiberias' (John 21^{1}). *the people*: a crowd is often in attendance on Jesus and sometimes a contrast is made between them and the inner circle of disciples to whom Jesus gives his more intimate teaching. *the word of God* is the message contained in 4^{18-21}, and a term which comes to have the same meaning as Gospel or 'good news'.

2 The lake enjoyed a prosperous fishing industry, some of the fish caught being pickled and exported as far afield as Rome. The fishermen were often men of means and standing.

3 As in 4^{38}, Simon comes on the scene suddenly as one who is well known.

-7 These verses stress that when Jesus is in control results follow. *Master*, used in Luke as a title of address to Jesus, is probably equivalent to 'teacher' (cp. 18^{18}), both probably translating 'rabbi'. *nets . . . sink* underlines the superabundance of fish.

8 Simon has his nickname *Peter* added—i.e. 'the rock' or (in Aramaic) Cephas (cp. Gal. 1^{18}). The tradition is strong that it was given by Jesus (6^{14}; Mark 3^{16}; John 1^{42}: for its significance see Matt. 16^{18-19}). Simon saw something supernatural in the unusual size of the haul, and sensed the presence of a 'holy man of God'. Hence his feeling of unworthiness and his cry *Depart . . . sinful man* (cp. Ps. 119^{115} and Isa.

astonished, and all that were with him, at the catch of fish
10 which they had taken; and so also were James and John, sons
of Zebedee, who were partners with Simon. And Jesus said
to Simon, 'Do not be afraid; henceforth you will be catching
11 men.' And when they had brought their boats to land, they
left everything and followed him.
12 While he was in one of the cities, there came a man full of

---

6^{1-5}). Peter's request is not granted; instead he is accepted as a close follower of Jesus despite his unworthiness, a living example of the Church's later teaching on justification by faith (cp. Rom. 3^{23-24}).

10 *James* and *John* appear in all our lists of the twelve, and always among the first four. They form part of an inner group of disciples present at decisive points in Jesus' ministry (e.g. 9^{28}). For James' death see Acts 12^{1-2}. John is associated closely with Peter in the early chapters of Acts (e.g. 3^{1}), and then passes from view, being by tradition the author of the Gospel according to John, of the Letters of John, and (sometimes) of the Revelation of John. *Zebedee*: the name means 'munificent' (cp. 1 Chr. 27^{27}). *catching*, or 'taking alive' (i.e. as prisoner), from the language of warfare, and not from that of fishing. Simon will capture people for God's kingdom and bring them into the living fellowship of the Church. Jesus proclaims 'release to the captives', and in turn they are to be captured by him!

11 *left everything*: the utter renunciation of these early disciples is stressed (cp. 18^{28}); it involved leaving a prosperous fishing business. *followed* contains the idea of adherence and committal to Jesus and his cause (cp. 1 Kgs. 19^{19-21}).

5: 12–16 The leper is healed

See also Matt. 8^{1-4}; Mark 1^{40-45}. Luke resumes his use of Mark, interrupted at 4^{44}. The incident connects Jesus with the great heroes such as Moses and Elisha, who were also involved in healing lepers (Num. 12^{9-16}; 2 Kgs. 5); but the cure effected by Jesus is his own action and is immediate. The healing is a sign of an unusual power at work defeating evil and inaugurating God's new era (cp. 7^{22}), and thus prepares for 5^{17}–6^{11}. The power of Jesus to cleanse the physical body of leprosy indicates his ability to cleanse the whole personality from sin through forgiveness.

12 *one of the cities*: vague, as the setting of the story is not important. *While . . . there came a man*: lit. 'and it came to pass while . . . that behold a man': a good example of Luke's 'Hebraic' or 'Old Testament'

leprosy; and when he saw Jesus, he fell on his face and be-
13 sought him, 'Lord, if you will, you can make me clean.' And
he stretched out his hand, and touched him, saying, 'I will;
14 be clean.' And immediately the leprosy left him. And he
charged him to tell no one; but 'go and show yourself to
the priest, and make an offering for your cleansing, as
15 Moses commanded, for a proof to the people.'[o] But so
much the more the report went abroad concerning him;
and great multitudes gathered to hear and to be healed
16 of their infirmities. But he withdrew to the wilderness and
prayed.

[o] Greek *to them*

---

style. *leprosy*: in ordinary Greek it could denote the skin disease, psoriasis, but in Biblical usage it meant leprosy proper, caused by Hansen's bacillus (as in Lev. 13–14, where regulations about lepers are laid down). *full of*: a bad case. *saw . . . besought him*: the leper, encouraged by the sight of Jesus and reports about him, came close, thus infringing Lev. 14^{45-46}. *make me clean*: a cure for leprosy was thought possible (though unusual), as is shown by the regulations of Leviticus and the healing of Naaman. *stretched out his hand*: Jesus thus incurs ritual uncleanness. But for Jesus the personal touch of reassurance and healing takes precedence over the ceremonial Law, and he claims an authority to dispense with the latter, together with a prerogative to have contact with lepers, reserved to the Jewish priests. *I will* takes up *Lord, if you will*.

4 Jesus wants the leper to go through the proper process for his restoration to society. It will thus be shown on good authority that the cure is genuine, and there will be both a *proof* (or 'witness') that the man need no longer be isolated, and a pointer to the presence of a new and important factor at work. *the people*, lit. 'them', may refer to Jewish society, or more probably to the priests, who, as a responsible group, are to take notice of the cure—a more probable explanation in view of Jesus' desire for secrecy and for the avoidance of the kind of popularity that might make him the centre of a political revolution (cp. John 6^{15}).

went abroad . . . gathered . . . withdrew . . . prayed: the tenses are imperfect and describe what kept happening.

17 On one of those days, as he was teaching, there were
Pharisees and teachers of the law sitting by, who had come
from every village of Galilee and Judea and from Jerusalem;
18 and the power of the Lord was with him to heal.[p] And behold,
men were bringing on a bed a man who was paralysed, and
19 they sought to bring him in and lay him before Jesus;[q] but

[p] Other ancient authorities read *was present to heal them*
[q] Greek *him*

5: 17–6: 11 *The claims of Jesus and controversy with the Jews*

Luke continues his use of Mark, retaining the controversy stories of Mark 2^{1}–3^{6}. They are linked together by theme rather than by chronology, the leading themes being (*a*) a veiled claim or hint that with the presence of Jesus something unusual is at work, and (*b*) controversy with the Jewish leaders. The atmosphere of controversy warns the reader of the coming sufferings and rejection of Jesus, though the climax (6^{11}) is not so poignant as that of Mark 3^{6}. There are three divisions: (i) 5^{17-32} (the forgiveness of sins: Jesus in the midst of forgiven sinners); (ii) 5^{33-39} (the unusualness of the present time: the old and the new); and (iii) 6^{1-11} (the authority of Jesus over the Sabbath).

5: 17–26 Jesus and the paralysed man: his claim to pronounce God's forgiveness of sins

17 In contrast with 2^{46}, *the teachers* now sit listening to Jesus. Luke's *Galilee, Judea,* and *Jerusalem* stress the wide interest that Jesus has aroused. The *Pharisees* formed a closely linked society for the strict observance of the Jewish Law, and constituted one of the religious parties of the Jews. *teachers of the law*: probably ordained rabbis, and not merely the teachers attached to the Jewish synagogues. *the Lord* refers to God, whose power is now effective in Jesus: with the reading in the RSV margin it could refer to Jesus, though this is unlikely, as the definite article in the Greek is missing. *power,* often used of divine power (e.g. Ps. 63^{2}), is also applied to Jesus (e.g. 4^{36}).

18 The more normal word for *bed* is used instead of 'pallet' or 'mattress' (Mark 2^{4}).

19 The details underline the undaunted faith of the man's friends. A Palestinian house would have a staircase leading to the roof. Mark suggests that a hole was dug through the roof. Luke is more

finding no way to bring him in, because of the crowd, they
went up on the roof and let him down with his bed through
20 the tiles into the midst before Jesus. And when he saw their
21 faith he said, 'Man, your sins are forgiven you.' And the
scribes and the Pharisees began to question, saying, 'Who is
this that speaks blasphemies? Who can forgive sins but God
22 only?' When Jesus perceived their questionings, he answered
23 them, 'Why do you question in your hearts? Which is easier,
to say, "Your sins are forgiven you," or to say, "Rise and
24 walk"? But that you may know that the Son of man has

---

explicit: the tiles of the covered gallery that ran round the courtyard of the house were removed, and an opening made in the framework that held them. Luke gives us the picture of the man coming right into the presence of Jesus as from nowhere!

20 Jesus usually requires *faith* (a firm trust in his God-given power of healing) as a condition of effecting a cure, either from the patient or those near to him. Jesus perhaps senses that the man has a guilt-complex through attributing his disability to punishment for sin (John 9²). He seeks to deal with this by declaring with authority that any obstacle between the man and God, created by sin, is removed.

21 Jesus is accused of claiming the prerogative of God, and so of blasphemy, an attempt to usurp the place of God. The claim is unexampled in Jewish literature, and denotes Jesus' consciousness of an exceptional relationship with God. Such forgiveness of human sins is sometimes connected with the new age promised by God to his people (e.g. Jer. 31³⁴), and so Jesus may be exercising his power as one who proclaims 'the acceptable year of the Lord' (4¹⁹). On the basis of this prerogative, vindicated by Jesus' resurrection, the Church in turn preaches forgiveness of sins (24⁴⁷).

22 The questionings, not openly expressed, were sensed by Jesus.

23 There is no real difference between the claim to heal bodily disease and the claim to forgive sins; in both Jesus is releasing people from the dominion of evil. His power to cure the body is a sign of his authority to restore the whole man to God.

24 The veiled hint is now given of the source of Jesus' *authority*: he is the *Son of man* exercising his prerogative *on earth*, which makes good sense if in the first century A.D. the Jews thought of the Son of man as a heavenly figure, God's agent in establishing his kingdom. Jesus then

authority on earth to forgive sins'—he said to the man who
was paralysed—'I say to you, rise, take up your bed and go
25 home.' And immediately he rose before them, and took up
26 that on which he lay, and went home, glorifying God. And
amazement seized them all, and they glorified God and were
filled with awe, saying, 'We have seen strange things today.'
27 After this he went out, and saw a tax collector, named Levi,
28 sitting at the tax office; and he said to him, 'Follow me.' And
he left everything, and rose and followed him.
29 And Levi made him a great feast in his house; and there
was a large company of tax collectors and others sitting at
30 table[r] with them. And the Pharisees and their scribes mur-

[r] Greek *reclining*

---

asserts that this figure is not merely heavenly, but one who operates *on earth*, and tacitly claims to be this figure. *rise, take up your bed and go home* are all actions that demonstrate the man's restoration to health.

25 *before them*: there were reliable witnesses of this event.

26 *strange* or 'wonderful'.

5: 27–32 Jesus and the outcasts

Jesus has claimed to forgive sins; he is now seen in contact with those whom respectable Jewish society classified as sinners.

27 *went out* could mean 'out of the house', but may refer to another occasion when Jesus went abroad. *saw*: Jesus and Levi may have met before, but Luke is interested only in recording the all-embracing demand of Jesus and the decisive response required of a disciple. In Matt. 9^{9} the same person is called 'Matthew'.

28 Cp. 5^{11}.

29 Jesus is concerned with all people, even those who in human eyes are 'beyond the pale' (cp. Gal. 3^{28}). *others*: those in the same category as the tax collectors. *sitting at table*: reclining on couches (see RSV margin).

30 *the Pharisees and their scribes*: some of the ordained rabbis belonged to the Pharisaic party (e.g. Gamaliel, Acts 5^{35}). *murmured*, or 'grumbled' (cp. Exod. 17^{3}). In Luke (contrast Mark and Matthew) the action of the disciples is challenged as well as that of Jesus. This is the first use of *disciples* to describe the close followers of Jesus—a term that includes

mured against his disciples, saying, 'Why do you eat and drink with tax collectors and sinners?' And Jesus answered them, 'Those who are well have no need of a physician, but those who are sick; I have not come to call the righteous, but sinners to repentance.'

And they said to him, 'The disciples of John fast often and

---

more than the twelve (6^{13}), and means 'pupils' or 'adherents'. The Jewish rabbis had their pupils, whom they trained in the understanding of the scriptures and to whom they passed on their teaching. The tax collectors did not observe the Law strictly, and so would be regarded as 'unclean' and would involve their associates in 'uncleanness'.

An efficient doctor is concerned with those who are ill, not with those in good health.

I have not come conveys Jesus' consciousness of his special appointment from God. In the Gospel according to John (e.g. 19^{37}) such words are seen to denote Jesus as God's Word who has come into the world. Jesus does not mean that there is a class of people who are virtuous or righteous, and so outside the scope of his mission. With a certain irony he suggests that those who are conscious of being virtuous will not see the need for his reconciling work. It is not the religious élite that respond to Jesus' message, but the outcasts of Jewish society. Luke clarifies *call* by the addition of *to repentance*, a change of attitude, outlook, and life in response to God's initiative. Jesus starts as always with the needs of people, and believes that this attitude fulfils the spirit of the Jewish Law, rather than the well-meaning attempt of the Pharisees to fulfil meticulously the ritual laws, which could set up a barrier between themselves and others (cp. 7^{36-50}, 15^{1-32}).

33–39 The new era

Jesus hints that the present time is a time of rejoicing, and that a new order of things is here that will not necessarily blend with the old.

they: in sense of 'people'. *The disciples of John*: either all the adherents of John, or his school of followers, after the pattern of the O.T. prophets (cp. Isa. 9^{16}). *the disciples of the Pharisees*: perhaps those who were applying for membership of the order, or more probably the members of the Pharisaic sect. Fasting might be practised twice a week by the pious Jew (for Jesus' attitude to it see Matt. 6^{16-18}). It might be a preliminary to prayer, or an expression of dedication to God or of sorrow. For John's disciples this fasting may have been a

offer prayers, and so do the disciples of the Pharisees, but
34 yours eat and drink.' And Jesus said to them, 'Can you make
35 wedding guests fast while the bridegroom is with them? The
days will come, when the bridegroom is taken away from
36 them, and then they will fast in those days.' He told them a
parable also: 'No one tears a piece from a new garment and

---

sign of their repentance and readiness to face God's judgement, and also of their sorrow at their master's imprisonment and a reinforcement of their prayers for his release (see also 7^{33-34}.)

34 Fasting, with its stress on asceticism and sorrow, would be out of place at a wedding. Luke's *make* suggests that it would be out of the question to enforce such a regulation. *wedding guests*, lit. 'the sons of the bride chamber', the bridegroom's friends, who played an important part in the wedding: here they stand for Jesus' disciples, while *the bridegroom* represents Jesus himself. The word sometimes describes God and his close relation to Israel, the bride (cp. Isa. 61^{10}), and so equates Jesus closely with the activity and person of God.

35 This verse has sometimes been seen as an addition to v. 34, due to a desire to justify weekday fasts in the early Church. But we have very little clear information about Christian fasting in the first century A.D. It is unlikely that anyone inventing such a saying would have referred to the 'removal' of Jesus without any reference to his resurrection and his continuing presence with his Church. A saying which suggests that the death of Jesus will lead to unmitigated sorrow is unlikely to have originated in the early Church, in view of the joy of Jesus' resurrection. The words fit better the situation of Jesus, who says that it will be time enough to give thought to mourning when people have done their worst to him (cp. John 16^{20-22}; and below, 23^{48}).

36 The *parable*, as elsewhere, takes the form of a statement of commonsense experience. The main point is the incompatibility of the old and new. With Jesus something new has entered the human situation, into which the observances of the old order will not fit. This tension between the old order of Judaism and the new and further revelation brought by Jesus was one that would tax the thought of the early Church, and raise the question how much of the old was to be retained, e.g., in the requirements to be made of Gentiles seeking admission to the Church (Acts 11^{1-18}, 15^{1-29}). *a piece from a new garment*: in attempting to clarify Mark, Luke has changed the picture, which in Mark is concerned with mending the hole in an old cloak with a

puts it upon an old garment; if he does, he will tear the new,
37 and the piece from the new will not match the old. And no
one puts new wine into old wineskins; if he does, the new
wine will burst the skins and it will be spilled, and the skins
38 will be destroyed. But new wine must be put into fresh wine-
39 skins. And no one after drinking old wine desires new; for
he says, "The old is good." '[s]

6: ON a sabbath,[t] while he was going through the grainfields,
his disciples plucked and ate some ears of grain, rubbing them

[s] Other ancient authorities read *better*

[t] Other ancient authorities read *On the second first sabbath* (on the second sabbath after the first)

---

piece of new cloth; the latter, being stiff, tends to pull, and causes the edges of the hole to fray once more, resulting in a still larger hole. Luke's picture is of the folly of spoiling a new garment or cloak to mend an old one, with the point that the piece put in will not match either in colour or texture.

37 *new wine*: wine still fermenting, and yet to reach maturity. Such wine containers would be made of animal skins. Unless they were in good condition the action of the wine, in addition to its weight, would cause them to split.

38 Two words are used for *new*: in the case of the wine, *νέος*; in the case of the skins, *καινός*. The first relates to time, the second to quality and condition.

39 This verse is peculiar to Luke, and, though omitted in certain MSS., it is very well attested. At first sight it suggests that the old is superior to the new, but is best taken as ironical: men cling to what is old and established, and are not prepared to face what is new and revolutionary. *better* (RSV margin) is a less likely reading.

6: 1–5 The observance of the Sabbath

The theme of the 'new' and its incompatibility with the old is now continued. Jesus claims an authority overriding the Sabbath regulations.

1 The RSV marginal reading would mean the Sabbath after the one mentioned in 4^{31}. The keeping of the Sabbath Day, now a firm characteristic of the Jewish religion, was both a humane institution to give rest from work to man and beast (Exod. 22^{12}), and also commemorative of the completion of creation (Exod. 20^{8-11}) and of the

2 in their hands. But some of the Pharisees said, 'Why are you
3 doing what is not lawful to do on the sabbath?' And Jesus
answered, 'Have you not read what David did when he was
4 hungry, he and those who were with him: how he entered
the house of God, and took and ate the bread of the Presence,
which it is not lawful for any but the priests to eat, and also
5 gave it to those with him?' And he said to them, 'The Son of
man is lord of the sabbath.'
6 On another sabbath, when he entered the synagogue and

Exodus from Egypt (Deut. 5^{12-15}). The rabbis had drawn up regulations for Sabbath observance, and a day originally meant to help human beings became hedged about with petty restrictive practices. *rubbing them in their hands*: a method of threshing and extracting the grain.

2 The action, not explicitly forbidden in the Law, would be thought by the Pharisees to contravene the general command, 'you shall do no work' (Exod. 20^{10}).

3 Jesus is talking to experts who would read the scriptures for themselves. For the incident cp. 1 Sam. 21^{1-6}. According to Jewish interpretation, David's action took place on the Sabbath, adding significance to Jesus' use of the example.

4 *the house of God*: the temple at Nob. To underline the holiness of the produce of the ground, bread was sometimes placed in ancient temples, including that of Jerusalem. Here the bread was known as 'the loaves of the presence' or 'presentation', as being placed in God's presence. A special table was used, and the custom was traced back to the wilderness wanderings (Exod. 25^{23-30}). The twelve loaves had to be wheaten and to be replaced every Sabbath. According to Lev. 24^{5-9}, the discarded loaves were to be eaten only by the priests. Jesus first challenges the Pharisees' exegesis of the Law by quoting a precedent where a personal need overrides the Law's regulations. Secondly, in appealing to what *David* did in unusual circumstances, Jesus is also hinting that the present situation is unusual and that a greater than David is here.

5 *The Son of man* is inaugurating God's new era and can use the Sabbath as suits his purpose (cp. vv. 6–11).

6: 6–11 The healing of the man with the withered hand

A 'captive' is again released. Jesus seems to make healing on the Sabbath a major issue. 'Sabbath' meant 'rest', and at this time each

7 taught, a man was there whose right hand was withered. And
the scribes and the Pharisees watched him, to see whether
he would heal on the sabbath, so that they might find an
8 accusation against him. But he knew their thoughts, and he
said to the man who had the withered hand, 'Come and stand
9 here.' And he rose and stood there. And Jesus said to them,
'I ask you, is it lawful on the sabbath to do good or to do
10 harm, to save life or to destroy it?' And he looked around on
them all, and said to him, 'Stretch out your hand.' And he did

---

Sabbath was probably regarded as a foretaste of the time when men would enjoy the real 'rest' of peace and fellowship with God (Heb. 4^{1-11}). Jesus is bringing this rest, seen in his healing and acts of forgiveness, and so the old Sabbath is abrogated (cp. John 5^{17}).

6 *withered*: shrunken and incapable of motion. *hand*, or perhaps 'arm'. Only Luke mentions that it was the *right* one, stressing further the man's disability.

7 Healing would be classified as work, and the argument would be that such a cure could be postponed until the next day (cp. 13^{14}). *accusation*: perhaps before the Jewish Sanhedrin or supreme council, which had authority in religious matters.

8 Jesus *knew their thoughts* from their looks and murmurings. By making the man stand out in front, Jesus brings the whole issue into the open.

9 The second possibility, that it is one's duty to do evil on the Sabbath, is inadmissible, while the admission of the first alternative would lead to the logical conclusion that Jesus was within his rights to heal the man. With his positive approach Jesus does not entertain the neutral position of postponing the cure until after the Sabbath, but again gives priority to the personal need. *life* could mean 'a living person' and *save* could also mean 'make whole' or 'restore': the two alternatives then become 'to restore to health a living person or to cause his death'. It might have seemed sufficient to ask whether 'doing good' was lawful, without raising the issue of 'doing evil'. But Jesus sees that failure to heal the withered hand at once is evil, as it allows an evil situation to remain unchecked. The attack on evil must go on, Sabbath or no Sabbath.

10 Jesus *looked round* by way of challenge. The command is partly aimed at making sure that people see what is done.

11 so, and his hand was restored. But they were filled with fury
and discussed with one another what they might do to Jesus.
12 In these days he went out into the hills to pray; and all
13 night he continued in prayer to God. And when it was day,

---

11 Their *fury* was called out by an inability to answer Jesus' challenge, and by Jesus' claim to authority. The note of opposition prepares for the final rejection of Jesus.

6: 12–19 *The twelve*

The section corresponds to Mark 3^{7-19} (see also Matt. 4^{23}–5^{1}, 10^{2-4}). But in addition to differences of language, there are slight divergences in the list of the twelve: also reference to the crowd follows the appointment of the twelve instead of preceding it as in Mark. Luke may, therefore, be following a different source or editing Mark fairly freely. The choice of the twelve follows the note of controversy and opposition: the Jews reject God's purposes, but Jesus founds the new people of God to carry on his work. The extensive area from which the crowds come probably looks forward to the time when people from all nations will be drawn into the Christian Church (cp. Acts 2^{1-11}).

6: 12–13 The choice of the twelve

12 *into the hills*, or 'into the mountain', may describe the highlands near the Jordan, but also suggests the mountain which was the scene of Moses' communication with God (Exod. 19^{20}). Jesus' prayer (only mentioned by Luke and probably concerned with the selection of the twelve) marks the occasion as important. One of the aims of prayer was to gain the guidance of God (Jer. 42^{4}).

13 For early evidence of 'the twelve' cp. 1 Cor. 15^{5}. The number suggests the twelve tribes of Israel, implying that the followers of Jesus constitute the real people of God, in a right relationship with him through their discipleship of Jesus. Only Luke records that Jesus gave the twelve the title of *apostles*, which in the first part of Acts is similarly reserved for them, but which later in Acts is also extended to others (Acts $14^{4, 14}$; cp. 1 Cor. 9^{1-5}). 'Apostle' in ordinary Greek sometimes had the meaning of 'ambassador', 'delegate', or 'messenger', and was later used to translate the Hebrew 'shaliach' ('one sent'), the official who represented the Jewish patriarch with plenipotentiary powers (a term, not, however, in use before the middle of the second century

he called his disciples, and chose from them twelve, whom
14 he named apostles; Simon, whom he named Peter, and
Andrew his brother, and James and John, and Philip, and
15 Bartholomew, and Matthew, and Thomas, and James the son
16 of Alphaeus, and Simon who was called the Zealot, and Judas
the son of James, and Judas Iscariot, who became a traitor.

A.D.). The title might, therefore, designate 'the twelve' as the plenipotentiaries of Jesus. Behind the word might also lie the thought of the Jewish proverb, 'the one sent is as he who sends him'.

6: 14–19 The names of the twelve: the crowds

–16 For *Simon* cp. 4[38], 5[3]. For *Andrew* see also John 1[40], 6[8], 12[52] (where he is presented as a decisive and practical man). For *James and John* cp. 5[10]. *Philip* occurs fifth in all our lists of the twelve (e.g. Acts 1[13]); he figures prominently in John (1[43–45], 6[5–7], 12[21–22], 14[8–9]). *Bartholomew* means 'son of Tolmai' (cp. 2 Sam. 3[3]). He has sometimes been identified with Nathanael (John 1[45–51], 21[2]). Matthew appears seventh here and in Mark's list, but eighth in the Gospel of Matthew and Acts (see also Matt. 9[9], 10[3], where his name takes the place of 'Levi' in Mark and Luke, and he is called the 'tax collector'). Thomas means 'twin', and an early addition to the name here is 'Didymus' ('the twin'), as in John 20[24]. He occurs in all our lists, and in John has the character of a firm realist (11[15], 20[24–27]). *James, the son of Alphaeus,* always comes ninth; the patronymic distinguishes him from James, the son of Zebedee. Alphaeus is also the surname of the father of Levi (Mark 2[14]), and possibly Levi and James were brothers. *Simon who was called the Zealot*: thus distinguishing him from Simon Peter. Matthew and Mark call him 'the Cananaean', which means 'enthusiast' or 'zealot'. The nickname has been thought to suggest his adherence to the Jewish nationalist party, the Zealots, but more probably describes his enthusiastic temperament, as 'called' implies. For *Judas, son of James,* cp. John 14[22]. The corresponding name in Matthew and Mark is 'Thaddaeus' (with a variant reading 'Lebbaeus'). The relation between Judas and Thaddaeus is not known. They could represent variant traditions, or Thaddaeus (if correct) could be a name by which Judas was known—'God-given', or perhaps 'large-hearted'. The identity of *James* is not clear: the son of Zebedee may be meant. *Judas Iscariot* (in John 6[71] 'Iscariot' is attached to the name of his father) is described dispassionately as the one who betrayed Jesus, i.e. later arranged the arrest of Jesus in connivance with the Jewish

17 And he came down with them and stood on a level place,
with a great crowd of his disciples and a great multitude of
people from all Judea and Jerusalem and the sea-coast of Tyre
and Sidon, who came to hear him and to be healed of their
18 diseases; and those who were troubled with unclean spirits
19 were cured. And all the crowd sought to touch him, for power
came forth from him and healed them all.
20 And he lifted up his eyes on his disciples, and said:
'Blessed are you poor, for yours is the kingdom of God.

---

authorities. *Iscariot* has sometimes been interpreted 'from Kerioth', a place in southern Judea (cp. the variant reading 'from Kerioth' in John 6^{71}). Hence the suggestion has been made that Judas as a southerner felt out of place with the Galilaean disciples, and in a disgruntled mood betrayed Jesus. The name has also been explained as 'assassin' or 'bandit': Judas had once been a bandit or had belonged to the Jewish nationalists or guerillas (cp. Acts 21^{38}), and so betrayed Jesus in disappointment that he did not start a revolution against Rome, or in an attempt to force his hand.

17 Contrast *on a level place* with Matthew's 'on the mountain' (5^{1}), which was probably intended to recall the picture of Moses receiving the Law on the mountain (e.g. Exod. 24^{12}). This episode may also have influenced Luke. In Exodus the following sequence recurs: (*a*) ascent of Moses into the mountain to commune with God (on one occasion the other leading men go with him, Exod. 24^{9-11}), (*b*) descent from mountain, (*c*) message to the assembled people (Exod. 19^{3-10}, 24^{1}). Luke may have this pattern in mind. First, just as some Israelites were privileged to set foot with Moses on the sacred mountain, so here certain of the disciples accompany Jesus (6^{13}). Secondly, Jesus, like Moses, descends and gives his message to the people *on a level place*, i.e. at the mountain's foot.

19 The picture is that of Jesus filled with the Holy Spirit, which becomes effective in *all* those who *touch him* (cp. 8^{43-46}).

6: 20–49 *The way of life for the disciples*

The section is similar to Matt. 5–7, and has material also found in Matt. 12. The early Church tradition probably contained a collection of sayings of Jesus headed by 'beatitudes', which Matthew and Luke used and adapted to suit their own

21 'Blessed are you that hunger now, for you shall be satisfied.
'Blessed are you that weep now, for you shall laugh.

---

purposes. The discourse links up with 4^{18-19}. It is part of the 'good news to the poor' (6^{20}), and is a call to a way of life that brings liberty, because one's conduct becomes independent of the reactions of others (6^{27-38}), and is solely controlled by the pattern of God's character. It also contains a warning of the dangers of 'blindness' (6^{39-42}) and of the need for 'recovery of sight'.

6: 20–26 The beatitudes and woes

Luke's four beatitudes resemble four of the nine beatitudes in Matt. 5^{3-12}. They are here balanced by four 'woes', both types of saying being used by Jesus elsewhere, and having a background in Jewish writings: the beatitude is common in the Wisdom literature (e.g. Prov. 3^{13}), and the woes in prophetic oracles (e.g. Isa. 10^{1}). The relation between the Matthaean and Lucan beatitudes is not easy to determine, and it is possible that Jesus gave them in different forms on different occasions. In Luke they bring reassurance to the disciples who can find no security in their immediate environment, whereas the woes are a warning to the self-satisfied. By commonly accepted standards 'blessed' would not fit the situations mentioned, nor would the term 'woe' be appropriate to the situations of wealth, etc.; but ordinary human judgements are reversed, because suffering in the cause of Jesus will be shown to have a future, while self-satisfaction will lead nowhere. The beatitudes in Matthew serve to assert that the faithful men of God and the qualities they represent will be vindicated.

20 *Blessed*, or 'happy' probably stands for a Hebrew term meaning 'O the happiness of', often used of those who are pleasing God (e.g. Ps. 1^{1}). Except in the fourth beatitude, it is not made clear that the beatitudes are in the second person plural; this has to be inferred from the clause beginning 'for'. Such sayings, normally in the third person, also occur elsewhere in the second. For the first beatitude cp. Matt. 5^{3}. *poor* refers partly to material poverty, but also (as in Matthew) to a lack of reliance on oneself. *for yours is the kingdom of God*, or better 'the kingdom of God belongs to you', suggests that with Jesus' mission the reign of God has broken in amongst men: the disciples, though poor in worldly possessions, and though having made a total renunciation in the cause of Jesus, have the true wealth of belonging to God's kingdom (cp. 1 Cor. 4^{8}).

21 Cp. Matt. 5^{6}, where, however, the 'hunger' is obviously metaphorical. Luke also inserts *now*, contrasting the present condition of

22 'Blessed are you when men hate you, and when they
exclude you and revile you, and cast out your name as evil,
23 on account of the Son of man! Rejoice in that day, and leap

---

the disciples with their future destiny. Luke is probably thinking of a literal hunger (cp. 1^{53}; Ps. 107^{5-9}): the disciples may suffer physical privations, but will be vindicated. *satisfied*, used elsewhere (e.g. Ps. 17^{14}) of God's 'filling' people, and meeting their need, here denotes the satisfaction of being on God's side and of enjoying fullness of life in his new age. *weep* probably refers to the trouble and sorrow of the faithful man of God (cp. Ps. 30^{5}) and to his longing for God's help (cp. Ps. 56^{8}). *laugh*: in the joy of sharing in the blessings that God has in store for his faithful people (cp. Ps. 126^{2}).

22 The last beatitude in both Matthew and Luke concerns persecution, with verbal differences, but with the common theme that such suffering is a ground for joy. *hate* (cp. Ps. 69^{4}): an expression of hostility to the faithful man of God. *exclude*, or 'separate', is normally followed by 'from', with a noun to show that from which the separation takes place, but here a phrase such as 'from themselves' or 'from the synagogue' has to be understood. *revile* in the Psalms (e.g. 55^{12}) describes the taunts suffered by the righteous at the hands of the ungodly. *cast out your name as evil* has sometimes been taken in the sense of issuing an evil report of Christians, or of disparaging them, or of endeavouring to remove all trace of their influence (cp. Ps. $74^{10, 18}$, 109^{13}). Perhaps the most likely meaning is that people will reject the name of Jesus, to whose cause the disciples are committed, as an evil influence. *the Son of man*: referring to Jesus, and connected elsewhere with suffering (e.g. 9^{22}). For the disciples' share in Jesus' suffering cp. 1 Pet. 4^{12-14}.

23 Cp. Matt. 5^{12}. *in that day*: the day of men's hatred and antagonism. For *leap for joy* cp. Ps. 114^{4-6}; Mal. 4^{2}, where the language is connected with God's rescue of his people. The *reward* (cp. Isa. 40^{10}, 62^{11}) is *in heaven*, i.e. sure and lasting, as guaranteed by God, in contrast with what 'men' can achieve by their opposition. Such reward in present participation in the new age of God brought by Jesus. *for so . . . prophets* gives another reason for joy, and also a high estimate of the disciples' sufferings, as on a level with those of the great prophets, e.g. Jeremiah. *their fathers*: Jesus dissociates himself from the Jews' past. The theme of the prophets' sufferings and martyrdom was prominent at that time, as is shown by the reverence paid to their tombs. The disciples are in the line of the O.T. prophets, and will declare to men the blessings of God's new age (cp. Acts 2^{16-21}).

for joy, for behold, your reward is great in heaven; for so
their fathers did to the prophets.
4 'But woe to you that are rich, for you have received your
consolation.
5 'Woe to you that are full now, for you shall hunger.
'Woe to you that laugh now, for you shall mourn and weep.
6 'Woe to you, when all men speak well of you, for so their
fathers did to the false prophets.
7 'But I say to you that hear, Love your enemies, do good to
8 those who hate you, bless those who curse you, pray for

---

4 *woe to you* expresses denunciation of what is contrary to God's will (cp. Isa. 5^{8-25}). The placing of 'beatitudes' and 'woes' side by side is unusual, and it is likely that Luke or his source has brought them together. Verse 27 shows that the 'woes' relate to an audience different from the disciples. Jesus warns people of the dangers of wealth, because it can blind them to the true place of God in their lives. *rich* has overtones of self-satisfaction. *consolation*, or 'source of strength', is also used of the strength given by God (cp. 2 Cor. 1^{3}): the rich men have comfort of their own making and so are in danger of ignoring that provided by God. *have received*, or 'have received in full': they have all the satisfaction that they hold worth while.

5 *you shall hunger*: in the day of God's judgement the *full* and self-satisfied will realize their lack of the things of value (cp. 16^{22-25}). The 'laughter' may denote an irresponsible enjoyment of life. The figure of the rich man in 16^{19-31} typifies what is meant by the 'rich', the 'full', and 'those who laugh'. *mourn and weep*, a description (cp. Isa. 56^{10}; Jer. 12^{4}) of God's judgement and of the recognition that there has been rebellion against him.

6 Universal popularity can be a warning-sign, as it can be the result of pandering to people's wishes, right or wrong, and of a failure to uphold God's will through fear of opposition. *False prophets* had often suited their message to their contemporaries' wishes (cp. 1 Kgs. 22^{5-28}; see also Deut. 18^{20-22}; Jer. 5^{31}; 1 John 4^{1-6}).

: 27–31 Love of enemies

8 Similar teaching is given in Matt. $5^{39-42,\ 44-48}$, 7^{12}.

The 'woes' have been addressed to those who are out of step with Jesus and his message; the teaching that follows is for *you who hear*, those who are ready to face God's demands. *love* is clarified further

29 those who abuse you. To him who strikes you on the cheek,
offer the other also; and from him who takes away your cloak
30 do not withhold your coat as well. Give to every one who begs
from you; and of him who takes away your goods do not ask
31 them again. And as you wish that men would do to you,
do so to them.

---

by *do good*, *bless*, and *pray*, while *enemies* is defined by *those who hate you*, *those who curse you*, and *those who abuse you*. One's conduct is not to be controlled by that of other people towards oneself, on a principle of measure for measure. Avoidance of revenge, or indifference, are not enough, for *love* is something positive, an attempt to give active help, a principle of conduct lived out by Jesus himself. *love* (ἀγαπᾶν) takes some of its meaning from its use to describe God's love for Israel, independent of the latter's merits (cp. Jer. 31^{3}), but also becomes coloured by the love of God experienced in Jesus—a love freely given to all (Rom. 5^{6-8}). Faced with his enemies' 'curse', the attempt to call down divine wrath upon him, the faithful man of God had thought fit to respond with a further 'curse', well illustrated in Ps. 109, where the Psalmist prays for the annihilation of his enemies, but asks God's blessing for himself. Jesus' teaching is, therefore, revolutionary; his followers are to *bless* their adversaries, i.e. pray that God will 'make his face to shine' upon them and will be 'gracious' to them (Num. 6^{25}), helping them to turn from their evil ways. *curse you*: for your loyalty to God. See also Rom. 12^{17-21}.

29–30 True love is now further explained: it involves a generous giving of oneself in ungrudging service to others. The vivid sayings all illustrate a generosity that is willing to go beyond what is required, and may be intended to drive home the principle of generosity, rather than to be pieces of advice for particular situations. *to him who strikes . . . the other also*: cp. Isa. 50^{6}. The *cloak* was the outer garment, while *coat* or 'shirt' was the undergarment. The picture is that of a readiness to give up both the garments, an essential part of a man's dress. *everyone*: there is no limit to the giving. *ask them again*, or, better, 'demand them back'.

31 The 'golden rule' is stated positively: do not merely abstain from conduct to others that you would not like as behaviour to yourself, but carry out the kind of action that you would like them to show to you. Jesus realistically appeals to the principle of 'self-love': if you expect other people to display a certain standard of conduct to you, it is illogical not to show the same in relation to them. In Jesus' time the rule was often stated in its negative and less demanding form: 'a man should not do what he hates to experience'.

32 'If you love those who love you, what credit is that to you?
33 For even sinners love those who love them. And if you do
good to those who do good to you, what credit is that to you?
34 For even sinners do the same. And if you lend to those from
whom you hope to receive, what credit is that to you? Even
35 sinners lend to sinners, to receive as much again. But love
your enemies, and do good, and lend, expecting nothing in

6: 32–36 Teaching on generosity

The first three verses are parallel, and then the three themes of *love, do good,* and *lend* are recapitulated in v. 35 and taken further. Jesus makes an appeal (*a*) to the adventurous side of human nature that likes to have demands made of it, and (*b*) to the fact that such conduct will show his disciples to be 'in the image of God' and to reflect his character.

32 It is easy to show affection to those who call it out from you. *credit,* or 'graciousness': what sort of graciousness of character does this conduct bring? Even *sinners,* perhaps outcasts from Jewish society, whose standards of conduct are not generally admired, show a staunch solidarity with each other.

33 As in Hebrew poetry, this verse repeats the thought of the previous one.

34 *lend*: in the widest sense of generosity. The instances here and in vv. 32–33 depict people whose conduct is controlled by that of others and by the principle of exact recompense (cp. the rabbinical saying, Tos. Megilla, iv. 16, 'Do [things for others] because they will do them for you, lend because they will lend to you, sorrow because they will sorrow for you, bury because they will bury you').

35 *expecting nothing in return* (μηδὲν ἀπελπίζοντες): the verb strictly means 'despair'; we are never to despair and think that such love is wasted. The parallelism with 'from whom you hope to receive' (v. 34) has suggested the translation as in RSV, though such usage is not attested until much later. Instead of *nothing* there is the alternative 'no one' or 'no man'. Perhaps originally Luke intended the verb in the sense of 'despair', and later it was taken to mean 'accept in return'. 'no one' or 'no man' may, therefore, be the original reading, with the translation 'despairing of no man' (RSV margin), an idea according well with the teaching of Jesus. With this unlimited kind of love contrast Ecclus. 12^{1-7}. The *reward* is that of being *sons* of God, i.e. in a right relationship with him and reflecting his character. This generous love of God is underlined in a Jewish interpretation of Ps. 145^{9}, 'his

return;[u] and your reward will be great, and you will be sons
of the Most High; for he is kind to the ungrateful and the
36 selfish. Be merciful, even as your Father is merciful.
37 'Judge not, and you will not be judged; condemn not, and
you will not be condemned; forgive, and you will be forgiven;
38 give, and it will be given to you; good measure, pressed down,

[u] Other ancient authorities read *despairing of no man*

---

mercies are over all his works, upon the just and the unjust' (*Tanch.* v. 49). For the early Christians it was demonstrated even more in the life, death, and resurrection of Jesus and the coming of the Holy Spirit.

36 *merciful*, or 'compassionate': cp. Ps. 78^{38}.

6: 37–38 A forgiving attitude

Four parallel clauses are placed side by side in the manner of Hebrew poetry: the first two are negative, and form opposites to the second two, which are positive. The last clause is extended to reinforce the importance of its teaching. The danger of allowing other people's attitudes and conduct to control one's own is again stressed, with the need for generous forgiveness and giving.

37–38 *Judge not*, like *condemn not*, is not aimed at our critical faculties and the work of law courts, but at our propensity to make carping criticism of others. *and you will not be judged* may have the force of a purpose clause. If our attitude is one of judgement, then logically we should expect the same attitude from both God and our fellow human beings—something that would be distasteful to us. It is far more constructive to *forgive* or 'acquit', which includes a willingness to see the best in people and to give them a new start without holding the past against them. *and . . . forgiven* may also be a purpose clause: it is illogical to expect forgiveness from God and other people unless you are prepared to exercise it yourself (cp. 11^{4}). *give*: in generous treatment of others. *and . . . given*: again perhaps a purpose clause. This 'givingness' will result in blessings, not merely in the sense of Eccles. 11^{1}, but in knowing that such conduct brings close fellowship with God. *good measure*: the picture is that of a measuring instrument in which the contents, compressed very tightly together, are allowed to pile up, and so the customer will receive a generous quantity. *will be put into your lap*, lit. 'they will put' or 'give . . .', a vague third person plural, probably referring to God. The *lap*, or the fold of a garment,

shaken together, running over, will be put into your lap. For
the measure you give will be the measure you get back.'
39 He also told them a parable: 'Can a blind man lead a blind
40 man? Will they not both fall into a pit? A disciple is not above
his teacher, but every one when he is fully taught will be like
41 his teacher. Why do you see the speck that is in your brother's

---

which was used as a pocket. *For the measure . . . you get back*: see also Matt. 7^{2}, and (in a different setting) Mark 4^{24} (a call to careful listening). It may be a proverb used by Jesus in different contexts, and sounds similar to the modern adage, 'What you put into life you get out of it'. The Jewish rabbis had a similar saying to express the principle of just retribution, but Jesus uses the saying differently, to show that a condemnatory attitude to others is inviting the judgement of being a loveless person, while a generous and forgiving attitude brings the blessing of closer fellowship and favour with God.

6: 39–42 The need for clarity of sight

39 See also Matt. 15^{14} (applied to the Pharisees). The *parable*, or 'proverb', stresses (*a*) the need for an adequate guide with insight into living, and (*b*) the disciples' need to have 'good sight' if they are to be Jesus' representatives. The implication is that Jesus is this guide who proclaims 'recovering of sight to the blind' (4^{18}).

40 See also Matt. 10^{24-25}; John 13^{16}, 15^{20}. Luke or his source has joined this saying to v. 39, and the sequence of thought may be: the followers of Jesus have an adequate guide in him, and, in the manner of pupils of a school of thought, are under obligation to conform to the manner of life the teacher prescribes. *fully taught*, or 'trained', which requires first the recognition that one is in need of 'sight', a point made clearer in what follows.

41 The saying first underlines the need to make sure that one's own vision and viewpoints are in order, and is secondly aimed at people's propensity to criticize others without realization of their poor ability to pass judgement. *speck*: a small piece of straw, chaff, or wood, something insignificant. It may be the picture of a piece of chaff being removed from the eye of a farm workman. *log*, or 'full-scale beam of wood': the direct opposite of the 'speck'. Jesus draws the humorous picture of someone with his own eye completely blocked by a huge beam trying to remove the tiny speck! The irony is increased by the fanciful suggestion that the person is unaware of having anything in his eye.

42 eye, but do not notice the log that is in your own eye? Or how
can you say to your brother, "Brother, let me take out the
speck that is in your eye," when you yourself do not see the
log that is in your own eye? You hypocrite, first take the log
out of your own eye, and then you will see clearly to take out
the speck that is in your brother's eye.
43 'For no good tree bears bad fruit, nor again does a bad tree
44 bear good fruit; for each tree is known by its own fruit. For
figs are not gathered from thorns, nor are grapes picked from
45 a bramble bush. The good man out of the good treasure of his
heart produces good, and the evil man out of his evil treasure
produces evil; for out of the abundance of the heart his mouth
speaks.

---

42 *hypocrite*: one who acts a part, and so lives in a world of 'make-believe'.

6: 43–45 The genuine disciple

For the *tree* see also Matt. 7^{16-19}, and for the *treasure* see also Matt. 12^{34-35}. Jesus may have expressed the first of the two analogies in different forms (cp. Matt. 12^{33}). Here both sayings are linked together with others on the subject of discipleship.

43–44 Cp. Ps. 92^{12-14}. A *good*, or 'sound' tree is demonstrated by the quality of its produce. The test laid down will be an indication whether the disciples have gained the new vision. *for each tree . . . fruit* goes best with what follows: just as the kind of fruit on a tree shows the type of tree from which it comes, so the quality of the disciples' lives will show them as belonging to Jesus. A contrast is drawn between the useless *thorns* and *bramble*, often of the cammock-weed type (cp. Gen. 3^{18}; Hos. 10^{8}), and the useful fig tree and vine.

45 The saying links in theme with vv. 43–44. The picture changes to a treasure house or store to which *the heart*, the inner and real personality of a person, is likened. In a *good man*, one loyal to God, the treasure store contains all kinds of valuables to be brought out for display in the manner of his life, while the opposite is true of the *evil man*, the one who leaves God out of the reckoning (cp. Ps. 140^{1}). The outward act, here a man's speech, can reveal the centre of his allegiance. *abundance*, or 'that of which the heart is full': either valuable or worthless treasure. *his mouth*: the person in his capacity of speaker (cp. 1 Kgs. 17^{24}).

46 'Why do you call me "Lord, Lord," and not do what I tell
47 you? Every one who comes to me and hears my words and
48 does them, I will show you what he is like: he is like a man
building a house, who dug deep, and laid the foundation upon
rock; and when a flood arose, the stream broke against that
house, and could not shake it, because it had been well built.[v]
49 But he who hears and does not do them is like a man who
built a house on the ground without a foundation; against
which the stream broke, and immediately it fell, and the ruin
of that house was great.'

7: AFTER he had ended all his sayings in the hearing of the

[v] Other ancient authorities read *founded upon the rock*

6: 46–49 The need for action

Cp. Jas. 1^{22-27}. For v. 46 see also Matt. 7^{21} (an extended version of the Lucan saying), and for vv. 47–49 see also Matt. 7^{24-27}. The two sayings here may have come from different contexts.

46 *Lord, Lord*: expressing recognition of Jesus' standing and authority, which must be shown not in words alone, but in actions.

47 Jesus is conscious of the authoritative nature of his teaching.

48 In Matthew the picture seems to be a Palestinian wady ('the sand'), dry in summer and presenting a tempting site for a house; the winter rains, however, fill the wady with a roaring torrent, and the only safety lies in building on the rock above. In Luke the builder appears to be erecting a house near a river, which for safety needs a deep and firm foundation; otherwise, if the building is just erected on the existing surface, the river may overflow its bank and carry the house away. Jesus himself may have varied the analogy in this way on different occasions.

: 1–17 *The centurion's slave; the widow's son*

Jesus continues to release 'the captives', the slave from approaching death, the widow's son from death itself. For the first episode see also Matt. 8^{5-13}; the second is peculiar to Luke.

2 people he entered Capernaum. Now a centurion had a slave
who was dear[w] to him, who was sick and at the point of death.
3 When he heard of Jesus, he sent to him elders of the Jews,
4 asking him to come and heal his slave. And when they came to
Jesus, they besought him earnestly, saying, 'He is worthy to
5 have you do this for him, for he loves our nation, and he built
6 us our synagogue.' And Jesus went with them. When he was

[w] Or *valuable*

7: 1–10 The centurion shows faith

The interest lies in Jesus' approval of the man's faith; he is a non-Jew, and so a type of the later Gentile believer. The story illustrates Jesus' concern for non-Jews (cp. Acts 10, Peter's dealings with the centurion, Cornelius).

1 *Capernaum*: the scene of Jesus' ministry from 4^{31}–8^{12}.

2 In the Greek *centurion* stands first, as the important character in the story. A centurion, strictly a commander of one hundred men in a Roman legion, was a key officer in that army's organization. Here he may have been seconded to train and command part of the forces of Herod, auxiliary troops for maintenance of internal order. *dear*: perhaps 'valuable' (RSV margin) or 'highly reliable'. *at the point of death* stresses the slave's critical state, and so underlines the centurion's confidence in Jesus.

3 Perhaps the centurion thought that the Jewish *elders* might have greater influence with Jesus. *heal*, or 'rescue from death'. In Luke (contrast Matthew) there is no direct contact between Jesus and the Roman. For the sending of the elders and 'the friends' (v. 6) cp. Acts 10^7. *come*: at first Jesus' presence is requested, then the word of healing is seen to be sufficient. Some of the differences in detail between Matthew and Luke may be due to the fact that the main interest was in the centurion's words and Jesus' reaction.

4–5 Perhaps the Jews felt that help given to a non-Jew had to be justified. *loves our nation*: the Jewish religion appealed to certain thinking Gentiles because of its monotheistic belief and high standard of morality; some, therefore, accepted the beliefs and moral obligations of Judaism, and attended synagogue worship, without becoming full members through circumcision, and were known as 'God-fearers' (cp. Acts 10^2).

6 Jesus is not deterred by the man's Gentile background. In contrast with vv. 4–5, the centurion is conscious of his own unworthiness, not just because Jesus is a Jew, but because he is 'a holy man of God', in whom God's power is at work.

not far from the house, the centurion sent friends to him,
saying to him, 'Lord, do not trouble yourself, for I am not
7 worthy to have you come under my roof; therefore I did not
presume to come to you. But say the word, and let my servant
8 be healed. For I am a man set under authority, with soldiers
under me: and I say to one, "Go," and he goes; and to another, "Come," and he comes; and to my slave, "Do this,"
9 and he does it.' When Jesus heard this he marvelled at him,
and turned and said to the multitude that followed him,
'I tell you, not even in Israel have I found such faith.'
10 And when those who had been sent returned to the house,
they found the slave well.
11 Soon afterward[x] he went to a city called Nain, and his
12 disciples and a great crowd went with him. As he drew near

[x] Other ancient authorities read *Next day*

---

7 *I did not presume*, or 'I did not count myself worthy'. *say the word*: give the appropriate command.

8 *authority*: the 'imperium' exercised by the Roman Emperor and his representatives, here the governor of Syria. In turn the centurion had control of others. His own experience of authority, and his exercise of it, bring him insight into what can be achieved by the command of proper authority, here Jesus' special power over sickness and disease.

9 *at him*: at his deep-rooted faith. Jesus *turned* to draw the attention of others to it. *not even in Israel*: not even among the people to whom God had made his special revelation.

10 The effectiveness of Jesus' command shows the centurion's faith to be justified.

: 11–17 The widow's son restored to life

Cp. Mark 5^{22-43}; John 11^{41-44}. Such acts are rare in the Gospel tradition, a reticence that points to its reliability, and place Jesus in line with the great prophets Elijah and Elisha (cp. 1 Kgs. 17^{17-24}; 2 Kgs. 4^{18-37}), thus giving him an unusual status. The Messiah was sometimes expected to raise the dead (cp. 7^{22}). Death was a sign of the devil's sovereignty (Wisd. 2^{24}), and so these acts of resurrection, like the exorcisms, demonstrate Jesus' power and victory over evil, and

to the gate of the city, behold, a man who had died was being
carried out, the only son of his mother, and she was a widow;
13 and a large crowd from the city was with her. And when the
Lord saw her, he had compassion on her and said to her, 'Do
14 not weep.' And he came and touched the bier, and the bearers
15 stood still. And he said, 'Young man, I say to you, arise.' And
the dead man sat up, and began to speak. And he gave him to
16 his mother. Fear seized them all; and they glorified God,
saying, 'A great prophet has arisen among us!' and 'God has
17 visited his people!' And this report concerning him spread
through the whole of Judea and all the surrounding country.
18 The disciples of John told him of all these things.

---

foreshadow the triumph of his own resurrection. They also indicate Jesus' power to raise a person from the life of death or purposelessness to that of fellowship with God.

11 *Soon afterward*: the chronology is probably vague. *Nain*: a town in Galilee.

12 *carried out*: to the burial place. *only son* and *widow* underline the woman's plight. The *large crowd* shows the strong sympathy felt for her.

13 *the Lord*: Jesus.

14 *touched the bier*, or 'coffin': a sign for the bearers to put it down. *Young man*: another tragic feature of the scene. *arise*, or 'be raised': also used of the resurrection of Jesus and of the raising of his followers to new life with him.

15 The man has his earthly faculties once more. Mother and son are reunited (cp. 1 Kgs. 17^{23}; 2 Kgs. 3^{36}). Perhaps Jesus is seen as the prophet expected in the last days (cp. Acts 3^{22}).

7: 18–35 *John the Baptist's question: his status discussed*

The section has three divisions: (*a*) vv. 18–23, John's inquiry about the status of Jesus; (*b*) vv. 24–30, Jesus' assessment of the importance of John's status; (*c*) vv. 31–35, the lack of response to both missions. See also Matt. 11^{2-19}.

7: 18–23 The status of Jesus

18 *told him*: Matthew records, as Luke implies, that John heard the news in prison (cp. 3^{19-20}). *all these things*: the activity of Jesus.

19 And John, calling to him two of his disciples, sent them to the
Lord, saying, 'Are you he who is to come, or shall we look for
20 another?' And when the men had come to him, they said,
'John the Baptist has sent us to you, saying, "Are you he who
21 is to come, or shall we look for another?"' In that hour he
cured many of diseases and plagues and evil spirits, and on
22 many that were blind he bestowed sight. And he answered
them, 'Go and tell John what you have seen and heard: the
blind receive their sight, the lame walk, lepers are cleansed,
and the deaf hear, the dead are raised up, the poor have good
23 news preached to them. And blessed is he who takes no offence
at me.'

---

19 *he who is to come*, or 'he who is coming', may have been a title of the Messiah, but may look back to 3^{16}: is Jesus the one whose coming John had predicted? Perhaps John had doubts because his news about Jesus did not tally with his own forecast of a figure exercising a fiery judgement.

21 Luke thus prepares for 'what you have seen and heard' (v. 22). This is the first reference to restoration of sight to the blind (cp. 18^{35-43}).

22 *seen* and *heard* refer to the mighty acts of Jesus and his verbal teaching. Both are signs of his God-given mission: (*a*) they are in line with O.T. passages about the coming of God's new era (e.g. Isa. 29^{18-19}, 35^{5-6}, 61^{1}), or (*b*) more generally they point to a new power at work, attacking evil and proclaiming God's favour to men. For *the lepers* and *the lame* cp. 5^{12-26}, and for the raising of *the dead* cp. above, vv. 11–17. The *good news* includes Jesus' acts and verbal instruction, the first showing God's love and power over evil, the second (with special reference to 6^{20-49}) giving assurance that the trust in God shown by *the poor* is not in vain, and setting forth the life of real freedom.

23 *takes . . . offence*: an *offence*, or 'stumbling block', sometimes denotes that which entices Israel away from God (Ezek. 7^{19}), or that which repels (Ecclus. 7^{6}). Jesus would repel many of his contemporaries, because his message did not fit in with Jewish nationalist hopes of liberation from the Roman power, or with the expectation of John. In a vivid way, therefore, he was also an enticement to sin, since rejection of him meant also rejection of God's purposes (cp. 1 Cor. 1^{23}).

24 When the messengers of John had gone, he began to speak
to the crowds concerning John: 'What did you go out into
25 the wilderness to behold? A reed shaken by the wind? What
then did you go out to see? A man clothed in soft raiment?
Behold, those who are gorgeously apparelled and live in
26 luxury are in kings' courts. What then did you go out to see?
27 A prophet? Yes, I tell you, and more than a prophet. This is
he of whom it is written,

> "Behold, I send my messenger before thy face,
> who shall prepare thy way before thee."

7: 24–30 The status of John

John's status as 'the forerunner' is underlined. Jesus confirms the prophecy of 1^{13-17}. The rhythmic form of the passage is based on question and answer.

24 For the crowds, who had been attracted to John, cp. $3^{7, 10}$. Something worth seeing must have drawn them into such an uninteresting place as the Judaean wilderness. Jesus suggests that people had invaded John's seclusion in the desert before he started his mission (3^3). The area had already been associated with uprisings against Rome, and perhaps in some quarters John was viewed as a possible nationalist leader. Humorously Jesus suggests that the natural scenery had little to offer people—perhaps a water reed easily swayed by the wind (cp. 1 Kgs. 14^{15}).

25 *soft raiment*: fastidious clothes. A fabulously dressed man, who might draw sightseers, is not likely to be found in such an 'out of the way' place. *kings' courts*, or 'palaces': in centres of civilization providing facilities for luxury. A contrast may be intended with the austere dress of John (Mark 1^6).

26 With greater plausibility, the attraction was the sight of someone in whom the line of the ancient prophets seemed to have revived. But this correct estimate needed to go further: John is a prophet with a difference, because he heralds and prepares for God's decisive intervention.

27 The quotation is close to Mal. 3^1, occurring also at Mark 1^2, but only cited by Matthew and Luke in the present context. The passage also resembles Exod. 23^{20} ('behold, I send an angel [or 'messenger'] before you [or 'before your face'] to guard you on the way . . .'), and may be a conflation of this and the Malachi quotation ('behold, I send

28 I tell you, among those born of women none is greater than
John; yet he who is least in the kingdom of God is greater
29 than he.' (When they heard this all the people and the tax
collectors justified God, having been baptized with the
30 baptism of John; but the Pharisees and the lawyers rejected

---

my messenger to prepare the way before me'). The use of the second person singular in Exod. 23^{20} perhaps accounts for its use here (*thy*, *thee*, probably referring to Jesus) instead of 'my' and 'me' in Mal. 3^{1}. Exod. 23^{20} relates to God's arrangements for the Exodus from Egypt, while Mal. 3^{1} would at this time be seen as a reference to Elijah. John is therefore closely connected with Elijah and with the new Exodus to be achieved by Jesus.

28 *among those born of women*: among human kind. The saying bears the stamp of authenticity, as the early Christians would never have admitted the possibility that John was as great as Jesus. Jesus means that the status of John and his reputation in relation to God's purposes are as great as those accorded to anyone previously, and his loyalty to God is not surpassed. *least*: lit. 'less', i.e. of lower seniority; but the comparative can have superlative force. The parallelism between the two parts of the verse is based on the word 'greater', on the two phrases 'among those born of woman' and 'in the kingdom of God' (both of which begin with the same preposition, ἐν), and on the contrast between *greater* and *least* or 'less'. But while John's place in past history is assured, he also has to be viewed against the perspective of the new order of things, the kingdom of God. The translation 'less' might refer to Jesus in the sense 'he who is junior', i.e. he who comes later, or is younger. But the phrase more probably describes 'the person who has far less reputation' or 'the person who is of the least standing'. Such a person may have a status far beyond that of John through his association with the new order that Jesus brings, and for which John prepares.

30 Only Luke records this reaction. *the people and the tax collectors*: contrasted with the learned aristocracy, the Pharisees and the rabbis. Matthew records the coming of Pharisees and Sadducees to John, but not their baptism. *having been baptized* and *not having been baptized* refer to action prior to the main verbs, *justified* and *rejected*, and give the reason for the present reaction. The first group *justified God*, acknowledged God's working and praised him for it: Jesus' assessment of John confirmed their own. The second group continued their prior refusal to be baptized, by their present rejection of God's *purpose*, his design

the purpose of God for themselves, not having been baptized
by him.)
31 'To what then shall I compare the men of this generation,
32 and what are they like? They are like children sitting in the
market place and calling to one another,

"We piped to you, and you did not dance;
we wailed, and you did not weep."

33 For John the Baptist has come eating no bread and drinking
34 no wine; and you say, "He has a demon." The Son of man
has come eating and drinking; and you say, "Behold, a

---

and plan for his world (cp. Ps. 33[11]; Wisd. 9[17]), of which John's mission is part. *for themselves*, omitted in some MSS. owing to its awkwardness, may mean 'intended for themselves' or 'among themselves'. *rejected*, or 'nullified'. The contrast may be of a legal kind between ratifying and declaring invalid.

7: 31–35 The unresponsiveness of Jesus' contemporaries

The note of rejection, the continuing theme of John (v. 34), and the word 'justified' (v. 35), all form links with the previous passage.

31 Jewish parables and those of Jesus often take this pattern of an extended simile, being introduced, as here, by a question.

32 The *market place* was a centre of social life, and is being used here as a public recreation ground. One group of children tries to start a game of 'weddings' or, as an alternative, a game of 'funerals', but neither game, one joyful, the other sad, suits, because the other group will not 'play'. *piped*, or 'played the flute', probably on toy pipes or flutes: a joyful tune to lead the dance is meant. *wailed*: like professional mourners employed at funerals. The children play-act scenes from 'grown up' life.

33 Cp. 1[15, 80]. John abstains from the normal agricultural and civilized life, and his asceticism is construed as that of a madman possessed by evil forces (mad people did sometimes live in desolate places: cp. 8[27]).

34 Jesus leads a normal social life, but is nevertheless condemned for being sociable and unjustly charged with over-eating and over-drinking, and with mixing with undesirables. There is no pleasing Jesus' contemporaries, who are in no state of mind to respond to God.

glutton and a drunkard, a friend of tax collectors and sinners!"
Yet wisdom is justified by all her children.'

One of the Pharisees asked him to eat with him, and he
went into the Pharisee's house, and sat at table. And behold,

---

wisdom, the knowledge of God's will and purpose for human life, revealed, e.g., in the Jewish Law, and sometimes personified poetically (Prov. 8^{22-31}), and even thought of as a kind of power mediating between God and his people (Wisd. 7^{22}–8^{1}), here refers particularly to God's plan for human beings, now being revealed through John and Jesus himself. Sentence is passed upon it by some as foolishness, but the real *children* of wisdom, those who belong to her family, give it 'the verdict of acquittal' and thus recognize its genuineness. The Pharisees and the rabbis would have claimed to be children of wisdom through observance of the Law. Jesus, therefore, connects himself very closely with the divine wisdom. Instead of *children* Matthew's original reading was almost certainly 'works', probably in the sense of 'results': the God-givenness of the missions of John and Jesus is shown in what they effect, and should not be assessed by superficial human judgements.

36–8: 3 *A woman anoints Jesus; the women companions of Jesus*

36–50 An outcast woman is offered forgiveness

The occasion is probably different from that in Matt. 26^{6-13}, Mark 14^{3-9}, and John 12^{1-8}. The details are very different and no connection is made with the death of Jesus. The main concern is Jesus' dealing with a woman who was not 'respectable', and links up with Luke's theme of God's search for 'the lost'. The Son of man now lives up to his reputation as a 'friend of sinners' (v. 34). The woman in wanting Jesus' help shows herself one of the 'children' of wisdom (v. 35). By his attitude the Pharisee aligns himself with those who reject God's purpose (v. 30). The forgiveness brought to a woman now balances that brought to a man (5^{17-26}).

For Jesus' social life cp. v. 34. Some *Pharisees* had friendly feelings towards Jesus, or at least found something attractive in him; there is no suggestion that the motive of the Pharisee was to trap Jesus in some way.

The *woman* has sometimes been equated with Mary Magdalene (8^{2}) without any clear evidence. *sinner* suggests that she was an outcast from society because of her loose living. *alabaster flask*: a vessel with a long neck which was broken to release the contents. *ointment*, or 'oil of myrrh', a perfume with a strongly aromatic character, was sometimes used for doing honour to a distinguished guest.

a woman of the city, who was a sinner, when she learned that
he was sitting at table in the Pharisee's house, brought an
38 alabaster flask of ointment, and standing behind him at his
feet, weeping, she began to wet his feet with her tears, and
wiped them with the hair of her head, and kissed his feet, and
39 anointed them with the ointment. Now when the Pharisee
who had invited him saw it, he said to himself, 'If this man
were a prophet, he would have known who and what sort of
40 woman this is who is touching him, for she is a sinner.' And
Jesus answering said to him, 'Simon, I have something to say
41 to you.' And he answered, 'What is it, Teacher?' 'A certain
creditor had two debtors; one owed five hundred denarii,
42 and the other fifty. When they could not pay, he forgave them
43 both. Now which of them will love him more?' Simon
answered, 'The one, I suppose, to whom he forgave more.'
44 And he said to him, 'You have judged rightly.' Then turning

---

38 *behind him*: the woman approached from the back of the couch unseen by Jesus. The *weeping* and the *tears* are a token of sorrow for her past life. *kissed*: an expression of homage. The woman's *hair* would be worn long (cp. 1 Cor. 11^{15}).

39 The less likely alternative reading 'the prophet' would denote Jesus as the special prophet expected in the last days (cp. Deut. 18^{15}). Jesus has impressed his contemporaries as being like the great prophets of old, but in the Pharisee's view he belies his reputation by not showing prophetic insight. Jesus makes it clear that his acceptance of the woman's action is not due to his lack of insight into her character, but to his love and feeling for others. His prophetic insight is shown in reading the mind and thoughts of Simon.

41–42 Jesus uses an analogy in the form of a story (cp. 10^{30-35}) to challenge the Pharisee's attitude: it is more constructive not to condemn, but to offer the woman forgiveness and so create a relationship of love and understanding. The denarius was a Roman silver coin, some workmen's daily wage. Sins were sometimes thought of as debts to God.

43 Jesus asks his audience to make a judgement for itself (cp. 10^{36}), on which he then builds his arguments. *I suppose*: 'I am of the opinion'.

toward the woman he said to Simon, 'Do you see this woman? I entered your house, you gave me no water for my feet, but she has wet my feet with her tears and wiped them with her hair. You gave me no kiss, but from the time I came in she has not ceased to kiss my feet. You did not anoint my head with oil, but she has anointed my feet with ointment. Therefore I tell you, her sins, which are many, are forgiven, for she loved much; but he who is forgiven little, loves little.' And he said to her, 'Your sins are forgiven.' Then those who were at

---

Do you see . . .?: Let us look more closely at this woman's action. The Pharisee in judging the woman has invited judgement on himself (cp. 6^{37}), which Jesus now makes by comparing the courtesy of the woman with the discourtesy of the Pharisee. Jesus starts with the best in her, while the Pharisee sees the worst. *water*: to remove the dust from the feet of the guests. The *kiss* was the eastern greeting between friends, accompanied by the greeting 'Peace be with you' (cp. 22^{47-48}). The *oil* would refresh the guests and show respect.

Therefore: because in paying these courtesies to Jesus, costly not only in price, but also in her courage in entering the crowded room, she had shown (unlike the Pharisee) a recognition of the importance of Jesus and of his power to help her, and had also revealed her need of help and forgiveness. In the Greek *are forgiven* is perfect passive in tense, indicating the statement of an accomplished fact, while *is forgiven* is present passive, i.e. 'is being forgiven little', or 'has little to be forgiven'. *which are many* and *for she loved much* are closely connected in the Greek, and are best taken together: her costly expression of respect for Jesus shows her consciousness of having many sins to be forgiven. Then the comment *but he who . . . little* states the grounds for the assertion. Another, less likely, interpretation might be: by her love the woman has shown her repentance, and her many sins are pronounced forgiven, a constructive action, as in turn the woman's knowledge of the great debt remitted to her will bring out yet more love from her. One MS. omits *for . . . little*, obviously because of its difficulty.

Cp. 5^{20}. *are forgiven*, the perfect passive tense, stresses the authority of Jesus in asserting that the sins are removed completely out of the way. 'forgive' is the same Greek word as that used for remitting a debt (cp. v. 42).

As in 5^{21}, the question of Jesus' status is raised.

table with him began to say among themselves, 'Who is this,
50 who even forgives sins?' And he said to the woman, 'Your
faith has saved you; go in peace.'

8: SOON afterward he went on through cities and villages,
preaching and bringing the good news of the kingdom of God.
2 And the twelve were with him, and also some women who
had been healed of evil spirits and infirmities: Mary, called
3 Magdalene, from whom seven demons had gone out, and
Joanna, the wife of Chuza, Herod's steward, and Susanna,
and many others, who provided for them[y] out of their means.

y Other ancient authorities read *him*

---

50 The woman's faith was her trust that Jesus could 'save' her, i.e. undo the shackles of her sins and give her a new start. She can *go in peace*, in a right relationship with God.

8: 1–3 The followers of Jesus

The thought passes from the 'woman . . . who was a sinner' (7^{37}) to the women mentioned here. In both cases the 'good news of the kingdom' has been seen to be effective. The passage is only found in Luke.

1 *cities*: better, 'large inhabited centres'. *preaching*, or 'proclaiming like a herald': a picture of a herald with news of a great event (cp. Isa. 40^{9}); here the verb may have *kingdom* as its object, or may be used absolutely (cp. Mark 1^{14-15}).

2 *infirmities*: any kind of sickness or disease. *Magdalene* distinguishes her from others with the same name, and probably means 'from Magdala', a place near Tiberias on the Lake of Galilee. This *Mary* (cp. 24^{10}) is one of the earliest witnesses of Jesus' resurrection.

3 *Chuza*: probably a non-Jew. *steward*: perhaps a manager of Herod's property, or a governor administering part of his kingdom. Herod Antipas is probably meant. For the inclusion of both men and women among the close circle of Jesus cp. Acts 1^{13-14}. Luke thus stresses the equal importance of each in the eyes of Jesus (cp. Gal. 3^{28}). *many others*: women. It was probably revolutionary for an itinerant teacher like Jesus to be accompanied by women as well as men. *them*: the whole company; the alternative 'him' (RSV margin) is an attempt to centre

4 And when a great crowd came together and people from

---

attention on Jesus. The provision made for Jesus and his company will tend against interpreting 9^{58} as a reference to physical privation. Was this sharing of resources in Jesus' lifetime the pattern of the practices of Acts 2^{44-45}, 4^{32}?

8: 4–21 *The good news of Jesus will make headway*

Luke returns to his use of Mark, which he left at 6^{11}, and follows closely Mark $4^{1-25, 31-35}$ (cp. Matt. 13^{1-23}, 12^{46-50}), omitting Mark $4^{26-29, 30-32}$ (two parables, the second of which occurs at 13^{18-19}, probably from a different source). The general theme of 'results come' sounds a note of encouragement, contrasting with 'the unresponsiveness' of 4^{29}, 6^{11}, 7^{31-35}, and illustrating that 'wisdom' has 'her children' (7^{35}). The different parts of the section are held together by (*a*) the language of 'hearing' or 'listening' (vv. 8, 10, 15, 21), and (*b*) the theme of the Gospel's success. (*b*) recurs in different forms. In the parable of the Sower (vv. 4–9) despite the wastage of seed there are results. Some are capable of being initiated into the secrets of God (v. 10), while the parable's interpretation stresses that the Gospel is grasped and held firm by some (v. 15). The message cannot remain hidden, any more than one thinks of shrouding a lamp, or any more than a secret can be kept indefinitely (vv. 16–17). The Gospel once held increases in value (v. 18). There are those who carry out God's will (v. 21). Probably several pieces of Jesus' teaching have been linked together for convenience.

: 4–10 The parable of the Sower

It is interpreted as an allegory in vv. 11–15, the different parts of the story having a further application and meaning. Such allegorical interpretations are often traced to the post-resurrection Christian community, and it has been suggested that originally this parable made one point: despite the failure of a quantity of seed, there is finally success and a harvest. Possible applications would then be: (*a*) despite apparent failure or setback the kingdom of God will have success; (*b*) despite the humiliation and seeming defeat of Jesus the victory of God's cause will come; (*c*) despite the lack of response to Jesus' message, and despite the wastage in missing its vital nature,

5 town after town came to him, he said in a parable: 'A sower
went out to sow his seed; and as he sowed, some fell along the
path, and was trodden under foot, and the birds of the air
6 devoured it. And some fell on the rock; and as it grew up, it
7 withered away, because it had no moisture. And some fell
among thorns; and the thorns grew with it and choked it.
8 And some fell into good soil and grew, and yielded a hundred-

---

some (i.e. the disciples) respond and are approved for it. But an element of allegory cannot be ruled out in Jesus' parables. The picture of the sower and the seed would suggest to Jews the idea of God's intervening to achieve his purpose and give his message, and the symbolism of growth and yield would typify alignment with God's will and the well-being arising from pleasing him. (*c*) is, therefore, likely to be the meaning intended by Jesus (as the interpretation in vv. 11–15 also suggests, however much some of the points in the story may have been given more detailed interpretation than Jesus perhaps intended). The saying in v. 10 then draws out the parable's implications.

4 The word 'parable' (which in the Gospels covers a wealth of material) sometimes denotes a challenging saying which contains divine teaching, but which for its understanding requires thought and sensitivity to God's purposes, and this seems to be the meaning of the term here. In the light of what follows, a contrast is implied between the crowd's superficial attraction to Jesus and the smaller number of his loyal followers.

5 The sower scattering the seed by hand would be a sight familiar to Jesus. *the path*: the footpath running along the side of the field, which (as Luke adds) *was trodden under foot* by the passers-by, and so did not give the seed a chance to penetrate the hard ground and to germinate.

6 *rock*, or rocky ground: the soil was thin. Unlike the first seed, the second *grew up*. Its failure in Luke is due to lack of moisture, a consequence of its not being able to put down roots (the point stressed by Matthew and Mark). Luke, however, retains the reference to 'root' in v. 13.

7 *the thorns* and the grain grow together, but the weeds (the cammock weed is perhaps meant) prevent its coming to maturity (cp. Jer. 12^{13}).

8 Luke mentions only the *hundredfold* yield, while Matthew and Mark refer also to 'thirtyfold' and 'sixtyfold'. The description of the successful seed marks the climax of the parable. The yield is paralleled elsewhere (e.g. in northern Africa), and this manner of stating it should

fold.' As he said this, he called out, 'He who has ears to hear,
let him hear.'
9 And when his disciples asked him what this parable meant,
10 he said, 'To you it has been given to know the secrets of the

---

not be confused with the modern way of calculating yields (e.g. thirty bushels of grain reaped per bushel of grain sown); the concern here is with seeds reaped for seeds sown, i.e. with the fertility of individual plants. Such a yield probably represented the best expected return in Palestine. To *hear* in Jewish thought was closely connected with understanding and obeying the demands of God (e.g. Deut. 4^{10}), and Jesus' summons is a call either to understand and act on his message, or to appreciate the implications of the parable.

9 *what this parable meant*, or 'what this parable might be': either the disciples wanted a complete explanation of the parable, or they grasped some of its meaning, but wanted its further implications drawn out, as Jesus now proceeds to do.

10 If the parable teaches that only a remnant in Israel responds to Jesus' message, then this verse goes on to make it clear that the disciples are this remnant who are to be initiated into God's secrets. *it has been given*: it is part of God's plan. In accordance with Jewish thinking the smallness of the response must somehow be part of a divine purpose. There is probably no difference of meaning between Luke's *secrets* (so also Matthew) and Mark's *secret*. Such language was common. The mystery religions claimed to have secret knowledge about the world and about coming to terms with it. The Jews spoke of the secrets of God, sometimes revealed through a study of the Law (cp. Wisd. 2^{21}, 6^{22}). The Jewish apocalyptic writings (e.g. Daniel) are in the form of secrets revealed to the great heroes of the past concerning the coming of God's reign over the forces opposed to him (e.g. Dan. $2^{30, 47}$). Again the Qumran community claimed a special insight into divine mysteries (especially about God's new age), which had been given to them by 'the teacher of righteousness' (cp. *Commentary on Habakkuk*, vii; *Hymns*, vii; Vermes, *the Dead Sea Scrolls in English*, pp. 236 and 160–4). Against this background the claim of Jesus to impart special knowledge to his disciples makes sense. He too claims to be an interpreter of God's mysteries or secrets about the coming of God's kingdom in his own mission, and his claim is based on his unique relationship to God (cp. 10^{21-22}). *others*, or 'the rest': the Qumran community believed that they were destined by God to walk in the ways of light, just as others walked in the path of darkness (cp. *The Community Rule*, iii; Vermes, *The Dead Sea Scrolls in English*, pp. 74–6).

kingdom of God; but for others they are in parables, so that
seeing they may not see, and hearing they may not under-
11 stand. Now the parable is this: The seed is the word of God.

The *others* (unlike the disciples) are not ready for God's purposes, and the message of Jesus remains *in parables*, i.e. in riddles. In Matthew, and probably also in Mark, the saying seems related specifically to Jesus' practice of using the parabolic form of speech: for certain reasons his message at the moment has to be shrouded in this way, and only the disciples can be initiated into it. For *so that seeing . . . understand* cp. Isa. 6^{8-10}, 29^{9-10}; Jer. 5^{21}: sometimes the lack of response to the prophet's message is attributed to the direct intention of God, as here, where we should express it in such terms as 'and the result is that . . .'. *seeing* and *hearing* refer to Jesus' teaching in words and action. Luke probably intends this reservation of Jesus' intimate teaching to the few to be seen in the light of 24^{45-48} and Acts 1^{8}: once the disciples are fully initiated into God's secrets with the resurrection of Jesus and the coming of the Holy Spirit, these secrets are open secrets for the whole world (cp. 1 Cor. 2^{7}, 4^{1}). Similarly Jesus' teaching in parables will become clear in the light of the disciples' later experience (cp. John 16^{25}).

8: 11–15 The interpretation of the parable of the Sower

This interpretation is often thought to have originated in an exposition of the parable by the Christian preacher. The parable is treated as an allegory, the different parts of the ground standing for different kinds of people. Jesus, it is said, did not intend his parables to be interpreted as allegories, but meant them to make one general point. But an allegorical element in the parables cannot be ruled out, and a parable such as that of 'the Sower' may have been intended as a thoroughgoing allegory, or at least Jesus may have 'spelt out' his original parable in greater detail on request, especially in the case of the present one, which according to Mark 4^{13} holds a key position. The rarity of such explanations as this could point to its genuineness. The interpretation fits the earthly-life situation of Jesus just as much as that of the early Church, though Luke's introduction into Mark's version of such phrases as 'believe and be saved' (v. 12), 'believe' (v. 13), 'fall away' (v. 13), and 'patience' (v. 15), all terms familiar in the early Christian literature, shows how the parable could be applied to the early preaching of the Gospel and response to it. The interpretation in Mark is compressed and complicated. The comparison between the different types of ground and the types of people

12 The ones along the path are those who have heard; then the
devil comes and takes away the word from their hearts, that
13 they may not believe and be saved. And the ones on the rock
are those who, when they hear the word, receive it with joy;
but these have no root, they believe for a while and in time of
14 temptation fall away. And as for what fell among the thorns,

---

is expressed in an unusual way, e.g. 'and these are the ones along the path where the word is sown . . .; when they hear . . .' (4^{15}), when one might expect 'the path on which some seed fell represents those who hear . . .'. The use of 'these', 'others', and 'those' (Mark $4^{15, 16, 18, 20}$) suggests that the appropriate part of the parable is to be read each time. Further, 'the ones sown upon rocky ground' (Mark 4^{16}; cp. vv. 18 and 20) is an awkward and strange expression. Luke attempts to iron out these difficulties in vv. 14 and 15, but (strangely) not in vv. 12 and 13.

12 Luke retains Mark's 'the ones along the path', which means 'the path, where the word is sown, represents those who have heard . . .'. The activity of the birds symbolizes the action of *the devil*. To take away *from their hearts* (which clarifies Mark) means to prevent the message from having any influence or effect on people's thought and wills. For further clarification there is added *that they may not believe and be saved*, i.e. commit themselves to Jesus and his message, and be brought to a full relationship with God (cp. 8^{48}; Acts 16^{31}).

13 The rocky ground gave no proper opportunity for the seed's growth and so represents a temporary loyalty. *receive*: welcome. *joy*: the happiness of being the recipient of God's love, and of knowing that he is acting to show his cause to be right (cp. 1 Thess. 1^{6}). *temptation*, or 'testing', including persecution and suffering for attachment to Jesus (cp. 1 Pet. 1^{6}), and so equivalent to Mark's 'tribulation' or 'persecution'. *fall away*: in the sense of deserting the one true God (cp. Jer. 3^{14}).

14 *cares*: the anxieties that arise out of people's environment, and that are traced by Jesus to lack of trust in the providence of God. For the danger of *riches* cp. 16^{19-31}, 18^{18-30}. Luke underlines the dangers of materialism by reference to the *pleasures of life* (instead of Mark's 'the desire for other things'). *their fruit does not mature*, lit. 'they do not bring forth fruit to perfection': their loyalty does not mature, but fades away. *as they go on their way* in the sense of 'conduct oneself' or 'live' does not normally occur without qualification, but

they are those who hear, but as they go on their way they are
choked by the cares and riches and pleasures of life, and their
15 fruit does not mature. And as for that in the good soil, they
are those who, hearing the word, hold it fast in an honest and
good heart, and bring forth fruit with patience.
16 'No one after lighting a lamp covers it with a vessel, or puts
it under a bed, but puts it on a stand, that those who enter
17 may see the light. For nothing is hid that shall not be made
manifest, nor anything secret that shall not be known and
18 come to light. Take heed then how you hear; for to him who

---

in the Greek 'life' immediately precedes it, and so 'through life' can be readily understood.

15 Finally, the seed on the good ground stands for those whose loyalty is unadulterated, e.g. the disciples of Jesus who have 'left everything and followed him' (5[11]), and the Christians of Acts who hold firm in face of persecution and suffering. The combination of *honest* and *good* is common in Greek. The first (*καλός*) is used in *good soil* earlier in this verse, and the second (*ἀγαθός*) in the similar 'good soil' of 8[8]. The two adjectives together mean 'perfect', describing persons, qualities, and actions. An *honest and good heart* therefore resembles the Jewish 'perfect (or "wholly true") heart' (e.g. 1 Kgs. 8[61], 11[4]), used of one who is wholly committed to God. Thus Luke draws out the meaning of Mark's 'accept'. The need for *patience* or, better, 'endurance', the quality of remaining firm, is stressed both by Jesus and by the early Church (cp. 2 Cor. 1[6]).

8: 16–18 Revelation will come

These three sayings, with their note of 'revelation', continue the theme of vv. 4–15: the disciples form a group who are to be initiated into the secrets of Jesus' mission.

16 Cp. 11[33]; Matt. 5[15]; Mark 4[21]. Jesus may have used the saying in different forms. *light* is something to be seen; the picture may be that of a house with an entrance-hall and a light shining in it to welcome the visitors.

17 Cp. 12[2]; Matt. 10[26]; Mark 4[22]. They sound like proverbial expressions with the theme 'secrets must come out'. The disciples are going to be the recipients of divine secrets.

18 *Take heed*: stressing the vital nature of Jesus' message. *for to him . . . away* (cp. 19[25–26]; Matt. 25[29]) is meant to provoke thought: in ordinary

has will more be given, and from him who has not, even what
he thinks that he has will be taken away.'
19 Then his mother and his brothers came to him, but they
20 could not reach him for the crowd. And he was told, 'Your
mother and your brothers are standing outside, desiring to
21 see you.' But he said to them, 'My mother and my brothers
are those who hear the word of God and do it.'
22 One day he got into a boat with his disciples, and he said to

---

life it would be considered wrong for a person who has wealth to be promised more, while the 'have not' is relieved of what little he has. *him who has*: probably the person who grasps the secret of God. Such a possession will have a 'snowball effect', bringing with it more and more understanding of God's purposes. But failure to grasp the secret means that 'what one thinks that one has', i.e. one's present knowledge of God, reaches a dead-end, because it does not come to its proper fulfilment through the further knowledge of God given to Jesus.

8: 19–21 The real relatives of Jesus

The incident is given this context (contrast Mark 3^{31-35}) to stress that those who accept the word of Jesus form a new family, not based on natural ties of kinship. The saying in v. 21 must have brought consolation to many early followers of Jesus, for whom discipleship meant the breaking of natural relationships (cp. 12^{51-53}).

20 The omission of Mark's introduction to the story (Mark 3^{31}), telling of the lack of understanding shown by the relatives of Jesus, obscures the background to Jesus' words in v. 21. *Your brothers* may refer to other children of Mary by Joseph, to half-brothers of Jesus by a former marriage of Joseph, or to relatives. The first possibility has too often been dismissed to uphold the doctrine of Mary 'ever-virgin'.

21 Cp. 11^{28}. The section ends, like the previous discourse (6^{46-49}), with the note of 'hearing' and 'doing'.

8: **22–56** ***Jesus' triumph over evil***

See also Matt. 8^{23-34}, 9^{18-26}; Mark 4^{35}–5^{43}. Luke gives four incidents from Mark, revealing the lordship of Jesus in face of the storm, demonic possession, hopeless illness, and death. Again he gives 'release to the captives' (4^{18}), and the disciples are initiated into 'the secrets of the kingdom of God.'

them, 'Let us go across to the other side of the lake.' So they
23 set out, and as they sailed he fell asleep. And a storm of wind
came down on the lake, and they were filling with water, and
24 were in danger. And they went and woke him, saying, 'Master,
Master, we are perishing!' And he awoke and rebuked the
wind and the raging waves; and they ceased, and there was a
25 calm. He said to them, 'Where is your faith?' And they were
afraid, and they marvelled, saying to one another, 'Who then
is this, that he commands even wind and water, and they
obey him?'

8: 22–25 Jesus controls the storm

Jesus exercises the prerogative of God (cp. Ps. 89^{9}); hence the question in v. 25. In the light of 'rebuked' (v. 24; cp. 4^{35}) the action can be classed as an exorcism. The storm is probably regarded as specially provoked by the forces of evil, who concentrate their efforts against the representative of God. Jesus deals with the situation and frees the disciples from their fears. The miraculous element has sometimes been explained away on the theory that sudden squalls arise on the Lake of Galilee and just as suddenly are followed by a calm; in this knowledge Jesus was able to reassure his disciples. The story would still attest the deep impression made by Jesus, who is presented as lord of creation. But just as Jesus controlled the disorder in men's bodies, so he may well have controlled his environment. The incident also illustrates Jesus' power to still the fears of human hearts.

22 *the other side*: the eastern side of the lake.

23 Luke (contrast Matthew and Mark) records the reference to Jesus' being *asleep* before the mention of the squall, probably to maintain the even flow of the story, and so the vivid picture of Jesus sleeping undisturbed by the storm around him is diminished.

24 Luke (like Matthew) tones down the disciples' cry, to make it less disrespectful to Jesus. The contrast between the storm and the resulting calm is stressed; once Jesus takes control all is well.

25 Both Luke and Matthew omit Jesus' question: 'Why are you afraid?' (Mark 4^{40}), probably out of respect for the disciples, who in their later witness to Jesus proved the very opposite of cowards. *faith*: in the power of Jesus to cope with the situation. The unusual power of Jesus calls for a decision about his personal identity. *commands . . . him*: cp. 4^{36}.

Then they arrived at the country of the Gerasenes,[z] which
is opposite Galilee. And as he stepped out on land, there met
him a man from the city who had demons; for a long time he
had worn no clothes, and he lived not in a house but among
the tombs. When he saw Jesus, he cried out and fell down
before him, and said with a loud voice, 'What have you to do
with me, Jesus, Son of the Most High God? I beseech you,

[z] Other ancient authorities read *Gadarenes*, others *Gergesenes*

26–39 The madman restored to sanity

The mania is attributed to demonic forces who speak through the person. The man's condition and his hostile reaction to Jesus (vv. 27–28) contrast with his later restoration to health and his willingness to serve Jesus (vv. 35–36, vv. 38–39); the difference that the encounter with Jesus makes is stressed.

The name of the place is given in three ways (see RSV margin). 'Gadarenes' is probably an assimilation to the text of Matthew. The original reading in Luke and Mark was almost certainly *Gerasenes*, which raised difficulties, as suggesting the well-known Gerasa, a town in Decapolis, situated 30 miles south-east of the lake, and so quite unsuitable to be the place of this incident (cp. 8^{27}). Hence Gergesa was suggested, a place according to Origen, on the eastern shore, where the precipice over which the pigs rushed was still pointed out. 'Gadara', the other possibility, a place about 4 miles inland from the lake, is the best-attested reading in Matthew, and may be his attempt to solve the difficulties of 'Gerasa'. A solution may be that at this time 'Gerasa' was another name for Khersa, a village in the centre of the lake's eastern shore.

The man's nakedness and his strange obsession with living in a graveyard show his abnormality. *for a long time* stresses further the power of Jesus.

fell down: faced with Jesus, God's representative, the evil forces recognize their superior. The personal address *Jesus* is rare in the Gospels (cp. 4^{34}, 17^{13}, 23^{42}). *torment*, or 'torture', described the torture of those standing trial, and was part of their examination or of the punishment after sentence was passed: it can thus denote (Rev. 14^{10}, 20^{10}) the final inquisition and sentencing of evil, of which Jesus' action is now an anticipation (cp. Matt. 13^{39}). The demon forces are pictured as dreading lack of embodiment in people, and the ineffective existence that results (cp. 11^{24-26}).

29 do not torment me.' For he had commanded the unclean
spirit to come out of the man. (For many a time it had seized
him; he was kept under guard, and bound with chains and
fetters, but he broke the bonds and was driven by the demon
30 into the desert.) Jesus then asked him, 'What is your name?'
And he said, 'Legion'; for many demons had entered him.
31 And they begged him not to command them to depart into
32 the abyss. Now a large herd of swine was feeding there on the
hillside; and they begged him to let them enter these. So he

---

29 Better, 'for he was commanding', an explanation of the demon's plea in v. 28: the process of exorcism had begun. The mention of the *unclean spirit* leads to Luke's insertion describing the person's uncontrollable state, which is thus brought into close relation with Jesus' power to control him. In popular thought the *desert* was the haunt of evil spirits. The mental derangement takes the form of desire for isolation.

30 Knowledge of a person's name meant power over the person (cp. Gen. 32[29]). In certain cases of mental trouble the patient identifies himself with some other character or object in history or fantasy, so here with a Roman legion, which consisted of about 6,000 men, supported by the same number of auxiliary troops. The answer shows the man's obsession with his unnatural strength.

31 Mark's 'not to send them out of the country' becomes the more definite *not to command them to depart into the abyss*, i.e. relegate them to final defeat and destruction (cp. Rev. 20[3]). Jesus' accession to the demons' request perhaps reflects the idea that, although in his earthly mission he showed his ultimate power over evil, its final overthrow is yet to come. Or does the sequel suggest that the demons' request to 'possess' the swine leads to their entering that water of the lake and so the dreaded abyss, which in popular mythology was thought to be connected with the 'waters that are under the earth'?

32 The breaking up of a powerful concentration of evil may have strange disruptive side-effects—here the herd of pigs rushing madly to destruction. If one believes in the demoniacal possession of persons, it is not a big step to believe in that of animals. Jesus' action here may seem strange and abhorrent. But we today may be more sensitive about animals than the people of those days. The Gospel writers and those in the tradition behind them do not feel such action to be derogatory to Jesus, and neither Luke nor Matthew emend Mark at

33 gave them leave. Then the demons came out of the man and
entered the swine, and the herd rushed down the steep bank
into the lake and were drowned.
34 When the herdsmen saw what had happened, they fled,
35 and told it in the city and in the country. Then people went
out to see what had happened, and they came to Jesus, and
found the man from whom the demons had gone, sitting at
the feet of Jesus, clothed and in his right mind; and they were
36 afraid. And those who had seen it told them how he who had
37 been possessed with demons was healed. Then all the people
of the surrounding country of the Gerasenes[z] asked him to
depart from them; for they were seized with great fear; so he
38 got into the boat and returned. The man from whom the
demons had gone begged that he might be with him; but he

---

this point. Perhaps Jesus knew that this was the price to be paid for the dispersal of evil and the restoration of a human being to a full life of usefulness to God. The Jews considered that the pig was unclean, and so may have thought that it was appropriate that swine should be used to dispose of evil. If the story were regarded as apocryphal, which is not necessary, it would testify to the impression made by Jesus' mysterious power on the superstitious inhabitants of this part of Galilee.

33 *down the steep bank*, or 'over the edge' (NEB). The picture is probably meant to be that of the headlong rush of evil from the presence of Jesus.

35 This verse and v. 36 suggest that the incident was attested by a number of witnesses. The contrast between the former and the present state of the man is very marked.

36 *those who had seen it* would include the disciples of Jesus.

37 The populace recognize supernatural power, but in their superstitious fear think that it may bring ill luck.

38 *be with him*: as a close companion (cp. Mark 3^{14}). It would not be easy at this stage for a non-Jew (as the man probably was) to join a Jewish group, and he would do more good by remaining where he was. The Gospel tradition suggests that Jesus' activity was mainly confined to Jews, his contact with Gentiles being seen as exceptional and pointing to the future, when Jew and Gentile would find a place together in the Church.

39 sent him away, saying, 'Return to your home, and declare
how much God has done for you.' And he went away, proclaiming throughout the whole city how much Jesus had done
for him.
40 Now when Jesus returned, the crowd welcomed him, for
41 they were all waiting for him. And there came a man named
Jairus, who was a ruler of the synagogue; and falling at Jesus'
42 feet he besought him to come to his house, for he had an only
daughter, about twelve years of age, and she was dying.
43 As he went, the people pressed round him. And a woman
who had had a flow of blood for twelve years[a] and could not

[a] Other ancient authorities add *and had spent all her living upon physicians*

---

39 Jesus wishes the man to correct the mistaken suspicions of the inhabitants: he is, therefore, to proclaim that it is *God*, and not an evil force, that has healed him.

8: 40–56 The woman suffering from haemorrhage; the restoration of Jairus' daughter to life

The insertion of one incident in the middle of another is characteristic of Mark, and here serves two purposes: (*a*) the healing of the woman who (by implication) was dying prepares us for the act of resurrection itself; (*b*) there is a certain dramatic effect, in that, while in v. 42 the girl is described as dying, on the resumption of the main incident (v. 49) she is now dead.

40 *returned*: to the western side of the lake. *the crowd*: Jesus is very much in demand.

41 For the name *Jairus* cp. Num. 32^{41}. *a ruler of the synagogue*: probably the president of the synagogue, responsible for some of the arrangements for worship (see also v. 49 below). A Jew of rank recognizes the extraordinary power of Jesus (cp. Acts 18^{8}). There may be a contrast between Jairus who besought Jesus *to come to his house*, and the centurion who felt himself unworthy for Jesus to do this (7^{6-7}).

42 The age of the child, together with Luke's additional reference to her as an *only daughter* (cp. 7^{12}, 9^{38}) stresses the tragedy. *twelve* forms another link between the stories (cp. v. 43). *pressed*, or 'stifled': hence NEB, 'he could hardly breathe for the crowds'.

43 *a flow of blood*: internal haemorrhage. According to Lev. 15^{25-30} the woman would be ritually unclean, and contact with her would bring

be healed by any one, came up behind him, and touched the fringe of his garment; and immediately her flow of blood ceased. And Jesus said, 'Who was it that touched me?' When all denied it, Peter[b] said, 'Master, the multitudes surround you and press upon you!' But Jesus said, 'Some one touched me; for I perceive that power has gone forth from me.' And when the woman saw that she was not hidden, she came trembling, and falling down before him declared in the presence of all the people why she had touched him, and how she had been immediately healed. And he said to her, 'Daughter, your faith has made you well; go in peace.'

[b] Other ancient authorities add *and those who were with him*

---

uncleanness. These laws of uncleanness were really laws of hygiene to prevent the spread of disease; people so classified had to be given a clean bill of health by a priest. The woman in her desperation and with her full confidence in Jesus is ready to break the law. *twelve years* underlines both her serious condition and Jesus' ability to succeed where others failed. 'and had spent all her living upon physicians' (RSV margin), added in some MSS., could be part of the original text. Luke might easily have included something derogatory to his profession, if it enhanced Jesus' reputation.

behind him: to make sure of touching Jesus before he saw her. *the fringe*: either the hem of the garment, or the tassel worn on the four corners of the outer garment (Num. 15^{38-41}), as a reminder of God's commandments. The instantaneous cure is stressed.

Mark gives here the reason for Jesus' question; Luke reserves it for the lips of Jesus (v. 46). He introduces Peter as the spokesman of the disciples (cp. 12^{41}) and tones down the answer to make it more respectful to Jesus.

Better, 'someone did touch me' (NEB). Just as, in helping another, one can feel drained of one's resources, so here physical healing has the same result.

Luke's *in the presence of all the people* underlines that the story is well attested. *trembling*: perhaps in fear of a rebuke, and also in awe at her cure.

Jesus brings reassurance, especially by the affectionate term *daughter*. He claims an authority higher than the Jewish Law; for

49 While he was still speaking, a man from the ruler's house
came and said, 'Your daughter is dead; do not trouble the
50 Teacher any more.' But Jesus on hearing this answered him,
51 'Do not fear; only believe, and she shall be well.' And when
he came to the house, he permitted no one to enter with him,
except Peter and John and James, and the father and mother
52 of the child. And all were weeping and bewailing her; but he
53 said, 'Do not weep; for she is not dead but sleeping.' And
54 they laughed at him, knowing that she was dead. But taking
55 her by the hand he called, saying, 'Child, arise.' And her
spirit returned, and she got up at once; and he directed that

---

according to Lev. 15^{28} such a woman would have to wait seven days for official discharge. In the early Church such faith would typify the convert's committal to Jesus, and the cure would symbolize reconciliation with God. *go in peace*: cp. 7^{50}; the woman can now lead a full and healthy life.

49 Jesus has given new life: now the news of death is brought. *the ruler's house*: he is now called 'president of the synagogue'. *trouble*, or 'bother'. *the Teacher*, or, better, 'the rabbi'.

50 Jesus is not deterred by the presence of death. *believe*: in the life-giving power of Jesus.

52 Probably this is the official lament of professional mourners, part of the funeral rites: the funeral is beginning and yet Jesus does not despair. Jesus' words (cp. John 11^{11}) might suggest that the girl had fallen into a swoon, mistaken for death; but more probably he is saying that death is like sleep (cp. 1 Thess. 5^{10}), easily dissipated (cp. Ps. 13^{3}; Dan. 12^{2}). Luke emphasizes both here and in v. 55 that the child was really dead.

54 *arise*, or 'get up': the normal word for 'getting up' from sleep, and also used of the resurrection of Jesus and of Christians.

55 Cp. 1 Kgs. 17^{21-22}. According to Hebrew psychology, a person is a living creature because of the 'breath' or 'spirit' given to him by God (Gen. 2^{7}); its withdrawal means physical death (cp. Ps. 104^{29}). The return of the breath denotes that the girl has come to life again. Luke stresses the immediacy of the girl's resurrection: death, with its overtones of purposelessness and disintegration, is out of place in the presence of Jesus and will have no lasting power in God's world (cp. 1 Cor. 15^{22}; Heb. 2^{14-15}).

56 something should be given her to eat. And her parents were
amazed; but he charged them to tell no one what had happened.

9: AND he called the twelve together and gave them power
2 and authority over all demons and to cure diseases, and he
3 sent them out to preach the kingdom of God and to heal. And
he said to them, 'Take nothing for your journey, no staff, nor

---

56 Secrecy might seem difficult to obtain, but it probably relates to Jesus' part in the events. His power over death is demonstrated to the few, and not to the wider public, who might misunderstand and wish to set him up as a nationalist leader.

9: 1–9 *The mission of the twelve; Herod's perplexity*

9: 1–6 Jesus' disciples now share his mission

See also Matt. 10; Mark 6^{7-13}; cp. below, 10^{1-20}. The commissioning of the twelve follows an act of resurrection from the dead, and so anticipates the later situation when the resurrection of Jesus himself will be followed by the mission of the Church.

1 *power and authority*: full power to act. Agreements between Matthew and Luke suggest that they are combining another source with Mark.

2 Luke explicitly refers to the sending out of the twelve (cp. Mark 3^{14-15}), and makes it clear that their acts will be demonstrations of the presence of God's kingdom. Jesus has already spoken (4^{43}) of his being 'sent', and now in turn 'sends' his disciples (cp. John 20^{21}).

3 The regulations are more severe in Luke and Matthew than in Mark, where the use of the staff and the wearing of sandals are allowed. The slight differences may be due to differences in the report of Jesus' instructions, or to a hardening of the rules imposed on missionaries in some of the early Church communities. The rules may, however, have hardened towards asceticism, to stress the abandonment of self-reliance required of the apostles. *bag*: a traveller's knapsack. In Mark the command is that two *tunics* are not to be worn, a practice sometimes thought effeminate; Luke's version could be a warning against even possessing two such under-garments, one for wear, one for change. The RSV leaves out 'each', i.e. 'nor are you each to have a second coat' (NEB). The Cynic itinerant preacher wore two tunics, and carried a stick and knapsack.

4 bag, nor bread, nor money; and do not have two tunics. And
whatever house you enter, stay there, and from there depart.
5 And wherever they do not receive you, when you leave that
town shake off the dust from your feet as a testimony against
6 them.' And they departed and went through the villages,
preaching the gospel and healing everywhere.
7 Now Herod the tetrarch heard of all that was done, and he
was perplexed, because it was said by some that John had
8 been raised from the dead, by some that Elijah had appeared,
9 and by others that one of the old prophets had risen. Herod
said, 'John I beheaded; but who is this about whom I hear
such things?' And he sought to see him.

---

4 One house is to be headquarters.

5 The action (cp. Acts 13^{51}) symbolizes the breaking off of all association, to show the seriousness of rejecting the message. *as a testimony*: that the message has been given and has not been heeded.

6 Luke compresses Mark's summary of the work of the twelve.

9: 7–9 Herod speculates about Jesus

The note of 'rejection' (v. 5) is taken up in the reference to John's death.

7 *all that was done*, or, better, 'all that was happening', i.e. the activities of Jesus. *raised from the dead* suggests 'brought to earth again'. This terminology, when later applied to Jesus, is often qualified by language of 'exaltation to God's right hand' (cp. Acts 2^{29-35}), to show that now 'resurrection' does not have its ordinary meaning of returning to earth, but rather refers to entering into a state of heavenly glory (cp. $24^{26, 46}$), the resurrection appearances of Jesus on earth being only a temporary arrangement to convince the disciples that Jesus is still their living Lord.

8–9 Cp. 1^{17}. Mark attributes to Herod the direct belief that John has come back from the dead. Similarly here Herod's question implies that he is having doubts whether he has finally disposed of John, and also keeps alive the problem of Jesus' identity, which is taken a stage further in 9^{18-22}. *beheaded*: Luke does not record the details in retrospect (cp. Mark 6^{17-29}), perhaps considering it bad literary taste to reintroduce a character who has played his part. *And he sought to see him*, or 'kept looking for an opportunity to meet him personally', a desire satisfied in 23^{6-12} (see also 13^{31}).

10 On their return the apostles told him what they had done.
And he took them and withdrew apart to a city called Beth-
11 saida. When the crowds learned it, they followed him; and
he welcomed them and spoke to them of the kingdom of God,
12 and cured those who had need of healing. Now the day began
to wear away; and the twelve came and said to him, 'Send the
crowd away, to go into the villages and country round about,
to lodge and get provisions; for we are here in a lonely place.'

9: 10–27 *The provision of food for the crowd; Jesus' identity; discipleship*

9: 10–17 Jesus provides food for the five thousand

See also Matt. 14^{13-21}; Mark 6^{30-44}; John 6^{1-13}. Luke, like John, only records one such incident. First, it is a sign of Jesus' concern for people (cp. v. 11). Secondly, Jesus is presented as master of the situation in contrast with the disciples (vv. 12–15), who are challenged to a decision about him. The episode (directly in Luke) leads to Peter's confession of Jesus as Messianic king (9^{20}). Thirdly, the scene is reminiscent of the provision of the manna for Israel (Exod. 16), which came to symbolize the life of God's new age, and lasting fellowship with him, that Jesus now makes possible. One explanation of the incident is that originally Jesus and his group set an example by sharing out their food, the rest did the same, and there was enough for all. But such a reconstruction is purely hypothetical, and the emphasis of the evangelists is on the power of Jesus to provide. If the story were regarded as a construction of the early Christians, it would still testify to the great impression created by Jesus. We should not be too ready to believe in the readiness of the early Christians to make up stories about Jesus, which people alive at the time could have declared to be untrue, and the tradition that Jesus did exercise control over his total environment is strong.

10 *Bethsaida* is given as the scene only by Luke, who knows it to be the centre of Jesus' work (cp. Mark 6^{32}).

11 Luke specifies the subject that Jesus is teaching, and with Matthew adds a reference to acts of healing, which, like the incident that follows, are signs of God's kingly power at work. God can 'provide . . . for his people' (Ps. 78^{20}) even in a desert place. The episode is a living illustration of 12^{31}.

12 About 3 or 4 p.m. For the disciples' scepticism cp. Ps. 78^{19}. *lonely*, or 'desert'.

13 But he said to them, 'You give them something to eat.' They
said, 'We have no more than five loaves and two fish—unless
14 we are to go and buy food for all these people.' For there were
about five thousand men. And he said to his disciples, 'Make
15 them sit down in companies, about fifty each.' And they did
16 so, and made them all sit down. And taking the five loaves
and the two fish he looked up to heaven, and blessed and
broke them, and gave them to the disciples to set before the
17 crowd. And all ate and were satisfied. And they took up what
was left over, twelve baskets of broken pieces.
18 Now it happened that as he was praying alone the disciples

---

13 *You* is emphatic. The disciples' helplessness is thus exposed. Luke makes their answer more respectful. *we* is emphatic: the disciples are only looking to their own resources, forgetting that the 'bread of life' is in their midst. The small amount of food highlights the power of Jesus. *all* and the number of people (v. 14) stress the problem. *five* and *two* add together to give the Jewish perfect number of seven, suggesting that the food is the perfect instrument for Jesus.

14 Jesus now takes charge. The arrangement into fifties suggests a military formation (see, e.g., *The War Rule*, vi; Vermes, *The Dead Sea Scrolls in English*, p. 132, 'fifty to each formation'). Jesus gives the people an army formation, not to engage in war, as some hoped, but to receive the bounty of God.

16 *looked up to heaven*: a common posture for prayer. Breaking of bread was a preliminary to Jewish meals, performed by the host, and accompanied by an act of praise. *them*, which occurs in the Greek after *blessed*, is read by most MSS.: Jesus made an act of praise over the bread and fishes (cp. 1 Cor. 10^{16}), as an alternative reading, 'over them', makes clear. The fourfold 'taking', 'blessing', 'breaking', and 'giving' was used by Jesus with a deeper purpose at the Last Supper (22^{19-20}; cp. 1 Cor. 11^{23-26}). The same familiar action (24^{30}) convinces his disciples that Jesus is still their living host and leader.

17 *all* is emphatic, and, with the abundant remains, underlines the all-sufficiency of Jesus. *ate and were satisfied*: cp. Ps. 22^{26}. *twelve* may suggest the twelve tribes of Israel for whom Jesus is the bread of life. The particular basket has Jewish associations.

9: 18–22 The question of Jesus: the answer of Peter and Jesus' further disclosure

were with him; and he asked them, 'Who do the people say
19 that I am?' And they answered, 'John the Baptist; but others
say, Elijah; and others, that one of the old prophets has risen.'
20 And he said to them, 'But who do you say that I am?' And
21 Peter answered, 'The Christ of God.' But he charged and
22 commanded them to tell this to no one, saying, 'The Son of
man must suffer many things, and be rejected by the elders
and chief priests and scribes, and be killed, and on the third
day be raised.'

See also Matt. 16^{13-23}; Mark 8^{27-33}; John 6^{67-69}. The acknowledgement of Jesus as the expected Messianic king is important only in so far as it points to him as the decisive figure in Jewish hopes, and leads to a more explicit definition of the course that his mission will take, i.e. it will involve suffering and death.

18 Luke is vague about the location (Caesarea Philippi in Mark and Matthew), perhaps because shortly he wishes to present Jesus as much further south, beginning his journey to Jerusalem. The reference to prayer marks the incident's importance.

19 Cp. 9^{7-9}.

20 *you*, as opposed to popular hearsay. Luke clarifies *The Christ* by adding 'of God'. No approval of the title is registered by Jesus except in Matthew, and secrecy is enjoined (v. 21). As the term would suggest an earthly king, delivering the Jews from outside domination, Jesus felt the inadequacy of the title. Significantly *The Christ* is followed by reference to 'the Son of man' both here and in 22^{67-69}, as though the latter is a more adequate and suitable description (cp. 20^{41-44}).

22 This is the first prediction of the Son of man's sufferings and vindication. *must*: as part of a divine plan. Jesus' thought and language on this theme have been traced to the influence of the 'servant figure' of Isa. 52^{13}–53^{12}. But explicit references to Isaiah are not proved. Further, the idea that the sufferings and death of the righteous could atone for sins was firmly established in Jewish thought of the time, and through his special relationship to God Jesus might well have believed that his own death would be even more effective. Two other questions arise: (*a*) Was the expected Jewish king sometimes pictured as suffering in the course of his mission? The evidence is by no means clear, and the Dead Sea Scrolls do not bear on the subject, as the connection between 'the righteous teacher', who was put to death, and 'the

23 And he said to all, 'If any man would come after me, let

Messiah' is very tenuous. Further, the disciples of Jesus are unfamiliar with such an idea, and 24$^{26, 46}$ suggests that the connection between kingship and suffering had to be established after Jesus' resurrection (cp. Acts 2^{36}). (*b*) Would Jesus have predicted his death and resurrection in such precise terms? The predictions are, therefore, sometimes attributed to the early Christians, or are thought to have been made more precise *post eventum*. But Jesus, in his consciousness of his God-given mission and of the experience of God's servants in the past, may well have seen both the inevitability and the necessity of his death, and, believing himself to be the representative of Israel, he may have expressed his hope of vindication after death in terms used of the restoration of Israel (cp. Hos. 6^{2}, 'after two days he will revive us; on the third day he will raise us up that we may live before him'). The predictions are couched in language descriptive of the suffering of God's servants in the O.T. Their general trustworthiness is also attested by the absence of reference to death by crucifixion (except in Matt. 20^{19}, an obviously editorial addition). *rejected*: not necessarily reminiscent of Isa. 53^{3}, the verb being common elsewhere in this sense, e.g., Ps. 118^{22}, quoted by Jesus (20^{17}). *The elders*: the Sanhedrin or council of the Jews. The *chief priests*: those belonging to the high-priestly families, or those who had previously held the office. The *scribes*: the professional rabbis. The three groups form 'official Judaism'. *on the third day* (the equivalent in eastern reckoning to Mark's 'after three days') would also suggest the sureness of God's action (Hos. 6^{2}; cp. Exod. 19$^{11, 15}$).

9: 23–27 The implications of being a disciple of Jesus: the crucial nature of correct response to him

See also Matt. 16$^{21-27}$; Mark 8^{31}–9^{1}; separate sayings have probably been brought together through similarity of theme.

23 *all*: the general public as well as the disciples. The demands and crucial importance of allegiance to Jesus can be shared with the wider public, but not the discussion of his person and the course of his mission. *come after*: in the sense of giving allegiance (cp. 1 Kgs. 11^{10}). *deny*, or, better, 'repudiate': here startlingly applied to the repudiation of oneself, i.e. of one's ability to control one's own life. The theme is continued in the drastic metaphor of *take up his cross*, based on the familiar picture of the criminal shouldering the wooden cross on the way to execution (cp. 23^{26}); it denotes the shattering of one's past life and ways, and the execution of self-interest, just as in going to the cross Jesus put self out of the question and completely submitted to God's purposes. Luke's *daily* shows that this is a continual condition of discipleship (cp. 1 Cor. 15^{31}).

him deny himself and take up his cross daily and follow me.
24 For whoever would save his life will lose it; and whoever
25 loses his life for my sake, he will save it. For what does it
profit a man if he gains the whole world and loses or forfeits
26 himself? For whoever is ashamed of me and of my words, of
him will the Son of man be ashamed when he comes in his
27 glory and the glory of the Father and of the holy angels. But

---

24 See also 17^{33}. To *save one's life* is to have a safety-first attitude. Such a person will lose the worthwhile life, because discipleship of Jesus means taking risks, and is the opposite of 'thinking of one's own skin'. The alternative translation is 'save oneself', i.e. 'gain union and fellowship with God', which involves 'losing oneself', dying to self in commitment to Jesus. In the first case there is a contrast between the two clauses of the verse, and in the second the thought is continuous.

25 *lose* links up with v. 24. Material prosperity resulting from the acquisition of the whole world is small compensation against the loss account of 'oneself', the failure to attain the life of harmony with God. *forfeits*: suffers the loss of. Jesus acts on this principle in rejecting the devil's suggestion (4^{5-8}).

26 One's attitude to Jesus influences the divine assessment of human beings in the day of judgement (cp. 12^{9}). 'The Son of man' is now used for the first time of a figure exercising God's future judgement; so far it has been used in connection with Jesus' earthly ministry, his death and resurrection. Jesus is sometimes thought to be distinguishing here between himself and a future Son of man, which would point to the unmistakable genuineness of the passage, as such a distinction would not have been made in the early Church; Jesus would then be claiming to be an even more important figure than the future Son of man. Jesus' interest, however, is not in the identity of the Son of man, which is left open, but in the fact that the latter's activity of judgement is already at work in people's assessment of himself. The saying presents Jesus as the all-decisive figure in God's dealings with human beings (cp. John 3^{18-19}). The picture is of the final triumph of God (*the Father*). In Luke's version the heavenly splendour surrounds *the Son of man*, *the Father*, and *the holy angels*; they are all involved in the divine action. A glimpse of the divine splendour surrounding the Son of man is seen in 9^{28-36}. The *angels*, important in God's dealings with creation, have a role in its renewal.

taste or 'experience'. *see the kingdom of God*: Mark has 'see the kingdom of God come with power', which is often interpreted as the final

I tell you truly, there are some standing here who will not
taste death before they see the kingdom of God.'
28 Now about eight days after these sayings he took with him
Peter and John and James, and went up on the mountain to

---

coming of God's reign, but could describe a decisive demonstration on God's kingship, e.g. the resurrection of Jesus. Luke might be removing any suggestion that Jesus is thinking of God's final kingdom, and so making an unfulfilled prediction. But he may have felt that 'come with power' was redundant. The passage expresses Jesus' faith and confidence that in the lifetime of some of the bystanders there will be a decisive expression of God's kingship, though he may not have seen in detail the form it would take.

9: 28–43a *The transfiguration; the epileptic boy*

9: 28–36 The vision of Jesus in glory

See also Matt. 17^{1-8}; Mark 9^{2-13}. The Gospel of John omits the incident, but there the whole ministry of Jesus is seen as a revelation of his glory. The interpretation of the scene as a resurrection appearance transferred to the earthly life of Jesus is improbable, as it has very little in common with the other accounts of such appearances. In contrast with his coming humiliation Jesus is now seen in his real majesty by the inner circle of disciples, a sign too of his coming vindication. 'the kingdom of God' (v. 27) leads to the thought here of Jesus' royal majesty, in whose reign that kingdom will be seen. In 2 Pet. 1^{16-18} the incident foreshadows Jesus' final coming in glory, an interpretation probably shared by the Gospel writers, though Luke also links the scene closely with Jesus' death, resurrection, and ascension. The parallelism with Moses and his experience on the mount of God (Exod. 34) was probably also thought important, and is particularly brought out by Matthew.

28 *about eight days after* (contrast Matthew and Mark, 'six days'): perhaps a divergent tradition. It could, however, allude to Jesus' resurrection, which takes place on the eighth day (the day after the sabbath or seventh day; cp. *Epistle of Barnabas*, xv. 9), and which the present incident foreshadows. *on the mountain*, or 'into the hills' (NEB), also suggests the mount of God, the scene of Moses' communion with God. The 'prayer' of Jesus once more marks the importance of the incident, and has led to its being interpreted as a personal experience of Jesus, meant to confirm him in his decision to face death. But although the conversation with Moses and Elijah concerns Jesus'

29 pray. And as he was praying, the appearance of his coun-
tenance was altered, and his raiment became dazzling white.
30 And behold, two men talked with him, Moses and Elijah,
31 who appeared in glory and spoke of his departure, which he
32 was to accomplish at Jerusalem. Now Peter and those who
were with him were heavy with sleep but kept awake, and
33 they saw his glory and the two men who stood with him. And
as the men were parting from him, Peter said to Jesus, 'Master,
it is well that we are here; let us make three booths, one for

---

coming death (v. 31), there is no hint that Jesus is in doubt about his future course of action or that this is the subject of his prayer. Luke probably felt it appropriate that the change in Jesus' appearance should take place while he was in communion with God, just as the Holy Spirit descends upon him at prayer (3^{22}).

29 Luke omits 'was transfigured' (so Matthew and Mark), perhaps because there was no change in the actual form or person of Jesus, or more probably because the word was associated with gods and other beings changing their form to deceive. *dazzling*, or 'flashing like lightning', is descriptive of supernatural beings (cp. Ezek. 1^{14}). Similarly, angelic beings are depicted as being robed in white (e.g. Mark 16^{5}).

30 *and behold two men*: see above, p. 32. Moses, the Law-giver, and Elijah, the great prophet, represent the covenant between God and his people, based on 'the law and the prophets' (cp. 16^{16}), now to be made new in the person of Jesus. Their presence may also denote the coming of God's new age, as Elijah at least had a role in preparation for it. His function has been performed by John the Baptist and now he is seen in person.

31 This verse and v. 32 are only found in Luke. *departure*, or 'exodus': see above, p. 32. For the first time Jerusalem is marked out as the scene of the completion of Jesus' mission, a constant theme from 9^{51} onwards.

32 The RSV suggests that the disciples managed to *keep awake*, although *heavy with sleep*. An alternative translation would be: 'Peter and his companions had been in a deep sleep; but when they awoke they saw . . .' (NEB). On either interpretation the experience is presented as solid reality and not a dream. The incident is important evidence for the disciples (*they saw*). The *glory* surrounds Jesus and so his status is carefully distinguished from that of *the two men*.

33 *as the men . . . from him* is Luke's preparation for the proposal of

you and one for Moses and one for Elijah'—not knowing
34 what he said. As he said this, a cloud came and overshadowed
35 them; and they were afraid as they entered the cloud. And a
voice came out of the cloud, saying, 'This is my Son, my
36 Chosen;[c] listen to him!' And when the voice had spoken, Jesus
was found alone. And they kept silence and told no one in
those days anything of what they had seen.
37 On the next day, when they had come down from the

[c] Other ancient authorities read *my Beloved*

Peter to perpetuate the scene. *we*: emphatic, and referring to the disciples who are available to do the work. Such living in *booths* or 'tents' would suggest the ideal period when Israel dwelt in tents in the wilderness (cp. Num. 9^{15-18}), with God in the midst of them in 'the tent of meeting'; it was also a picture of the new age of God, when God would again 'tabernacle' with his people. *not knowing what he said*: despite Peter's muddled state, there was some truth in what he said about 'booths': God was now present in the person of Jesus. Peter seems to put all the figures on a level.

34 *As he said this*: the sequel is a direct answer to Peter's remark. *a cloud . . . overshadowed*: descriptive of the divine presence and protection (cp. Exod. 13^{21}; Ps. 36^{10}).

35 This divine testimony is a link between the baptism of Jesus and the present vision of him in glory, his sonship being in the former case connected with his lowliness, as he stoops to share a baptism for sinners, and in the latter with his divine splendour. Instead of Mark's 'beloved', Luke has 'chosen': both underline the special relationship between God and Jesus in language already used of Israel. Peter's suggestion of the equality of the three figures (v. 33) is now corrected by stress on the unique place of Jesus. The important point is not a perpetuation of the scene, but careful attention to the words of Jesus. *listen to him* has sometimes been connected with Deut. 18^{15} (cp. Acts 3^{22-23}), thus linking Jesus with the expected prophet of the last days, but such a particular reference is unnecessary.

36 *alone*: implying that only Jesus had lasting significance. Jesus gives no command to secrecy, but it is implied in the *silence* of the disciples. The episode's full meaning only becomes clear after Jesus' resurrection (cp. John 2^{22}, 12^{16}, 13^{7}).

9: 37–43 The healing of the epileptic boy

See also Matt. 17^{14-21}; Mark 9^{14-29}. The serenity and splendour of vv. 28–36 contrast with Jesus' return to the distresses of ordinary life.

mountain, a great crowd met him. And behold, a man from the crowd cried, 'Teacher, I beg you to look upon my son, for he is my only child; and behold, a spirit seizes him, and he suddenly cries out; it convulses him till he foams, and shatters him, and will hardly leave him. And I begged your disciples to cast it out, but they could not.' Jesus answered, 'O faithless and perverse generation, how long am I to be with you and bear with you? Bring your son here.' While he was coming, the demon tore him and convulsed him. But Jesus rebuked the unclean spirit, and healed the boy, and gave him back to his father. And all were astonished at the majesty of God.

But while they were all marvelling at everything he did, he said to his disciples, 'Let these words sink into your ears; for

---

The man's son appears to have had some kind of epilepsy, here attributed to demonic possession. The glory of Jesus is seen in the service of his fellow men (similarly in the Gospel of John the glory of God and of Jesus is linked with the latter's humiliation and death in human service).

Luke emphasizes the man's distress at losing his *only child* (cp. 7^{12}, 8^{42}). *look upon*: help (cp. Ps. 102^{19}).

The helplessness of the disciples contrasts with Jesus' mastery of the situation.

Jesus, as elsewhere (e.g. 11^{29}), attacks the lack of faith shown by his contemporaries. The man's hopelessness is out of place in the presence of Jesus. *faithless*, *perverse*, and *and how long . . . bear with you?* all express Jesus' disappointment at his contemporaries' lack of insight into his mission and his God-given power.

This is the demon's last demonstration of power before his overthrow by Jesus. *gave him back*: the boy is returned to his parents in a healthy and normal state.

majesty, or 'greatness': used elsewhere both of the grandeur of God, and of Jesus himself (e.g. Josephus, *Antiquities*, i. 24; 2 Pet. 1^{16}).

43b–50 *Jesus' coming arrest: related teaching*

See also Matt. 17^{22-23}, 18^{1-9}; Mark 9^{30-32}. The sayings that follow Jesus' prediction of his death are concerned with status,

45 the Son of man is to be delivered into the hands of men.' But
they did not understand this saying, and it was concealed
from them, that they should not perceive it; and they were
afraid to ask him about this saying.
46 And an argument arose among them as to which of them
47 was the greatest. But when Jesus perceived the thought of
48 their hearts, he took a child and put him by his side, and said

---

the disciples' arguments about greatness contrasting with Jesus' coming humiliation.

9: 43b–45 Jesus for the second time foretells his coming death

43b Luke emphasizes that wonder must give way to sober reality.

44 *Let these words . . . sink into your ears*: take them to heart (cp. Ezek. 3[10]). Luke omits any explicit reference to death, already mentioned in 9[22]: he perhaps wishes to stress that this Jesus, whose grandeur has been seen, will be given completely into the control of human beings. *delivered into the hands of men*: a reference to Isa. 53[3, 12] is not necessarily intended. If *the Son of man* denotes a heavenly and exalted figure, then there is a paradox in that this exalted figure receives such a humiliation.

45 Luke (perhaps to excuse the disciples) suggests that the ignorance was divinely planned: the significance of Jesus' words would only become clear in God's own time.

9: 46–48 Real greatness

46 Cp. 22[24–27], also in the context of Jesus' death. The disciples are thinking of earthly forms of precedence.

47 Jesus uses an enacted parable to show that true greatness consists in willing service to all, even to those who appear least important in human eyes.

48 The saying takes the form of Hebrew progressive parallelism (see also Matt. 10[40]; John 13[20]). *in my name*: on my behalf, or as my representative. To welcome a child is to welcome Jesus, because service to a fellow human being is service to Jesus (cp. Matt. 25[30]), and so in turn is service to God. *him who sent me*, a term common in the Gospel of John (e.g. 16[5]). Jesus is conscious of himself as the plenipotentiary of God. *he who . . . great*: see also 22[26]; Matt. 20[26]; Mark 10[43–44]; cp. Matt. 23[11]. *great*, normally describing those with influence in society and state, is applied here to those of little outward status, who are content to perform the most insignificant of tasks.

to them, 'Whoever receives this child in my name receives
me, and whoever receives me receives him who sent me;
for he who is least among you all is the one who is great.'
49 John answered, 'Master, we saw a man casting out demons
in your name, and we forbade him, because he does not follow
50 with us.' But Jesus said to him, 'Do not forbid him; for he
that is not against you is for you.'
51 When the days drew near for him to be received up, he set
52 his face to go to Jerusalem. And he sent messengers ahead of
him, who went and entered a village of the Samaritans, to
53 make ready for him; but the people would not receive him,

9: 49–50 The exorcist outside the company of Jesus

-50 The disciples are jealous of their privileged position. A person's *name* was often thought to convey his power, and the name 'Jesus' was used by the early Christians in baptism and healing. The exorcist is on the side of Jesus, because he at least believes in his power (contrast 11[23], in a different situation).

III. THE SECOND JOURNEY-NARRATIVE—JESUS' JOURNEY TO JERUSALEM (CHAPTERS 9:51–19:27)

9: **51–62** *Jesus in Samaria; the demands of discipleship*

9: 51–56 Jesus is rejected in a Samaritan village

The incident only occurs in Luke, who with John (4[1–12]) shows an interest in Jesus' activity in Samaria. His love is seen to embrace non-Jews, and the episode foreshadows Acts 8[2–25].

51 *days drew near*: Jesus' movements are determined by God's time-scheme. The train is being laid for the decisive events mentioned in 9[31]. *for him to be received up*, lit. 'of his being received up' or 'of his ascension', i.e. into heaven (cp. 2 Kgs. 2[1]): 'receive up' is used in Acts 1[2, 11], and 2[22], of the triumphant return of Jesus to God after the completion of his earthly mission: Luke looks forward to the victorious end of the events now beginning. *set his face* denotes firm resolution of purpose, probably without the note of hostile judgement, present when 'against' is added (cp. Ezek. 13[17]).

2 Perhaps the picture is of a king heralding his approach.

3 For this hostility cp. Ecclus. 50[25–26]. *his face was set* (or 'was going') describes the direction of Jesus' activity.

54 because his face was set toward Jerusalem. And when his
disciples James and John saw it, they said, 'Lord, do you
want us to bid fire come down from heaven and consume
55, 56 them?'[d] But he turned and rebuked them.[e] And they went
on to another village.
57 As they were going along the road, a man said to him,
58 'I will follow you wherever you go.' And Jesus said to him,
'Foxes have holes, and birds of the air have nests; but the
59 Son of man has nowhere to lay his head.' To another he said,
'Follow me.' But he said, 'Lord, let me first go and bury my
60 father.' But he said to him, 'Leave the dead to bury their

[d] Other ancient authorities add *as Elijah did*

[e] Other ancient authorities add *and he said, 'You do not know what manner of spirit you are of; for the Son of man came not to destroy men's lives but to save them'*

---

54 If the nickname 'sons of thunder', given to *James and John* (Mark 3^{17}), refers to their hot-tempered natures, then this suggestion accords with it (cp. the action of Elijah, 2 Kgs. 1^{10}; hence some MSS. add 'as Elijah did', RSV margin). James and John can claim the authority of Elijah for their proposed action, but, as 9^{35} has made clear, they have now a higher authority, Jesus, who has laid down the principle of generous love (6^{27-36}).

55 The longer text (see RSV margin), probably not original, gives the reason for Jesus' rebuke.

56 *another village*: presumably in Samaria.

9: 57–62 Discipleship and its challenge

For the first two incidents see Matt. 8^{18-22}; the third is found only in Luke. The picture of Jesus accompanied by his disciples gives the opportunity for Luke to introduce three replies of Jesus on the subject of discipleship and its demands: such allegiance involves cost and takes precedence over all existing ties.

58 Discipleship means sharing the unsettled and (humanly speaking) insecure existence of *the Son of man* who *has nowhere to lay his head*, in the sense that he must be ever moving on to travel the road appointed by God (cp. Heb. 13^{14}).

59–60 The man's reply, probably to be taken seriously, suggests that he wished to wait until his father was dead and he had discharged his

own dead; but as for you, go and proclaim the kingdom of
61 God.' Another said, 'I will follow you, Lord; but let me first
62 say farewell to those at my home.' Jesus said to him, 'No one
who puts his hand to the plough and looks back is fit for the
kingdom of God.'

0: AFTER this the Lord appointed seventy[f] others, and sent

[f] Other ancient authorities read *seventy-two*

---

filial duties, or that his father was already dead and that he wished first to carry out his duty of burying him (cp. Exod. 20^{12}). Jesus' severity links up with his claim that nothing, not even the most solemn obligation, has priority over his own demands for loyalty (cp. 14^{26}). The present juncture must not be occupied with the thought of death, but with the living good news of God's reign breaking out among men, and with the shattering of death's power. *leave . . . dead*: perhaps a proverb.

1 Cp. 1 Kgs. 19^{20}, the call of Elisha (he was ploughing when summoned by Elijah, hence perhaps v. 62). *first*: the man did not realize the urgency of being a disciple, which can demand the disregard of old ties.

2 The ploughman, to run a straight furrow, must keep his eyes fixed ahead and must not be constantly looking back: there is need for uncompromising singleness of purpose in those who are worthy of *the kingdom of God. looks back*, or 'keeps looking back'. There is an alternative reading: 'no one who looks back as he sets his hand to the plough'.

: **1–20** *The seventy: their return*

: 1–16 The commission given to the seventy.

The appointment of this group is only found in Luke, who makes it the occasion for a discourse, a collection of sayings connected with the theme of 'mission'. Some instructions given to the twelve are repeated, and material found also in Matt. 9^{36}–10^{42} is incorporated.

seventy, or 'seventy-two' (RSV margin; the MSS. evidence is divided) could be reminiscent of the seventy or seventy-two (if Eldad and Medad are included) elders who were appointed to assist Moses in the leadership of Israel (Num. 11^{10-30}). More probably, however, the number is meant to suggest the Jewish idea, based on Gen. 10, that

them on ahead of him, two by two, into every town and place
2 where he himself was about to come. And he said to them,
'The harvest is plentiful, but the labourers are few; pray
therefore the Lord of the harvest to send out labourers into
3 his harvest. Go your way; behold, I send you out as lambs in
4 the midst of wolves. Carry no purse, no bag, no sandals; and
5 salute no one on the road. Whatever house you enter, first
6 say, "Peace be to this house!" And if a son of peace is there,
your peace shall rest upon him; but if not, it shall return to
7 you. And remain in the same house, eating and drinking what

---

there were seventy or (as sometimes reckoned) seventy-two nations in the world, and so for Luke the present mission foreshadows the Church's preaching to the wider Gentile world, described in Acts. *two by two*: cp. Mark 6^{7}; Acts 3^{1}. Again the picture is of a king sending his heralds before him.

2 *harvest*: a metaphor of bringing people to God (cp. John 4^{35-36}). Here the farmer in charge of the harvesting is God. Intercession among the early Christians was much concerned with the spread of the Gospel (cp. Col. 4^{3}), and was perhaps encouraged by this saying.

3 See also Matt. 10^{16}: cp. John 10^{12}; Acts 20^{28-29}. Jesus' blunt warning of hostility from the outside world (cp. 21^{17}) was taken seriously (cp. 1 Thess. 2^{14-16}; 1 Pet. 4^{12}). Balancing such a warning is Jesus' assurance of the loving protection of God (cp. 12^{22-24}).

4 Cp. 9^{3} and contrast 22^{35}. The disciples are to abandon self-reliance. Only Luke adds the command about 'no greetings', a vivid way of forbidding 'dawdling *en route*' (cp. 2 Kgs. 4^{29}).

5 *peace*, part of the conventional greeting of friendship, also means that the *house*, or household, is being offered reconciliation with God (cp. 2^{14}, 19^{38}).

6 *a son of peace* (only found in Luke) means one who is ready to respond to such a message of *peace*. The future tenses that follow may have the force of imperatives: 'let the household receive your friendship and its blessings', but otherwise 'let it be withdrawn or withheld' (cp. vv. 10–11).

7–8 *the same house*, or better 'that very house' (NEB), the one that welcomes you. For one house as headquarters cp. 9^{4}; Acts 18^{7}, and for the instruction about hospitality cp. Matt. 10^{10}; 1 Tim. 5^{18}. The second principle perhaps lay behind the free maintenance due to the apostles (1 Cor. 9^{3-18}).

they provide, for the labourer deserves his wages; do not go
8 from house to house. Whenever you enter a town and they
9 receive you, eat what is set before you; heal the sick in it and
say to them, "The kingdom of God has come near to you."
10 But whenever you enter a town and they do not receive you,
11 go into its streets and say, "Even the dust of your town that
clings to our feet, we wipe off against you; nevertheless know
12 this, that the kingdom of God has come near." I tell you, it
shall be more tolerable on that day for Sodom than for that
town.

13 'Woe to you, Chorazin! woe to you, Bethsaida! for if the
mighty works done in you had been done in Tyre and Sidon,
they would have repented long ago, sitting in sackcloth and
14 ashes. But it shall be more tolerable in the judgement for Tyre
15 and Sidon than for you. And you, Capernaum, will you be
exalted to heaven? You shall be brought down to Hades.

---

9 Cp. Mark 6^{7}; see also above, 9^{2}.

11 Cp. 9^{5}. The meaning of 'for a witness against them' is here explained.

12 Cp. Matt. 10^{15}, 11^{24}. *on that day*: the day of judgement. Sodom was a classic example of disobedience to God (cp. Gen. 13^{12-13}), but the case against her will be smaller than that of those who reject the messengers of Jesus. Thus the vital nature of God's present revelation is underlined.

13 The saying (see also Matt. 11^{21-23}) links up with v. 12, continuing the theme of unresponsiveness and judgement. Again the all-importance of people's response to Jesus is stressed. *Chorazin* may have been on the site of the present ruins of Kerazeh, north-west of Tell Hum. These Jewish towns of Galilee are contrasted with *Tyre* and *Sidon*, Gentile cities of Phoenicia, and will have much more to answer for in the judgement day because of their experience of Jesus' mighty works. *sackcloth and ashes*: deep mourning. Once more we note the authority of Jesus to speak about God's judgement.

15 The language, reminiscent of Isa. 14^{13}, suggests 'pride having a mighty fall'.

16 'He who hears you hears me, and he who rejects you rejects
me, and he who rejects me rejects him who sent me.'
17 The seventy[f] returned with joy, saying, 'Lord, even the
18 demons are subject to us in your name!' And he said to them,
19 'I saw Satan fall like lightning from heaven. Behold, I have
given you authority to tread upon serpents and scorpions, and
over all the power of the enemy; and nothing shall hurt you.
20 Nevertheless do not rejoice in this, that the spirits are subject
to you; but rejoice that your names are written in heaven.'
21 In that same hour he rejoiced in the Holy Spirit and said,

[f] Other ancient authorities read *seventy-two*

---

16 Cp. 9^{48}; Matt. 10^{40}. Again Jesus claims to be the plenipotentiary of God.

10: 17–20 The victory over Satan

The group's commission is followed at once by the account of its return. The exorcisms' importance lies in their demonstration of God's sovereignty over evil; their performance is not to be a source of pride for the disciples.

17 *even*: exorcisms were not mentioned in their commission; they may have been thought more difficult than other acts of healing. The seventy's power is traced to Jesus' authority.

18 *I saw*, or 'had a vision': Jesus in the absence of the seventy had a mental vision of the downfall of Satan, and was, therefore, prepared for the news. *from heaven* can go (*a*) with *lightning* (a metaphor of suddenness), or (*b*) with *fall*. (*b*) would mean that Satan is dethroned from his heavenly status, *heaven* sometimes describing the sphere of superhuman beings (cp. Rev. 12^{7-8}).

19 *serpents* (or 'snakes') and *scorpions* (cp. Deut. 8^{15}) symbolize evil forces, just as *the enemy* describes the devil (cp. Matt. 13^{39}). *nothing shall hurt* the disciples, because they belong to the dominion of God, against which evil cannot prevail.

20 The point of significance is that *your names are written in heaven* (cp. Exod. 32^{33}; Rev. 13^{8}): they have a real and lasting fellowship with God. For an unhealthy interest in the miraculous cp. 11^{29} and John 14^{11}.

10: 21–34 *Jesus' act of praise; the privilege of the disciples*

10: 21–22 The Son's unique status

See also Matt. 11^{25-27}. The saying has a poetical structure, and in Luke consists of two stanzas, while Matthew adds a third (11^{28-30}).

'I thank thee, Father, Lord of heaven and earth, that thou hast
hidden these things from the wise and understanding and
revealed them to babes; yea, Father, for such was thy gracious
22 will.[g] All things have been delivered to me by my Father; and

[g] Or *so it was well-pleasing before thee*

---

21 There is the continuing theme of the revelation of God's purposes, and of Jesus' authority and status. If *Holy* is read (it is well attested), then Jesus' joy was inspired by God's Holy Spirit (cp. Gal. 5^{22}): Jesus' close union with the Holy Spirit (3^{22}) enables him to see God's hand in the present situation. The omission of *Holy* could give the same meaning, or the reference could be to Jesus' 'spirit': he rejoiced with his whole being. *thank*: a way of acknowledging God's greatness and adequacy (cp. Ps. 7^{17}). While *Father* brings out the idea of God's accessibility and loving care, *Lord of heaven and earth* suggests the transcendent ruler of the whole creation. *these things* probably refers to the demonstration of God's sovereignty in Jesus' ministry (cp. 10^{23-24}). *the wise and understanding* specialists, like the rabbis, in the interpretation of the Law, as distinct from *babes*, people who lack such specialist training (cp. 18^{17}). God does the unusual and reverses human status (cp. 1^{51-53}; 1 Cor. 1^{18-31}). The thought of the whole verse is Jewish (cp. 8^{10}). *revealed*: the normal word for God's unfolding of his secrets. The last part of the verse is lit. 'yes, Father, because thus was good pleasure before thee' or 'that thus was . . .' (with the clause still dependent on 'thank'). *before thee*: willed and desired by God.

2 *all things*: perhaps the whole task of demonstrating God's sovereignty, or else the whole creation, which is under the authority of Jesus as God's Wisdom (cp. Matt. 28^{18}, where Jesus' claim to authority over the whole creation is vindicated by his resurrection). Once more Jesus' sense of being a plenipotentiary of God is stressed. The rest of the saying has features that are found in the Gospel of John to describe the relationship between God and Jesus: (*a*) the terminology of *the Father* and *the Son*, rare in the first three Gospels (but cp. Mark 13^{32}); (*b*) the idea of the mutual knowledge of *the Father* and *the Son* (e.g. John 10^{15}); (*c*) the emphasis on the distinctive role of the *Son* as the unique revealer of God (cp. John 1^{18}, 14^{6}). Luke's *knows who . . . is* seems to be an exact equivalent of Matthew's 'recognizes' (better than RSV 'knows'). In the background may be the relation between God and Israel, which was described in terms of 'the father' and 'the son'. The full purpose and implications of Israel's status, as the special people of God, are known only to him, while Israel is the sole repository of God's truth, and so is to be the means of revealing him to other

no one knows who the Son is except the Father, or who the
Father is except the Son and any one to whom the Son
chooses to reveal him.'
23 Then turning to the disciples he said privately, 'Blessed
24 are the eyes which see what you see! For I tell you that many
prophets and kings desired to see what you see, and did not
see it, and to hear what you hear, and did not hear it.'
25 And behold, a lawyer stood up to put him to the test, saying,

---

nations. Jesus' language could easily be a contemporary description of the place and function of Israel (cp. Rom. 2^{17-20}), but strikingly he now claims them for himself. On the one hand, the full implications of his status are known only to God, which gives it a secure basis; on the other hand, Jesus is conscious of being the repository of God's truth, and so the fullness of God's being can be known only through him. If, as the Gospel tradition suggests, Jesus was firmly convinced of his unique place in the unfolding of God's purposes, then he may well have viewed himself in this way as the true representative of Israel. The original feature is that, whereas particular groups in Israel saw themselves in this light (e.g. the Qumran community), now such a claim is made by an individual. *no one knows who the Son is except the Father* is only appropriate on the lips of Jesus himself: after his resurrection the early Christians would have claimed to be in the secret (cp. Gal. 1^{16}). The Gospel of John could be regarded as a development of the whole saying.

10: 23–24 The disciples' unique position

See also Matt. 13^{16-17}. Luke places the beatitude here to continue the preceding theme of revelation. *prophets*: both the O.T. prophets and the apocalyptic writers. *kings* (Matthew 'righteous men') may refer to the national hopes of Jewish kings (including the Maccabaean kings) that by God's intervention Israel would be made into a great nation. In Jesus the varied Jewish hopes are given an answer. *what you see*: the mighty works of Jesus. *what you hear*: Jesus' verbal message of the good news of the kingdom.

10: 25–42 *Neighbourliness: Martha and Mary*

10: 25–37 The story of the neighbourly Samaritan

The opening (vv. 25–28) has connections with Mark 10^{17} (part of an episode found below, 18^{18-30}) and with Mark 12^{28-31} (omitted by

26 'Teacher, what shall I do to inherit eternal life?' He said to
27 him, 'What is written in the law? How do you read?' And he
answered, 'You shall love the Lord your God with all your

Luke), but is probably taken from Luke's special sources. Matthew and Mark record 'parables' of Jesus usually drawn from the world of nature. In addition Luke includes a number of 'parables' of the type found here, which take the form of a story, and occur mainly in the section 9^{51}–19^{28}. The interest centres on the characters, often consisting of opposites, one of whom may be surprisingly approved. The story seeks to establish a principle to be applied to God or man, and sometimes employs an argument from the 'lesser' to the 'greater'. For this type of parable cp. 7^{41-42}, 12^{16-21}, 14^{16-24}, 15^{11-32}, $16^{1-8, 19-31}$, $18^{1-5, 9-13}$, 19^{12-27}.

25 *put him to the test*: either in an attempt to trap Jesus, or in an honest desire to see whether Jesus could make a contribution to this controversial subject. *eternal life*, or 'the life of the age to come', i.e. God's new era. The question is: 'What are the qualifications for making sure of a place in God's new era?'

26 As a good Jew, Jesus makes *the law* the basis of the discussion, and issues a challenge by a further question, to test the man's motive. *read*: interpret.

27 In Mark this two-part command is given by Jesus in reply to a rabbi's question about the 'heads' under which the Law might be summarized. Although in Luke this combination of Deut. 6^{4} with Lev. 19^{18} is attributed to the rabbi, it is often thought to be original to Jesus, no parallels to it being found in contemporary Jewish literature. *love . . . God*: show allegiance and give obedience to him. *with all your heart . . . mind*: with one's whole being. *with all your mind* is not in the Hebrew, while in the LXX it is a variant reading for *with all your heart*. By this time it may have become part of a Jewish interpretation of the passage. After the resurrection of Jesus the command would be reinforced by the experience of God's love seen in the cross of Jesus (Rom. 5^{5}). Similarly *neighbour* (originally a fellow Jew) would be broadened in the light of the story that follows, and in the universal significance attached to Jesus' death. Again, love of neighbour, which meant doing good to him, would receive a deeper content from Jesus' teaching on generous, self-giving love (6^{27-36}), shown also in his own life and his death. *as yourself*: the kind of conduct that we expect to be shown to ourselves should have an effect on what we do to others. The passage stresses that love of neighbour must spring from our love for God and be inspired by it. In conjunction with 18^{22}, the implication is that to love God will include following Jesus.

heart, and with all your soul, and with all your strength, and
28 with all your mind; and your neighbour as yourself.' And he
said to him, 'You have answered right; do this, and you will
live.'
29 But he, desiring to justify himself, said to Jesus, 'And who
30 is my neighbour?' Jesus replied, 'A man was going down from
Jerusalem to Jericho, and he fell among robbers, who stripped

---

28 *you will live*: you will attain the age to come.

29 *justify himself*: either in the sense of vindicating himself for having come forward with the question, or of making an impression (cp. 16^{15}). A neat definition of neighbour is required.

30 In its present context the main point of the story is that good neighbourliness involves the help of all whom we meet in trouble: the Samaritan (introduced here for his 'shock value' on a Jewish audience) does not stop to ask, 'Who is my neighbour?, but goes at once to the man's assistance. The rabbi's question is not directly answered, but instead the challenge is presented: which of the three proved to be a neighbour? (v. 36). It is sometimes thought that the original emphasis was on the contrast between the priest and the Levite on the one hand, and the Samaritan on the other. Jesus paints a picture of an outsider or outcast who proved to be a better observer of the spirit of the Jewish law than members of the chosen people. The audience is expecting Jesus to say that, while the priest and Levite fell short, an Israelite—an ordinary Israelite—rose to the occasion. Jesus' substitution of 'Samaritan' shocks his listeners, and teaches that non-Jews as well as Jews have value in God's sight (cp. 4^{25-30}, 17^{11-19}). But the supposed conflict between question and answer should not be pressed, because it is not unusual to rephrase a question in giving an answer. The contrast between the Samaritan and the other two figures is important: into a story that from the start was probably concerned with neighbourliness Jesus introduces the Samaritan to challenge the Jewish sense of superiority. If the story in its first setting was solely concerned with approval of a non-Jew, then in view of the early Church's interest in the Gentiles, would that original context have been lost?

a man: he remains anonymous; the Samaritan does not know whom he is helping. The journey covers a dangerous and lonely terrain with rocks where brigands could hide. *stripped*: robbed of his possessions.

31 him and beat him, and departed, leaving him half dead. Now
by chance a priest was going down that road; and when he saw
32 him he passed by on the other side. So likewise a Levite, when
he came to the place and saw him, passed by on the other side.
33 But a Samaritan, as he journeyed, came to where he was; and
34 when he saw him, he had compassion, and went to him and
bound up his wounds, pouring on oil and wine; then he set
him on his own beast and brought him to an inn, and took
35 care of him. And the next day he took out two denarii[h] and
gave them to the innkeeper, saying, "Take care of him; and
whatever more you spend, I will repay you when I come
36 back." Which of these three, do you think, proved neighbour
37 to the man who fell among the robbers?' He said, 'The one
who showed mercy on him.' And Jesus said to him, 'Go and
do likewise.'
38 Now as they went on their way, he entered a village; and

[h] The denarius was worth about eight new pence

---

2 For the combination of *priest* and *Levite* cp., e.g., 2 Chr. 30[27]. The Aaronic priests were responsible for the various temple offerings and sacrifices. The Levites now performed only some of the lowlier tasks in the temple ritual. The action of the two men here has been traced to fear of incurring ritual uncleanness while on duty: Jesus is then highlighting an obsession with ritual cleanness that results in neglect of moral duty. If this were so, we should expect the motives behind the action to be clearly stated.

oil was used as an emollient, *wine* as a disinfectant. *his own*, together with other details of his action, stresses the care taken by the Samaritan.

The generosity of the Samaritan is underlined.

The need is for action as a neighbour to those in need, and not for neat definitions of the word.

38–42 Jesus' approval of Mary

Only Luke records the incident. For the characters see also John 11–12. The story, in which the practical woman, Martha, is rebuked,

39 a woman named Martha received him into her house. And
she had a sister called Mary, who sat at the Lord's feet and
40 listened to his teaching. But Martha was distracted with much
serving; and she went to him and said, 'Lord, do you not care
that my sister has left me to serve alone? Tell her then to help
41 me.' But the Lord answered her, 'Martha, Martha, you are
42 anxious and troubled about many things; one thing is needful.[i] Mary has chosen the good portion, which shall not be
taken away from her.'

[i] Other ancient authorities read *few things are needful, or only one*

---

forms a contrast with the previous parable, where the practical Samaritan is approved. The apparent harshness of Jesus' reply, in which the episode culminates (v. 42), is in line with the ruthlessness of his demand for absolute priority to be given to himself and his teaching. Mary has her priorities right, and is approved because she has obeyed the divine voice (9^{35}). Jesus is concerned that Martha is 'fussing' unnecessarily over the food and so does not have time to attend to his vital teaching. Jesus is not approving the person who is impervious to practical issues, but is stressing that practical living must stem from listening to him.

38 The *village* may have been Bethany (John 12^{1}). *received*: welcomed with hospitality, which throws into relief Jesus' words in v. 41.

39 Mary takes up the position of the pupil at the master's feet.

40 *distracted*: from listening to Jesus. Another translation would be 'kept busy'.

41 *anxious and troubled*, or 'fretting and fussing' (NEB). Some MSS. omit *you . . . things*, obviously because of their apparent harshness.

42 Instead of *one thing is needful* there is another reading, 'few things are needful, or only one' (RSV margin). The reading in the text is slightly the better attested, the other perhaps being an attempt to make the transition easier from 'many' to 'one'. There may be humour underlying the word *portion*, which can mean a 'dish' or 'course' at a meal (cp. Gen. 43^{34}): Martha has been occupied preparing a varied menu of dishes, but Mary has chosen the one *good* and really adequate dish: listening to Jesus. Otherwise choice of *the good portion* may be a metaphor of taking the best action.

11: He was praying in a certain place, and when he ceased,
one of his disciples said to him, 'Lord, teach us to pray, as
2 John taught his disciples.' And he said to them, 'When you
pray, say:
3 'Father, hallowed be thy name. Thy kingdom come. Give

11: 1–13 *Teaching on prayer and on the accessibility of God*

Luke has brought together various sayings of Jesus: (*a*) the prayer given to the disciples (vv. 1–4; see also Matt. 6^{9-13}); (*b*) the story of the friend (vv. 5–8; only found in Luke); (*c*) encouragement to be expectant (vv. 9–13; see also Matt. 7^{7-11}). (*a*) and (*b*) are linked by the theme of 'giving bread' (vv. 3, 5), while (*a*), (*b*), and (*c*) are joined together by 'father' (vv. 2, 7, 13) and by 'give' (vv. 3, 7–8, 13).

11: 1–4 The way to pray

1 The rabbis sometimes taught their disciples prayers.

2 The prayer is both a model for prayer and a prayer to be used. Matthew's parallel is sometimes seen as an expansion of that in Luke for use in the worship of the Church. Jesus may, however, have given a shorter and longer version and the prayer's main themes are identical. The direct address of God as *Father* is probably original to Jesus, who now calls his disciples to the same close relationship with God. Matthew's 'our Father' would be the more normal Jewish usage. *hallowed be thy name* and *thy kingdom come* are both imperatives. When God 'hallows his name' (e.g. Ezek. 36^{23}), he acts to vindicate his honour and show the rightness of his cause. The prayer is thus for the achievement of God's purposes, like the second petition, which is for the establishment of God's sovereignty. A similar petition is found in Jewish prayers. These petitions receive some fulfilment in Jesus' mission: the name of God is hallowed through the perfect loyalty to God shown by Jesus, and God's sovereignty is demonstrated in Jesus' triumphant death and resurrection. The poorly attested alternative reading 'let thy Holy Spirit come upon us and cleanse us' instead of 'thy kingdom come' goes back to Marcion and may be his comment on *kingdom*.

3 After God's purposes, human needs are mentioned. Except for a possible occurrence in a papyrus fragment, *daily* (ἐπιούσιος) is found only here, in the parallel in Matthew, and in quotations of this passage in the Church Fathers. Origen's translation 'supernatural' is unlikely, while other early interpretations are 'continual' and 'for our

4 us each day our daily bread;[j] and forgive us our sins, for we ourselves forgive every one who is indebted to us; and lead us not into temptation.'

[j] Or *our bread for the morrow*

---

needs'. More probable meanings are 'for today' or 'for the following day': then the prayer would be for bread for the immediate future (cp. Exod. 16, where Israel is given only a day's portion of the manna at a time, to test their loyalty): so Christians are to pray for the coming day's bread and no more, to show their trust in God (cp. Matt. 6^{34}). *bread* could include the needs of the whole man. On the other hand, eating bread and the giving of the manna symbolized the new age of God, and 'bread for the morrow' might have this latter meaning: we pray to enjoy 'today' (Matthew) or *each day* (Luke) the fruits of God's coming age. Such a prayer makes sense both in Jesus' ministry, where the power of God's new age is already at work (e.g. 4^{18-21}, 7^{22-23}), and after Jesus' death, resurrection, and ascension, and the coming of the Holy Spirit, when this new age is firmly established (cp. Heb. 6^{4}). It has already been symbolized under the form of bread (9^{10-17}), and the continuing fellowship between Jesus and his followers, a feature of the new era, will continue to be so symbolized (22^{19}, 24^{30}; Acts 2^{46}).

4 Jewish prayers contain a petition for God's forgiveness, based on his compassion. Jesus claims an authority to pronounce that forgiveness, and so here encourages prayer for it. *we ourselves forgive*, or are in the habit of forgiving: it is illogical to expect from God a forgiveness that we do not practise ourselves (cp. Matt. 5^{23}, 6^{14}, 18^{23-35}). *indebted*: to fail in our duty to our fellow human beings (and also to God) was sometimes described as the running up of a debt. For such readiness to forgive cp. 23^{34}, and for the further assurance of God's forgiveness cp. 23^{43}. *and lead us not into temptation* has a parallel in Jewish prayers. *temptation*, or 'testing', was used of (*a*) testing God (cp. 4^{12}), and (*b*) being put to the test by God. With (*a*) the petition could mean: may we not be brought to the situation where we doubt the capacity of God to achieve his purposes. With (*b*) the idea is that God sometimes creates situations to test the mettle of his people, and also allows them to be tested by their living in an environment opposed or indifferent to his will. Then the prayer is for deliverance from situations that will test one's loyalty to God, with perhaps reference to the 'tribulation' which would precede the final triumph of God, and in which the power of evil would severely strain his people's loyalty. Perhaps the kind of 'testing' involved is seen in 22^{39-46}, where Jesus, the repre-

5 And he said to them, 'Which of you who has a friend will
go to him at midnight and say to him, "Friend, lend me three
6 loaves; for a friend of mine has arrived on a journey, and I
7 have nothing to set before him"; and he will answer from
within, "Do not bother me; the door is now shut, and my
children are with me in bed; I cannot get up and give you
8 anything"? I tell you, though he will not get up and give him
anything because he is his friend, yet because of his im-
9 portunity he will rise and give him whatever he needs. And

---

sentative of God's cause, is brought to the brink of putting himself completely into the control of his enemies and facing apparent defeat, a situation where God's demands create a breaking-point and doubt. Then *temptation* would be used in senses (*a*) and (*b*), and *lead* would refer to God's leading along a path that brings this impasse (from which the disciples are to pray for deliverance, $22^{40, 45}$). Against the apparent cowardice of such a prayer there must be placed the Jewish horror of falling away from the living God, the consciousness of human frailty, and the principle that there is not any merit in 'putting oneself into the lion's den'. Jesus' mission involves this kind of testing and he comes through triumphant.

11: 5–13 'The persistent friend' and related sayings

Jesus uses a less admirable type of humanity to make an analogy: even this man under constant pestering responded to the other's request; how much more, says Jesus, will a loving God, who treats you as friends, be accessible to you and your prayers, and be ready to give you his gifts—his kingdom, daily bread, and forgiveness. This is a time to be expectant. If the friend's 'importunity' is important for the analogy, it would point to the need for earnest prayer, or for eager receptiveness.

5 *Which of you . . .?*: 'Suppose one of you . . .' Jesus frequently introduces his analogies in this way (cp. 14^{28-32}, 15^{3-9}).

7 The man and his family would be settled on the house's raised platform, and to reach the door he would have to find a way through the animals bedded down on the ground floor itself—and in darkness!

8 *importunity*: because the friend is not ashamed to keep up the pressure.

9 The saying (in a different context in Matthew) here links up with the preceding theme of expectancy or need for prayer. It may have

I tell you, Ask, and it will be given you; seek, and you will
10 find; knock, and it will be opened to you. For every one who
asks receives, and he who seeks finds, and to him who knocks
11 it will be opened. What father among you, if his son asks for[k]
12 a fish, will instead of a fish give him a serpent; or if he asks
13 for an egg, will give him a scorpion? If you then, who are
evil, know how to give good gifts to your children, how much
more will the heavenly Father give the Holy Spirit to those
who ask him!'

[k] Other ancient authorities insert *bread, will give him a stone; or if he asks for*

---

been part of Jesus' call for readiness to receive God's kingdom. *ask, seek, knock* all denote an eager reaching out.

11–13 The argument is similar to 11^{5-8}: if human parents, deficient in so many ways, show loving care and attention to the needs of their children, how much more is such readiness to give to be expected of God, the perfect heavenly Father. *What father . . .?*: 'Suppose one of you is a father'. '*bread . . . asks for*' (RSV margin) is an assimilation to Matthew, who does not record v. 12. Jesus probably put forward the three suppositions, but each Gospel writer has chosen two of them, according to his own predilections: Matthew preferred the combination of bread and fish (cp. 9^{15}), while Luke recorded the two sayings that referred to poisonous creatures. The *serpent* was a snake, the *scorpion* a species of vermin, four or five inches long, common in southern latitudes, and feared for its sting; so that both, apart from their being uneatable, were positively dangerous. Instead of 'good things' (Matt. 7^{11}), Luke has *the Holy Spirit* (the best-attested reading). Perhaps Luke or his source has made 'good things' more explicit in view of the early Church's experience of the Holy Spirit, which figured large among God's blessings. This mention of the Holy Spirit could have led to the insertion of the prayer for the Holy Spirit's coming (v. 2). *heavenly*, or 'the one from heaven' (denoting the perfect and transcendent existence of God) contrasts with the earthly father.

11: 14–36 *Controversy over Jesus' power*

11: 14–23 Jesus' power is attributed to alliance with evil

See also Matt. 12^{22-27}; Mark 3^{22-27}. Luke is perhaps drawing on a common source with Matthew. The section is in a non-Marcan context, and there are parallels between Luke and Matthew with no

14 Now he was casting out a demon that was dumb; when the
demon had gone out, the dumb man spoke, and the people
15 marvelled. But some of them said, 'He casts out demons by
16 Beelzebul, the prince of demons'; while others, to test him,
17 sought from him a sign from heaven. But he, knowing their
thoughts, said to them, 'Every kingdom divided against itself
18 is laid waste, and house falls upon house. And if Satan also is
divided against himself, how will his kingdom stand? For

---

corresponding agreement in Mark. Luke also has unique features, suggesting his continued use of the common source where Matthew abandons it. The arguments of Jesus would be useful in rebutting similar charges against the early Christians, but the main point is the significance that Jesus attaches to his work.

14 The demon is *dumb* because it causes this detriment in the person.

15 *Beelzebul* means 'lord of the house'; the alternative 'Beelzebub' (not so well attested) means 'lord of flies', a derogatory term developed by a change of consonant in 'Beelzebul'. Both terms, which described originally a Philistine deity, now denote the *prince* or 'ruler' *of the demons*, not necessarily identical with Satan, but part of his kingdom: like the good angels organized under their prince, the archangel Michael, the demons are marshalled under their leader. *by*, or 'in': in alliance with or in the power of.

16 Cp. Matt. 12^{38}, 16^{1}; Mark 8^{11}. *test him*: see whether his claims were genuine. *from heaven*: given by God: the servants of God (including the Messiah) were expected to make their presence known by undisputed signs; for the discerning the exorcisms are such signs.

17 In Luke *house falls on house* describes the result of 'division' and 'being made waste'. The picture could be of the destruction of buildings resulting from internal strife, or of one dynasty rapidly falling after another.

18 A *kingdom*, faced with internal division, collapses in ruin, and is ineffective: if Jesus conquers the evil forces by alliance with their leader, then logically the kingdom of Satan must be in a state of collapse and disintegration, which is contrary to experience. Jesus testifies to his sense of the reality of evil, never minimized in Christian thought. So far from Satan's power being in a state of collapse, Jesus' whole mission is concerned with breaking it, and right to the end Satan is active (22^{3}). *for you say . . . Beelzebul*: perhaps an editorial addition to make the transition easier.

19 you say that I cast out demons by Beelzebul. And if I cast
out demons by Beelzebul, by whom do your sons cast them
20 out? Therefore they shall be your judges. But if it is by the
finger of God that I cast out demons, then the kingdom of
21 God has come upon you. When a strong man, fully armed,
22 guards his own palace, his goods are in peace; but when one
stronger than he assails him and overcomes him, he takes
away his armour in which he trusted, and divides his spoil.
23 He who is not with me is against me, and he who does not
gather with me scatters.

---

19 The saying in this and the following verse, once an independent unit, is placed here (as in Matthew) for convenience. The *kingdom of God* now balances 'the kingdom of Satan' (v. 18). Jesus throws out a positive challenge. Exorcism is a feature common to Jesus and the Jewish *sons*, perhaps the pupils of the rabbis, or the adherents of the Pharisees, but more probably members of the Jewish nation; it is illogical to say that the source of power is different in each case. If their *sons* exorcized with the power of God, why should it be denied that Jesus does the same? If he is accused of an unholy league with Satan, why should not they be?

20 *I* is emphatic (in contrast with *sons*). *If it is*: 'as I claim it to be'. The source of Jesus' success may be God, and certain consequences then follow: his exorcisms are unique, because they are indications of God's special intervention to assert his sovereignty over evil. *has come*, or 'has come by anticipation'.

21 The general sense of the analogy is the same as in Mark and Matthew, but the picture is of a palace or castle guarded by a man possessing the equipment of a heavy armed soldier and on the watch against border raids. As teachers do, Jesus may well have developed a similar analogy in different ways on different occasions. Jesus is subtly suggesting that, in contrast with the Jewish accusation, he himself may be the stronger one sent by God to crush the evil power (cp. Isa. 49^{24}; Ps. of Sol. 5^{3}). *guards*: is capable of guarding.

22 *armour*: the full range of armour and weapons of a Roman soldier. The success is stressed by the distribution of the *spoil*, the sequel to a victorious raid or battle (a special reference to Isa. 53^{12} may not be intended).

23 Cp. 9^{50}. Jesus denies the possibility of a neutral position in face of hostility, and stresses the seriousness of failure to see his mission as

24 'When the unclean spirit has gone out of a man, he passes
through waterless places seeking rest; and finding none he
25 says, "I will return to my house from which I came." And
26 when he comes he finds it swept and put in order. Then he
goes and brings seven other spirits more evil than himself,
and they enter and dwell there; and the last state of that man
becomes worse than the first.'
27 As he said this, a woman in the crowd raised her voice and
said to him, 'Blessed is the womb that bore you, and the
28 breasts that you sucked!' But he said, 'Blessed rather are
those who hear the word of God and keep it!'

God-given. *with me*: on my side. *gather*: perhaps a metaphor from shepherding the flock. The person who does not help Jesus to gather the flock plays the same part as the wolf or enemy who scatters the flock; he is disruptive of God's plans. The Jews hoped that God would 'gather' Israel from all lands into a new promised land.

24–26 The return of the evil spirit

The coincidence of language with Matt. 12^{43-45} suggests the use of a common source: in both Gospels the general context is the 'Beelzebul' controversy. The theme of 'demons' and 'exorcism' and of the danger of the Jewish attitude is continued. Jesus uses the popular idea that demons, when expelled from one body, sought rest in another, and, if possible, returned to their first home; their disembodiment defeated their aim of creating disintegration in people. Such a popular mythology expresses the truth that evil's effectiveness depends on using people as its instrument. The main point is probably that the house, not being put to any good use, is all ready to give a welcome to the demons: Jesus' contemporaries are 'a sitting target' for evil, because of their barrenness where God's purposes are concerned, shown in their non-committal attitude towards himself.

A person might sometimes be compared to a house. *put in order*: well furnished.

seven, the perfect number, is emphatic: the forces of evil have a perfect situation.

27–28 The true happiness

The incident is found only in Luke; cp. 8^{21}.

hear: in contrast with the scepticism of vv. 15–16. The main

29 When the crowds were increasing, he began to say, 'This
generation is an evil generation; it seeks a sign, but no sign
30 shall be given to it except the sign of Jonah. For as Jonah

---

concern is not paying compliments to Jesus, but the more costly way of hearing the word of God, given in speech and action, and of 'keeping' or 'guarding' it from escape (cp. 8^{15}).

11: 29–36 *The danger of scepticism and need for clear sight*

11: 29–32 The crucial nature of the present situation

See also Matt. 12^{38-42}; (cp. Matt. 16^{1-4}); Mark 8^{11-12}. Matthew and Luke are probably drawing on a common source.

29 In Matthew the audience is 'the scribes and Pharisees'; the original context has been lost. *generation*: the contemporaries of Jesus. *evil*: out of tune with God. This looking for spectacular signs of the genuineness of Jesus' mission could prove to be an unhealthy obsession, showing lack of trust in God, and preventing a serious consideration of what Jesus was doing. The *sign of Jonah* sounds like a term well known to the Jews. It ought to refer to something characteristic of Jonah rather than of anyone else; the *sign* is not, therefore, likely to be Jonah's preaching of repentance, as this was not peculiar to him. The sign, or miraculous happening, that marked out Jonah as having a genuine God-given mission was that he was swallowed up by the sea monster (Jonah 1^{17}) and yet kept safe for God's purposes (2^{10}). So Jesus may be saying that the only sign in his case (which ironically his contemporaries would not recognize as in this category) will be the fact of his being swallowed up and apparently finished, i.e. by death. But as in the case of Jonah, so with Jesus, such apparent death will prove to be 'life'.

30 Jonah himself is now described as a *sign*, i.e. a person chosen by God to reveal to his contemporaries the will and purpose of God (cp. Ezek. 12^{6}). The meaning might, therefore, be that Jesus, as the Son of man, is like Jonah confronting men with God's demand for a change of heart. But this explanation ignores (*a*) the future tense *will be*, and (*b*) *became* (probably the correct translation of the Greek verb ἐγένετο, which could also mean 'was'): 'just as' (i.e. 'in the same way as') 'Jonah became a sign, so will the Son of man be . . .'. Just as Jonah's death was the preliminary to his confronting the Ninevites with the judgement of God, so through death Jesus will confront men with God and his demands, and challenge people to a response. Matt. 12^{40} could then be regarded as an early exposition of Jesus' words.

became a sign to the men of Nineveh, so will the Son of man
31 be to this generation. The queen of the South will arise at the
judgement with the men of this generation and condemn them;
for she came from the ends of the earth to hear the wisdom of
Solomon, and behold, something greater than Solomon is
32 here. The men of Nineveh will arise at the judgement with
this generation and condemn it; for they repented at the
preaching of Jonah, and behold, something greater than Jonah
is here.
33 'No one after lighting a lamp puts it in a cellar or under a
bushel, but on a stand, that those who enter may see the light.
34 Your eye is the lamp of your body; when your eye is sound,
your whole body is full of light; but when it is not sound,

-32 In Luke the two parts of the saying follow the O.T. order of events. *Jonah* forms a link with the previous teaching. For *the queen of the South*, a non-Jewish queen of Sheba, see 1 Kgs. 10^{1-10}. For Jonah and the Ninevites see Jonah 3: the Ninevites are non-Jews, symbolizing the worst of sinners. These non-Jews, without Jewish advantages, recognized God's presence in Solomon's wisdom and in Jonah's preaching: all the more serious is the lack of response by Jesus' Jewish contemporaries to *something greater* than either, Jesus' mission and message. In the O.T. God is sometimes pictured as a prosecutor conducting a lawsuit with Israel (cp. Mic. 6^{1-2}); here a similar picture is used of the final judgement day. *arise*: as witnesses for the prosecution against Jesus' contemporaries.

1: 33–36 The need for clear vision

See also Matt. 5^{15}, 6^{22-23}.

33 Cp. 8^{16}, where Luke is probably following Mark. Here he draws on a special source. The light is there to be seen: Jesus is stressing the importance of having insight and vision into his mission.

35 *lamp* and *light* form a link with v. 33. In ancient thought the *eye* allowed light into the body and so gave it sense of direction. Good eyesight results in co-ordination of the body; deficient eyesight causes the body to fumble. There is need for clear vision in discerning the purposes of God. *therefore . . . darkness*: it is dangerous to believe in

35 your body is full of darkness. Therefore be careful lest the
36 light in you be darkness. If then your whole body is full of
light, having no part dark, it will be wholly bright, as when a
lamp with its rays gives you light.'
37 While he was speaking, a Pharisee asked him to dine with

---

the possession of good eyesight when it is lacking. Self-deception about insight into the affairs of God has serious consequences (cp. John 9^{40-41}).

36 This verse, found only in Luke, and at first sight stating the obvious, has been attributed to an early scribal comment. It is omitted in some MSS. and sometimes replaced by: 'If the light that is in you is darkness, how great is the darkness!', an assimilation to Matt. 6^{23}. But the saying is well attested, and its literal translation is: 'If then your whole body is full of light, it will be full of light, the whole of it, as when . . .' (*full of light* and *bright* in RSV translate the same adjective). The emphasis may be on the simile: if you are a centre of insight into God's purposes, then you will be like a lamp or beacon throwing light on others (cp. Eph. 5^{7-14}).

11: 37–54 *Jesus' criticism of the Pharisees and rabbis*

See also Matt. 23^{1-36}, where many of these sayings are found in a different order and in varying language. Jesus' assessment of these leading Jews was probably preserved to show where he differed from some of those who were instrumental in having him executed, and to indicate the dangers inherent in the spirit of their teaching. The attack has often been thought to present an unfair picture, and also to reflect later controversy between the Christian Church and the Jews. But Jesus may not be implying that all the Pharisees are like this, but may be speaking of them collectively to show certain dangerous tendencies in them (cp. Mark 7^{1-13}, 12^{38}). Even if the sayings are taken as the product of the early Church, the charges must have had some substance of truth, and so could well have applied equally to Jesus' generation of Pharisees. We are probably dealing with a collection of remarks made on different occasions, and so their cumulative effect may seem harsh. We have no contemporary account of the Pharisees for comparison, but people of this kind, who had developed a minute and

38 him; so he went in and sat at table. The Pharisee was aston-
39 ished to see that he did not first wash before dinner. And the
Lord said to him, 'Now you Pharisees cleanse the outside of
the cup and of the dish, but inside you are full of extortion
40 and wickedness. You fools! Did not he who made the outside
41 make the inside also? But give for alms those things which
are within; and behold, everything is clean for you.

---

complicated system of regulations for the observance of the Law, could easily have forgotten its central purpose, i.e. to be a reminder of God's love and a means of response to it; hence Jesus' urgent warnings here. Luke begins with criticism of the Pharisees and passes to particular reference to the rabbis (vv. 45, 52). With this unfavourable estimate of the Jewish religious authorities we should also compare that held in the Qumran community during the same period (e.g. *Hymns*, vii: 'Teachers of lies . . . have led them astray; they perish without understanding. . . . And they, teachers of lies and seers of falsehood, have schemed against me a devilish scheme. . . . And they withhold from the thirsty the drink of knowledge, and assuage their thirst with vinegar'; see Vermes, *The Dead Sea Scrolls in English*, p. 161).

11: 37–41 The right kind of cleansing

37 Cp. 7^{36}.

38 *wash*: carry out certain ablutions to secure ritual cleanness, often a development of the Law's demands. The Pharisees tried to be meticulous in such observances, the intricacy of which can be seen in the Jewish *Mishnah*.

39 A fine distinction was sometimes made between the outer and inner part of a utensil in discussions of uncleanness. Such an obsession can cause forgetfulness of the danger arising from one's innermost being, where *extortion*, or 'greed', may be lurking together with *wickedness*, the selfish disregard of God.

40 The Pharisees are *fools* because their concern with outward ritual cleanness can blind them to God's vital concern with a man's *heart* or innermost being. A man's outlook can affect his whole being.

41 *those things which are within* (τὰ ἐνόντα) is difficult in the sense either of 'the contents of the cup' or 'that which is possible', while *alms* forms

42 'But woe to you Pharisees! for you tithe mint and rue and
every herb, and neglect justice and the love of God; these
43 you ought to have done, without neglecting the others. Woe
to you Pharisees! for you love the best seat in the synagogues
44 and salutations in the market places. Woe to you! for you are
like graves which are not seen, and men walk over them without knowing it.'

45 One of the lawyers answered him, 'Teacher, in saying

---

an awkward apposition. The giving of money to the poor was a primary religious duty (Tob. 4^{16}; cp. Matt. 6^{1-4}). Jesus' point may be that the prior almsgiving is the giving of one's innermost being to God: then the whole of life is clean. An alternative is to suppose a mistranslation from Aramaic, and to translate: 'cleanse the innermost being', i.e. give oneself unreservedly to God (cp. Matt. 23^{26}).

11: 42–44 The dangerous example of the Pharisees

42 To *tithe* meant to give one-tenth of the value of the product to God, and this practice was a primary object of the Pharisaic sect. Detailed rules are given in the Jewish *Mishnah*, where there is no mention of tithing of *mint*, and where *rue* is definitely exempted, while not all garden herbs are subject to tithing. This obsession with over-generous tithing can cause *neglect* of *justice*, right dealing with other people, which is the true expression of one's *love of God*. With the O.T. prophets (e.g. Amos 5^{24}) Jesus stresses the priority of personal relationships.

43 Cp. 14^{7-10}. *best seats*: perhaps the synagogue seats in front of the ark, reserved for prominent men. The rabbinical writings refer to similar pride in the title of honour, 'Rabbi' (contrast 22^{24-27}).

44 Just as people in walking over unmarked graves unknowingly incur ritual uncleanness, or just as people may be in the presence of death without knowing it, so the dangerous influence of the Pharisees may pass unnoticed. The parallel in Matt. 23^{27}, different in details, may be a separate saying of Jesus.

11: 45–54 The terrible responsibility of the rabbis

Luke introduces a special reference to the lawyers or rabbis, perhaps because of the appropriateness of the 'woe' to them, or under the influence of his source.

45 *us also*: they belong to the Pharisaic party.

46 this you reproach us also.' And he said, 'Woe to you lawyers
also! for you load men with burdens hard to bear, and
you yourselves do not touch the burdens with one of your
47 fingers. Woe to you! for you build the tombs of the prophets
48 whom your fathers killed. So you are witnesses and consent
to the deeds of your fathers; for they killed them, and you
49 build their tombs. Therefore also the Wisdom of God said,
"I will send them prophets and apostles, some of whom they
50 will kill and persecute," that the blood of all the prophets,

---

46 *burdens*: the minute and burdensome regulations, evolved by the rabbis to apply the Jewish Law to contemporary life, and known as 'the tradition of the elders' (Mark 7^{8-9}). The rabbis do not *lift a finger* to help people to bear the load: they have no feeling for people's difficulties, and so a situation is created that is alien to God himself, who is compassionate (6^{36}).

48 The veneration paid to *the prophets* was expressed by the erection of *tombs* or 'sepulchral monuments' on the sites of their burial. Later generations of Jews might thus be thought to be dissociating themselves from their ancestors' notorious rejection of the prophets, but Jesus paradoxically draws the opposite conclusion. The lawyers are concerned with the prophets as dead people, and not as those who gave the living oracles of God, the spirit of which is lacking from their own teaching. The concluding sentence is ironical: if your ancestors did the killing, you are insuring the effective burial of their message! (See also Matt. 23^{29-31}, which may have a different point.)

9 *the Wisdom of God* (peculiar to Luke) has been explained as Jesus himself, who is giving a decree of the divine Wisdom, or as a reference either to the O.T. or to a Jewish book of Wisdom. The words probably form part of Jesus' saying: 'God in his wisdom has said . . .', i.e. what follows is his divine purpose revealed to Jesus. *I will send*, or 'I am sending'. *prophets*: Zechariah, Elizabeth, Simeon, Anna, and John the Baptist, together probably with Jesus himself, while *apostles* includes Jesus himself and those (e.g. the twelve) who are commissioned by him. The present heralds of God's greatest revelation will be treated with scant respect, like the rest of God's messengers.

Just as God's approach to the Jews reaches its climax with Jesus' mission, so retribution for their rejection of it is near at hand. The Jews are heading for disaster (cp. 19^{42-44}), which can be interpreted as God's judgement on their past rebellion against him (cp. 20^{1-18}).

shed from the foundation of the world, may be required of
51 this generation, from the blood of Abel to the blood of
Zechariah, who perished between the altar and the sanctuary.
52 Yes, I tell you, it shall be required of this generation. Woe to
you lawyers! for you have taken away the key of knowledge;
you did not enter yourselves, and you hindered those who
were entering.'
53 As he went away from there, the scribes and the Pharisees
began to press him hard, and to provoke him to speak of many
54 things, lying in wait for him, to catch at something he might
say.

12: In the meantime, when so many thousands of the multi-

---

51 *Abel*: here seen as a prophet, because he witnessed to the righteousness required by God (Gen. 4^{1-11}). *Zechariah*: probably the one mentioned in 2 Chr. 24^{20-22}, who was stoned to death in the temple. The description of him in Matthew 23^{35} as 'the son of Barachiah' may be a scribal gloss due to confusion with the well-known prophet Zechariah (Zech. 1^{1}). The reference is to the first and last servants of God who are recorded in the O.T. (in the Hebrew canon Chronicles is the last book) as having been murdered.

52 The house of *knowledge* or God's wisdom (cp. Prov. 9^{1}) is locked up and the entrance key removed. The *knowledge* is probably that of God's revelation of himself now being offered in Jesus. By their own rejection of his mission, and by their attempt to dissuade others from responding to it, the lawyers set a bad example, and so bar entrance.

53–54 Cp. 6^{11}. *provoke . . . to speak* is a translation of ἀποστοματίζειν, which usually means 'teach by dictation' or 'repeat from memory', but which is here given the meaning as in RSV, or is taken to mean 'trap in speech' or 'ply with questions' (NEB). *catch*: in order that a plausible charge of blasphemy or treason might be brought.

12: 1–59 *The right centre of allegiance; the need for readiness*

The section consists of a collection of sayings found in other contexts in Matthew and Mark.

12: 1–12 Various warnings

1 Cp. Matt. 16^{6}; Mark 8^{15}. The saying continues the criticism of the Pharisees and may be from Luke's special source. *hypocrisy*, or 'play

tude had gathered together that they trod upon one another,
he began to say to his disciples first, 'Beware of the leaven of
2 the Pharisees, which is hypocrisy. Nothing is covered up that
3 will not be revealed, or hidden that will not be known. Whatever you have said in the dark shall be heard in the light, and
what you have whispered in private rooms shall be proclaimed upon the housetops.
4 'I tell you, my friends, do not fear those who kill the body,
5 and after that have no more that they can do. But I will warn
you whom to fear: fear him who, after he has killed, has
6 power to cast into hell;[l] yes, I tell you, fear him! Are not five
sparrows sold for two pennies? And not one of them is for-
7 gotten before God. Why, even the hairs of your head are all

[l] Greek *Gehenna*

---

acting': the Pharisees are one thing on the surface, another underneath. In Matthew and Mark the *leaven*, or evil influence, of the Pharisees consists in their incredulity. Jesus may well have seen their bad example to take both forms (cp. Mark 7^{5}). *first*: vv. 1–12 are intended for the disciples.

-3 Cp. 8^{17}; Matt. 10^{26}; Mark 4^{22}, where similar sayings occur in different contexts: here the impossibility of hiding anything from God is stressed. The Pharisees' play-acting cannot escape the notice of God—a theme leading directly to vv. 4–7.

-5 Paradoxically, God alone is to be feared as the ultimate authority over our lives, and yet *fear him* is accompanied by the assurance 'fear not' (v. 7), because this ultimate authority is not tyranny, but loving concern for each person. Jesus' disciples are called *friends*, as being taken into close confidence (cp. Wisd. 7^{27}; John 15^{15}). Mortal enemies can only end a person's physical existence (*the body*); cp. Wisd. 2^{1}–3^{9}; 4 Macc. 13^{14}. Only God can end the much more important relationship with himself. *cast into hell*: discard from the presence of God, which alone gives fullness of life, *hell* having become in Jewish thought the place of punishment for the wicked after death.

7 If God cares for the animal world, how much more can we be assured of his love for human beings, to whom he has subjected the

numbered. Fear not; you are of more value than many
sparrows.
8 'And I tell you, every one who acknowledges me before
men, the Son of man also will acknowledge before the angels
9 of God; but he who denies me before men will be denied
10 before the angels of God. And every one who speaks a word
against the Son of man will be forgiven; but he who blas-
11 phemes against the Holy Spirit will not be forgiven. And
when they bring you before the synagogues and the rulers
and the authorities, do not be anxious how or what you are
12 to answer or what you are to say; for the Holy Spirit will
teach you in that very hour what you ought to say.'

---

rest of creation (Gen. 1^{28}). *pennies*: Roman copper coins of small value. The numbering of the *hairs* vividly portrays the complete love of God for each individual. The Jewish idea of God's being involved in his world is taken much further by Jesus.

8–9 *acknowledges me*: owns up to an acceptance of me. The claim is striking: one's attitude to Jesus determines the attitude of approval or disapproval on the part of the Son of man, God's agent in the final judgement, with the implication that rightness with God depends on accepting Jesus. The judgement is depicted as taking place in the presence of *the angels*, the heavenly court. *denies*, or better 'disowns'. Cp. 9^{26}; Matt. 10^{32}; Mark 8^{38}.

10 The *Son of man* forms a link with v. 8 (cp. Matt. 12^{32}, in a different context). In this passage 'Son of man' has sometimes been given the sense of 'men' (cp. Mark 3^{38}), with a contrast between abuse aimed at men and blasphemy against the Holy Spirit. But the saying makes sense as it stands. The person who speaks a word against Jesus (cp. 23^{35-39}) can be *forgiven* by God. But such an attitude may be symptomatic of an unreadiness to respond to *the Holy Spirit* of God, and so can sever fellowship with him, with the result that restoration of relations with him becomes impossible.

11–12 See also Matt. 10^{19-20}; Mark 13^{11}; cp. 21^{14-15}. There is a link with v. 8 (the acknowledgement of the Son of man) and with v. 10 (the Holy Spirit). *synagogues*: Jewish tribunals. *rulers and . . . authorities*: the Roman jurisdiction. *answer*, or, better, 'make your defence' (cp. 21^{14}; Acts 19^{23}). Jesus can promise his disciples the help of *the Holy Spirit*, because he sees them as the community of God's new era (cp. Acts 2^{15-21}).

13 One of the multitude said to him, 'Teacher, bid my brother
14 divide the inheritance with me.' But he said to him, 'Man,
15 who made me a judge or divider over you?' And he said to
them, 'Take heed, and beware of all covetousness; for a man's
life does not consist in the abundance of his possessions.'
16 And he told them a parable, saying, 'The land of a rich man
17 brought forth plentifully; and he thought to himself, "What
18 shall I do, for I have nowhere to store my crops?" And he
said, "I will do this: I will pull down my barns, and build
larger ones; and there I will store all my grain and my goods.
19 And I will say to my soul, Soul, you have ample goods laid
20 up for many years; take your ease, eat, drink, be merry." But

---

12: 13–34 Teaching on concern with wealth and possessions

The parable of the rich fool (vv. 16–21), peculiar to Luke, leads to further sayings about earthly possessions (vv. 22–32; see also Matt. 6[25–33]) and real wealth (vv. 33–34; cp. Matt. 6[19–21]).

13 The man is concerned only with himself and the possibility that Jesus can exercise moral pressure on his brother.

14 There are the official channels for the consideration of his case. The question is a way of disclaiming authority in the matter (cp. Exod. 2[14]; Acts 7[35]).

15 *beware of*, or 'guard yourselves from'. *covetousness* represents an attitude that is always grasping for selfish gain.

16 The illustration shows that wealth as a basis of life has limitations. The rich man's monologue of obsession with himself is contrasted with the words of God, which make the monologue into a dialogue and demonstrate that the man cannot live as a self-contained unit.

17 *my* (as in v. 18) is emphatic.

19 *soul*, or 'self'. *ample* and *many* are the same Greek adjective and stress the man's self-confidence. *eat, drink, and be merry*: probably a proverbial expression, denoting a philosophy of life based on enjoyment of material things and on pessimism about any existence after death (cp. Isa. 22[13]; 1 Cor. 15[32]).

20 *God* is emphatic. *fool*: the person who leaves God out of account. *is required*, by God (lit. 'they are demanding back'). In Jewish thought a person was a *soul*, or 'living person', because of God's creative goodness, and so one's earthly existence could be pictured as a loan to be repaid (cp. Wisd. 15[8]). *whose will they be?*: someone else's, and certainly not the rich man's (cp. Eccles. 2[18–21]).

God said to him, "Fool! This night your soul is required of
you; and the things you have prepared, whose will they be?"
21 So is he who lays up treasure for himself, and is not rich
toward God.'
22 And he said to his disciples, 'Therefore I tell you, do not be
anxious about your life, what you shall eat, nor about your
23 body, what you shall put on. For life is more than food, and
24 the body more than clothing. Consider the ravens: they
neither sow nor reap, they have neither storehouse nor barn,
and yet God feeds them. Of how much more value are you
25 than the birds! And which of you by being anxious can add
26 a cubit to his span of life? [m] If then you are not able to do as

[m] Or *to his stature*

---

21 The verse, omitted in some MSS., could be a later scribal comment. *so*: in this predicament. There is a contrast between the person who is self-centred, and the person who finds riches in serving God (cp. Prov. 3^{13-16}).

22 The sayings that follow have a rhythmic structure. *life*, 'the living personality', is parallel to *body*, 'the whole human person' (cp. Rom. 12^{1}). Concern for one's well-being should not be related solely to food and clothing.

23 Human personality is not something purely biological, but is concerned with personal fellowship with God.

24 The *ravens* have no organized farming operations! Man has a more important part than the birds in God's creation, and can trust his providence (cp. Ps. 8^{5-8}). Jesus is not recommending the casual attitude of 'if we just trust God, he will provide for all our needs without any effort on our part', but is arguing that we can confidently expect our material needs to be satisfied, so that we may not be deflected from the weightier matters of life.

25 Anxiety achieves nothing. A *cubit*, lit. 'a forearm', can be a measure of length (about eighteen inches) or of time (an hour). *span of life*, or 'age', also means 'height' or 'stature'. The reference is, therefore, to adding to height or to length of life. The latter is the more likely, as something very insignificant is in question, and a cubit is used elsewhere of an infinitesimal period of time (cp. Mimnermus, ii. 3).

26 The comment is peculiar to Luke: if worry cannot achieve the smallest of feats, why let it dominate the bigger necessities of life?

small a thing as that, why are you anxious about the rest?
27 Consider the lilies, how they grow; they neither toil nor
spin;[n] yet I tell you, even Solomon in all his glory was not
28 arrayed like one of these. But if God so clothes the grass
which is alive in the field today and tomorrow is thrown into
the oven, how much more will he clothe you, O men of little
29 faith! And do not seek what you are to eat and what you are
30 to drink, nor be of anxious mind. For all the nations of the
world seek these things; and your Father knows that you
31 need them. Instead, seek his[o] kingdom, and these things shall
be yours as well.
32 'Fear not, little flock, for it is your Father's good pleasure

[n] Other ancient authorities read *Consider the lilies; they neither spin nor weave*

[o] Other ancient authorities read *God's*

---

27 The question of anxiety over clothing (vv. 22–23) is now expanded. *lilies*: the autumn crocus or the anemone may be meant. *they neither toil nor spin* is well attested, though it could be an assimilation to Matt. 6^{28}, with the original reading, as in RSV margin, 'they neither spin nor weave'. The splendour of Solomon's kingdom had become proverbial (cp. 2 Chr. 1^{12}).

28 Jesus now turns to another natural feature, *the grass*. *But*, or, better, 'And'. *clothes*: with colour and beauty, even though the grass's life is short. *the oven*: used for baking bread, and heated by the burning of grass. *little faith*: in the providence of God and his loving care.

29 *you*: emphatic, 'you of all people'. *seek*: make your main concern.

30 *the nations*: those who do not belong to God's people, the Jews, and are, therefore, deficient in the knowledge of God. The disciples, as Jews and witnesses of Jesus' own trust in God's loving care, are to have a very different attitude. *your*: emphatic, 'but you have a Father who knows . . . .'

31 An obsession with material considerations is especially dangerous, as the primary consideration now must be alert expectation for God's *kingdom*, breaking out amongst men in the ministry of Jesus. *as well*: bodily needs matter, but priorities must be right.

32 The saying is only found in Luke. For *give you the kingdom* cp. Dan. 7^{13-18}, where 'the saints of the most high' or faithful Israel reign with

33 to give you the kingdom. Sell your possessions, and give
alms; provide yourselves with purses that do not grow old,
with a treasure in the heavens that does not fail, where no
34 thief approaches and no moth destroys. For where your
treasure is, there will your heart be also.

35, 36 'Let your loins be girded and your lamps burning, and be
like men who are waiting for their master to come home from

God in his final kingdom. Jesus is addressing his followers as the true representatives of Israel, as is also implied by the use of *flock* (cp. Ezek. 34^{31}). The early Christians would see a partial fulfilment of this promise in Jesus' establishment as king after his resurrection, and in their belonging to his kingdom (Col. 1^{13}), and would look forward to its complete fulfilment in God's final kingdom (1 Cor. 15^{24-28}).

33 Transitory possessions are contrasted with those that are lasting: it is a good thing to part with the first to show one's readiness for the second (cp. 18^{18-23}). *purses*, or 'money bags'. The *treasure*, a term used of winning merit and standing with God (cp. Tobit 4^{9}, connected with almsgiving as here), is gained by membership of God's kingdom, and is lasting because it is *in the heavens*, i.e. dependent on God (cp. Wisd. 7^{14}).

34 A man's *heart*, his whole being, becomes committed to his *treasure*, the thing which he accounts most worth while.

12: 35–48 A call to readiness

Jesus' formation of his disciples into a special community within Israel to await God's decisive intervention makes sense of this call. See also Matt. 24^{43-51}. Verses 35–38 and 47–48 are found only in Luke. The note of preparedness continues the theme of having right priorities.

35 *loins . . . girded*: the long eastern robe was caught up by a girdle during active work, and the metaphor means 'be ready' (cp. Exod. 12^{11}). The *lamps burning* suggests readiness for someone's reception (cp. Matt. 25^{1}), and also vigorous activity (cp. 2 Sam. 21^{17}, where 'quench the lamp' means 'render powerless').

36 The main point is alertness, stressed by *at once* and by the note of uncertainty about the master's return. The *marriage feast* could be that of someone else or of the master himself. The early Christians might have seen in the master's return a reference to the final return or advent of Jesus in glory.

the marriage feast, so that they may open to him at once when
37 he comes and knocks. Blessed are those servants whom the
master finds awake when he comes; truly, I say to you, he
will gird himself and have them sit at table, and he will come
38 and serve them. If he comes in the second watch, or in the
39 third, and finds them so, blessed are those servants! But
know this, that if the householder had known at what hour
the thief was coming, he would have been awake and[p] would
40 not have left his house to be broken into. You also must be
ready; for the Son of man is coming at an hour you do not
expect.'
41 Peter said, 'Lord, are you telling this parable for us or for
42 all?' And the Lord said, 'Who then is the faithful and wise
steward, whom his master will set over his household, to give
43 them their portion of food at the proper time? Blessed is that

[p] Other ancient authorities omit *would have been awake and*

---

37 The master's action in waiting on the *servants*, or 'slaves', seems strange (contrast 17^{7-8}). Jesus did perform a menial task for his disciples (John 13^{1-16}), but such an act was contrary to notions of propriety in normal life (cp. 22^{24-27}). Perhaps this practice formed part of celebrations at a wedding.

38 According to Roman custom the period 6 p.m.–6 a.m. was divided into four parts called 'watches', while among Greeks and Jews three night 'watches' were known and are probably in mind here.

39 The theme is once more one of readiness. *broken into*, lit. 'dug into', presents the picture of a burglar digging through the sun-dried brick of a house.

40 Preparedness is set against the background of the coming of *the Son of man*, a term conjuring up the final triumph of God and his judgement.

41 *us* may refer to the followers of Jesus, while *all* refers to Israel. Then the illustrations that follow stress the special responsibilities of Jesus' own circle; the teaching would perhaps be later applied to the Church's leaders. This *parable*, or 'analogy' looks back to vv. 35–40.

42 A *steward* exercised a post of special responsibility in all kinds of spheres, being sometimes, as here, of slave status.

servant whom his master when he comes will find so doing.
44 Truly I tell you, he will set him over all his possessions.
45 But if that servant says to himself, "My master is delayed in
coming," and begins to beat the menservants and the maid-
46 servants, and to eat and drink and get drunk, the master of
that servant will come on a day when he does not expect him
and at an hour he does not know, and will punish[q] him, and
47 put him with the unfaithful. And that servant who knew his
master's will, but did not make ready or act according to his
48 will, shall receive a severe beating. But he who did not know,
and did what deserved a beating, shall receive a light beating.
Every one to whom much is given, of him will much be required; and of him to whom men commit much they will
demand the more.

49 'I came to cast fire upon the earth; and would that it were

[q] Or *cut him in pieces*

---

44 The steward will be given promotion.

46 *punish*, lit. 'cut in pieces' (RSV margin), denotes the execution of the slave, which is out of keeping with the context. Perhaps both here and in Matt. 24^{51} the Greek word is a mistranslation of an Aramaic original meaning 'segregate'. The master now classes him among his unreliable slaves, since he has forfeited his good name of 'faithful'.

47–48a This saying, only found in Luke, and based on practices relating to the punishment of slaves, illustrates the point that being taken into confidence brings with it responsibility. The disciples are in a special relationship to Jesus and their accountability will be all the greater.

48b A position of trust makes big demands; the metaphor may be from banking. The first part of the clause suggests that a certain amount of trust merits an equal amount of responsible action; the second part says that this demand is too small and a responsibility far greater than the amount of trust can be expected (cp. 6^{32-36}). The faithfulness demanded here is tested when the disciples are given the dangerous responsibility of proclaiming the death and resurrection of Jesus.

12: 49–59 Jesus' coming creates a crisis

Jesus' death will have an inflammatory effect. His mission will cause division and face people with a challenge.

50 already kindled! I have a baptism to be baptized with; and
51 how I am constrained until it is accomplished! Do you think
that I have come to give peace on earth? No, I tell you, but
52 rather division; for henceforth in one house there will be five
53 divided, three against two and two against three; they will be
divided, father against son and son against father, mother
against daughter and daughter against her mother, mother-

-50 This self-contained saying, peculiar to Luke, consists of two lines of poetry in the form of Hebrew parallelism, and links up with vv. 51–53 in similarity of language and general theme. *to cast fire* may not refer to divine judgement or to the fire of the kingdom of God, but rather suggest that the mission of Jesus will set the world ablaze through the *baptism* that he is to undergo. The word pictures the passing through affliction and distress (cp. Ps. 69^{1-2}, where the sufferings of the righteous are described in terms of being engulfed in water; see also Mark 10^{39}). Jesus may have seen his baptism in the Jordan and his immersion beneath the waters as symbolical of the distress and suffering awaiting him. *how I am constrained* is sometimes interpreted 'how I am hemmed in' or 'restricted': Jesus' work is hampered until his death has taken place. A better translation is 'how distressed I am', meaning that Jesus, though full of longing for the completion of his mission, is at the same time full of anguish, because such completion will involve abandonment of himself to his enemies and his rejection by God's people. The saying, emphasizing the cruciality of Jesus' coming death, sounds authentic, as this use of 'baptism' in the Gospels is rare, and there is no reference either to crucifixion or resurrection.

51 For this verse and vv. 52–53 see also Matt. 10^{34-36}. Jesus' mission will provoke divisions at the most intimate level of family relationships; there is the implication that an allegiance to him is to outweigh all others. In the early Church commitment to Jesus often caused a rift with nearest relations. Although the purpose of Jesus' work is *peace* (2^{14}; Col. 1^{20}), or reconciliation with God, offering also a basis of peace between man and man (Eph. 2^{14}), yet ironically the result will also be disharmony, according as some accept his challenge and others refuse it (cp. John 7–11). In Matthew the stronger term 'sword' is used.

3 Cp. Mic. 7^{6}, a lament about the breakdown of family bonds before the coming of God's kingdom.

in-law against her daughter-in-law and daughter-in-law
against her mother-in-law.'
54 He also said to the multitudes, 'When you see a cloud
rising in the west, you say at once, "A shower is coming";
55 and so it happens. And when you see the south wind blowing,
you say, "There will be scorching heat"; and it happens.
56 You hypocrites! You know how to interpret the appearance
of earth and sky; but why do you not know how to interpret
the present time?
57 'And why do you not judge for yourselves what is right?
58 As you go with your accuser before the magistrate, make an
effort to settle with him on the way, lest he drag you to the
judge, and the judge hand you over to the officer, and the
59 officer put you in prison. I tell you, you will never get out till
you have paid the very last copper.'

---

54 In vv. 54–56 and vv. 57–59 there are two analogies from (*a*) weather forecasting and (*b*) legal action, both concerned with correct assessments of phenomena or a situation. Jesus is hinting at the critical nature of the present time. In (*a*) Jesus contrasts people's ability to predict the weather from natural occurrences with their inability to put a correct interpretation on the present juncture. In (*b*) the illustration is taken from the legal procedure for debts, when the defendant has to face his predicament squarely and do his utmost to achieve a settlement out of court: there is the same need to come to terms with the present situation.

55 *scorching heat*: the scorching east wind and the heat that it brings.

56 *You hypocrites!*: they do not show consistency; they observe nature, but do not concern themselves with the much more important task of discerning the significance of contemporary events. *the present time*: this decisive moment (cp. 19^{44}).

58 In Matt. 5^{25-26} the saying (in a different context) reinforces teaching on reconciliation, and is perhaps a reapplication of Jesus' saying to the living situation of the early Church. *the officer* was in charge of the debtors' prison and his duties included the collection of debts under order from the judge.

13: THERE were some present at that very time who told him
of the Galileans whose blood Pilate had mingled with their
2 sacrifices. And he answered them, 'Do you think that these
Galileans were worse sinners than all the other Galileans,
3 because they suffered thus? I tell you, No; but unless you
4 repent you will all likewise perish. Or those eighteen upon
whom the tower in Siloam fell and killed them, do you think
that they were worse offenders than all the others who dwelt

3: 1–17 *Repentance; a woman healed*

13: 1–9 The opportunity for change of heart

The need for repentance (vv. 1–5) is stressed further in the parable of the fig tree (vv. 6–9), continuing the theme of the need to face the challenge of the present hour. The section is found only in Luke.

1 *at that very time*: Jesus had been issuing a solemn challenge, but these people were complacently passing judgement on others. The incident is not recorded elsewhere, but *the Galileans* must have been in Jerusalem for one of the Jewish festivals. Josephus records several massacres in this period, when the Roman garrison had to deal with turbulent crowds. *mix their blood with their sacrifices*: Pontius Pilate had killed them at the same time as the animals for sacrifice were being killed.

2 The incident had been reported to Jesus not to provoke his indignation against the governor's action, but to suggest that the calamity was the just punishment for the Galileans' sins (cp. Job 4^{7}; John 9^{2-3}). Jesus points out the complacency of believing that extent of misfortune goes in proportion to that of sin.

3 The audience must concern themselves with their own need to *repent*, i.e. to change their ways and turn to God (especially at this time, when 'the acceptable year of the Lord' is being proclaimed). *likewise*: death will again be the result, in this case, perhaps, that of alienation from God (cp. Rom. 2^{12}). Or is Jesus thinking that, unless the Jews respond to his Gospel of peace (19^{42}), their nationalist passions will lead to utter destruction?

4 The accident is described only here. The *tower*, on which these men were perhaps working, was probably part of the Jerusalem water-supply system, called *Siloam*. The fate of the Galileans may have been brought up by people who believed in the inferiority of Galilean Jews to those of Judea; hence Jesus' illustration is taken from a fatality that happened in Judea.

5 in Jerusalem? I tell you, No; but unless you repent you will
all likewise perish.'
6 And he told this parable: 'A man had a fig tree planted in
his vineyard; and he came seeking fruit on it and found none.
7 And he said to the vinedresser, "Lo, these three years I have
come seeking fruit on this fig tree, and I find none. Cut it
8 down; why should it use up the ground?" And he answered
him, "Let it alone, sir, this year also, till I dig about it and
9 put on manure. And if it bears fruit next year, well and good;
but if not, you can cut it down." '
10 Now he was teaching in one of the synagogues on the
11 sabbath. And there was a woman who had had a spirit of
infirmity for eighteen years; she was bent over and could not

---

6 This parable has sometimes been regarded as the raw material out of which the story of Jesus' 'cursing of the fig tree' was created (Mark $11^{12-14, 20-21}$). But it is not easy to see why out of this relatively easy parable the more difficult miracle arose, and in spite of some similarity of language, the main theme of each is different. Here the point is that God is offering an opportunity for repentance (cp. 4^{18-19}). There is no clear reason for believing that Luke has included the story to explain the delay in the final advent or coming of Jesus. *vineyard*, or perhaps 'orchard': a fig tree would seem out of place in a vineyard, unless it had grown unplanned by the owner. NEB is better: 'a man had a fig tree growing . . .'.

7 The tree is 'using up' the resources of the soil with no result.

8–9 *to dig round*: partly to make room for the manure. The stress is on the respite and new chance of life being given to the tree.

13: 10–17 The woman with a stoop

The new chance of life is now symbolized in an act of healing, found only in Luke. The reply of Jesus (vv. 15–16) reveals his attitude to such acts.

11 The woman's complaint is traced to a *spirit* (or 'demon') *of infirmity* that crippled her. Perhaps she had a deformity of the spine, a case unique among the healings of Jesus. The long-standing nature of the trouble throws Jesus' power into relief.

12 fully straighten herself. And when Jesus saw her, he called
her and said to her, 'Woman, you are freed from your infir-
13 mity.' And he laid his hands upon her, and immediately she
14 was made straight, and she praised God. But the ruler of
the synagogue, indignant because Jesus had healed on the
sabbath, said to the people, 'There are six days on which work
ought to be done; come on those days and be healed, and not
15 on the sabbath day.' Then the Lord answered him, 'You
hypocrites! Does not each of you on the sabbath untie his ox
16 or his ass from the manger, and lead it away to water it? And
ought not this woman, a daughter of Abraham whom Satan
bound for eighteen years, be loosed from this bond on the
17 sabbath day?' As he said this, all his adversaries were put to
shame; and all the people rejoiced at all the glorious things
that were done by him.
18 He said therefore, 'What is the kingdom of God like? And
19 to what shall I compare it? It is like a grain of mustard seed

---

12 *you are freed*: perfect tense of completed action.

14 Strict rules existed about the observance of the Sabbath, and, unless life was in danger, even the work of healing had to be suspended.

15 The hypocrisy consists in the discrepancy of caring for one's livestock even on the Sabbath, while denying such care to a fellow human being. *lead . . . away*: to the well. *untie . . . from* and 'be loosed from' (v. 16) are the same Greek verb and preposition in each case.

16 It is an insult to God that this *woman, a daughter of Abraham*, a member of the chosen people of God, should be left even a day longer under the dominion of Satan. Jesus' attack on the work of *Satan* must go on, Sabbath or no Sabbath (cp. John 5^{17}).

17 *put to shame*: shown to be in the wrong (cp. Ps. 53^{5}). *glorious*: because done by the glory and power of God.

: **18–35** *Teaching on the kingdom of God; the death and rejection of Jesus*

: 18–21 Two parables on the kingdom of God

For (*a*) the parable of the mustard seed see also Matt. 13^{31-32}; Mark 4^{30-34}; and for (*b*) the parable of the leaven see also Matt. 13^{33}. In

which a man took and sowed in his garden; and it grew and
became a tree, and the birds of the air made nests in its
branches.'
20 And again he said, 'To what shall I compare the kingdom
21 of God? It is like leaven which a woman took and hid in three
measures of meal, till it was all leavened.'
22 He went on his way through towns and villages, teaching,
23 and journeying toward Jerusalem. And some one said to him,

---

(*a*) the language differs from Mark, but has similarities with Matthew, suggesting that Matthew and Luke are drawing on a non-Marcan source for that parable as also for (*b*). These parables on the kingdom of God link up closely with the victory over Satan (vv. 10–17). The concern in each parable seems to be with something small and unobtrusive which achieves great success: the reign and cause of God, despite all appearances, will prevail and triumph, and the preceding incident is a token and sign of it.

18 A similar formula introduces some Jewish parables (e.g. 'to what is the thing like?' 'To . . .').

19 *tree*, or, better, 'shrub'. For the analogy of the birds roosting to describe a great kingdom cp. Dan. 4^{21}.

21 The quantity is lit. 'three seahs', a Jewish measure for grain, equivalent to about a peck and a half or thirteen litres (cp. Gen. 18^{6}). The leaven is something small but has an effect on the whole mixture in the making of it into bread. *all* is emphatic.

13: 22–30 Warnings about entry into the kingdom of God

See also Matt. $7^{13-14,\ 22-23}$, 8^{11-12}, 20^{16}, 25^{10-12}; but, with the exception of vv. 28–29, the sayings are best regarded as different sayings of Jesus with similar themes.

22 This note is a reminder of Jesus' important destination, and prepares for vv. 31–35. The mention of *Jerusalem* in the context of the kingdom of God (vv. 18–21) may suggest that the coming events in Jerusalem are vitally connected with it.

23 *those who are saved*: better, 'those who are destined to be saved', which would mean to a Jew the passing of God's final judgement or scrutiny, and the admission to God's new age of full fellowship with himself. Speculation ranged over the number of people to be admitted, whether the Gentiles would be included, and whether the whole of the Jewish nation or only a part would be accepted.

'Lord, will those who are saved be few?' And he said to them,
24 'Strive to enter by the narrow door; for many, I tell you, will
25 seek to enter and will not be able. When once the householder
has risen up and shut the door, you will begin to stand outside and to knock at the door, saying, "Lord, open to us." He
will answer you, "I do not know where you come from."
26 Then you will begin to say, "We ate and drank in your
27 presence, and you taught in our streets." But he will say, "I
tell you, I do not know where you come from; depart from

---

24 The 'new age' was sometimes pictured as a city with gates, or as a house (cp. 2 Esd. 7^{7}. where the entrance to the new Jerusalem is narrow and difficult of approach; see also Rev. 21^{20-27}). Perhaps the picture is that of a narrow door, difficult to squeeze through. Contrast Matt. 7^{13-14}, where the picture is of two different gates and roads. Jesus does not give statistics but warns his hearers against complacency and resting on privilege, as entry will make demands.

25 The illustration of vv. 25–27 may originally have belonged to a context different from that of v. 24, the connecting link being *door*. The passage is constructed by parallel clauses, the appeal of those 'outside' being twice followed by the reply of *the householder*. The main theme is the terrible nature of exclusion, against which no appeal, even on grounds of familiarity with the householder, prevails: it is probably a warning to Jews not to rest on their privileged position. The picture, not necessarily true to life, could be that of guests arriving late for a banquet (see also Matt. 25^{1-13}). But the situation could be that of 11^{5-7}, where the householder has locked up for the night and refuses to admit visitors, suspecting that they may be robbers in disguise. *will begin to stand*, or 'will go on to stand'; see also v. 26.

26 *in your presence*: with the householder as host. He is strangely depicted as *having taught in our streets*; perhaps he was the local synagogue teacher, now visited by some of his former pupils. The figure would probably be interpreted in the early Church as referring to Jesus: to be admitted to the friendship of Jesus (including the Lord's Supper) and to receive his teaching is not enough; there must be some practical proof of discipleship.

27 For *depart . . . iniquity* cp. Ps. 6^{9}. The words of scripture would be appropriate from the synagogue teacher.

28 me, all you workers of iniquity!" There you will weep and
gnash your teeth, when you see Abraham and Isaac and Jacob
and all the prophets in the kingdom of God and you your-
29 selves thrust out. And men will come from east and west, and
from north and south, and sit at table in the kingdom of God.
30 And behold, some are last who will be first, and some are first
who will be last.'
31 At that very hour some Pharisees came, and said to
him, 'Get away from here, for Herod wants to kill you.'

---

28 A further warning against complacency is given (see also Matt. 8^{11-12}, which has a different arrangement and a more poetical structure). *there* (adverb of place) comes in abruptly, as it refers forward to *the kingdom of God*. *gnash your teeth*, often taken to mean the anguish of utter despair, is normally a metaphor of indignation (cp. Ps. 35^{16}), here perhaps denoting chagrin at previous obtuseness and disregard of God. For *weep*, relating to the experience of God's judgement, cp. Ps. 102^{9-10}; Isa. 15^{3}. A claim to belong to a nation, descended from the patriarchs, and productive of the great spokesmen of God, is not sufficient. *you yourselves*: the Jews of Jesus' time.

29 In Luke this part of the saying forms the climax, and is linked closely with his theme of the world-wide Gospel (he mentions the four points of the compass). The gathering of God's people (sometimes including Gentiles, as here) formed part of Jewish expectations. The prophecy is partly fulfilled in the triumphant advance of the Church (cp. Acts 1^{8}).

30 For this proverb-like saying cp. Matt. 19^{30}, 20^{16}; Mark 10^{31}. Commonly accepted ideas of precedence and privilege are going to be broken down, perhaps the Jewish sense of superiority over the Gentiles.

13: 31–35 Jesus' reply to Herod; the lament over Jerusalem

The passage falls into two parts: (*a*) vv. 31–33 (found only in Luke), and (*b*) vv. 34–35 (see also Matt. 23^{37-39}). They have been combined by Luke or his source because of their common themes, 'Jerusalem' and 'rejection'. Luke returns again to Jesus' journey to Jerusalem to die.

31 Such an intimation of Herod's intention is only given here and may not reflect his mind.

32 And he said to them, 'Go and tell that fox, "Behold, I cast
out demons and perform cures today and tomorrow, and
33 the third day I finish my course. Nevertheless I must go on
my way today and tomorrow and the day following; for
it cannot be that a prophet should perish away from Jeru-
34 salem." 'O Jerusalem, Jerusalem, killing the prophets and
stoning those who are sent to you! How often would I have
gathered your children together as a hen gathers her brood
under her wings, and you would not! Behold, your house is

---

32 *fox*: denoting Herod's craftiness. Jesus will not be deterred by fear of Herod from his divinely appointed ministry, which will last a short time longer and will reach its goal in Jerusalem (as v. 33 makes clear). *I finish my course*, or 'I am made perfect' (i.e. through obedience to death Jesus' character reaches perfection). But the RSV translation is more likely: Jesus again sees his death as vital for the completion of his mission. *the third day* here does not refer to the resurrection of Jesus, and this fact, together with lack of any reference to crucifixion, suggests the saying's authenticity.

33 *today . . . day following* recapitulates the thought of v. 32, but now adds the further point that his leaving Galilee is due to God's will and time-scheme, and not to Herod's threats. Jesus associates himself with the prophets of the O.T. If a prophet is to die in witnessing to God, then the most appropriate place for him to do so is Jerusalem, the centre of the worship of the one true God.

34 The repetition of Jerusalem brings out Jesus' feeling and compassion (cp. 19^{41}). The city is viewed as a mother with children (cp. Jer. 22^{26}; Gal. 4^{24-26}). *killing . . . and stoning*, or, better, 'she who is in the habit of killing and stoning': cp. Neh. 9^{26}, and the treatment meted out to the 'teacher of righteousness' of the Qumran community (*Commentary on Habakkuk*, iv, ix; Vermes, *The Dead Sea Scrolls in English*, pp. 232 and 238). Ironically, stoning was the punishment for blasphemy. One Jewish hope was that God would gather the Jews to a newly built Jerusalem with a new and glorious temple for the perfect worship of God. Jesus has come to unite the Jews in such a worship (cp. John 4^{21-24}), but is rejected. *sent to you*: *you*, like *your*, is singular, referring to Jerusalem. Instead of *you*, another well-attested reading is 'her'. *you would not* is plural, denoting the people of Jerusalem.

35 forsaken. And I tell you, you will not see me until you say,
"Blessed is he who comes in the name of the Lord!"'

ONE sabbath when he went to dine at the house of a ruler
14: who belonged to the Pharisees, they were watching him. And
2 behold, there was a man before him who had dropsy. And
3 Jesus spoke to the lawyers and Pharisees, saying, 'Is it lawful
to heal on the sabbath, or not?' But they were silent. Then he
4

---

35 Lit. 'your house is abandoned to you': forsaken by God and left to you as your own property. Perhaps Jerusalem is regarded, like Israel, as a *house* or household, which is now being deserted by God, as the result of her disobedience and lack of response (cp. Jer. 12[7]). More likely, however, the *house* is the temple, which symbolizes the presence of God among men, but, as the Jews are rejecting Jesus and so God's purposes, it can no longer be the centre of God's presence, which by implication is now centred in Jesus. As the rest of the verse suggests, the divine presence only returns in Jesus himself, and with his occupation of the temple for his teaching (cp. 19[47]). The whole saying probably belonged originally to a visit to Jerusalem (cp. e.g. John 4[44]), when Jesus sees that his work there is finished until he returns for the Passover festival, and is greeted as a pilgrim with the words *Blessed . . . Lord* (Ps. 118[26]; cp. 19[38]).

14: 1–35 *Membership of the kingdom of God*

There are the following sections: (*a*) a healing on the Sabbath (vv. 1–6); (*b*) the desire for places of honour (vv. 7–11); (*c*) instructions on invitations (vv. 12–14); (*d*) the parable of the dinner party (vv. 15–24); (*e*) various sayings on the cost of discipleship (vv. 25–35).

(*a*)–(*d*) have the common theme of a 'meal', while (*e*) stresses the cost of entry into the feast of the kingdom of God. Most of the material is found only in Luke.

14: 1–6 The man suffering from dropsy

Cp. 13[10–17], in the light of which the present story is to be read. See also 7[36].

2 *dropsy*: a disease producing watery fluid which collects in the body.

5 took him and healed him, and let him go. And he said to them,
'Which of you, having an ass[r] or an ox that has fallen into a
well, will not immediately pull him out on a sabbath day?'
6 And they could not reply to this.
7 Now he told a parable to those who were invited, when he
marked how they chose the places of honour, saying to them,
8 'When you are invited by any one to a marriage feast, do not
sit down in a place of honour, lest a more eminent man than
9 you be invited by him; and he who invited you both will
come and say to you, "Give place to this man," and then you
0 will begin with shame to take the lowest place. But when you
are invited, go and sit in the lowest place, so that when your
host comes he may say to you, "Friend, go up higher"; then
you will be honoured in the presence of all who sit at table
1 with you. For every one who exalts himself will be humbled,
and he who humbles himself will be exalted.'
2 He said also to the man who had invited him, 'When you
give a dinner or a banquet, do not invite your friends or your
brothers or your kinsmen or rich neighbours, lest they also

[r] Other ancient authorities read *a son*

---

5 The other reading, 'a son' (RSV margin), instead of *an ass*, is preferable.

: 7–11 The chief places

For v. 11 see also 18^{14}; Matt. 23^{12}. For the danger of self-exaltation and outward show cp. 22^{25-27}; Matt. 6^{1-18}; Mark 8^{34}, 12^{39}.

7 The places of honour would be on the couches near the host.

1 The saying provides a convenient summary of the preceding teaching: self-renunciation is the way of status, especially with God, a principle lived out in Jesus himself (cp. Phil. 2^{5-11}).

: 12–14 Invitations

Cp. 6^{27-36}, and for Luke's interest in the poor cp. 16^{19-31}.

2 *lest . . . repaid*: it is easy to love those who return love, and to confine one's attention to them.

13 invite you in return, and you be repaid. But when you give a
14 feast, invite the poor, the maimed, the lame, the blind, and
you will be blessed, because they cannot repay you. You will
be repaid at the resurrection of the just.'
15 When one of those who sat at table with him heard this, he
said to him, 'Blessed is he who shall eat bread in the kingdom
16 of God!' But he said to him, 'A man once gave a great
17 banquet, and invited many; and at the time for the banquet

---

14 *blessed*: because such love is patterned on the generous love of God, and is not controlled by hope of return. There will, however, be a reward—a full life with God at *the resurrection of the just*. Jewish hope sometimes looked forward to the raising of the faithful people of God from the shadowy existence of Sheol to close fellowship with him (cp. Dan. 12^{1-4}), and so present injustices would be corrected. An anticipation of this resurrection of 'the just' or 'righteous' is seen in the resurrection of the 'righteous' Jesus.

14: 15–24 The great banquet

See also Matt. 22^{1-14}, which is best regarded as a separate parable with a similar theme. Apart from the theme of 'the meal', there is a link with vv. 1–14, because 'the resurrection of the just' (v. 14) and 'the kingdom of God' are closely connected, and 'the poor' (v. 13) again appear. One interpretation would stress the excuses: will people be ready for God's kingdom when it comes? Another would emphasize the kind of people that became the guests: they could merely accept the invitation without hope of giving hospitality in return; i.e. a place at the banquet of God's kingdom cannot be earned, but can only be accepted at the hands of God. But the main point seems to be the difficulty of finding guests for the banquet. The 'many' (v. 16) who were first invited were not attracted by the prospect (hence the trivial excuses), and the host has to go outside his immediate circle to find guests in the most unlikely quarters, and even 'compel' people to come. So far from the comment of the guest (v. 15) finding an echo in human hearts, human beings may not be eager to answer God's call and to pay the cost (see also vv. 25–33 below). The early Christians may have seen a further reference: even if the Jews reject the Gospel, those further afield, the Gentiles, will accept it.

15 A feast was a natural metaphor for the happiness of the new golden age, or *kingdom of God*. The guest may have wished to say the pious thing.

he sent his servant to say to those who had been invited,
18 "Come; for all is now ready." But they all alike began to
make excuses. The first said to him, "I have bought a field,
and I must go out and see it; I pray you, have me excused."
19 And another said, "I have bought five yoke of oxen, and I go
20 to examine them; I pray you, have me excused." And another
said, "I have married a wife, and therefore I cannot come."
21 So the servant came and reported this to his master. Then
the householder in anger said to his servant, "Go out quickly
to the streets and lanes of the city, and bring in the poor and
22 maimed and blind and lame." And the servant said, "Sir,
what you commanded has been done, and still there is room."
23 And the master said to the servant, "Go out to the highways
and hedges, and compel people to come in, that my house may
24 be filled. For I tell you, none of those men who were invited
shall taste my banquet." '
25 Now great multitudes accompanied him; and he turned

---

8 The *excuses*, humorous and frivolous, showed a casual treatment of the invitation. Inspection of the field would normally precede purchase! *have*, or 'consider'.

9 *examine* (or 'test') their capacity for farmwork, something done before purchase.

0 The Jewish law laid down certain regulations about the separation of newly-weds (Deut. 24^5) but they did not apply here.

1 The refusals could be thought an insult, especially if the host were senior in rank. *servant*, or 'slave'. The *householder* acts on the advice given by Jesus (vv. 12–14), but only as a last resort and under compulsion.

3 *compel*, or perhaps 'urge', but in any case the drastic measures needed are underlined.

: 25–35 The cost of discipleship

Discussion of entry into the kingdom of God, followed here by the theme of discipleship of Jesus, suggests that the two are closely

26 and said to them, 'If any one comes to me and does not hate
his own father and mother and wife and children and
brothers and sisters, yes, and even his own life, he cannot be
27 my disciple. Whoever does not bear his own cross and come
28 after me, cannot be my disciple. For which of you, desiring
to build a tower, does not first sit down and count the cost,
29 whether he has enough to complete it? Otherwise, when he
has laid a foundation, and is not able to finish, all who see it
30 begin to mock him, saying, "This man began to build, and
31 was not able to finish." Or what king, going to encounter
another king in war, will not sit down first and take counsel
whether he is able with ten thousand to meet him who comes
32 against him with twenty thousand? And if not, while the other
is yet a great way off, he sends an embassy and asks terms of
33 peace. So therefore, whoever of you does not renounce all
that he has cannot be my disciple.

---

connected. Most of the material in its present form is found only in Luke, though certain of its themes are found elsewhere.

25 The popularity of Jesus contrasts with the probable unpopularity of the demands that follow.

26–27 Cp. 9^{23}; Matt. 10^{37-38}; Mark 8^{34}. The severity of the saying sounds authentic. Jesus may have made this demand in different ways on different occasions. *hate* is a startling expression, because it seems to contradict the principle of love towards one's fellow human beings (6^{32-36}) and to rule out even self-love of the right kind (implicit in 10^{27}), and also because it seems to ignore the natural affection for kinsfolk, as well as the instinct for self-preservation. It is, however, a drastic way of saying that all one's closest attachments must be counted as nothing compared with one's loyalty to Jesus.

28–32 These illustrations occur only here; both underline the need to count the cost, and indicate the downright honesty of Jesus in stressing the price of discipleship. The *tower*: perhaps part of a vineyard (cp. Mark 12^{1}).

33 As renunciation of possessions has not been mentioned, *so therefore* is awkward; the sense probably is that in counting the cost this particular condition must not be forgotten (cp. 18^{18-25}). Luke may, however,

34 'Salt is good; but if salt has lost its taste, how shall its salt-
35 ness be restored? It is fit neither for the land nor for the dung-
hill; men throw it away. He who has ears to hear, let him
hear.'

15: Now the tax collectors and sinners were all drawing near

---

have inserted the saying from another context. The instruction applied to Jesus' close group of disciples in his earthly life; it was not generally practised by the early Christians, though the practice of Acts 2^{44-45} may have been based on it. The council of the Qumran community renounced their own possession of personal property and gave it into a common pool. *renounce*, or 'say farewell to'.

-35 See also Matt. 5^{13}; Mark 9^{15}. The salt produced by natural evaporation on the shores of the Dead Sea is never pure; when the dampness decomposes it, the residue is useless as a fertilizer. *lost its taste*: its property of seasoning. The metaphor suggests something that is effective, provided that it possesses its special characteristic, and probably describes discipleship, which depends for its effectiveness on its quality of renunciation.

5: 1–32 *The joy of finding what is lost*

The section contains three parables: (*a*) the lost sheep (vv. 3–7); (*b*) the lost coin (vv. 8–10); (*c*) the lost son (vv. 11–32). (*a*) and (*b*) are appeals to life situations; (*c*) is in the form of a story. The sequence is from loss of possessions to loss from the family circle of a valued son. For (*a*) see also Matt. 18^{12-14}, in a different context. (*b*) and (*c*) are found only in Luke. (*a*) and (*b*) are constructed on parallel lines. The context in Luke is the protest of the Jewish leaders and is likely to be original. All three parables make the point that, just as in ordinary life the recovery of something or someone lost is a joyful occasion, so the recovery of people who are 'lost' must bring God joy, 'lost' being a Jewish description of those alienated from God (Ps. 119^{176}; Jer. 50^{6}). Jesus may have intended other features of the parables to be important. In (*a*) and (*b*) the search for the sheep and the coin is sometimes taken to denote God's search for lost humanity, the first underlining the importance of the one lost person, the second the keenness of the search; but these may

2 to hear him. And the Pharisees and the scribes murmured,
saying, 'This man receives sinners and eats with them.'
3, 4 So he told them this parable: 'What man of you, having a
hundred sheep, if he has lost one of them, does not leave the
ninety-nine in the wilderness, and go after the one which is
5 lost, until he finds it? And when he has found it, he lays it on
6 his shoulders, rejoicing. And when he comes home, he calls
together his friends and his neighbours, saying to them,
"Rejoice with me, for I have found my sheep which was lost."
7 Just so, I tell you, there will be more joy in heaven over one
sinner who repents than over ninety-nine righteous persons
who need no repentance.
8 'Or what woman, having ten silver coins,[s] if she loses one

[s] The drachma, rendered here by *silver coin*, was about seven new pence

---

be incidental features. In (*c*) importance is sometimes attached to the change of heart in the son (thus stressing the need for repentance), and to the father's unqualified welcome of his son (pointing to God's unconditional acceptance of the sinner). Further, the elder brother's attitude may be intended to represent the Pharisaic position of 'justification by works'. All three parables contain a hint that Jesus has a special responsibility to recover 'the lost' (cp. 19^{10}).

15: 1–7 The search for the one lost sheep

4 Israel is often seen as the flock of God, and some may have taken this imagery (drawn from a familiar Palestinian scene) in that sense (cp. Ezek. 34). *wilderness*: the grassland.

7 *heaven* suggests the picture of God surrounded by his heavenly court of angels. *repent*: turns towards God. Jesus is not necessarily suggesting that there are such perfect people; there may be an ironic reference to the self-opinionated Pharisees. God's *joy* is connected with the achievement of his purpose (Isa. 62^5), which includes the recovery of 'the lost'. Jesus speaks with authority of the attitude of God, and challenges the Pharisees' viewpoint that there was joy before God when those who provoked him perished from the world.

15: 7–11 The search for the lost coin

8 Greek *silver coins*, or 'drachmas', had considerable purchasing power. The money may have formed part of the woman's dowry.

coin, does not light a lamp and sweep the house and seek
9 diligently until she finds it? And when she has found it, she
calls together her friends and neighbours, saying, "Rejoice
10 with me, for I have found the coin which I had lost." Just so,
I tell you, there is joy before the angels of God over one sinner
who repents.'

, 12 And he said, 'There was a man who had two sons; and the
younger of them said to his father, "Father, give me the share
of property that falls to me." And he divided his living be-
13 tween them. Not many days later, the younger son gathered
all he had and took his journey into a far country, and there
14 he squandered his property in loose living. And when he had
spent everything, a great famine arose in that country, and
15 he began to be in want. So he went and joined himself to one
of the citizens of that country, who sent him into his fields
16 to feed swine. And he would gladly have fed on[t] the pods that
17 the swine ate; and no one gave him anything. But when he
came to himself he said, "How many of my father's hired

[t] Other ancient authorities read *filled his belly with*

---

10 The *angels of God*, God's heavenly court, and his messengers to men, share his concern for human beings.

5: 11–32 The return of the lost son

2 Such a disposal of ancestral property is similar to that found in Indian traditions, where at the youngest son's majority any of the sons can demand a division of the property, the father taking one share, which passes to the eldest son on the father's death (cp. v. 31).

5 *swine*, together with the method of inheritance, suggests a non-Jewish setting.

6 'filled his belly with' (RSV margin) is preferable to *fed on. would gladly*: but could not bring himself to do it. *pods*: the fruit of the carob tree, yielding a bean nutritious for cattle and horses.

7 *came to himself*: to his senses. *hired*, or 'paid', *servants*: distinct from slaves who received no wages but belonged completely to their master.

servants have bread enough and to spare, but I perish here
18 with hunger! I will arise and go to my father, and I will say
to him, 'Father, I have sinned against heaven and before you;
19 I am no longer worthy to be called your son; treat me as one
20 of your hired servants.' " And he arose and came to his father.
But while he was yet at a distance, his father saw him and had
21 compassion, and ran and embraced him and kissed him. And
the son said to him, "Father, I have sinned against heaven
and before you; I am no longer worthy to be called your
22 son."[u] But the father said to his servants, "Bring quickly the
best robe, and put it on him; and put a ring on his hand, and
23 shoes on his feet; and bring the fatted calf and kill it, and let
24 us eat and make merry; for this my son was dead, and is alive
again; he was lost, and is found." And they began to make
merry.
25 'Now his elder son was in the field; and as he came and
26 drew near to the house, he heard music and dancing. And he
27 called one of the servants and asked what this meant. And he
said to him, "Your brother has come, and your father has

[u] Other ancient authorities add *treat me as one of your hired servants*

---

18 For the Jew sin was an act of rebellion against God. *before*, or, better, 'against' (NEB): he had let his father down by his lack of responsibility. Different prepositions (εἰς, ἐνωπίον) are used to distinguish the offence against God and the offence against man.

20 The father takes the initiative.

21 'treat me as one of your hired servants' (RSV margin) is probably an assimilation to v. 19.

22 The son is at once given the status and treatment due to an honoured son of the family.

23 The *fatted calf*: an animal specially fattened and used for an honoured guest.

24 *dead* and *lost*: partly because of his absence from the family circle and partly because of the degenerate life that he had lived. The repetition of *make merry* underlines the joy at recovery of the lost.

killed the fatted calf, because he has received him safe and
28 sound." But he was angry and refused to go in. His father
29 came out and entreated him, but he answered his father,
"Lo, these many years I have served you, and I never dis-
obeyed your command; yet you never gave me a kid, that I
30 might make merry with my friends. But when this son of
yours came, who has devoured your living with harlots, you
31 killed for him the fatted calf!" And he said to him, "Son, you
32 are always with me, and all that is mine is yours. It was fitting
to make merry and be glad, for this your brother was dead,
and is alive; he was lost, and is found." '

16: HE also said to the disciples, 'There was a rich man who

---

29 *a kid*: much less than the fatted calf.

30 *this son of yours*: he will not say 'my brother'. *harlots* have not been mentioned and so the accusation may be a malicious inference.

32 The father appreciates the qualities of his elder son, but this does not rule out joy at the recovery of the lost son.

16: 1–31 *Teaching on wealth and on the Law and the Prophets*

The section is a compilation of parables and sayings of Jesus, held together by certain key ideas and words. Most of the material is found only in Luke, but for vv. 13, 16, 17, and 18, see also Matt. 6^{24}, 11^{12-13}, $5^{18, 32}$. Two parables, one at the beginning and one at the end (vv. 1–9: vv. 19–31), hold the chapter together, while the intervening part is a series of sayings (vv. 10–18) divided by the reference to the Pharisees into two sets of three (vv. 10, 11–12, 13; vv. 15, 16–17, 18).

16: 1–9 The parable of the astute steward

Jesus takes an illustration from the selfish side of life: a man who summoned up all his astuteness and energy to secure his future. Verse 8 makes the point that if such a worldly person behaved like this, how much more should Jesus' followers direct their attention to securing their future—entry into God's kingdom and new age; v. 9 adds more

had a steward, and charges were brought to him that this
2 man was wasting his goods. And he called him and said to
him, "What is this that I hear about you? Turn in the account
3 of your stewardship, for you can no longer be steward." And
the steward said to himself, "What shall I do, since my master
is taking the stewardship away from me? I am not strong
4 enough to dig, and I am ashamed to beg. I have decided what
to do, so that people may receive me into their houses when
5 I am put out of the stewardship." So, summoning his master's
debtors one by one, he said to the first, "How much do you
6 owe my master?" He said, "A hundred measures of oil."
And he said to him, "Take your bill, and sit down quickly
7 and write fifty." Then he said to another, "And how much
do you owe?" He said, "A hundred measures of wheat." He

---

positive instruction on what this involves. The teaching is relevant to the disciples, whom Jesus had formed into a community to be ready for God's decisive intervention.

1 The *steward*, or 'bailiff', probably had wide discretionary powers as the manager of his master's farms let out to tenants. Not normally paid a salary, he made his own commission by fixing the rents at a suitable level. *wasting*, or 'squandering', could mean the misuse of the master's resources for his own interest, or the fixing of the tenants' rent so high that they were in danger of ruin, with resultant loss of revenue. *charges were brought*: perhaps by the tenants.

2-3 The employer found the charges convincing. Perhaps the manager was given so much notice, during which he had to *Turn in the account*, i.e. make up the balance sheet and final report. *I am not strong enough to dig*: perhaps a proverb used of shirking hard work. On the other hand, the man could not face turning professional beggar.

5 *into their houses*: the bailiff intends to secure a life of ease at least for the immediate future.

6 The rents were paid in kind, and the rebate may have been possible through reduction of the bailiff's own commission. The clients' trust seems surprising, but perhaps the news of the manager's impending departure was not yet known, or they were ready to grasp any concessions. *bill*: the original agreement about the rent.

8 said to him, "Take your bill, and write eighty." The master
commended the dishonest steward for his prudence; for the
sons of this world[v] are wiser in their own generation than the
9 sons of light. And I tell you, make friends for yourselves by
means of unrighteous mammon, so that when it fails they
may receive you into the eternal habitations.

[v] Greek *age*

---

8 *the master*, lit. 'the lord' (ὁ κύριος), could refer (*a*) to Jesus, or (*b*) to the employer. Against (*a*) it is urged that Jesus would not have approved of such a character; but by his very use of the illustration Jesus is giving approval at least to the man's astuteness. More telling is the literary consideration. If (*a*) is correct, then the parable ends with v. 7; in 8a we pass into narrative; and finally, without any preparatory 'and he said' there follow further words of Jesus, an awkward and unlikely sequence. (*b*) is, therefore, more probable, 'lord' or *master* having already been used of the employer (vv. 3, 5). Perhaps the latter *commended* his bailiff because: (i) 'one rogue knows another', and the master, himself adept at underhand dealings, felt a 'sneaking regard' for his clever employee; or (ii) at the cost of his own commission the bailiff reached a settlement, and so his master's revenue was assured. *this world*, or, better, 'age' (RSV margin), is dominated by powers hostile to God and by human selfishness and materialism. The bailiff belongs to it and represents its viewpoint. The *sons of light*, also a description of the members of the Qumran community, who are involved in God's conflict with the darkness of evil, can now be applied to Jesus' disciples, as the recipients of God's secrets and the witnesses of God's decisive intervention (cp. 1 Thess. 5^{5}). *in their own generation*: in their dealings with their own kind, and in their own limited sphere.

9 The saying (originally perhaps in another context) may have been placed here because it echoes themes of the parable, e.g. 'make friends' and 'receive'. *unrighteous mammon*: wealth that can be used for selfish purposes. It is to be redeemed and used for God through acts of charity, and then it becomes the stepping-stone to something more permanent, *the eternal habitations*, the age to come, with its full fellowship with God. *friends* could refer to God, or to the people helped by one's charity, who in the day of judgement will witness to one's unselfish use of money (cp. Matt. 25^{34-41}).

10 'He who is faithful in a very little is faithful also in much;
and he who is dishonest in a very little is dishonest also in
11 much. If then you have not been faithful in the unrighteous
12 mammon, who will entrust to you the true riches? And if you
have not been faithful in that which is another's, who will
13 give you that which is your own? No servant can serve two
masters; for either he will hate the one and love the other, or

---

16: 10–13 The faithfulness required in disciples

Trustworthiness and loyalty are the common themes of this collection of sayings, and contrast with the bailiff's lack of these qualities; 'mammon' connects vv. 11–12 and v. 13, and looks back to v. 9.

10 The real test of faithfulness is seen in performance of the least important things.

11 The *true*, or 'real', riches: a part in the carrying out of God's purposes. Originally the warning may have been aimed at the tax collectors and the rich who had not been scrupulous over money matters, and who wished to join Jesus.

12 The problems are: (*a*) the meaning of *that which is another's*, or 'that which is foreign'; and (*b*) the interpretation of *your own*, or 'our own' (an alternative reading). The background may be that of inheritance: there may be reluctance to entrust the heir with the property due to him, if he has not shown himself responsible with property that does not belong to him. The real test of loyalty is found in concern for others' interests, here the cause of God. On the other hand, if the parallelism with v. 11 is stressed then the meaning might be: if there has been unfaithfulness in dealing with 'that which is foreign', i.e. worldly wealth and not your real wealth, there may be reluctance to entrust to you that which is *your own* (or 'our own') proper riches, the responsibilities of service of God. Perhaps vv. 10–12 are aimed at any easy-going professions of loyalty to Jesus: if this quality is not present in ordinary life, it cannot be expected in the service of God.

13 See also Matt. 6[24]. A hired servant could presumably be employed by different masters, but such a divided allegiance would invite comparison between the two, one calling out more affection than the other. Similarly, there is an incompatibility between giving ultimate allegiance both to God and to the acquisition of money, because obsession with the latter gives priority to material gain and self, and so leaves no room for God and his demands.

he will be devoted to the one and despise the other. You cannot serve God and mammon.'

14 The Pharisees, who were lovers of money, heard all this,
15 and they scoffed at him. But he said to them, 'You are those who justify yourselves before men, but God knows your hearts; for what is exalted among men is an abomination in the sight of God.

16 'The law and the prophets were until John; since then the

16: 14–15 The Pharisees are answered

14 Only Luke describes the Pharisees as *lovers of money* (cp. 20[47]).

15 *justify yourselves*: make a good name for yourselves. A distinction is drawn between the superficial human estimate, based on outward appearance, and that of God, who sees into the innermost being (cp. 1 Sam. 16[7]). Before *for . . . God* some such phrase as 'and judges you accordingly' is understood. *what is exalted*, i.e. what is often given status in human judgement, *is an abomination*, i.e. the worship of a false god. An alternative, but less likely, translation would be 'what is exalted within men', i.e. human pride.

16: 16–18 The Law and the Prophets

These three sayings, loosely connected by the theme of 'law', have been brought together by Luke or at an earlier time. Their introduction at this point might suggest a looseness in Luke's arrangement of his material, but, strikingly, both here and in vv. 19–31 a warning on the dangers of wealth is followed by reference to 'the law and the prophets'. First, the Pharisees' concern with themselves is contrasted with the concern of prior importance, i.e. the revelation of God through the Mosaic Law and the prophetic writings, and the extension of that revelation now taking place. Secondly, the brothers of Lazarus need to attend to God's demands in 'the law and the prophets', if they are to be saved from themselves. In each case attention to the special revelation to Israel is the starting-point for turning away from self to God.

16 *until*, according to normal N.T. usage, means 'up to but not including': John's ministry is not part of the era of *the law and the prophets*, but is part of the new era of God now being initiated. *enters it violently*, or 'forces his way in', could suggest an eager rush to respond to the good news, which is contrary to the Gospel picture. Another translation might, however, be: 'acts with violence against', a

good news of the kingdom of God is preached, and every one
17 enters it violently. But it is easier for heaven and earth to pass
away, than for one dot of the law to become void.
18 'Every one who divorces his wife and marries another commits adultery, and he who marries a woman divorced from her husband commits adultery.
19 'There was a rich man, who was clothed in purple and fine

---

reference to the opposition to Jesus' message (cp. Matt. 11^{11-13}, a similar saying spoken perhaps on a different occasion). John is in prison, or is even by now put to death, but the proclamation of the good news goes on in the person of Jesus, for whom John prepares the way.

17 See also Matt. 5^{18}. The assurance about the Law's permanence forms a paradoxical contrast with v. 16. *one dot*: a projection on letters of the Hebrew script, used metaphorically of something insignificant. For God's creation as a symbol of permanence cp. Ps. 104^{5}. The meaning is not that every regulation of the *law* will be binding for ever, but that the Law's whole aim and purpose, so far from losing its force, will find its full expression and completion in the new order (cp. Matt. 5^{21-48}, where the moral laws of the O.T. have their deeper meaning drawn out; similarly the O.T. sacrificial system was seen by the early Christians to receive its fulfilment in the perfect sacrifice of Jesus on the cross).

18 See also Matt. 5^{32}, 19^{9}; Mark 10^{11}. Luke omits the discussion about divorce in Mark 10^{1-12}, but inserts this saying on divorce here, as an example of how the Law does not 'become void' but has its true spirit drawn out by Jesus. From the theme of putting aside the Law, we pass to that of putting aside the wife by divorce, which is treated (as in Jewish Law) as the prerogative of the husband. The lifelong nature of the marriage bond is stressed by the unanimous teaching of the Gospels that remarriage after divorce is a form of adultery (cp. 1 Cor. 7^{10-11}). Here the saying may also stress that God in introducing his new order is not 'divorcing' his people Israel (cp. Jer. 3^{8}).

16: 19–31 The rich man and Lazarus

The story, found only in Luke, links up with vv. 1–18 because of its theme of wealth, and of 'the law and the prophets'. Jesus may be using a popular fable. There are three divisions to the story: (*a*) the reversal of the two men's positions in the after-life, with the thought that obsession with wealth has no future (vv. 19–23); (*b*) the rich man's

20 linen and who feasted sumptuously every day. And at his
21 gate lay a poor man named Lazarus, full of sores, who desired
to be fed with what fell from the rich man's table; moreover
22 the dogs came and licked his sores. The poor man died and
was carried by the angels to Abraham's bosom. The rich man
23 also died and was buried; and in Hades, being in torment, he
lifted up his eyes, and saw Abraham far off and Lazarus in
24 his bosom. And he called out, "Father Abraham, have mercy
upon me, and send Lazarus to dip the end of his finger in

---

continuing sense of his own privileged position, shown in his request for special treatment for himself and his brothers, and in his view of Lazarus as one who exists purely to serve his own ends (vv. 24 and 27); (*c*) the refusal of special privilege to the brothers, for whom, as for others, 'the law and the prophets' is the meeting-point with God. The important theme is that wealth has no lasting value and does not carry rights: God deals with the rich as with others. The story is not giving detailed instructions about the after-life.

9 *purple* suggests high position. *sumptuously* is emphatic.

0 *Lazarus*: a form of Eleazar. *gate* (πυλῶν) suggests an important residence. *sores*, or 'ulcers'.

1 *what fell . . . table*: the pieces of bread, used by the guests to wipe their fingers, and then thrown into the street. *desired*: would have been glad. The beggar did not always obtain this satisfaction. The *dogs* would be the wild street dogs: does this mean that he was at their mercy, or that this was the only mark of affection that he received?

3 Cp. 2 Esd. 7^{75-101}, in which *Hades*, or Sheol, the place of the departed, becomes the temporary abode of both righteous and wicked, where each experience a foretaste of their final destiny: in the case of the wicked, torment, in the case of the righteous, rest and contentment. Abraham and the patriarchs were thought to enjoy a living relationship with God (cp. 20^{37-38}; 4 Macc. 16^{25}); Abraham is seen here as a protector of an oppressed member of the nation whose ancestor-founder he is.

mercy, or 'pity': a quality which the rich man expected for himself, but which he had not shown to Lazarus. In vv. 19–21 there is no indication that the two had ever met. In 2 Esdras seven torments for the wicked are mentioned.

water and cool my tongue; for I am in anguish in this flame."
25 But Abraham said, "Son, remember that you in your lifetime
received your good things, and Lazarus in like manner evil
things; but now he is comforted here, and you are in anguish.
26 And besides all this, between us and you a great chasm has
been fixed, in order that those who would pass from here to
you may not be able, and none may cross from there to us."
27 And he said, "Then I beg you, father, to send him to my
28 father's house, for I have five brothers, so that he may warn
29 them, lest they also come into this place of torment." But
Abraham said, "They have Moses and the prophets; let them
30 hear them." And he said, "No, father Abraham; but if
some one goes to them from the dead, they will repent."
31 He said to him, "If they do not hear Moses and the prophets,
neither will they be convinced if some one should rise from
the dead." '

---

25 The injustices of this world do not go unnoticed by God. The *anguish* may include the self-knowledge of his former wasted life. *son*: he is addressed affectionately as a member of Abraham's family. Thus the note of compassion is not lacking: the rich man's torment may be remedial, to bring home to him the folly of his self-centredness.

26 *the great chasm* perhaps symbolizes the gulf created between the rich man and God.

27 *house*, or 'family': presumably the five brothers were men of wealth and self-centred like their brother.

29 *Moses*: the Jewish Law.

30 *if . . . dead*: Lazarus. This would be a miraculous event, in view of the common belief that no one came back *from the dead* (Job 10^{21-22}, 14^{12}), and so might startle them into repentance.

31 Unless the brothers already have a desire to serve God by response to his existing revelation of himself, a sudden miraculous event will not suddenly work a transformation. In the early Church the saying would be related to Jesus' resurrection from the dead, which only makes sense if seen as part of the fulfilment of God's purposes, to which the O.T. scriptures look forward (cp. 24^{13-49}).

17: AND he said to his disciples, 'Temptations to sin[w] are sure
2 to come; but woe to him by whom they come! It would be
better for him if a millstone were hung round his neck and he
were cast into the sea, than that he should cause one of these
3 little ones to sin.[x] Take heed to yourselves; if your brother
4 sins, rebuke him, and if he repents, forgive him; and if he
sins against you seven times in the day, and turns to you
seven times, and says, "I repent," you must forgive him.'

[w] Greek *stumbling blocks* [x] Greek *stumble*

17: 1–19 *Further instructions to the disciples; the one thankful leper*

17: 1–10 Teaching on stumbling-blocks and duty

Jesus introduces two sayings, and then gives two more in response to the disciples' request (v. 5). Verses 7–10 are found only in Luke, while teaching similar to that of the other verses is found in (*a*) Matt. 18^{6-7}; Mark 9^{42}; (*b*) Matt. $18^{15, 21-22}$; (*c*) Matt. 17^{20}, 21^{21}; Mark 11^{22-23}. We probably have here a collection of independent sayings brought together for convenience.

1–2 The danger of riches, just stressed, perhaps leads to this theme of *temptations to sin*, or 'stumbling-blocks' (RSV margin)—obstacles that come between God and the recognition of his purposes. Originally the warning may have been applied to the Pharisees and Jewish leaders who were deterring the people (*these little ones*) from serious attention to Jesus; perhaps it was then reapplied to the leaders of the early Church in their responsibilities to their flock, and also to the individual members of the Church in their relations with others (cp. Rom. 14^{33}; 1 Cor. 8). *millstone*: a heavy stone in a large mill, which was worked by donkey power. The picture in a drastic way stresses the seriousness of being a bad influence. *these little ones*: small in influence and position, and needing the help and guidance of others.

3–4 *take heed to yourselves* could refer back to vv. 1–2, or (as intended by RSV) to what follows. The disciples by their lack of forgivingness can cause stumbling-blocks, in thus encouraging bad relationships. *brother*: referring in Jesus' lifetime to one of his intimate group or to a fellow Jew, and in the early Church to a fellow Christian. *your* is singular, and so are *rebuke* and *forgive* (cp. Deut. 11^{18}): Jesus is la this command on each of his followers. *sins*: does you a wrong. *rebuke*: the offence has to be brought into the open and cleared up. *repents*: expresses his regret. No limit can be set to attempts at reconciliation.

5, 6 The apostles said to the Lord, 'Increase our faith!' And the
Lord said, 'If you had faith as a grain of mustard seed, you
could say to this sycamine tree, "Be rooted up, and be planted
in the sea," and it would obey you.

7 'Will any one of you, who has a servant ploughing or keeping sheep, say to him when he has come in from the field,
8 "Come at once and sit down at table"? Will he not rather say
to him, "Prepare supper for me, and gird yourself and serve
me, till I eat and drink; and afterward you shall eat and drink"?
9 Does he thank the servant because he did what was com-
10 manded? So you also, when you have done all that is commanded you, say, "We are unworthy servants; we have only
done what was our duty." '

11 On the way to Jerusalem he was passing along between

5–6 The use of *sycamine tree*, probably a mulberry tree, as a metaphor of something firmly fixed, instead of the more usual 'mountain', suggests the authenticity of the saying. *Increase our faith*, or perhaps 'give us faith', i.e. such trust in God as to accept the demands of the God-centred life. *a grain of mustard seed*, proverbially the smallest of seeds: a fraction of the right kind of faith would have big results.

7–10 The theme of obedience (v. 6) is taken further, and the thought of 'faith' is succeeded by that of 'action'. The disciples have no reason for pride in being chosen to play an important part in God's plans. The illustration from everyday life teaches that service of God is not a subject for God's congratulation and gratitude. Even if, hypothetically, one carried out all God's commands perfectly, it would not constitute merit, as in obeying God human beings are only performing the function assigned to them in the universe.

17: 11–19 The one thankful leper

The incident continues the theme, gratitude of (v. 9), which is in place as a response to God's goodness. The interest lies in the reaction of the Samaritan (vv. 15–16) and in Jesus' comment (vv. 17–18). His approval of a non-Jew ('this foreigner', v. 18) typifies for Luke the later reception of Gentiles into the Church, and the Samaritan's burst of praise (v. 16) also anticipates the later joy of the Samaritan and Gentile convert (cp. Acts $8^{8, 39}$, 16^{34}).

12 Samaria and Galilee. And as he entered a village, he was met
13 by ten lepers, who stood at a distance and lifted up their
14 voices and said, 'Jesus, Master, have mercy on us.' When he
saw them he said to them, 'Go and show yourselves to the
15 priests.' And as they went they were cleansed. Then one of
them, when he saw that he was healed, turned back, praising
16 God with a loud voice; and he fell on his face at Jesus' feet,
17 giving him thanks. Now he was a Samaritan. Then said Jesus,
18 'Were not ten cleansed? Where are the nine? Was no one
found to return and give praise to God except this foreigner?'
19 And he said to him, 'Rise and go your way; your faith has
made you well.'
20 Being asked by the Pharisees when the kingdom of God

---

11 The note suggests that Jesus is on the border where Samaria adjoins Galilee.

12 The lepers observe the Jewish Law by standing at a distance.

13 The personal address *Jesus* is unusual.

14 The lepers are asked to make the leap of faith and behave as if they were already cured.

16 *fell on his face*: in recognition of his debt to Jesus. *Samaritan* comes in dramatically and singles out this non-Jew from the rest. In face of a common plight old animosities had been forgotten.

18 *give praise*: acknowledge the mighty power of God at work in Jesus.

17: 20–18: 8 *The kingdom of God and the coming of the Son of man*

17^{20-21} (peculiar to Luke) is linked to 17^{22-24} (see also Matt. 24^{26-27}) by the similar language of vv. 21 and 23, while 17^{26-30} (partly parallel to Matt. 24^{37-39}) continues the theme of suddenness and of the Son of man. 17^{31-33} (see also Matt. 25^{17-18}; Mark 13^{15-16}) is joined to the preceding verses by the reference to 'day' and to 'Lot's wife', while 17^{33} (see also Matt. 10^{39}; Mark 8^{35}; cp. above, 9^{24}) continues the theme of decisive response. 17^{34-35} (partly parallel to Matt. 24^{40}) links up with 17^{31}, 'in that night' contrasting with 'on that day', while 17^{37} (see also Matt. 24^{28}) results from the question of the audience. 18^{1-8}

was coming, he answered them, 'The kingdom of God is not
21 coming with signs to be observed; nor will they say, "Lo,
here it is!" or "There!" for behold, the kingdom of God is in
the midst of you.'[y]

[y] Or *within you*

(only recorded by Luke) continues the theme of the coming of God's kingdom and the vindication of God's faithful people. The passage is best regarded as a collection of separate sayings of Jesus, and is sited to follow the incident of 17^{11-19}, which would be viewed as a sign of the presence of God's kingdom.

17: 20–21 The kingdom of God

20–21 This subject was a vital part of Jesus' message, and so the question—a topical one—was natural. Jesus' reply consists of a contrast, the nature of which depends on the interpretation of 'for behold . . . in the midst of you' (ἰδοὺ γάρ ἡ βασιλεία τοῦ Θεοῦ ἐντὸς ὑμῶν ἐστίν), which can be variously explained. (*a*) 'for suddenly the kingdom of God will be in the midst of you', ἐντός meaning 'in the midst of' or 'among', and ἐστίν representing a future tense: it will not be possible to see advance signs and evidence of the kingdom's coming (a reference to the Jewish idea that signs will herald 'the end'), because it will come suddenly—an explanation linking up with vv. 22–27 below. But ἐστίν does not necessarily stand for a future tense, and 'suddenly' has to be awkwardly introduced. *with signs to be observed* is lit. 'with observation', and may not refer to advance signs, but to the kingdom's not being found in the visible and observable. (*b*) 'for behold the kingdom of God is in the midst of you' (RSV): it is not something to be detected approaching in the future, but is already present with the coming of Jesus. But the supposed contrast between present and future is forced: in the first part of the saying the emphasis is not on the future aspect of the kingdom, but on the fact that it is not something that can be observed or located. Further, against (*a*) and (*b*) it is questionable whether ἐντός can mean 'among', or 'within your grasp', the other suggested translation. (*c*) 'for behold, the kingdom of God is within you' (*so* AV): ἐντός then has its well-attested meaning of 'within', and there is a telling contrast with the first part of the verse. Jesus is rejecting the popular conception of an outward and localized kingdom, involving the overthrow of Israel's enemies: the decisive factor will be one of inward response to certain events that are taking place and will take place, and that centre on Jesus.

22 And he said to the disciples, 'The days are coming when
you will desire to see one of the days of the Son of man, and
23 you will not see it. And they will say to you, "Lo, there!" or
24 "Lo, here!" Do not go, do not follow them. For as the lightning flashes and lights up the sky from one side to the other,
25 so will the Son of man be in his day.[z] But first he must suffer
26 many things and be rejected by this generation. As it was in
the days of Noah, so will it be in the days of the Son of man.

[z] Other ancient authorities omit *in his day*

17: 22–37 The coming of the Son of man

The disciples are to be ready for the final achievement of God's purposes.

22 *one of the days* might imply that there were various such days or decisive moments, i.e. the transfiguration, the resurrection, the ascension. This thought is unexampled elsewhere, and there may be no difference of meaning between 'the days of the Son of man' and 'the day of the Son of man' (vv. 24–26), 'days' meaning 'the time of one's activity'. *one of the days of the Son of man* might, therefore, mean 'the slightest indication of the Son of man's final activity'. Suffering and persecution will have to be endured without the immediate hope of vindication.

24 The contrast is between something elusive and something, such as lightning, that travels from one end of the horizon to the other and makes itself clearly visible: the Son of man will make his final and triumphant presence known without room for doubt. *his day*: 'the day of the Lord' (cp. Amos 5^{18}) now becomes 'the day of the Son of man', as the latter is the agent of God in the achieving of his purposes.

25 Cp. 9^{22}. The saying, which may owe its present position to Luke, stresses that the vital activity of the Son of man in the near future will be his suffering.

30 There is a parallelism between vv. 26–27 and vv. 28–30. The main point is the contrast between the normal existence of one moment and the thoroughgoing and sudden intervention of God at the next. The teaching is aimed at both complacency and despair, engendered by the thought that things seem to be going on as ever and that God's judgement seems far away (cp. 2 Pet. 3^{3-4}). The early Christians had to live in the tension between a normal organized existence and readiness for a sudden end to the present order. For *Noah* see Gen. 7–9,

27 They ate, they drank, they married, they were given in
marriage, until the day when Noah entered the ark, and the
28 flood came and destroyed them all. Likewise as it was in the
days of Lot—they ate, they drank, they bought, they sold,
29 they planted, they built, but on the day when Lot went out
from Sodom fire and brimstone rained from heaven and
30 destroyed them all—so will it be on the day when the Son of
31 man is revealed. On that day, let him who is on the housetop,
with his goods in the house, not come down to take them
away; and likewise let him who is in the field not turn back.
32, 33 Remember Lot's wife. Whoever seeks to gain his life will
34 lose it, but whoever loses his life will preserve it. I tell you,
in that night there will be two men in one bed; one will be
35 taken and the other left. There will be two women grinding
37 together; one will be taken and the other left.'[a] And they

[a] Other ancient authorities add verse 36, '*Two men will be in the field; one will be taken and the other left*'

---

and for *Lot* see Gen. 19. *all* (vv. 27 and 29) is emphatic, stressing the completeness of the catastrophe. *revealed*: a term used of the final coming of Jesus in triumph (cp. 2 Thess. 1^{7}).

31 See also Matt. 24^{17-18}; Mark 13^{15-16}, where a similar saying is in the context of the fall of Jerusalem: here it reinforces the theme of readiness for the day of the Son of man. *let him . . . back*: cp. Gen. 19^{26}.

32 *Lot's wife*, as a result of her disobedience, was turned into a pillar of salt.

33 The saying (cp. 9^{24}) is inserted here to underline the sense of urgency needed to be ready for the triumph of God's purposes.

34–35 The saying is a couplet, the first part about men, the second about women. One interpretation is that this was originally Jesus' description of how some respond to his challenge and others do not. *in that night* suggests the night of judgement created by the coming of the Son of man. This will cause a division between people who on the human level are equal and closely associated. *taken*: perhaps in the sense of being received into the presence of the risen Christ in the day of his triumph (cp. 21^{36}; see also John 14^{3}).

36 This verse (RSV margin) is an assimilation to Matt. 24^{40}.

37 *where* may be related to the place of the Son of man's appearance.

said to him, 'Where, Lord?' He said to them, 'Where the
body is, there the eagles[b] will be gathered together.'

18: AND he told them a parable, to the effect that they ought
2 always to pray and not lose heart. He said, 'In a certain city
there was a judge who neither feared God not regarded man;
3 and there was a widow in that city who kept coming to him
4 and saying, "Vindicate me against my adversary." For a
while he refused; but afterward he said to himself, "Though
5 I neither fear God nor regard man, yet because this widow
bothers me, I will vindicate her, or she will wear me out by

[b] Or *vultures*

Jesus will not give a direct answer, his reply sounding like a proverb of inevitability: the decisive point is the sureness of the Son of man's coming. *eagles*, or 'vultures', have an uncanny ability to detect a corpse or carcass.

: 1–8 The parable of the unscrupulous judge

The themes of 'vindication' and of 'the Son of man' form a link with 17^{22-37}. Verse 1 might suggest that the purpose is to teach persistence in prayer to God, but the words 'and not lose heart' imply that the prayer meant is for the coming of the Son of man and God's kingdom. The argument is: even the unscrupulous judge in the end heeded the widow's plea, and saw that she had her rights; how much greater is the certainty that in answer to human prayers for vindication God will do the right by his loyal followers, an assurance later reinforced by God's vindication of Jesus at his resurrection. In the early Church the parable would be a message of hope in time of persecution.

them: probably the disciples.

adversary: an opponent in a lawsuit, against whom the widow was bringing claims. *vindicate me*: see that I get justice.

refused: perhaps he knew that the widow had no influence and might be ignored with impunity.

or . . . coming: lit. 'lest coming she finally wears me out'. The last verb can mean 'give a black eye': the judge may have feared actual violence.

6 her continual coming." ' And the Lord said, 'Hear what the
7 unrighteous judge says. And will not God vindicate his elect,
who cry to him day and night? Will he delay long over them?
8 I tell you, he will vindicate them speedily. Nevertheless, when
the Son of man comes, will he find faith on earth?'
9 He also told this parable to some who trusted in themselves

---

6 *the Lord*: Jesus.

7 For such prayers cp., e.g., Ps. 43^{1}, and for *cry . . . day and night* cp. Ps. 88^{1}. *his elect*: used of Israel, or of a group within Israel, selected for God's purposes, and now of the followers of Jesus (cp. Col. 3^{12}). *Will he delay long over them?*: before vindicating their cause. The alternative translation 'while he listens patiently to them' does not fit in very well with the note of urgency.

9 The reference must be to a coming of *the Son of man* in the future, and not to one which has already taken place in the mission of Jesus. The saying, perhaps originally in another context, forms a fitting conclusion to a section dealing with the Son of man. God's vindication of his cause will surely come, but, tragically, will also throw into relief human lack of loyalty to him.

18: 9–30 *A parable; the children brought to Jesus; the ruler's question; the future reward*

The qualities of a right relationship with God, and the conditions of entry into his kingdom, are now discussed. The themes of 'kingdom' (17^{20}) and of 'faith' (18^{8}) are thus continued. The opening parable is found only in Luke, while in 18^{15-30} the use of Mark is resumed.

18: 9–14 The Pharisee and the tax collector

The story is based on a contrast between the first character, who typified the religious man, and the second, who typified 'the sinner' or 'religious outcast'. Jesus reverses contemporary opinion by suggesting that the latter had something to teach the former, the less respectable character being again put forward as an example. Morally the tax collector was not as good as the Pharisee, but in his attitude to God he was sounder: in contrast with the Pharisee and his self-satisfied boastfulness, he realized his creatureliness before God, while the other almost treated God as an equal and failed to realize that he was only giving God his just due (cp. 17^{10}). One's relationship to God cannot be based on a sense of one's own merit (cp. Rom. 1–3).

10 that they were righteous and despised others: 'Two men went
up into the temple to pray, one a Pharisee and the other a tax
11 collector. The Pharisee stood and prayed thus with himself,
"God, I thank thee that I am not like other men, extortioners,
12 unjust, adulterers, or even like this tax collector. I fast twice
13 a week, I give tithes of all that I get." But the tax collector,
standing far off, would not even lift up his eyes to heaven, but
beat his breast, saying, "God, be merciful to me a sinner!"
14 I tell you, this man went down to his house justified rather
than the other; for every one who exalts himself will be
humbled, but he who humbles himself will be exalted.'

---

9 *righteous*: in the sense both of carrying out God's law and of being right with him. The *others* (shockingly enough!) can give a lesson to the Pharisees.

10 *prayed*: another link with 18^{1-8}.

11 *with himself*, or 'to himself', underlines the concern of the Pharisee with himself, and suggests that he was addressing himself rather than God. The alternative 'by himself' would bring out his aloofness. *stood*: the normal position of prayer, perhaps also denoting the man's self-assured stance. Not all Pharisees were guilty of pride, nor did all tax collectors show contrition: Jesus is contrasting two extremes that he has experienced. The Pharisee made the mistake of comparing himself with others. *not like other men*, or perhaps 'not like the rest of mankind'. *extortioners*: thus breaking the tenth commandment (Exod. 20^{14}). *even*, or 'also'.

12 The tithing of all income was not required: the Pharisee gave more generously than was stipulated by the rules.

13 *far off*: at a distance from the Pharisee, whom he felt unworthy to approach. *lift up . . . heaven*: he would not dare to face God. *beat*, or 'kept beating', an expression of sorrow. *be merciful*: a term connected with reconciliation to God, who alone can heal the breach.

14 *I tell you*: introducing a provocative comment. *justified*, or 'right with God'. The concluding saying (cp. 14^{11}) may be Jesus' further comment, or may be a separately preserved saying placed here to round off the parable: it leads to the theme of self-renunciation in vv. 15–30.

15 Now they were bringing even infants to him that he might
touch them; and when the disciples saw it, they rebuked
16 them. But Jesus called them to him, saying, 'Let the children
come to me, and do not hinder them; for to such belongs the
17 kingdom of God. Truly, I say to you, whoever does not
receive the kingdom of God like a child shall not enter it.'
18 And a ruler asked him, 'Good Teacher, what shall I do to
19 inherit eternal life?' And Jesus said to him, 'Why do you call

---

18: 15–17 Jesus' reaction to the children

Luke returns to his use of Mark (probably for the first time since 9^{50}) but omits Mark 9^{41}–10^{12} (cp. however, above, 14^{34-35}, 16^{12}, 17^{1-2}). This and the following two incidents (vv. 18–27 and vv. 28–30) share the theme of self-negation, and lead to the third prediction of Jesus' death (vv. 31–34).

15 *infants*, or 'babes': the parallel in Mark and Matthew, 'children', can also be used of infants as well as older children, and Luke retains it in v. 16. *even*: suggesting that not only people who could walk came to Jesus, but also young children who had to be carried. *touch*: give them his blessing. The disciples meant to spare Jesus trouble, or thought that babies were beneath his notice.

16 Language similar to *do not hinder them* is sometimes used in connection with baptism (e.g. Acts 8^{36}, 10^{47}), but it is unlikely to be in view here. *such*: people who are like these babies. *belongs* suggests that the kingdom of God is a present reality with the coming of Jesus.

17 *like a child*: if a particular characteristic of children is being singled out, it is probably their dependence and their readiness to trust others. But Jesus may be saying that entry into the kingdom of God involves beginning life all over again, starting like a baby or child (cp. John 3^{3-5}). *receive*: the kingdom is something offered by God.

18: 18–27 The rich ruler: the danger of riches

'eternal life' (v. 18) links closely with the preceding theme of 'the kingdom of God'. The incident not only illustrates the uncompromising demands of Jesus, but implies that the way to eternal life is through discipleship of him and not merely through observance of the Jewish Law.

18 Only Luke calls him a *ruler*, or 'elder'.

19 Jesus is not disclaiming goodness, but is asking the speaker's meaning in using so glibly a term which, though sometimes applied to man

20 me good? No one is good but God alone. You know the
commandments: "Do not commit adultery, Do not kill, Do
not steal, Do not bear false witness, Honour your father and
21 mother."' And he said, 'All these I have observed from my
22 youth.' And when Jesus heard it, he said to him, 'One thing
you still lack. Sell all that you have and distribute to the poor,
and you will have treasure in heaven; and come, follow me.'
23 But when he heard this he became sad, for he was very rich.
24 Jesus looking at him said, 'How hard it is for those who have
25 riches to enter the kingdom of God! For it is easier for a camel
to go through the eye of a needle than for a rich man to enter
26 the kingdom of God.' Those who heard it said, 'Then who
27 can be saved?' But he said, 'What is impossible with men is

---

(e.g. in Prov. 14^{14}), Jesus feels is a suitable description only of God (cp. Ps. 135^{3}).

20 The ten *commandments* (Exod. 20^{1-17}; Deut. 5^{6-21}) are here regarded as summing up the demands of the Jewish Law. Jesus is testing the man: 'You know the moral law of the O.T.; is not observance of that sufficient to gain your end?'

1 This was said probably with sincerity and without boasting.

2 Jesus' demand tests the man's willingness to sacrifice in the service of God; so far, his very circumstances had made it easy for him to keep the moral law. *treasure in heaven*: the wealth of pleasing God, contrasted with material wealth. The acceptance of Jesus' challenge would have meant beginning life afresh (cp. above, v. 17).

3 The omission of reference to the man's departure softens his refusal.

5 The *camel*, a symbol of something very large, is contrasted with *the eye of a needle*, something very small. The saying is probably a proverbial expression denoting an impossibility. The interpretation of *the eye of a needle* as 'a postern gate' lacks evidence, while the alternative reading 'cable' for *camel* is not original, being the result of failure to realize the proverbial nature of the expression.

The question strangely suggests that rich men should find entrance into the kingdom easy. Perhaps the hearers held the view that possession of riches indicated the favour of God. *saved*: find full fellowship with God in his kingdom.

Human self-centredness and other obstacles can be broken down only by God.

28 possible with God.' And Peter said, 'Lo, we have left our
29 homes and followed you.' And he said to them, 'Truly, I
say to you, there is no man who has left house or wife or
brothers or parents or children, for the sake of the kingdom
30 of God, who will not receive manifold more in this time, and
in the age to come eternal life.'
31 And taking the twelve, he said to them, 'Behold, we are

18: 28–30 The reward of self-sacrifice

28 The disciples' conduct contrasts with that of the rich man. Peter is really asking about the reward of discipleship (cp. Matt. 19^{27}). Instead of 'all' (Matthew and Mark) Luke has *homes*, or, better, 'possessions', and so makes a parallel with 'all that you have' (18^{22}).

29 Luke adds *wife*, but does not refer to 'lands' (cp. 14^{26}). *for the sake of the kingdom of God* replaces 'for my sake and the Gospel's' (Mark), and so brings the language into line with the preceding discussion with no difference of meaning.

30 *manifold more*, or 'many times more': including the knowledge of furthering the purposes of God, and also the reception into a new family, the community of Jesus. We note that Jesus claims authority to pronounce on these future rewards.

18: 31–19: 27 *Preparations for events in Jerusalem*

For 18^{31-43} see Matt. $20^{17-19, 29-34}$; Mark $10^{32-34, 46-52}$. Luke omits Mark $10^{35-40, 41-44}$, the first section perhaps because it places the disciples in a bad light, the second probably because it overlaps with 22^{24-27}. 19^{1-27} is found only in Luke. The first and last episodes (18^{21-34}, 19^{11-27}) are introduced with a reference to Jerusalem, while the second and third (18^{35-43}, 19^{1-10}) are centred on Jericho. The first and third are linked together by reference to the Son of man (18^{31}, 19^{10}), while the second and fourth have reference to kingship (18^{38-39}, $19^{11-15, 27}$). Perhaps the sequence of events gives us the following line of thought; Jerusalem is to be the scene of Jesus' death and resurrection, events which give Jesus the right to the kingly title 'son of David', but the nature of his kingship is revealed in an act of mercy to a blind man (symbolical too of the insight into God's purposes that Jesus brings), and also in his function as Son of man of seeking and saving the lost; but will Jerusalem be ready for its king?

going up to Jerusalem, and everything that is written of the
32 Son of man by the prophets will be accomplished. For he will
be delivered to the Gentiles, and will be mocked and shame-
33 fully treated and spit upon; they will scourge him and kill
34 him, and on the third day he will rise.' But they understood
none of these things; this saying was hid from them, and they
did not grasp what was said.

35 As he drew near to Jericho, a blind man was sitting by the
36 roadside begging; and hearing a multitude going by, he
37 inquired what this meant. They told him, 'Jesus of Nazareth
38 is passing by.' And he cried, 'Jesus, Son of David, have mercy

---

18: 31–34 The third prediction of Jesus' death

Luke omits Mark's reference to betrayal to the Jewish authorities (already mentioned at 9^{22}) and to their condemnation of Jesus to death (cp. 22^{66-71}).

32 *the prophets*: perhaps here the O.T. as a whole, with special reference to Pss. 16, 22, and 69; Isa. 53. The Gentiles are mentioned for the first time in this connection. Luke focuses attention on the Roman power, and so prepares us for the trial before Pilate (23^{1-25}).

33 Scourging or whipping was a method of eliciting evidence and of punishment. A Roman citizen was normally exempt from this treatment, but Jesus is not one of the privileged class.

34 Cp. 9^{45}, 24^{16}. *hidden* suggests a supernatural blinding. Luke thus explains the ignorance of the disciples, but he may also be suggesting that the future course of events was far from their thoughts, and that the truth would be made clear in God's good time, after Jesus' resurrection (cp. John 2^{22}).

18: 35–43 The restoration of a blind man's sight

The healing is a sign of the presence of God's new age (cp. 7^{21}).

35 In Mark and Matthew the episode occurs when Jesus is leaving Jericho. Luke, who wishes to place 19^{1-27} as a preface to Jesus' entry into Jerusalem, puts the present incident earlier as part of his literary rearrangement of Mark. The blind man's disability had forced him to become a professional beggar.

38 The personal address *Jesus* is uncommon. *Son of David*: the fame of Jesus leads the blind man to think that he might be the expected Saviour-king.

39 on me!' And those who were in front rebuked him, telling
him to be silent; but he cried out all the more, 'Son of David,
40 have mercy on me!' And Jesus stopped, and commanded him
to be brought to him; and when he came near, he asked him,
41 'What do you want me to do for you?' He said, 'Lord, let me
42 receive my sight.' And Jesus said to him, 'Receive your sight;
43 your faith has made you well.' And immediately he received
his sight and followed him, glorifying God; and all the people,
when they saw it, gave praise to God.

19: 2 HE entered Jericho and was passing through. And there
was a man named Zacchaeus; he was a chief tax collector,
3 and rich. And he sought to see who Jesus was, but could not,
4 on account of the crowd, because he was small of stature. So
he ran on ahead and climbed up into a sycamore tree to see
5 him, for he was to pass that way. And when Jesus came to
the place, he looked up and said to him, 'Zacchaeus, make
6 haste and come down; for I must stay at your house today.' So
he made haste and came down, and received him joyfully.

---

39 The motive was to prevent Jesus from being pestered, or perhaps the title was felt objectionable. *those who were in front* suggests a small procession, with the advance party trying to silence the blind man before Jesus came level with him.

42 The blind man's persistence shows his *faith*, his belief in Jesus' God-given power to help him.

43 Luke sounds the note of praise and removes Mark's 'on the way', which in that Gospel leads at once to the entry into Jerusalem.

19: 1–10 Jesus and Zacchaeus

Jesus associates with an unacceptable member of society, and even gives him his approval.

4 The *tree* was probably the fig-mulberry.

5 The implication is that Jesus knew of the presence of Zacchaeus by divine prescience.

7 And when they saw it they all murmured, 'He has gone in to
8 be the guest of a man who is a sinner.' And Zacchaeus stood
and said to the Lord, 'Behold, Lord, the half of my goods I
give to the poor; and if I have defrauded any one of anything,
9 I restore it fourfold.' And Jesus said to him, 'Today salvation
has come to this house, since he also is a son of Abraham.
10 For the Son of man came to seek and to save the lost.'
11 As they heard these things, he proceeded to tell a parable,

---

7 Cp. 5^{30}, 15^{2}.

8 *stood*: out of respect to Jesus. The present tenses *give* and *restore* mean that Zacchaeus is going to make an immediate act of restitution, thus showing a change of heart. *defrauded*: extorted more taxes than could be rightly assessed. According to Num. 5^{7}, the restoration of the full amount plus one-fifth would have been enough.

9 God's deliverance, or rescue, *has come to this house* (a vivid way of describing the occupant), because in response to the presence of God's representative, the Son of man, Zacchaeus has been released from the bondage of his past life, and has made a new start. *son of Abraham*: Zacchaeus (despite his malpractices, and his undoubted condemnation by respectable religious society) is none the less accepted at once by Jesus and classed as a true member of God's people.

: 11–27 The parable of the pounds

See also Matt. 25^{14-30}, with which there are many similarities of language and theme. Underlying both there might be an original parable which has undergone modifications. On the other hand, they may be separate parables of a similar kind, but used on different occasions. Luke has sometimes been thought to have expanded an original parable about a man who gave his servants money for trading, with material about a man who was installed as a king against the will of his subjects (are vv. 12*b*, 14–15, and 27 additions to the original story?). The story, however, may be regarded as a unity (note that in vv. 17 and 19 the slaves are put in charge of the cities of which the nobleman is now king), and the twofold disloyalty of the citizens and of the third slave is not pointless repetition but an intentional emphasis on this theme. The parable is intended as a sobering influence: will the Jews be ready for the kingdom of God in the form in which it appears (cp., e.g., Acts 28^{25-28})? 'into a far country' (v. 12), best taken as merely a feature of the story, should not be pressed to mean that Luke is suggesting that the final advent of Jesus will be interminably delayed.

because he was near to Jerusalem, and because they supposed
12 that the kingdom of God was to appear immediately. He said
therefore, 'A nobleman went into a far country to receive
13 kingly power[c] and then return. Calling ten of his servants, he
gave them ten pounds,[d] and said to them, "Trade with these
14 till I come." But his citizens hated him and sent an embassy
after him, saying, "We do not want this man to reign over
15 us." When he returned, having received the kingly power,[c]
he commanded these servants, to whom he had given the
money, to be called to him, that he might know what they
16 had gained by trading. The first came before him, saying,
17 "Lord, your pound has made ten pounds more." And he said
to him, "Well done, good servant! Because you have been
faithful in a very little, you shall have authority over ten
18 cities." And the second came, saying, "Lord, your pound has
19 made five pounds." And he said to him, "And you are to be
20 over five cities." Then another came, saying, "Lord, here is

[c] Greek *a kingdom*
[d] The mina, rendered here by *pound*, was equal to about £7

---

11 The introduction may give the correct context, as the arrival of Jesus near Jerusalem may have caused an outburst of enthusiasm and speculation in the shape of nationalist hopes.

12 The picture may be that of the heir apparent to a client kingdom going to Rome for confirmation of his kingship by the Roman emperor.

13 *pounds*, lit. 'minas', a Greek monetary unit, equalling 100 drachmas. In Matthew's similar parable the talent, a far higher unit of coinage, is used. *servants*, or 'slaves', who could occupy important administrative posts. The commission tests the initiative and loyalty of the slaves, as the amount concerned is infinitesimal (cp. 16[10]).

14 When Archelaus, son of Herod the Great, went to Rome to seek the emperor's confirmation of his father's will, a Jewish embassy followed, representing those who hoped for the abolition of the rule of the Herods.

15 Just as Archelaus was confirmed as king of Judea.

20 The third servant had shown no initiative about his master's business interests. *a napkin*: a face-cloth for wiping perspiration.

21 your pound, which I kept laid away in a napkin; for I was
afraid of you, because you are a severe man; you take up what
22 you did not lay down, and reap what you did not sow." He
said to him, 'I will condemn you out of your own mouth,
you wicked servant! You knew that I was a severe man, taking
up what I did not lay down and reaping what I did not sow?
23 Why then did you not put my money into the bank, and at
24 my coming I should have collected it with interest?" And he
said to those who stood by, "Take the pound from him, and
25 give it to him who has the ten pounds." (And they said to
26 him, "Lord, he has ten pounds!") "I tell you, that to every
one who has will more be given; but from him who has not,
27 even what he has will be taken away. But as for these enemies
of mine, who did not want me to reign over them, bring them
here and slay them before me." '
28 And when he had said this, he went on ahead, going up to

---

severe, or 'exacting'. *take up . . . sow*: perhaps a proverbial expression for a grasping person.

26 Cp. 8^{18}.

27 This rounds off the story of the nobleman's entry into his kingdom. *reign* forms a link with the theme of kingship in vv. 28–40, which follows.

IV. THE SECOND JERUSALEM-TEMPLE SCENE—THE THE CLIMAX (CHAPTERS 19: 28–24: 53)

19: 28–48 *The state entry into Jerusalem: Jesus in Jerusalem*

19: 28–40 Jesus enters Jerusalem.

See also Matt. 21^{1-9}; Mark 11^{1-10}; John 12^{12-19}. The regal procession of Jesus (9^{51} onwards) now enters its final stage. The present incident opens a passage terminating at 21^{38}, with reference to 'the mount of Olives' at beginning and end; another recurring theme is Jesus' use of the temple (19^{45-47}, 20^{1}, $21^{1, 37-38}$). 19^{29-35} suggests Jesus' intention to make a demonstration of his authority, in addition to entering Jerusalem like any other pilgrim for the Passover festival. Luke wishes to present Jesus' entry as one of kingly state, and clarifies the nature of his kingship.

29 Jerusalem. When he drew near to Bethphage and Bethany,
at the mount that is called Olivet, he sent two of the disciples,
30 saying, 'Go into the village opposite, where on entering you
will find a colt tied, on which no one has every yet sat; untie
31 it and bring it here. If any one asks you, "Why are you untying
32 it?" you shall say this, "The Lord has need of it." ' So those
who were sent went away and found it as he had told them.
33 And as they were untying the colt, its owners said to them,
34 'Why are you untying the colt?' And they said, 'The Lord
35 has need of it.' And they brought it to Jesus, and throwing
36 their garments on the colt they set Jesus upon it. And as he
37 rode along, they spread their garments on the road. As he

---

28 *ahead*: a picture of Jesus as leader of his disciples.

29 *Bethphage*, *Bethany*, and *Olivet* (or 'the Olive Grove') were all places close to Jerusalem.

30 Either Bethphage or Bethany is probably meant. *colt* (πῶλος) is usually interpreted as an 'ass's foal' or 'young donkey', The normal use of the word, however, suggests that, when used in association with another animal, it describes the young of that animal, but that, when used alone, it means a 'horse', which may be the sense intended by Mark and Luke. The occurrence of πῶλος in the sense of 'ass's foal' in the LXX of Zech. 9^{9} (quoted by Matthew and John) has enabled them to connect Jesus with the lowly king of that passage, who there rides the ass, the animal of peace. But for Mark and Luke the common assumption that Jesus chooses the ass, the animal of peace, as opposed to the horse, the animal of war, may be unjustified. Further, the classification of a horse as an animal of war would depend on the context in which it was used; it need only denote a regal animal. *no one has ever sat*: and so for a special person. The whole atmosphere is mysterious and suggestive of secret preparation.

31 *The Lord has need of it* is the password allowing the disciples to proceed. *The Lord*, i.e. our master who is known to you.

35 The *garments*, or 'cloaks', form the saddle.

36 The carpeting of the road is treatment due to an important person (cp. 2 Kgs. 9^{13}).

37 Luke stresses that the acclamation comes from Jesus' own disciples. Jesus' kingly action is seen in his *mighty works* of compassion and not in an attempted rebellion against Rome.

was now drawing near, at the descent of the Mount of Olives,
the whole multitude of the disciples began to rejoice and praise
God with a loud voice for all the mighty works that they had
38 seen, saying, 'Blessed is the King who comes in the name of
39 the Lord! Peace in heaven and glory in the highest!' And
some of the Pharisees in the multitude said to him, 'Teacher,
40 rebuke your disciples.' He answered, 'I tell you, if these were
silent, the very stones would cry out.'
41 And when he drew near and saw the city he wept over it,
42 saying, 'Would that even today you knew the things that make
43 for peace! But now they are hid from your eyes. For the days
shall come upon you, when your enemies will cast up a bank
about you and surround you, and hem you in on every side,

---

38 All four accounts refer to the acclamation 'Blessed . . . the Lord' (part of the greeting given to pilgrims at the Jewish Passover), and they also connect it with kingship. Luke omits reference to 'the kingdom of our father David' (Mark): Jesus has not come to establish an earthly kingdom. *Peace in heaven and glory in the highest!* (cp. 2^{14}) is perhaps Luke's translation of Mark's 'Hosanna in the highest', which meant 'Grant salvation, thou who art in highest heaven'. It is best regarded as a prayer that God's *peace* and *glory* may now be revealed.

39 *rebuke*: disown the kingly office being attributed to him.

40 If all the onlookers were blind to the crucial nature of the situation, even lifeless objects, such as *stones*, would have to bear their witness.

19: 41–48 Jesus' concern for Jerusalem

The section is from a special source, except for vv. 45–46, which may be dependent on Mark. In rejecting Jesus the Jews are missing the way that leads to 'peace', a full life with God, and the road is being opened up for the free play of nationalist feelings, resulting in the destruction of Jerusalem. The decisive nature of Jesus' mission is stressed (v. 42, 'today'; v. 44, 'the time of your visitation'). Luke, who omits Mark $11^{12-14, 20}$, replaces it with the pronouncement here on the same theme—the barrenness of Israel's response.

41 This is an occasion of sorrow as well as of joy (v. 37).

42 *now* suggests that the obtuseness is too deep-rooted to be overcome. *hid* could denote a supernatural blinding: it is so great that it must be God-sent.

44 Cp. Isa. 29^{3}, 37^{33}; Jer. 52^{4-5}; Ezek. 4^{1-3}. *the time*: the decisive moment.

44 and dash you to the ground, you and your children within
you, and they will not leave one stone upon another in you;
because you did not know the time of your visitation.'
45 And he entered the temple and began to drive out those
46 who sold, saying to them, 'It is written, "My house shall be a
house of prayer"; but you have made it a den of robbers.'
47 And he was teaching daily in the temple. The chief priests
and the scribes and the principal men of the people sought to
48 destroy him; but they did not find anything they could do,
for all the people hung upon his words.

20: ONE day, as he was teaching the people in the temple and

45–46 For the clearing of the temple area see also Matt. 21^{12-17}; Mark 11^{15-19}; John 2^{12-17}. John, probably for theological reasons, places the incident at the beginning of Jesus' ministry. Luke's account is short and continues the theme of the barrenness of Israel, shown in the use of the temple for these practices. In Mark and John the incident also seems to typify the cleansing of the old order of Judaism and the creation of a new order in Jesus. Luke's interest is that Jesus clears the area of improper practices and then puts the temple (his rightful sphere, 2^{49}) to its proper use by occupying it for his teaching.

45 *the temple*: the whole area, with the courts. The part concerned is often thought to be the court of the Gentiles, but the direct evidence is missing. The things *sold* were those required for the sacrificial offerings; the traders were probably profiteering.

46 The quotation is partly Isa. 56^7 and and partly Jer. 7^{11}. Matthew and Luke omit from it Isaiah's 'for all the nations', included by Mark, who wishes to stress the place of the Gentiles in the new order. Luke perhaps wishes to avoid any suggestion that the Jewish temple, as opposed to Jesus himself, will be the centre of Gentile worship.

47 Cp. 22^{53}. Luke stresses Jesus' teaching in the temple. He is thus closely connected with the centre of the Jewish religion, from which the gospel goes out into the world. *the principal men*: the Jewish elders, who with the other two groups formed the Sanhedrin.

20: 1–21: 4 *Jesus in controversy with the Jews*

See also Matt. 21^{23}–22^{46}; Mark 11^{27}–12^{44}. Luke now follows Mark closely, except for the omission of Mark 12^{28-34} (but

preaching the gospel, the chief priests and the scribes with
2 the elders came up and said to him, 'Tell us by what authority
you do these things, or who it is that gave you this authority.'
3 He answered them, 'I also will ask you a question; now tell
4 me, Was the baptism of John from heaven or from men?'
5 And they discussed it with one another, saying, 'If we say,
"From heaven," he will say, "Why did you not believe him?"
6 But if we say, "From men," all the people will stone us; for
7 they are convinced that John was a prophet.' So they
8 answered that they did not know whence it was. And Jesus
said to them, 'Neither will I tell you by what authority I do
these things.'

---

cp. Luke 10^{25-28}). The emphasis on the claims of Jesus and on the Jewish opposition prepares for Jesus' coming death. 20^{19-26} and 20^{41-44} are meant to show that Jesus is no threat to the Roman power, while 20^{27-40} points to the common ground between Jesus and some of the Jews (see especially v. 39).

20: 1–8 The question about authority

The official leaders of the Jews were incapable of expressing an unbiased opinion on Jesus, as they were of giving an honest opinion on John the Baptist.

2 *these things*: Jesus' authoritative teaching and his action in clearing the temple area. The question shows that Jesus had not been ordained as a rabbi.

4 *heaven*: God. *from men*: having no place in God's purposes. For the distinction cp. Acts 5^{38-39}.

5 If *him* denotes Jesus, the meaning could be: if John was inspired in his prediction of 'the mightier one' (3^{16}), who was coming soon, and for whom John's baptism prepared, then it is reasonable to believe that Jesus fulfils this role. But *him* could refer to John, the question turning on the refusal of the Jewish leaders to give recognition to John's mission (cp. 7^{30}).

6 Popular opinion would regard such an assessment of John as worthy of the punishment for blasphemy.

8 The Jews' inability to give an impartial answer about John makes it futile to discuss his own authority.

9 And he began to tell the people this parable: 'A man
planted a vineyard, and let it out to tenants, and went into
10 another country for a long while. When the time came, he
sent a servant to the tenants, that they should give him some
of the fruit of the vineyard; but the tenants beat him, and
11 sent him away empty-handed. And he sent another servant;
him also they beat and treated shamefully, and sent him away
12 empty-handed. And he sent yet a third; this one they
13 wounded and cast out. Then the owner of the vineyard said,
"What shall I do? I will send my beloved son; it may be they
14 will respect him." But when the tenants saw him, they said to
themselves, "This is the heir; let us kill him, that the in-

20: 9–18 The story of the treacherous tenants

The parable is a commentary on the history of Israel as the scene of God's revelation: the latter reaches its climax with the coming of the Son of God, as does also the readiness of Israel to reject God's messengers. The story is allegorical, the different features standing for something further: the owner for God, the vineyard for Israel, the tenants for the people of Israel, the servants for the prophets, and the owner's son for Jesus. If, as is reasonable to suppose, Jesus was conscious of having a unique place in God's purposes and of the consequences to himself, the parable is appropriate on his lips, though sometimes later embellishment is seen, e.g., in v. 13, reminiscent of Jesus' death outside the walls of Jerusalem. The seriousness of Israel's obtuseness in the face of God's greatest revelation is further underlined in vv. 17–18.

9 *the people*: but the leaders are particularly in mind. The opening is abbreviated, and so the reference to Isa. 5^{1-2} (clear in Mark and Matthew, and equating the vineyard with Israel) is obscured. *tenants*, or 'vinegrowers'.

10 Luke has a straightforward sequence of three servants and the heir, with an ascending scale of harsh treatment ('beat', 'beat and treated shamefully', 'wounded and cast out', 'cast out and killed').

13 Would the absentee landlord in real life have risked his son in this way? But not all Jesus' parables are true to life, and the present one illustrates the risk that God took.

14 Perhaps the tenants thought to intimidate the owner from asserting his rights.

15 heritance may be ours." And they cast him out of the vineyard and killed him. What then will the owner of the vine-
16 yard do to them? He will come and destroy those tenants,
and give the vineyard to others.' When they heard this, they
17 said, 'God forbid!' But he looked at them and said, 'What
then is this that is written:

> "The very stone which the builders rejected
> has become the head of the corner"?

18 Every one who falls on that stone will be broken to pieces;
but when it falls on any one it will crush him.'

19 The scribes and the chief priests tried to lay hands on
him at that very hour, but they feared the people; for they

---

16 God's plans will not be frustrated: he will use *others*—the Gentiles.

17 Jewish lack of harmony with God is foretold in scripture, i.e. in Ps. 118^{22}, which originally probably applied to the nation Israel, persecuted by other nations, but given status by God, and which is now reapplied to Jesus, as the representative of Israel: despite his rejection by the Jewish authorities, he will be vindicated by God. *the head of the corner*, or 'the main corner stone': sometimes thought to be the keystone in the arch over the building's entrance, but more likely a foundation stone of importance, binding together the walls and the foundation (cp. Eph. 2^{20-22}). God reverses human assessment. For the quotation see also Acts 4^{11}; 1 Pet. 2^{6}.

18 The stone of v. 17 is now equated with 'the stone of stumbling' (Isa. 8^{14}; cp. Rom. 9^{33}; 1 Pet. 2^{7-8}). *crush*: this translation seems demanded by the parallel 'broken in pieces', though the Greek word (λικμᾶν) usually means 'sift', 'shake', or, more rarely, 'make an end of'. The stone is viewed as (*a*) an obstacle and (*b*) a weapon of offence, and so from being a key feature in construction becomes, when rejected, a source of destruction: Jesus is the meeting-place between God and man, but rejection of him means alienation from God.

19–26 The payment of taxes to the emperor.

The incident culminates in Jesus' saying of v. 25, and stresses that Jesus is no political revolutionary, challenging Roman authority.

20 perceived that he had told this parable against them. So they
watched him, and sent spies, who pretended to be sincere,
that they might take hold of what he said, so as to deliver him
21 up to the authority and jurisdiction of the governor. They
asked him, 'Teacher, we know that you speak and teach
rightly, and show no partiality, but truly teach the way of
22, 23 God. Is it lawful for us to give tribute to Caesar, or not?' But
24 he perceived their craftiness, and said to them, 'Show me a
coin.[e] Whose likeness and inscription has it?' They said,
25 'Caesar's.' He said to them, 'Then render to Caesar the things
26 that are Caesar's, and to God the things that are God's.' And
they were not able in the presence of the people to catch him
by what he said; but marvelling at his answer they were silent.

[e] Greek *denarius*

---

20 Only Luke mentions the *spies*, or secret agents, and makes it clear that the Jewish authorities desired to establish a capital charge of treason (cp. 22^{67-71}).

21 *the way of God*: God's plan for human life (cp. Ps. 119^1; Acts 9^2). Jesus is flattered as a *teacher* or rabbi, who gives a correct interpretation of the Law.

22 *lawful*: in accordance with God's revealed will. The request for Roman rule had come from a Jewish embassy in A.D. 6, but the payment of taxes that it entailed had become a living issue of contention, some Jews asserting that they owed loyalty to God alone.

23 For Jesus' insight, cp. John 2^{24-25}.

24 The denarius (see RSV margin) was a silver coin of the Roman currency in which the taxes would be paid. The inscription contained the emperor's name, to which his titles were sometimes added.

25 Jesus might be giving a non-committal answer: since the coin bears the head and inscription of the emperor, it must belong to him and so should be given back to him in taxes! There might then be a play on the word *render*, which also means 'give back'. Jesus' answer, however, probably makes the serious point that, in view of the circulation of the emperor's coinage, his responsibility for law and order is not in doubt, and in return for this provision taxes should be paid. Jesus gives a place to God and to the State or organized society: the two are not irreconcilable (cp. Rom. 13^{1-7}; Tit. 3^1; 1 Pet. 2^{13-15}).

26 The aim was to trap Jesus into a seditious statement.

27 There came to him some Sadducees, those who say that
28 there is no resurrection, and they asked him a question,
saying, 'Teacher, Moses wrote for us that if a man's brother
dies, having a wife but no children, the man[f] must take the
29 wife and raise up children for his brother. Now there were
seven brothers; the first took a wife, and died without
30, 31 children; and the second and the third took her, and likewise
32 all seven left no children and died. Afterward the woman
33 also died. In the resurrection, therefore, whose wife will the
woman be? For the seven had her as wife.'
34 And Jesus said to them, 'The sons of this age marry and are
35 given in marriage; but those who are accounted worthy to attain
to that age and to the resurrection from the dead neither marry
36 nor are given in marriage, for they cannot die any more,
because they are equal to angels and are sons of God, being
37 sons of the resurrection. But that the dead are raised, even

[f] Greek *his brother*

20: 27–40 Resurrection from the dead

Jesus' disagreement with some of his fellow Jews was of a religious and non-political kind (cp. Acts 26^{4-8}). The belief that the dead would be brought to life again, either to face God's judgement or to share the blessings of God's new age, had come to prominence only in the last two centuries before Jesus.

27 The Sadducees, only mentioned here in this Gospel, later lead the opposition to Christianity (e.g. Acts 4^{1}). Josephus classifies them as one of the important Jewish sects. Their scepticism about the resurrection of the dead is well attested, and followed from their recognition of the Pentateuch as the sole authoritative scripture.

28 For this law, aimed at securing the continuance of a man's name and ancestral line, see Deut. 25^{5-6} (cp. Gen. 38^{8}). The example is extremely hypothetical and is based on a crudely materialistic view of the resurrection.

35 Luke clarifies Mark by drawing the distinction between the conditions of the present age, and those of God's new era, whose members, including those raised from the dead, will be immortal, living in a different manner of life (cp. 1 Cor. 15^{35-53}).

38 *they cannot die any more* explains what similarity to *angels* means. *sons*

Moses showed, in the passage about the bush, where he calls
the Lord the God of Abraham and the God of Isaac and the
38 God of Jacob. Now he is not God of the dead, but of the
39 living; for all live to him.' And some of the scribes answered,
40 'Teacher, you have spoken well.' For they no longer dared to
ask him any question.

41 But he said to them, 'How can they say that the Christ is
42 David's son? For David himself says in the Book of Psalms,

---

of God is sometimes a description of angels (e.g. Job 1^{6}), and those who are *sons of* (i.e. share in) *the resurrection* enjoy their deathless status.

The concern seems at first sight to be with life after death rather than with resurrection, but the argument may be: the so-called dead are not disintegrated shadowy beings in Sheol, whose possibility of life with God is ended, but are still real living beings, and so belief in their resurrection to full life with God in his new age must not be ruled out. Jesus' argument is based on Exod. 3^{6}, where God is still described as the patriarchs' God, although they have died, with the suggestion that they are still in a living relationship with him. Rabbi Gamaliel II used a similar argument, based on Deut. 11^{9}; see Talmud, *Sanh.* 90 *b*. *for all . . . him* is an explanation added in Luke: perhaps *all* refers to the patriarchs, i.e. they are all alive in his sight or as far as he is concerned (cp. 4 Macc. 16^{25}).

39 These *scribes* may have belonged to the Pharisees, who believed in the resurrection of the dead.

20: 41–44 The status of the Messiah

Jesus now asks a question himself.

41–42 *they*: the scribes. Jesus is not disputing such a king's coming, but the assumption that he will conform to the pattern of David's kingship. The quotation is from Ps. 110^{1}, which originally applied to a king who was also priest, but which in Jesus' time had probably been re-applied to the Messiah. *David* is seen, in the manner of the time, as the author of the Psalm, and also as addressing the king with the title 'my Lord', implying that the king so addressed is of superior status. *sit at my right hand*, originally a reference to the receiving of God's protection, is now taken to mean the sharing of God's throne and dominion: the Messiah is seen as one who reigns as a heavenly figure, with the implication that Jesus' kingship will not be of an earthly kind (see also 22^{69}; Acts 2^{33}: cp. Rom. 8^{34}; Heb. 1^{2-4}).

"The Lord said to my Lord,
Sit at my right hand,
43 till I make thy enemies a stool for thy feet."
44 David thus calls him Lord; so how is he his son?'
45 And in the hearing of all the people he said to his disciples,
46 'Beware of the scribes, who like to go about in long robes, and
love salutations in the market places and the best seats in the
47 synagogues and the places of honour at feasts, who devour
widow's houses and for a pretence make long prayers. They
will receive the greater condemnation.'

1: HE looked up and saw the rich putting their gifts into the
2 treasury; and he saw a poor widow put in two copper coins.

---

3 This would later be seen as a reference to Jesus' triumph over all the forces that tried to silence him for ever.

: 45–47 The dangerous example of the Scribes

Luke has already (11^{37-54}) recorded some of Jesus' warnings on this subject, from another source, and now gives Mark's short account of Jesus' criticism.

6 *long* flowing *robes* look impressive and suggest importance. *salutations*: e.g. 'Rabbi', 'Master', or 'greatest'. In the rabbinical writings regulations are given about the assignment of *seats* of honour among the rabbis.

7 *devour widows' houses*: appropriate them illegally, with the implication that the scribes take advantage of such unprotected people (cp. Talmud, *Sot.* 21 b;). For *long prayers* cp. Matt. 6^{7}. *the greater condemnation*: they should know that God does not look on the outward appearance, but on the heart.

1–4 The widow's contribution

The incident links up with 'widows' (20^{47}), while 'treasury' (of the temple) looks forward to 21^{5-7}. The widow has given her all, and this, in another sense, is what Jesus is going to do in his coming death.

treasury: there were thirteen chests in the shape of trumpets for contributions to the upkeep of the temple.

The *coins* mentioned were of very low value.

3 And he said, 'Truly I tell you, this poor widow has put in
4 more than all of them; for they all contributed out of their
abundance, but she out of her poverty put in all the living
that she had.'
5 And as some spoke of the temple, how it was adorned with

---

4 A startling paradox, but true, because the worth of a contribution is shown by the sacrifice involved.

21: 5–38 *The discourse of the future*

See also Matt. 24^{1}–25^{46}; Mark 13^{1-37}.

(1) Luke follows Mark closely in vv. 5–11a, 17, 21a, 26b–27, and 29–33. 11b may be an editorial amplification of Mark, while vv. 12–16 overlap with the latter in theme and language, and could be a rewriting of Mark, but are probably best regarded as from another source; the same applies to vv. 20 and 21b. vv. 18–19, 22, 23b–24, 28, and 34–36 are from a non-Marcan source. Luke may have had a special source or sources which covered the following themes: (*a*) warning about persecution and reaction to it; (*b*) the future fate of Jerusalem and its significance; (*c*) world upheaval; (*d*) the need of the disciples to be ready for the final intervention of God and for acceptance by the Son of man. Luke has combined this special material with Mark, an explanation preferable to the suggestion that the whole form of this chapter is to be traced to a rewriting and editing of Mark 13.

(2) The purpose of the discourse is to prepare the followers of Jesus for future events, and can be viewed as a collection of his sayings on this theme.

(3) Certain similarities of theme and certain contrasts link this section with the account of Jesus' death and resurrection:

Chapters 21^{5-38}	*Chapters* 22–24
false Messiahs (vv. 8–9)	the true Messiah ($24^{26, 46}$)
the disciples before kings and governors (v. 12)	Jesus on trial before Pilate and Herod (23^{1-25})
the disciples handed over to synagogues (v. 12)	Jesus before the Sanhedrin (22^{66-71})

the witness of the disciples	Jesus' witness (22^{69}, $24^{25-27, 44-46}$); the disciples as witnesses (24^{48})
the disciples betrayed by friends (v. 16)	Jesus' betrayal by his friend, Judas (22^{47-48})
the disciples hated (v. 17)	Jesus hated (22^{63}, $23^{18, 35-39}$)
God's protection assured (v. 18)	Jesus' faith in God's protection (23^{46}), later confirmed (24)
endurance demanded of the disciples (v. 19)	Jesus shows endurance in going to death (22^{7}–23^{46})
Jerusalem under God's judgement (vv. 20–24)	judgement passed in Jerusalem on Jesus (22^{71}, 23^{24})
fulfilment of O.T. (v. 22)	fulfilment of O.T. (22^{37}, 24^{44-46})
Jesus' sorrow for those who have, or are expecting children (v. 23)	Jesus pronounces the childless blessed (23^{28-29})
the times of the Gentiles (v. 24)	the proclamation of the gospel to the Gentiles (24^{47})
signs in the sun (v. 25)	the failure of the sun's light (23^{44-45})
the coming of the Son of man in glory (v. 27)	the entry of the Son of man into his glory at the resurrection ($24^{26, 46}$)
redemption (v. 27)	Jesus, the one to redeem Israel (24^{21})
revelation to the whole earth (v. 27)	revelation to disciples (24^{1-52})
Jesus' call to prayer 'that you may have strength to escape all these things . . .' (v. 36)	Jesus is strengthened by an angel after prayer (22^{43}), and comes safely through his ordeal
standing before the Son of man (v. 36)	the disciples in the presence of the Risen Jesus (24^{13-52})

These close parallels bring out several important points. The pattern of Jesus' life will be reproduced in his followers (e.g. they will be persecuted). The triumph of God's cause is foreshadowed in Jesus' triumph and establishment as king (cp. Col. 1^{13}). The disciples are encouraged to endure and hope for vindication of their cause by the vision of Jesus' endurance and by his triumphant emergence from his ordeal. The apparent defeat of Jesus will be reversed for all to see; his triumph, known at present only to his close followers, will be manifested to all (cp. Col. 3^{3-4}). Future events that seem to spell out disintegration and despair must be seen in the light of Jesus' sufferings and death, which seemed 'the hour of darkness' (22^{53}), but which were proved far otherwise. The theme that the disciples are not to be daunted by future events is expanded also in the present discourse. Some of the most shattering events (e.g. persecution, vv. 12–19; upheavals of war, vv. 9–11; the destruction of Jerusalem, vv. 20–24) have a purpose in God's sight. All these future happenings are to be seen against the background of the triumph of God's plans (v. 27), so that catastrophes can be faced in hope. The disciples have a future, whatever happens (vv. 28 and 36).

(4) Luke is also thought to be suggesting that the end of the present order is further away than is implied by Mark, and so to be facing the problem of the delay in the advent of Jesus. He omits (v. 11) Mark's reference to 'the beginning of the sufferings', or, better, 'the birth pangs of the new age' (Mark 13^{8}), and the warning of v. 8 is reinforced by the addition of 'the time is at hand'. The denial of the immediacy of 'the end' seems more emphatic (v. 9) than in Mark 13^{7}. Luke prefaces the prediction of the disciples' sufferings with 'before all this', thus putting the phenomena of vv. 8–11 even further in the future. In Mark 13^{14-22} the destruction of Jerusalem is connected with 'the tribulation' or 'the distress', which in Jewish thought was the prelude to God's ultimate triumph, while Luke (vv. 20–24) removes it from this context and presents it as an historical event in which God's judgement on the Jews is to be discerned. The reference to 'the times of the Gentiles' and 'Jerusalem will be trodden down by the Gentiles' (v. 24) suggest a long period of future history. The stronger emphasis on endurance (vv. 19, 36) might also point in the same direction. vv. 25–27 (the signs that culminate in the Son of man's coming) are only loosely connected with vv. 20–24, giving the impression that these signs lie well in the future, and it is these alone that announce final 'redemption' (v. 28) and God's final 'kingdom' (v. 31). Luke, therefore, in spite of his retention of v. 32, may be suggesting that 'the end' will be delayed. Some of the features may, however, be the result of Luke's combination of different sources, and the extent to which Luke was occupied with this problem is still much disputed.

6 noble stones and offerings, he said, 'As for these things which
you see, the days will come when there shall not be left here
7 one stone upon another that will not be thrown down.' And
they asked him, 'Teacher, when will this be, and what will
be the sign when this is about to take place?' And he said,
8 'Take heed that you are not led astray; for many will come
in my name, saying, "I am he!" and, "The time is at hand!"
9 Do not go after them. And when you hear of wars and
tumults, do not be terrified; for this must first take place, but
the end will not be at once.'
10 Then he said to them, 'Nation will rise against nation, and
11 kingdom against kingdom; there will be great earthquakes,

1: 5–9 The question about the destruction of the temple

The temple's future raises the question of the future in general. Such a momentous upheaval as the destruction of the temple could not be separated from the issue of the coming of God's final day of triumph and judgement.

5 The rebuilding of the temple, begun by Herod the Great, was not completed until A.D. 62, only eight years before its destruction in A.D. 70. The new temple was famed for its magnificence. *votive offerings*: gifts of ornaments and other articles for beautification and use.

8 *in my name*: claiming the name of Messiah. *the time*: when God will make his kingdom finally effective. The period A.D. 70–130 saw the appearance of such claimants. *do not . . . them*: do not become their disciples.

9 Such happenings were sometimes thought to herald the end of the present world order, and are perhaps here connected with the coming destruction of the temple, as *tumults*, or, better, 'insurrections', suggests Jewish rebellions against the Romans. *must*: such discords, the result of human disobedience to God (cp. 19^{42-44}), are catered for in God's plans.

: 10–19 Various disturbances; the persecution of the disciples

Cp. Isa. 19^{2}. *Then he said to them*, only found in Luke, suggests that vv. 10–36 are an expansion of the theme of vv. 8–9, and also makes it clear that 'all this' (v. 12) refers to vv. 10–11.

From war we pass to other kinds of distress on earth, and then to unusual heavenly phenomena, all evidence of God's coming judgement,

and in various places famines and pestilences; and there will
12 be terrors and great signs from heaven. But before all this
they will lay their hands on you and persecute you, delivering
you up to the synagogues and prisons, and you will be
13 brought before kings and governors for my name's sake. This
14 will be a time for you to bear testimony. Settle it therefore
in your minds, not to meditate beforehand how to answer;
15 for I will give you a mouth and wisdom, which none of your

---

and so no reason for surprise. To Mark's 'famines' Luke adds *pestilences*, a common combination in Greek, with a play on words (λιμός: λοιμός). *terrors*, or 'portents', combined with *signs*, suggest happenings that augur some future event.

12 In the light of his own destiny, Jesus may well have predicted sufferings for those who joined him, though the predictions may in some respects have become more precise in the light of the Church's experience. *the synagogues*: synagogue jurisdiction, either at the level of local elders or of the Sanhedrin itself; the charge would be that of teaching unacceptable doctrine or of causing disturbance in the congregation. *delivering up*, the same word in Greek as that used to describe Judas' betrayal of Jesus (22^{4}), links up master and disciple. *kings*: the client kings of Rome, such as Herod Agrippa I and II (Acts 12^{1}, 25^{13}). *governors*: including proconsuls, legati, and procurators, such as Gallio (Acts 18^{12-17}), Felix (Acts 23^{26}), and Festus (Acts 24^{27}). *for my name's sake*: because of allegiance to me.

13 *This will be a time for you*, or 'the result will be to you', stresses that the persecution has an important positive result. The statement of the disciples' case will not only be legal evidence, but testimony to the gospel, the preaching of which has been the cause of their arrest (cp. Phil. 1^{13}).

14 *Settle it therefore in your minds*: resolve. *answer*: make defence in answer to a charge.

15 Cp. 12^{12}. The omission of reference to the Holy Spirit, together with the difference of language, suggests that Luke is not dependent on Mark 13^{11}. It is perhaps a sign of Luke's faithfulness to his special sources that, despite his obvious interest in the Holy Spirit, he prefers this version of Jesus' promise. The saying underlines the authority of Jesus, who claims the prerogative of God to give *a mouth* and *wisdom*, i.e. the power to speak with insight into God's purposes (cp. Exod. 4^{11-12}; Isa. 51^{16}; Wisd. 10^{21}; Ecclus. 34^{8}). For the promise's fulfilment cp., e.g., Acts 6^{10}. *which none of . . . contradict*: cp. Acts 26^{30-32}.

16 adversaries will be able to withstand or contradict. You will
be delivered up even by parents and brothers and kinsmen
17 and friends, and some of you they will put to death; you will
18 be hated by all for my name's sake. But not a hair on your
19 head will perish. By your endurance you will gain your lives.
20 'But when you see Jerusalem surrounded by armies, then
21 know that its desolation has come near. Then let those who
are in Judea flee to the mountains, and let those who are

---

16 Cp. 12^{52-53}. Only Luke mentions betrayal by friends (cp. $22^{3, 47-48}$). For the disciples' deaths cp. Acts 7^{54-60}, 12^{2}.

18 Cp. 12^{7}. For the metaphor see also 1 Sam. 14^{45}. There is no contradiction with v. 16, as the reference is not just to physical safety (Acts 27^{34}), but to the assurance that in all circumstances (even beyond death) the disciples are under God's protection.

19 The disciples' troubles are a positive opportunity for showing *endurance*, the quality of standing firm in the cause of Jesus (see also 8^{15}). The result will be to *gain your lives*, i.e. fullness of living in fellowship with God.

21: 20–24 The coming judgement on Jerusalem

The definitely Marcan sections here seem to be intrusions into the text. In v. 21 'Then . . . mountains' (Mark 13^{14}) breaks the transition, as 'inside the city' is lit. 'in the midst of her', and, like 'it' or 'her' must refer back to 'Jerusalem' (v. 20) and not to 'Judea'. In v. 23 'Alas . . . days!' (Mark 13^{17}) also breaks the sense, as the rest of v. 23, and also v. 24, which contain references to the O.T., follow more naturally on 'all that is written' (v. 22). Luke may, therefore, be using from a special source an extended saying about God's judgement on the Jewish people, into which he has inserted sections of Mark. In that case v. 20, with its difference of form from Mark 13^{14}, may be due to Luke's special source rather than to his own editing of the Marcan passage (the Lucan version could be an early elucidation of the Marcan).

20 *desolation*: used of the dereliction of a place or nation, seen as part of God's judgement (e.g. Jer. 22^{5}).

21 The language probably reinforces the idea of desolation: Jerusalem is under the judgement of God and is to be avoided (cp. Isa. 64^{10}). The command would have been impossible to carry out once the city had been encircled.

inside the city depart, and let not those who are out in the
22 country enter it; for these are days of vengeance, to fulfil all
23 that is written. Alas for those who are with child and for those
who give suck in those days! For great distress shall be upon
24 the earth and wrath upon this people; they will fall by the
edge of the sword, and be led captive among all nations; and
Jerusalem will be trodden down by the Gentiles, until the
times of the Gentiles are fulfilled.
25 'And there will be signs in sun and moon and stars, and
upon the earth distress of nations in perplexity at the roaring
26 of the sea and the waves, men fainting with fear and with

---

22 Cp. Jer. 46^{10}; Hos. 9^{7}. *all that is written*: passages in the O.T. about the coming judgement of God. *days of vengeance*: disobedience to God brings disaster and disintegration.

23 *Alas . . . those days*: it is a situation into which one would not wish to bring children. For *distress* and *wrath* cp. Zeph. 1^{15}. *earth*, or, perhaps better, 'land', i.e. of the Jews, and so parallel to *this people*.

24 *led captive among all nations*: such a procedure, not used by the Romans in A.D. 70, was regularly used by the Assyrian and Babylonian kings in dealing with subject peoples, including Israel, in whose case it was seen as part of God's judgement (cp. 2 Kgs. 18^{11}, 25^{11}; Ezek. 6^{8-10}). *trodden down*: a common description of the fate of God's enemies (cp. Isa. 63^{6}). For *Gentiles*, or non-Jews, as the instrument of God's punishment cp. Isa. 28^{11}. *the times of the Gentiles*: the period in which the Jews are subject to the foreigners, and the period in which the Gentiles have the opportunity to hear the gospel (cp. Mark 13^{10}; Rom. 11^{11-25}).

21: 25–38 Signs of the end; exhortation to hold firm

Again certain features suggest that Luke has combined another source with portions of Mark. Vv. 26b–27, 29–33 appear to be taken from Mark. Verse 25a, 'And . . . stars', is similar to Mark 13^{24} but differently phrased, and so probably from the other source. Verse 28 follows more satisfactorily after v. 26a, 'men . . . would', while vv. 29–31 repeat the sense of v. 28, which is more naturally followed by vv. 34–36. Further, 'all these things that will take place' (v. 36) would be easier in close proximity to vv. 25–26a.

25–26 Disturbances are part of the picture imagery used in descriptions of the Day of the Lord: God can achieve his purposes in the face of

foreboding of what is coming on the world; for the powers of
27 the heavens will be shaken. And then they will see the Son of
28 man coming in a cloud with power and great glory. Now when
these things begin to take place, look up and raise your heads,
because your redemption is drawing near.'

29 And he told them a parable: 'Look at the fig tree, and all
30 the trees; as soon as they come out in leaf, you see for your-
31 selves and know that the summer is already near. So also,
when you see these things taking place, you know that the
32 kingdom of God is near. Truly, I say to you, this generation

---

world upheaval, however great. *signs*: unusual phenomena, which, rightly understood, are indications of the nearness of the end. Human uncertainty, revealed in people's *perplexity*, *fear*, and *foreboding*, is contrasted with the certainty of God's triumph and the confident assurance to be shown by the disciples. *the powers of the heavens* (cp. Isa. 34[4]) probably refers to evil supernatural forces.

27 *they will see*: human beings will have an unmistakable demonstration that God is all in all. For the *coming* of the *Son of man* see above, pp. 39–40. *cloud*, *power*, and *glory*, all portray the triumphal presence of God. *cloud* (instead of Mark's 'clouds'), suggests the cloud that symbolized God's presence at the Exodus from Egypt, and brings the passage into line with 9[34] and Acts 1[9], where the cloud is associated with the triumph of Jesus, to the open demonstration of which our present verse looks forward.

28 *these things*: perhaps all the events mentioned from the beginning of the discourse. *look up and raise your heads*: take courage. *redemption*, with its sense of 'emancipation' or 'release' (e.g. of slaves), denotes the setting free of the disciples from the troubles of earth through their being received into full fellowship with the Son of man (v. 36), the climax of the liberation offered by Jesus.

31 Luke adds *and all the trees* perhaps because not all his readers would be familiar with the fig tree, and he amplifies the vaguer 'he is near' or 'it is near' of Mark.

32 *this generation*: Jesus' contemporaries; the other possible translation 'this nation' is not plausible. If *all* refers to all that has preceded, there is an unfulfilled prediction. In its present context it may express the early Church's eagerness for 'the end'. The saying may originally have related to the destruction of Jerusalem, like Mark's 'all these

33 will not pass away till all has taken place. Heaven and earth
will pass away, but my words will not pass away.
34 'But take heed to yourselves lest your hearts be weighed
down with dissipation and drunkenness and cares of this life,
35 and that day come upon you suddenly like a snare; for it will
come upon all who dwell upon the face of the whole earth.
36 But watch at all times, praying that you may have strength
to escape all these things that will take place, and to stand
before the Son of man.'
37 And every day he went teaching in the temple, but at night

---

things' or 'all those (former) things' (13^{30}), which contrasts with 'this (latter) day' (13^{32}). Another possibility is that in its original context the saying expressed Jesus' firm conviction of the proximity of happenings decisive for the coming of God's kingdom, a hope fulfilled in his own death and resurrection.

33 *pass away* forms a link with v. 32. The saying, a striking testimony to Jesus' confidence in the durability of his teaching, can mean: (*a*) Jesus' message will prove as lasting as God's creation, 'which stands fast for ever' (Ps. 93^{1}), or (*b*) even God's creation may come to an end (Ps. 102^{25}), but Jesus' words will never lose their force.

34 *dissipation* and *drunkenness* together suggest a self-centredness and self-indulgence that throws one's outlook on life off balance (cp. Isa. 19^{14}, 24^{20}). *that day*: of the Son of man's coming. *like a snare*: a trap that acts suddenly (cp. 17^{26-30}; 1 Thess. 5^{1-3}). The warning stresses that overhanging the whole of human life are the kingship of God and its demands.

35–36 Cp. Gen. 11^{4}. *all* mankind are accountable to God. *watch*, or 'keep awake and alert', a contrast with v. 34. *escape*: pass safely through, by remaining faithful despite all these challenges to faith (cp. Joel 2^{32}). The faithful people of God were sometimes thought of as going through a trying period before the end. *to stand before the Son of man* presents probably the picture of people admitted to a king's court to form his intimate circle. The general theme is that faithful service of God will be vindicated (cp. e.g. *Hymn* vii of the Qumran Community, 'But those who please Thee shall stand before Thee for ever'; Vermes, *The Dead Sea Scrolls in English*, p. 162).

37 In Luke *Olivet* is the scene of Jesus' triumphal entry into Jerusalem (19^{29}), of his place of retirement (as here), of his agony (22^{39}), and of his ascension (Acts 1^{12}).

38 he went out and lodged on the mount called Olivet. And early in the morning all the people came to him in the temple to hear him.

2: Now the feast of Unleavened Bread drew near, which is

---

38 Jesus' popularity is again stressed—ironic in the light of what follows.

2: 1–23: 56 *The arrest, trial, and execution of Jesus*

(1) As will be suggested in the commentary, Luke is drawing on a special source or sources, into which he has incorporated parts of Mark 14 and 15.

(2) As the death of Jesus had a vital place in the earliest Christian belief, a narrative of the events that led up to the crucifixion would probably be in use from an early date, both in preaching, instruction, and apologetics, and for recital in the Christian Eucharist or Lord's Supper.

(3) These chapters, with chapter 24, form the climax for which 9^{51}–19^{27} was a preparation.

(4) There is a contrast between the atmosphere of Luke's narrative and that of Mark: (*a*) The tragedy and horror of Mark's account are toned down by Luke or in the source that he is using. Mark's grim introduction (14^{3-9}) is omitted, the build-up of the Gethsemane scene is far less tense (22^{29-46}; cp. Mark 14^{32-43}), the betrayal by Judas does not overshadow the last supper (22^{21-23}; cp. Mark 14^{17-21}), the disciples' desertion of Jesus is not described, and Peter's denial of Jesus is mollified by the promise of his future important role (22^{31-34}); (*b*) Mark's picture of the loneliness of Jesus, who treads the path of God and of redemption in solitary greatness, is relieved by Luke, who records the sympathy of the women (23^{27}), of the penitent criminal (23^{29-43}), and of the crowds (23^{48}), and has no reference to the cry of dereliction (Mark 15^{34}); (*c*) Luke lays much more stress on the triumph of Jesus' closing hours, seen in his confidence about the future and his undying love for people, his death being the path to a heavenly splendour (24^{26}); (*d*) Mark and Luke are emphasizing two different

2 called the Passover. And the chief priests and the scribes
were seeking how to put him to death; for they feared the
people.
3 Then Satan entered into Judas called Iscariot, who was of

---

aspects of the crucifixion story, the first stressing the horror and sordidness of what men did to Jesus, and the dark and solitary agony through which he went, the other sensing the triumph and joy of an event by which he triumphed and Satan was defeated.

(5) In Luke, as in Matthew and Mark, Jesus' situation is partly described in language from the Psalms, relating to the sufferings of God's faithful servants (23^{34-35}, Ps. $22^{7, 18}$; 23^{36}, Ps. 69^{21}; 23^{46}, Ps. 31^{5}; 23^{49}, Ps. 38^{11}). Such suffering must be included in the role of the Messiah ($24^{26, 44}$).

(6) The death of Jesus in Luke, as in Matthew and Mark, takes place on the Passover feast day itself (contrast John, where, probably for theological reasons, the crucifixion is set during the Preparation for the feast, e.g. 19^{14}); see also J. Jeremias, *The Eucharistic Words of Jesus*, pp. 1–88.

(7) The background to the trial of Jesus is well discussed in A. N. Sherwin-White, *Roman Society and Roman Law in the New Testament*, pp. 1–47.

22: 1–6 The plot to kill Jesus

See also Matt. $26^{1-5, 14-16}$; Mark $14^{1-2, 10-11}$; John 13^{2}. Luke may also be using a special source in addition to Mark.

1 *Passover* and *Unleavened Bread* were names for the same festival, which lasted seven days beginning on Nisan 15. All the evangelists connect Jesus' crucifixion closely with this season, and later his death was seen as a new Passover festival, with himself as the new paschal victim (cp. 1 Cor. 5^{7-8}).

3 On the motives of Judas there is almost complete silence (but see John 12^{6}). Luke (cp. John $13^{2, 27}$) attributes the action of Judas to *Satan*. This is not just an attempt to find extenuating circumstances for Judas, but is intended to depict the sufferings and death of Jesus as a battle-ground between God and the forces of evil, in which God is victorious (cp. $22^{31, 53}$). *of the number of the twelve* stresses the horribleness of the action.

4 the number of the twelve; he went away and conferred with
the chief priests and captains how he might betray him to
5 them. And they were glad, and engaged to give him money.
6 So he agreed, and sought an opportunity to betray him to
them in the absence of the multitude.

7 Then came the day of Unleavened Bread, on which the
8 passover lamb had to be sacrificed. So Jesus[g] sent Peter and
John, saying, 'Go and prepare the passover for us, that we
9 may eat it.' They said to him, 'Where will you have us prepare
10 it?' He said to them, 'Behold, when you have entered the
city, a man carrying a jar of water will meet you; follow him
11 into the house which he enters, and tell the householder,
"The Teacher says to you, Where is the guest room, where
12 I am to eat the passover with my disciples?" And he will
show you a large upper room furnished; there make ready.'

[g] Greek *he*

---

4 *captains*: of the temple guard (cp. Acts 4^{1}, 5^{24}).

5 Matthew gives the amount as thirty pieces of silver (cp. Zech. 11^{12}).

6 *in the absence of the multitude*, or 'without causing a disturbance'.

2: 7–13 The preparations to observe the Passover

See also Matt. 26^{17-19}; Mark 14^{12-16}. Luke is probably using Mark. Jesus had very likely prearranged plans, in the interests of secrecy, with the owner of the house both for leading the disciples to the house and for the use of the room. *the day of Unleavened Bread* is a strange, but perhaps legitimate description of Nisan 14, as, according to rabbinical rulings, the law about abstention from leavened bread came into force from 12 noon on that day in the period of 'the preparation'). In this period the paschal lambs were sacrificed for the Passover meal, which followed in the early part of Nisan 15, and had to be eaten in Jerusalem.

0 The sight of a man carrying a *jar* or pitcher would be unusual; such work would normally be done by a woman.

1 *with my disciples*: the Passover was eaten in a family or similar group.

2 *a large upper room*: with access from an outside staircase. There would be need of unleavened bread, wine for the Passover cups, and the Paschal lamb. *furnished*: with tables and couches.

13 And they went, and found it as he had told them; and they
prepared the passover.
14 And when the hour came, he sat at table, and the apostles
15 with him. And he said to them, 'I have earnestly desired to
16 eat this passover with you before I suffer; for I tell you I shall

---

22: 14–18 The end of the Jewish Passover

Verse 18 is similar to Mark 14[25], but Luke is probably using a special source, where the Marcan saying was given in a more extended form.

14 Jesus would be the host or president at the meal, with important duties.

15 There is close parallelism between vv. 15–16 (*A*) and vv. 17–18 (*B*):

A	*B*
eating of Passover	drinking of cup
'I shall not eat'	'I shall not drink'
'fulfilled in the kingdom of God'	'until the kingdom of God comes'

Each saying stresses the distinctiveness of the present Passover as the last before God's new order, the kingdom of God, comes in full force. Jesus goes to his death believing that the old order based on the Exodus from Egypt, and commemorated at the Jewish Passover, is now giving way to a new deliverance, through which God will assert his kingship and bring in his kingdom. The genuineness of these sayings is suggested by the vague, though confident, reference to the future kingdom, and the lack of any clearly defined connection between this event and Jesus' death.

I have earnestly desired: because it is the prelude to decisive events. *before I suffer*, or 'endure death' (cp. Mark 8[31]). A play on words may be intended between *passover* (πάσχα) and *suffer* (παθεῖν).

16 *I shall not eat it* is the original reading rather than the alternative 'I shall never eat it again' (RSV margin), which will then be an amplification of the first. The negative (οὐ μή) adds firmness and certainty to a future statement. *until*, or, better, 'before': before Jesus can join in another Jewish Passover, and even before the present one is finished, it is already giving way to something better. At this time each Passover was a foretaste of a new order, when God would establish his sovereignty over his world, and Jesus is confident of the nearness of this event: the kingdom of God, already demonstrated in

17 not eat it[h] until it is fulfilled in the kingdom of God.' And he
took a cup, and when he had given thanks he said, 'Take this,
18 and divide it among yourselves, for I tell you that from now
on I shall not drink of the fruit of the vine until the kingdom
19 of God comes.' And he took bread, and when he had given

[h] Other ancient authorities read *never eat it again*

---

his ministry, is to receive a more explosive and vital demonstration through going to death.

-18 *a cup*: one of the Passover cups passed round during the meal. *took*: into his hands. The implication is that Jesus drinks of the cup: the interpretation of *I shall not drink* as an oath of abstention by which Jesus consecrates himself to death is, therefore, doubtful; like v. 16, it is best taken as a firm prophecy about the future. *until*, or, better, 'before' (as in v. 16). The sharing of the cup with the disciples associates them with Jesus in this confident hope.

2: 19–20 Jesus gives meaning to his coming death

The RSV ends at 19a, adopting what is known as the 'shorter text' (the 'longer text' being given in the RSV margin). This longer text forms a parallel with vv. 15–16:

Vv. 15–18	*Vv.* 19–20
The old Passover, with its eating of unleavened bread in remembrance of the Exodus (v. 15)	Jesus takes bread and connects it with remembrance of himself (v. 19)
The future holds something decisive for God's purposes (v. 16)	The decisiveness of Jesus' coming death (v. 19)
The Passover cup (v. 17)	The cup after the meal (v. 20)
The confidence that the immediate future will be momentous (v. 18)	The new covenant to be made through Jesus' death (v. 20)
'when he had given thanks' (v. 17)	'when he had given thanks' (v. 19)
The old order ends	The way in which the new order is inaugurated

The longer text may be original. The MSS. evidence strongly supports it (only D and the Old Latin version omitting it), while the shorter text ends very abruptly. The omission of 19b–20 may be due to a failure to understand the mention of two cups (only found in Luke),

thanks he broke it and gave it to them, saying, 'This is my
21 body.[i] But behold the hand of him who betrays me is with me

[i] Other ancient authorities add *which is given for you. Do this in remembrance of me.* [20] *And likewise the cup after supper, saying, 'This cup which is poured out for you is the new covenant in my blood.*

---

which led to the various rearrangements of the whole section found in some versions. The importance of the parallelism between vv. 15–18 and vv. 19–20, which passes from the thought of the coming of the new order to that of the means by which it is inaugurated, may not have been appreciated, and so led to the shortening of the text. Further, the close connection of vv. 17–18 with vv. 15–16 rather than with v. 19 may not have been recognized. Luke may be drawing on a special source, which represents a tradition similar to 1 Cor. 11^{23-25} (cp. Matt. 26^{26-28}; Mark 14^{22-24}).

19 A Jewish meal usually included breaking of bread (here unleavened) by the host, accompanied by praise and thanksgiving to God. Jesus makes the action symbolical by the additional *This is my body*: his body, his person or himself, will be broken in death, and (like bread in the physical sense) will bring the life of God to his disciples. *Do this in remembrance of me* (margin; cp. 1 Cor. 11^{24-25}): his death will be worthy of continual remembrance (cp. Exod. 12^{14}). *in remembrance of me*, or 'for my memorial', might include the idea of making effective in the present the benefits of Jesus' death. *gave* suggests that Jesus is binding his followers into a close fellowship based on his death.

20 'he took' is probably to be understood from v. 19. *likewise*: Jesus now uses the cup of wine for symbolical action, as previously he used the bread. *the cup*: the definite article contrasts with v. 17 ('a cup'), implying the one and single cup that followed the meal, or suggesting the cup to which Christians are accustomed in the Lord's Supper. The relationship between God and Israel was based on a *covenant* or 'agreement', established by the blood of sacrificial animals (representing 'life'), which was sprinkled on the people and the altar, thus effecting a new life relationship between God and Israel (Exod. 24^{3-8}). Similarly for Jesus the red wine of the cup is his blood and his life about to be given in death, which will bring about a *new covenant* (cp. Jer. 31^{31}) and a new living relationship between God and human beings. *which is poured out for you* could go with *the cup*, but from its sense and position in the sentence qualifies *blood*, the construction being loose, perhaps the result of translation from Aramaic.

22: 21–23 The Betrayer

See also Matt. 26^{21-25}; Mark 14^{18-21}; cp. John 13^{21-30}. But differences between Luke and Mark suggest that he is using another source.

22 on the table. For the Son of man goes as it has been de-
23 termined; but woe to that man by whom he is betrayed!' And
they began to question one another, which of them it was
that would do this.

24 A dispute also arose among them, which of them was to be
25 regarded as the greatest. And he said to them, 'The kings of
the Gentiles exercise lordship over them; and those in
26 authority over them are called benefactors. But not so with
you; rather let the greatest among you become as the youngest,
27 and the leader as one who serves. For which is the greater,
one who sits at table, or one who serves? Is it not the one who
sits at table? But I am among you as one who serves.

---

21 The Gospels are not interested in answering the question why steps were not taken to prevent the betrayer's action. *But*: introducing a jarring note. *the hand . . . is with me*: the hand of Judas, now connected with fellowship and friendship, will be raised against Jesus.

22 *as it has been determined*: in God's purposes. *woe to that man* stresses the seriousness of Judas' action (cp. Acts 1^{18-19}).

24–27 The real greatness

See also Matt. 20^{24-28}; Mark 10^{41-45}; cp. John 13^{4-16}. The general theme is the same as in Matthew and Mark, but the context and language are different, the saying here having greater rhythm and structure. Luke is probably drawing on a special source. Jesus' self-renunciation, and the self-centredness on the disciples, are contrasted.

4 *the greatest*: in the earthly kingdom that they were expecting.

5 In the outside world it is the exercise of power over others that gains the name of 'benefactor', a title conferred on princes and other outstanding men, especially in the East.

7 *the youngest*: the juniors, or least important. Ordinary standards are reversed: true greatness is assessed as a willingness to serve others, a principle seen in the selfgivingness of Jesus himself.

28–30 The privileges of the disciples

See also Matt. 19^{28} (in another context and with certain differences). The saying links up here with the theme of the disciples' status: although the disciples should not be quarrelling about precedence, yet Jesus can offer them an important place in his kingdom.

28 'You are those who have continued with me in my trials; as
29 my Father appointed a kingdom for me, so do I appoint for
30 you that you may eat and drink at my table in my kingdom,
and sit on thrones judging the twelve tribes of Israel.
31 'Simon, Simon, behold, Satan demanded to have you,[j]
32 that he might sift you[j] like wheat, but I have prayed for you
that your faith may not fail; and when you have turned again,

[j] The Greek word for *you* here is plural; in verse 32 it is singular

---

28 *continued with me*: stood firmly by me. Others had deserted Jesus (cp. Jesus 6[66]), while the twelve, despite their failings, had made sacrifices and had been loyal in their friendship with him. *trials*: both controversies with official Judaism, and testings by the devil.

29–30 *appointed*, or 'appointed by deed of covenant': just as the Israelite king's appointment was often based on a covenant with God (cp. 2 Kgs. 11[17]), so here God has entered into a covenant with Jesus (probably at his baptism) to establish him as Messianic king. In turn, under the covenant made by his death (v. 20), Jesus 'appoints' or 'bequeathes' to his disciples a place in his kingdom. Ironically, in the face of death, Jesus is sure that he will prove to be a king with a kingdom (a confidence in God's cause justified in 24[1–53]), and can give places at court to his disciples. For Luke the promise is probably fulfilled in the position of the apostles as the leaders of the Christian Church—a privilege which also involves sharing their master's sufferings. They judge *the twelve tribes of Israel*, the Jewish nation, by their preaching of the gospel, before which the Jews are shown up in their true light.

22: 31–34 The role of Simon Peter

Verse 34 is parallel to Mark 14[30]. Otherwise the section seems to be derived from another source (to which the use of 'Simon' also points).

31 *sift*: see what is good in you. The evil power is trying not only to do away with Jesus, but also to disrupt the fellowship that Jesus leaves behind him. *demanded*, better than 'has been given leave' (cp. Plutarch, *Moralia*, 417 D, 'violent spirits who demand a human soul').

32 The demands of Satan are countered by Jesus' prayer (cp. vv. 39–44 below). *you* is singular, contrasting with the plural 'you' of v. 31 (see RSV margin). *faith*: belief in the rightness of Jesus' cause and claims. *when you have turned again*, i.e. 'have returned in loyalty to Jesus', or 'have come to yourself', suggests that Simon may have a

33 strengthen your brethren.' And he said to him, 'Lord, I am
34 ready to go with you to prison and to death.' He said, 'I tell
you, Peter, the cock will not crow this day, until you three
times deny that you know me.'
35 And he said to them, 'When I sent you out with no purse or
bag or sandals, did you lack anything?' They said, 'Nothing.'
36 He said to them, 'But now, let him who has a purse take it,
and likewise a bag. And let him who has no sword sell his
37 mantle and buy one. For I tell you that this scripture must be
fulfilled in me, "And he was reckoned with transgressors";
38 for what is written about me has its fulfilment.' And they

---

temporary failure of nerve, but he is to be a stabilizing influence, holding the fellowship of the disciples together in readiness for future events. The disciples kept together as a group even before Jesus' resurrection (cp. $24^{9, 22, 33}$). Simon's position of leadership in the early Church most likely goes back to an arrangement made by Jesus.

:3 For Simon Peter's later imprisonment and death see Acts 5^{17-18}, 12^{4}; John 21^{18}; 2 Pet. 1^{14}. When Luke–Acts was written, Peter's death during Nero's persecution may well have been known.

4 *the cock will not crow this day*: before morning comes. *three times*: perhaps Jesus meant it in the sense of 'decisively'.

: 35–38 Coming hostility

The section is found only in Luke. On their previous mission (cp. 9^{3}, 10^{4}) the disciples relied on a hospitable reception, but now hostility must be expected and they must fend for themselves.

5 Only in dire circumstances would a person sell his *mantle*, or 'cloak', the outer garment. A *sword* symbolizes the present situation, in which hostility against Jesus is soon to reach its climax (cp. Matt. 10^{34}).

7 *this scripture*: Isa. 53^{12} (cp. Acts 8^{32}; 1 Pet. 2^{21-25}). Like the Suffering Servant, Jesus is classed with criminals and hunted down like one of them. *for what . . . fulfilment*, lit. 'the matter concerning me has an end': (*a*) the role of the servant who suffers to bring human beings to God receives its perfect embodiment in Jesus, or (*b*) 'my career is reaching its completion' (cp. 13^{32}).

The disciples misunderstand Jesus' words, just as, contrary to his wishes, they later use their swords (22^{49-51}). Jesus' reply may be ironic ('two swords will be more than enough'), or may be his way of dismissing the subject.

8369107 S

said, 'Look, Lord, here are two swords.' And he said to them,
'It is enough.'
39 And he came out, and went, as was his custom, to the
40 Mount of Olives; and the disciples followed him. And when
he came to the place he said to them, 'Pray that you may not
41 enter into temptation.' And he withdrew from them about
42 a stone's throw, and knelt down and prayed, 'Father, if thou
art willing, remove this cup from me; nevertheless not my
43 will, but thine, be done.' And there appeared to him an angel
44 from heaven, strengthening him. And being in an agony he

22: 39–46 Jesus in prayer on the Mount of Olives.

See also Matt. 26^{36-46}; Mark 14^{35-42}; cp. John 12^{27-28}, 18^{11}. Luke's version is sometimes thought to be a rewriting of Mark's, in an attempt to smoothe the tragic contrast between the picture of Jesus engaged in inner conflict and that of his disciples who are asleep, and also to tone down the agony of Jesus and present him as unperturbed (a view difficult to hold if vv. 43–44 are original). Luke may, however, be relying on another source.

39 *the Mount of Olives* contained Gethsemane, the scene in Mark and Matthew of what follows. *the place*: either the Mount of Olives or the spot there chosen by Jesus.

42 *cup*: destiny of suffering and death, already symbolized in the literal use of the cup at 22^{20}.

43–44 These verses are best regarded as original. Their later omission by some important MSS. may be traced to a desire to stress the sufficiency of Jesus' own strength, and to tone down the anguish that the thought of the cross brought to Jesus. For angelic help in time of testing cp. Mark 1^{13}. *agony*, or 'anxiety', in Stoical writings a mental state to be overcome, means the anguish that results from a conflict of mind. It has been attributed to Jesus' horror at the coming cleavage between God and his people in their rejection of 'his chosen one', or to Jesus' consciousness that in his coming death he is going to feel the impact and dreadfulness of human sin, as though his own. Perhaps, however, the agony is connected with the prospect of abandoning himself and God's cause completely into the hands of his enemies and seeing it apparently defeated. Jesus is thus in line with the faithful men of God of the past (e.g. Ps. 22^{1}), and as a full human being shares our fears (cp. Heb. 5^{1-10}).

prayed more earnestly; and his sweat became like great drops
45 of blood falling down upon the ground.[k] And when he rose
from prayer, he came to the disciples and found them sleeping
46 for sorrow, and he said to them, 'Why do you sleep? Rise and
pray that you may not enter into temptation.'
47 While he was still speaking, there came a crowd, and the
man called Judas, one of the twelve, was leading them. He
48 drew near to Jesus to kiss him; but Jesus said to him, 'Judas,
49 would you betray the Son of man with a kiss?' And when
those who were about him saw what would follow, they said,
50 'Lord, shall we strike with the sword?' And one of them struck
51 the slave of the high priest and cut off his right ear. But Jesus
said, 'No more of this!' And he touched his ear and healed
52 him. Then Jesus said to the chief priests and captains of the

[k] Other ancient authorities omit verses 43 and 44

---

45 Only Luke accounts for the sleep—nervous exhaustion arising from sorrow and anxiety at the crisis facing Jesus.

46 In this critical situation they should be praying that they may not come to the point of doubting and deserting God's purposes (cp. 11^{4}).

2: 47–53 The arrest of Jesus

See also Matt. 26^{47-56}; Mark 14^{43-50}; cp. John 18^{3-9}. Luke's account is shorter than Mark's, with the same main features. The only clear parallel with Mark is vv. 52b–53, suggesting Luke's use of a special source.

8 *still speaking*: the time of testing is beginning. In Mark the kiss of greeting is a prearranged signal. Jesus' words mean: 'Are you marking this act of treachery with a greeting that betokens friendship?'

9 Cp. 22^{38}.

1 John (18^{10}) identifies the striker as Simon Peter. Luke and John tell us that it was *the right ear*. *no more of this*, i.e. of violence. *slave* suggests that it was an improvised company drawn partly from the high priest's household. Jewish slavery was limited to a period of years and not lifelong.

3 The presence of such high dignitaries (only mentioned by Luke) shows the seriousness with which they viewed the matter. *captains of*

temple and elders, who come out against him, 'Have you come
53 out as against a robber, with swords and clubs? When I was
with you day after day in the temple, you did not lay hands
on me. But this is your hour, and the power of darkness.'
54 Then they seized him and led him away, bringing him into
55 the high priest's house. Peter followed at a distance; and
when they had kindled a fire in the middle of the courtyard
56 and sat down together, Peter sat among them. Then a maid,
seeing him as he sat in the light and gazing at him, said, 'This
57 man also was with him.' But he denied it, saying, 'Woman,
58 I do not know him.' And a little later some one else saw him
and said, 'You also are one of them.' But Peter said, 'Man,
59 I am not.' And after an interval of about an hour still another
insisted, saying, 'Certainly this man also was with him; for he

---

the temple: here probably part of the guard that the temple's overseer (Acts 4^{1}) had at his disposal. *swords* and *clubs* suggest a hunt for a *robber* or 'bandit' operating in secret, whereas Jesus acted in the open. *your hour*: when Jesus' captors dictate events. Yet in another sense Jesus is doing this, as the crucifixion is part of God's plan and the way to his own glory. Behind the Jewish action lies *the power of darkness* (cp. Eph. 6^{12}), the forces of evil, who in this attack on Jesus are challenging God's sovereignty.

22: 54–61 Peter disowns Jesus

See also Matt. $26^{58,\ 69-75}$; Mark $14^{54,\ 66-72}$; cp. John $18^{15,\ 25-27}$. The differences between Luke and Mark once again suggest Luke's use of a special source. Perhaps the story was preserved to show how Jesus was left to face his fate alone, and to contrast Peter's refusal to own Jesus with his subsequent rock-like witness to him.

55–56 Peter was brave enough to risk the danger of being recognized. The middle of the night would be cold in the Palestinian spring; hence the *fire* that showed up Peter's features.

59 Peter's Galilean accent must have betrayed his origin (cp. Matt. 26^{73}). The Galileans pronounced Aramaic differently from their Jewish brethren in Judaea.

60 is a Galilean.' But Peter said, 'Man, I do not know what you
are saying.' And immediately, while he was still speaking, the
61 cock crowed. And the Lord turned and looked at Peter. And
Peter remembered the word of the Lord, how he had said to
him, 'Before the cock crows today, you will deny me three
62 times.' And he went out and wept bitterly.
63 Now the men who were holding Jesus mocked him and
64 beat him; they also blindfolded him and asked him, 'Prophesy!
65 Who is it that struck you?' And they spoke many other words
against him, reviling him.

---

60 *the cock crowed*: heralding the morning and fulfilling Jesus' prediction (v. 34 above).

61 Only Luke mentions the glance of Jesus, not necessarily one of reproach, but more probably one of reassurance, and a reminder that despite his present feeling of failure Peter still has an important part to play.

2: 63–65 The mocking of Jesus

See also Matt. 26^{67}; Mark 14^{65}. Some variations from Mark suggest a different source. This treatment of Jesus places him in line with the faithful men of God (e.g. Ps. 22^{6-8}).

63 *holding*: in Luke the incident fills the time before the first and only hearing of Jesus' case before the Sanhedrin.

64 The taunt reflects the reputation that Jesus had of being a prophet.

2: 66–71 Jesus before the Sanhedrin.

See also Matt. 26^{59-66}; Mark 14^{55-64}; cp. John 18^{19-24}. Luke records only one meeting of the Jewish council at dawn. The sole aim is to establish Jesus' claim to kingly power, and there is no discussion of blasphemy. Luke's narrative does not raise the issue of the council's power to pass and execute the death penalty (an unlikely privilege; cp. John 18^{31}). Luke's account has certain similarities with Mark's, but in essentials differs widely. He is sometimes thought to be tidying up Mark's account, but if he is mainly using Mark, his omission of the charge of blasphemy is strange, as it would have enabled him to stress (cp. Acts 24^{20}, 26^{6-8}) that Jesus' activity was one involving the Jewish religion and not the Roman state. Luke may, therefore, be following another source, with, perhaps, some Marcan additions.

66 When day came, the assembly of the elders of the people
gathered together, both chief priests and scribes; and they
67 led him away to their council, and they said, 'If you are the
Christ, tell us.' But he said to them, 'If I tell you, you will not
68, 69 believe; and if I ask you, you will not answer. But from now
on the Son of man shall be seated at the right hand of the
70 power of God.' And they all said, 'Are you the Son of God,
71 then?' And he said to them, 'You say that I am.' And they
said, 'What further testimony do we need? We have heard it
ourselves from his own lips.'

---

66 The *assembly* would include, with others, the two groups mentioned. The Roman custom was to use existing councils for purposes of law and order.

67–68 Jesus' stress on the futility of saying anything (only mentioned by Luke) links up with the description in Matthew and Mark of Jesus' silence in face of accusation. *if I tell you*: that I am the expected Saviour. *not believe*: because the Jewish leaders would not see royalty in such a helpless person. For an unanswered question cp. 20[1–8]. The Jews will not join in unbiased discussion.

69 Jesus is confident of the future, whatever the Jews' reaction: *the Son of man* (the title he himself prefers, and not carrying the same political and nationalist overtones) will be *seated at the right hand of the power of God*, a phrase which suggests vindication at the hands of God and the triumph of his cause, and also the non-earthly nature of Jesus' kingship (cp. 20[43]). *from now on* expresses the absolute certainty of vindication. Here, as elsewhere (e.g. 9[51]), Luke's interest is in the triumphal exhaltation of Jesus to share God's throne, the prelude to the coming of the Holy Spirit and the Church's mission. Mark has just 'the power', itself a reverent description of God'

70 The change from 'Son of man' to *Son of God* is probably a return to the original question of v. 67, 'the Son of God' being an alternative title of 'the Christ'. If this title could be fastened on Jesus, then a charge of sedition could be plausibly brought against him. *all*: this was the question they all wanted answered. Jesus' reply, as in the text, suggests a non-committal answer; the reaction in v. 71 is then a deduction from Jesus' refusal to deny the charge. But Jesus' answer might mean: 'You are right; for I am.' He will not refuse the title, though it has to be qualified as in v. 69 (cp. Mark's 'I am').

23: THEN the whole company of them arose, and brought him
2 before Pilate. And they began to accuse him, saying, 'We
found this man perverting our nation, and forbidding us to
give tribute to Caesar, and saying that he himself is Christ a
3 king.' And Pilate asked him, 'Are you the King of the Jews?'
4 And he answered him, 'You have said so.' And Pilate said to
the chief priests and the multitudes, 'I find no crime in this
5 man.' But they were urgent, saying, 'He stirs up the people,
teaching throughout all Judea, from Galilee even to this place.'
6 When Pilate heard this, he asked whether the man was a
7 Galilean. And when he learned that he belonged to Herod's
jurisdiction, he sent him over to Herod, who was himself in

23: 1–25 The investigation of Jesus' case by Pilate and Herod

See also Matt. 27^{1-26}; Mark 15^{1-15}; cp. John 18^{28}–19^{16}. The hearing before Herod is only found in Luke (cp. Acts 25^{23}–26^{32}). The linguistic parallels between Mark and Luke are so small that Luke may be drawing on a special source (v. 19 may be derived from Mark 15^{7}, and v. 22a. from Mark 15^{14a}). The belief of Herod and Pilate in Jesus' innocence is strongly emphasized.

1 Before this there would be an interval while Pilate was warned of a case impending. It was Roman governors' practice to hear such cases at an early hour.

2 This charge, the only one to carry weight with the Roman authorities, is made clear from the start. *a king* brings out the meaning of *Christ*, and, being the emperor's title, would suggest treason.

3 Jesus' answer may mean: 'The term is one that you are using; I have never used it of myself.'

4 *the multitudes*: the sightseers in court. Pilate doubts whether there is a case to answer.

5 The dangerous extent of Jesus' activity now reinforces the charge (cp. Acts 10^{37}, 13^{31}). *Galilee* leads directly to Pilate's determination to consult Herod, tetrarch of Galilee. *stirs up*: to rebellion.

7 *sent him over*, or 'remitted him': used of referring someone or something to a higher, or, as here, an appropriate authority. Pilate did not pass the case entirely to Herod, as the law did not demand that a person should be passed for trial to the authority of his native place. Herod was in Jerusalem for the Passover festival.

8 Jerusalem at that time. When Herod saw Jesus, he was very
glad, for he had long desired to see him, because he had heard
about him, and he was hoping to see some sign done by him.
9 So he questioned him at some length; but he made no answer.
10 The chief priests and the scribes stood by, vehemently
11 accusing him. And Herod with his soldiers treated him with
contempt and mocked him; then, arraying him in gorgeous
12 apparel, he sent him back to Pilate. And Herod and Pilate
became friends with each other that very day, for before this
they had been at enmity with each other.

13 Pilate then called together the chief priests and the rulers
14 and the people, and said to them, 'You brought me this man
as one who was perverting the people; and after examining
him before you, behold, I did not find this man guilty of any
15 of your charges against him; neither did Herod, for he sent
him back to us. Behold, nothing deserving death has been
16 done by him; I will therefore chastise him and release him.'[l]

[l] Here, or after verse 19, other ancient authorities add verse 17, *Now he was obliged to release one man to them at the festival*

---

8 Cp. 9^9. Herod was not interested in the real significance of Jesus, but in satisfying his own thirst for a *sign* or for the miraculous.

9 *made no answer*: Jesus knew that Herod was not out to discover the truth.

10 The Jewish authorities are there to present their case.

11 *soldiers*: probably Herod's personal bodyguard. *gorgeous apparel*, fit for a king and given in irony, but none the less appropriate to Jesus' real majesty. The case now goes back to Pilate.

12 The reason for the enmity is not known, unless it was concerned with the governor's treatment of the Galileans (13^1). Herod was probably flattered by Pilate's courtesy in consulting him.

13 The public may have been 'packed' by the Jewish leaders to make a demonstration to influence the governor. Luke may also wish to show that the Jewish people bear some responsibility.

16 *chastise*, or 'flog': as a warning. Roman citizens were protected against such treatment. *release*, or 'acquit'.

18 But they all cried out together, 'Away with this man, and
19 release to us Barabbas'—a man who had been thrown into
prison for an insurrection started in the city, and for murder.
20 Pilate addressed them once more, desiring to release Jesus;
21, 22 but they shouted out, 'Crucify, crucify him!' A third time he
said to them, 'Why, what evil has he done? I have found in
him no crime deserving death; I will therefore chastise him
23 and release him.' But they were urgent, demanding with loud
cries that he should be crucified. And their voices prevailed.
24 So Pilate gave sentence that their demand should be granted.
25 He released the man who had been thrown into prison for
insurrection and murder, whom they asked for; but Jesus he
delivered up to their will.
26 And as they led him away, they seized one Simon of

---

17 This verse is given in RSV margin; it is a later comment based on Matt. 27^{15}; Mark 15^{6}; cp. John 18^{39}. Our knowledge of such amnesties is very incomplete, but such a concession at a great festival should by no means be ruled out.

18 *together*: a public demonstration of feeling. *Barabbas* may also have had the name 'Jesus' (see Matt. 27^{16-17}), Barabbas itself being a patronymic, 'son of Abbas'. We only meet with him here.

19 Thus the iniquity of the Jewish choice is stressed; such insurrections were frequent in this period. Ironically, one who had definite *insurrection* proved against him is released, while Jesus, who was innocent of any such act, is condemned.

21 This is the first mention of crucifixion in Luke, the method of execution of a non-Roman citizen.

23 Pilate yields to the public demand, a small price to pay for the avoidance of disturbance in the city.

24 The governor passes official sentence. *their demand*: for the death penalty on Jesus and for the release of Barabbas. The unvarnished repetition of the man's offence stresses once more (cp. v. 19) the enormity of the action.

23: 26–49 The crucifixion of Jesus

See also Matt. 27^{31-56}; Mark 15^{20-41}; cp. John 19^{16-37}. The main part of the section is peculiar to Luke. Vv. 26, 33–34, 38, 44–45, and perhaps v. 35, are taken from Mark.

Cyrene, who was coming in from the country, and laid on
27 him the cross, to carry it behind Jesus. And there followed
him a great multitude of the people, and of women who be-
28 wailed and lamented him. But Jesus turning to them said,
'Daughters of Jerusalem, do not weep for me, but weep for
29 yourselves and for your children. For behold, the days are
coming when they will say, "Blessed are the barren, and the
wombs that never bore, and the breasts that never gave suck!"
30 Then they will begin to say to the mountains, "Fall on us";
31 and to the hills, "Cover us." For if they do this when the
wood is green, what will happen when it is dry?'
32 Two others also, who were criminals, were led away to be
33 put to death with him. And when they came to the place
which is called The Skull, there they crucified him, and the

---

26 Contrast John 19^{16}. The condemned criminal usually carried his own cross. Jesus may have been physically too weak, or he may have carried his cross some distance until *Simon* took over.

27 Jesus receives more sympathy in Luke's account than is reported in Mark.

28 *weep not*: no appeal to pity Jesus is found in the Gospels, a sentiment out of keeping with his regal figure.

29 Childlessness, usually a sign of adversity, will be considered a blessing in the dreadful time coming.

30 The language (cp. Hos. 10^{8}) expresses human terror at God's judgement and a desire to escape from it (cp. Rev. 6^{16}).

31 For *green* and *dry wood* cp. Ezek. 20^{47}. The contrast is between what is easily ignited and what is not. The reference may be to (*a*) the Romans: if they can act so discriminately and unjustly in a situation where there is little to inflame their passion (with an innocent man before them), what enormities will they commit in a situation where their passions will be fully roused by an inane rebellion of the Jews! Or it may be to (*b*) the Jews: if they act so spitefully with so little provocation, what horrors will they commit when tempers run high in rebellion against Rome?

32 Jesus, in life and in death, mixes with sinners.

33 *The Scull*, or Golgotha (its Aramaic name), an eminence near Jerusalem, named after its shape. *they*: the Roman soldiers.

34 criminals, one on the right and one on the left. And Jesus
said, 'Father, forgive them; for they know not what they do.'[m]
35 And they cast lots to divide his garments. And the people
stood by, watching; but the rulers scoffed at him, saying, 'He
saved others; let him save himself, if he is the Christ of God,
36 his Chosen One!' The soldiers also mocked him, coming up
37 and offering him vinegar, and saying, 'If you are the King of
38 the Jews, save yourself!' There was also an inscription over
him,[n] 'This is the King of the Jews.'
39 One of the criminals who were hanged railed at him, saying,

[m] Other ancient authorities omit the sentence *And Jesus . . . what they do*
[n] Other ancient authorities add *in letters of Greek and Latin and Hebrew*

---

34 The verse, though omitted by some important MSS., is almost certainly part of the original text (cp. Acts 7^{60}). *they*: the Roman soldiers or everyone concerned, who do not know the seriousness of what is happening (cp. Acts 3^{17}). Again Jesus' thought for others is stressed, and so he lives out the prayer of 11^{4}, and his command of 6^{27-36}: contrast Neh. 4^{4-5}; Jer. 15^{5}. *and they cast . . . garments*: cp. Ps. 22^{19}, quoted only at John 19^{11}. The executioners' squad had the right to share out the minor possessions of their victims.

35 Cp. Ps. 22^{7}. The common theme of vv. 35–39 is the taunting of Jesus by various groups, and the constant reference to the kingship of Jesus. *saved others*: a description of Jesus' healing work and acts of resurrection. *chosen*: a term used of the Israelite king, and so naturally transferred to the Messianic king. *save himself*: by delivering himself from the cross in some miraculous way. Yet, ironically, Jesus becomes *the Christ* not by saving himself, but by committing himself into God's hands and by being vindicated at his resurrection.

36 Cp. Matt. 27^{48}; Mark 15^{36}; John 19^{28}. This sour wine (cp. Ps. 69^{21}) was the common drink of the lower classes.

38 The scroll over each criminal's cross gave the reason for execution, and so accounts for the soldiers' jeers. Some important MSS. add (RSV margin) that the writing was in 'Greek and Latin and Hebrew', stressing the world-wide relevance of Jesus' death, but this is probably an assimilation to John 19^{20}.

39 Matthew and Mark record only the reviling of Jesus by the other criminals. For *hanged*, which occurs only here in the Gospels as a description of crucifixion, cp. Deut. 21^{22-23}; Acts 5^{30}, 10^{39}. Despite the

40 'Are you not the Christ? Save yourself and us!' But the other
rebuked him, saying, 'Do you not fear God, since you are
41 under the same sentence of condemnation? And we indeed
justly; for we are receiving the due reward of our deeds; but
42 this man has done nothing wrong.' And he said, 'Jesus, re-
43 member me when you come in your kingly power.'[o] And he
said to him, 'Truly, I say to you, today you will be with
me in Paradise.'

44 It was now about the sixth hour, and there was darkness

[o] Greek *kingdom*

---

fact that under Jewish Law such a person, who was punished by hanging, was thought accursed in God's sight, the early Christians were, strikingly enough, convinced of the God-given mission of Jesus, a conviction to be traced to Jesus' resurrection appearances to them.

41 Again Luke stresses the innocence of Jesus.

42 *remember*: 'think of' or 'care for'. *in your kingly power*, or 'kingdom' (RSV margin): other readings are 'into your kingdom' and 'in the day of your coming', the first of which could well be original. The criminal believes that, in spite of Jesus' apparent humiliation, he will prove to be a king—a hope in contrast with the ironic mockery.

43 *paradise*, a 'park' or 'pleasure garden', also describes the garden of Eden (Gen. 2^{8}), a state of prosperity or happiness (Ezek. 28^{13}, 31^{8}), and the blessedness of the righteous in God's new age (Rev. 2^{7}). Even now Jesus is confident of the triumph of his cause, and in the midst of death can offer the criminal a happy future of fellowship with God. The implication may be that through the death of Jesus God's new era is opened up. The passage does not give direct teaching on the state of the departed, but suggests that the Christian dead are still personal beings in a personal relationship to Jesus. Strikingly, the reward of the righteous is offered here and now to the brigand, who, in however imperfect a way, has accepted the sovereignty of Jesus—a living illustration of Paul's teaching on 'justification by faith'. Once again Jesus accepts sinners as they are, and forgives them.

44 The time, 12 noon–3 p.m., points to an unusual and unnatural *darkness*, regarded as a portent. *darkness* denoted the displeasure of the Deity, or the activity of evil, and the Jews believed that such a phenomenon might precede the time of God's decisive intervention. It may also suggest that the earth is in mourning for this treatment of Jesus, and adds to the general sense of mystery.

45 over the whole land[p] until the ninth hour, while the sun's
light failed;[q] and the curtain of the temple was torn in two.
46 Then Jesus, crying with a loud voice, said, 'Father, into thy
hands I commit my spirit!' And having said this he breathed
47 his last. Now when the centurion saw what had taken place,
he praised God, and said, 'Certainly this man was innocent!'
48 And all the multitudes who assembled to see the sight, when
they saw what had taken place, returned home beating their
49 breasts. And all his acquaintances and the women who had
followed him from Galilee stood at a distance and saw these
things.

50 Now there was a man named Joseph from the Jewish town

[p] Or *earth*

[q] Or *the sun was eclipsed.* Other ancient authorities read *the sun was darkened*

---

5 In giving the reason for the darkness Luke may be influenced by, e.g., Joel 2^{28-32} (cp. Acts 2^{17-20}). *the curtain* is the partition between the Holy of Holies and the rest of the temple building. In Mark this happening, sited between the death of Jesus and the centurion's acknowledgement of him, symbolizes the opening of the presence of God to all men. For Luke it may mean that the temple has now fulfilled its usefulness and purpose.

The loud shout, probably a shout of victory, expresses Jesus' sure hope of vindication, now carried further by words from Ps. 33^{5}. Like the Psalmist, Jesus is entrusting himself to God in the face of persecution, knowing that God will prove his cause to be right. *breathed his last*: or 'died'.

what had taken place: probably the confident way in which Jesus died. For Luke the Gentile *centurion*, in charge of the execution squad (cp. Acts 27^{1}), probably typifies all the later non-Jews who will praise God and acknowledge Jesus. *innocent*, or 'righteous' (instead of Mark's 'Son of God'), may suggest that Jesus has divine approval.

The sightseers too had a revulsion of feeling about Jesus.

Cp. Ps. 38^{11}. For the woman cp. 8^{1-3}. The friends of Jesus were able to appreciate the reality of his resurrection, because they had seen him die a real death.

50–56 The burial of Jesus

See also Matt. 27^{57-66}; Mark 15^{42-47}; cp. John 19^{38-42}. Luke is probably following Mark, with the exception of vv. 54–56. The

of Arimathea. He was a member of the council, a good and
51 righteous man, who had not consented to their purpose and
52 deed, and he was looking for the kingdom of God. This man
53 went to Pilate and asked for the body of Jesus. Then he took
it down and wrapped it in a linen shroud, and laid him in a
54 rock-hewn tomb, where no one had ever yet been laid. It was
55 the day of Preparation, and the sabbath was beginning.[r] The
women who had come with him from Galilee followed, and
56 saw the tomb, and how his body was laid; then they returned,
and prepared spices and ointments.

On the sabbath they rested according to the commandment.

[r] Greek *was dawning*

---

interest here and in 24^{1} is in the desire to give Jesus a proper burial, as incorrect burial was repugnant to a Jew. The reality of Jesus' death is also being underlined (cp. 1 Cor. 15^{3-4}).

50 *Arimathea*: perhaps the modern Rentis, about twenty miles north-west of Jerusalem. *good and righteous*: he tried to observe the Jewish Law, *purpose* or 'plan': of disposing of Jesus.

52 Joseph's influential position gained him access to the governor. Jesus' body would normally have been thrown on the common rubbish heap.

53 Jewish tombs usually consisted of caves in the limestone rock, the hard strata being left as a roof, and the softer strata below being cut. *where no one had ever yet been laid* stresses the honoured treatment (cp. John 19^{41}).

54 According to the first three Gospels, Jesus was executed on the Passover Day, which was also the day before the Sabbath: Jesus died in the late afternoon, and the Sabbath would begin at 6 p.m., the same evening. Hence the haste of burial and the delay in the last funeral rites. *was beginning*, lit. 'was dawning': the verb means 'draw on', and does not imply that the Sabbath began at daybreak.

55 The women who have seen Jesus die (v. 49) now witness his burial, and note carefully the actual tomb and the position of the body. They would know, therefore, to which tomb to return.

56 *spices* and *perfumes* were used in the embalming of corpses. *the commandment*: forbidding work on the Sabbath (Exod. 20^{8}). *they rested*: in contrast with 24^{1}.

24: But on the first day of the week, at early dawn, they went
2 to the tomb, taking the spices which they had prepared. And
3 they found the stone rolled away from the tomb, but when
4 they went in they did not find the body.[s] While they were
perplexed about this, behold, two men stood by them in

[s] Other ancient authorities add *of the Lord Jesus*

24: 1–53 *The resurrection of Jesus*

24: 1–12 The tomb found empty

See also Matt. 28^{1-8}; Mark 16^{1-8}; cp. John 20^{1-11}. Though the Gospel writers naturally differ in details in describing such an unexpected shattering event, all agree that the tomb was found empty, and so posed a problem (cp. 24^{23}), without providing convincing evidence that Jesus was still alive, in a living relation to his disciples. This could only be supplied by the resurrection appearances of Jesus himself. Without such an experience it would be difficult to account for the disciples' conviction that, despite his accursed death by crucifixion, he was the agent of God's revelation. In Luke (and even more so in Mark) the scene at the empty tomb is marked by a splendid reversal of circumstances: the women go to the tomb equipped to deal with death and a dead body, but find instead living witnesses to someone who is alive, and no body requiring their services. God is one move ahead. Luke emphasizes that the women who had witnessed Jesus' death (23^{49}) and his burial (23^{55-6}) now believed that the only remaining duty was to complete the funeral rites: he thus rules out fabrication or hallucination on their part.

on the first day of the week: the day after the Sabbath, later called 'the Lord's day' (Rev. 1^{10}; cp. Acts 20^{7}). The women set out as soon as there was sufficient light to see their way.

Luke makes no mention of the difficulties of rolling back the stone.

of the Lord Jesus (RSV margin) is probably a later clarification. *not find the body*: despite the fact that they knew where to look (23^{55}). Although it would have been important evidence against the Christians, no body, whether that of Jesus or one purporting to be his, was ever found.

perplexed: about the absence of the corpse. Resurrection, the idea that Jesus had come to life again by a resuscitation of his body, or by his body being taken up into a higher existence, was not the only explanation. The body could have been stolen (cp. Matt. 27^{64}, 28^{13}; John 20^{13}). *behold, two men*; perhaps Moses and Elijah; see above, *in dazzling apparel* suggests non-earthly beings.

5 dazzling apparel; and as they were frightened and bowed
their faces to the ground, the men said to them, 'Why do you
6 seek the living among the dead?[t] Remember how he told you,
7 while he was still in Galilee, that the Son of man must be
delivered into the hands of sinful men, and be crucified, and
8, 9 on the third day rise.' And they remembered his words, and
returning from the tomb they told all this to the eleven and to
10 all the rest. Now it was Mary Magdalene and Joanna and
Mary the mother of James and the other women with them
11 who told this to the apostles; but these words seemed to them
an idle tale, and they did not believe them.[u]

[t] Other ancient authorities add *He is not here, but has risen*

[u] Other ancient authorities add verse 12, *But Peter rose and ran to the tomb; stooping and looking in, he saw the linen cloths by themselves; and he went home wondering at what had happened*

---

5 The women knew themselves to be in the presence of the supernatural. The *dead* were often thought to be confined to Sheol and to have no influence in the affairs of men. Jesus still belongs to the *living*—those whose power in human affairs is still effective. The addition in RSV margin is probably due to Mark.

6–7 Instead of Mark's 'he is going before you into Galilee.' Luke has *while he was still in Galilee*, a change supposed to reflect Luke's intention of recording appearances of Jesus in Jerusalem rather than Galilee. Luke may, however, be drawing on a variant tradition: present happenings make sense in the light of Jesus' long-standing prediction, which had never been understood, and had been forgotten in the shattering circumstances that had arisen. In Jesus' predictions of his coming death *crucified* and *sinful* are not used ($9^{22, 44}$, 18^{31-33}), but here a rough summary is given. *third day*: here a literal fact. *remember*: cp. 22^{62}; Acts 20^{25}.

9 Cp. Matt. 28^{8}; contrast Mark 16^{8} (the women's initial reaction). *the eleven*: the twelve now lacked Judas.

10 A better translation would be: 'They [i.e. the women of v. 9] were Mary Magdalene . . . James: and the rest of the women with them kept saying these things to the apostles.' The picture is probably that of the rest of the women pressing home the points made by the first three. *mother of James*: strictly 'daughter of' or 'wife of', the translation in the text being influenced by Mark 16^{1}. The identity of James is uncertain.

11 The scepticism about Jesus' resurrection is likely to be historical,

13 That very day two of them were going to a village named
14 Emmaus, about seven miles[v] from Jerusalem, and talking
with each other about all these things that had happened.

[v] Greek *sixty stadia*; some ancient authorities read *a hundred and sixty stadia*

---

as it had no place in Jewish expectations about the expected Saviour-king. The disciples had to be convinced in the face of their own deep scepticism, an important piece of early Christian apologetic (cp. Matt. 28^{17}; Mark 16^{11-13}; John 20^{25}; see also 24^{22-24} below).

12 This verse (given in RSV margin) is probably an interpolation based on John 20^{3-7}.

4: 13–35 The first resurrection appearance of Jesus

The story, only found in Luke, is probably drawn from a special literary source. The vocabulary contains words found only here, or very rarely, in Luke: e.g. 'talking . . . discussing together' (v. 15), 'holding' (v. 17), 'sad' (v. 17), 'amazed' (v. 22), 'slow' (v. 25), 'interpreted' (v. 27), 'appeared' (v. 28), 'constrained' (v. 29). There are also certain constructions and expressions unusual in Luke: e.g. 'one' (v. 18), 'how' (v. 20), 'yes, and besides all this' (v. 21), 'burn' (v. 32). The story is written in a good literary style and is vividly told. It is marked by a dramatic reversal of circumstances: the disciples' gloom is changed to happiness (vv. 17; 22), and the unrecognized Jesus is finally recognized (vv. 16; 31, 35). The story aims at showing how it was brought home to the disciples that Jesus was still their living leader (he is recognized in the act that he had performed so often for them, v. 30). Further, a right understanding of the O.T. makes it reasonable to believe that one who has suffered and been raised from the dead can fulfil the role of the expected Messiah—an important feature of early Christian apologetic.

3 *two of them*: not necessarily from the eleven. *about seven miles*: lit. 'sixty stadia' (RSV margin), a stade being about 607 English feet. The possibilities for the site of Emmaus are: (*a*) the Emmaus of Maccabaean times, later Nicopolis, and now 'Anwas, which would appear to be too far from Jerusalem (the alternative reading 'a hundred and sixty stadia' (RSV margin) may be an attempt to make the equation easier); (*b*) the present day El-Kubêbe; (*c*) the later military colony of Vespasian, called Ammaus (Josephus, *Jewish War*, vii. 217, where a variant reading gives the distance from Jerusalem as 64 stades).

all these things: the death of Jesus.

8369107 T

15 While they were talking and discussing together, Jesus him-
16 self drew near and went with them. But their eyes were kept
17 from recognizing him. And he said to them, 'What is this
conversation which you are holding with each other as you
18 walk?' And they stood still, looking sad. Then one of them,
named Cleopas, answered him, 'Are you the only visitor to
Jerusalem who does not know the things that have happened
19 there in these days?' And he said to them, 'What things?'
And they said to him, 'Concerning Jesus of Nazareth, who
was a prophet mighty in deed and word before God and all
20 the people, and how our chief priests and rulers delivered
1 him up to be condemned to death, and crucified him. But
we had hoped that he was the one to redeem Israel. Yes, and
besides all this, it is now the third day since this happened.
22 Moreover, some women of our company amazed us. They
23 were at the tomb early in the morning and did not find
his body; and they came back saying that they had even seen
24 a vision of angels, who said that he was alive. Some of those

---

16 *their eyes were kept* implies a divine withdrawal of sight (cp. Isa. 44^{18}). The implication is that the appearance of Jesus was different from his earthly one (cp. John 20^{14}). Perhaps his identity can only become clear in the performance of the familiar action of v. 30.

18 *Cleopas* (a Greek name) is short for Cleopatros. A Jewish form of the name occurs at John 19^{25}; it is uncertain whether the two people are identical. The question can also be translated: 'Are you the only one living in Jerusalem . . .?' or 'Have you been staying by yourself in Jerusalem, seeing that you do not know . . .?'

19 *before . . . people*: Jesus had the stamp of divine authority upon him and received some popular respect.

21 *it is now the third day*: the events are old news, yet they are about to become fresh, with Jesus' appearance to them, alive and undefeated.

23 Again the absence of the body is stressed. The 'two men' of 24^{4} are now described as angels.

24 Cp. John 20^{1-10}. Again the problem of the missing body is posed.

who were with us went to the tomb, and found it just as the
25 women had said; but him they did not see.' And he said to
them, 'O foolish men, and slow of heart to believe all that the
26 prophets have spoken! Was it not necessary that the Christ
27 should suffer these things and enter into his glory?' And
beginning with Moses and all the prophets, he interpreted to
them in all the scriptures the things concerning himself.

28 So they drew near to the village to which they were going.
29 He appeared to be going further, but they constrained him,
saying, 'Stay with us, for it is toward evening and the day is
now far spent.' So he went in to stay with them.

30 When he was at table with them, he took the bread and
31 blessed, and broke it, and gave it to them. And their eyes
were opened and they recognized him; and he vanished out
32 of their sight. They said to each other, 'Did not our hearts

---

5 *foolish*: out of touch with God's purposes. *slow of heart*: not ready to commit themselves. The death and resurrection of Jesus had to be shown to be in line with the O.T., and so part of God's plans. Jewish exegesis would not be tied to the original context of passages.

6 *necessary*: in accordance with God's plans. *enter into his glory*: assume his regal majesty, i.e. at his resurrection (cp. John 17^{5}; 1 Pet. 1^{11}). The Messiah's sufferings are not incompatible with his glory and kingship.

all the scriptures: including *Moses* (the Pentateuch) and the prophetic writings, but also containing 'the rest of the writings' (Ecclus., Prologue), e.g. the Psalms and Wisdom literature. Apart from Isa. 52^{13}–53^{12}, other relevant texts were probably parts of Psalms 16, 22, 69, and 110. The sufferings of the prophets would also probably be seen as types of the suffering of the Messiah.

This could mean either that Cleopas and his fellow disciple lived in the village, or that they were going to stay at an inn there.

Jesus, though the invited guest, performs the duty of the host who would preside at table. Perhaps this unexpected action made the others see that this was no ordinary guest. The connection of the risen Jesus with the breaking of bread would facilitate the subsequent idea of Jesus' presence with his followers at the Lord's Supper (1 Cor. 10^{14-22}).

eyes were opened: in the sense of recognition and understanding.

our hearts burn: with new hope and encouragement. The thrill that

burn within us while he talked to us on the road, while he
33 opened to us the scriptures?' And they rose that same hour
and returned to Jerusalem; and they found the eleven
34 gathered together and those who were with them, who said,
'The Lord has risen indeed, and has appeared to Simon!'
35 Then they told what had happened on the road, and how he
was known to them in the breaking of the bread.
36 As they were saying this, Jesus himself stood among them.[w]
37 But they were startled and frightened, and supposed that they
38 saw a spirit. And he said to them, 'Why are you troubled, and
39 why do questionings rise in your hearts? See my hands and

[w] Other ancient authorities add *and said to them, 'Peace to you!'*

---

they experienced as the unknown stranger made sense of events was now explained by their recognition of Jesus. *opened*: explained.

33 *the same hour*: without delay, even if it meant a journey in the darkness.

34 For the appearance to *Simon* cp. 1 Cor. 15^5.

35 *in*: by the action of.

24: 36–43 Another resurrection appearance.

Cp. John 20^{19-23}. Some of the resurrection stories stress that, though Jesus now belongs to a different order of existence from that of his earthly humanity, he yet retains material characteristics (cp. v. 39, 'flesh and bones'). Perhaps Jesus during the time of his appearance to his disciples had to adopt such a form in order to make himself known to them. The important point, however, is not the description of the risen Jesus, but the conviction of the disciples that the crucified Jesus was alive and capable of a living relationship with them. The passage stresses the unwillingness of the disciples to believe the truth (cp. vv. 11–12), and also the real personality of Jesus.

36 The addition in RSV margin is probably an assimilation to John 20^{19}.

37 The spirits or ghost of those who had died young or had met a violent death were sometimes supposed to return to earth and haunt people that had known them.

39 *hands . . . feet* are mentioned probably not because they bore the marks of crucifixion (John 20^{24-27}), but because they point to Jesus as being a real human being, and not a ghost (cp. also vv. 42–43).

my feet, that it is I myself; handle me, and see; for a spirit
41 has not flesh and bones as you see that I have.'[x] And while
they still disbelieved for joy, and wondered, he said to them,
42 'Have you anything here to eat?' They gave him a piece of
43 broiled fish, and he took it and ate before them.
44 Then he said to them, 'These are my words which I spoke
to you, while I was still with you, that everything written
about me in the law of Moses and the prophets and the psalms
45 must be fulfilled.' Then he opened their minds to understand
46 the scriptures, and said to them, 'Thus it is written, that the

[x] Other ancient authorities add verse 40, *And when he had said this, he showed them his hands and his feet*

---

40 This verse (see RSV margin) is an assimilation to John 20^{19}.
41 *joy*: it was too good to be true.

4: 44–53 Jesus' final instructions

Cp. Matt. 28^{16-20}; John 20^{21-23}, 21^{15-25}; Acts 1^{1-11}. The passage is found only in Luke.

4 *these are my words . . . you*: 'this is what I meant when I said to you'. Jesus had claimed a role in God's purposes—a role to be found in the O.T., and now *fulfilled* in the events that have happened. *must*: as part of the divine plan.

7 *and that repentance . . . name*: the mission of Jesus has been concerned with the search of God for humanity, with the demonstration of his love, and with his offer of forgiveness, and Jesus' kingship is seen in the victorious accomplishment of this kind of mission. The task of the disciples will, therefore, be to proclaim the consequences of this kingship: (*a*) the need for *repentance*, an active response to God's approach, and the change of outlook that goes with it, both to be symbolized in the rite of baptism (cp. Acts 2^{38}); (*b*) the *forgiveness of sins*, the restoration of the broken relationship between God and human beings. *all nations*: the relevance of Jesus to non-Jews has already been hinted at in the Gospel, and becomes the main theme of Acts. *in his name*: on Jesus' authority, now vindicated by his resurrection. Verse 47 is not strictly Jesus' command, but is dependent on *it is written* (v. 46). Perhaps the many calls of the prophets to the people of Israel to repent are here reapplied to the mission of *the Christ*, together with passages where God promises forgiveness of the nation's sins (e.g.

Christ should suffer and on the third day rise from the dead,
47 and that repentance and forgiveness of sins should be preached
48 in his name to all nations,[y] beginning from Jerusalem. You
49 are witnesses of these things. And behold, I send the promise
of my Father upon you; but stay in the city, until you are
clothed with power from on high.'
50 Then he led them out as far as Bethany, and lifting up
51 his hands he blessed them. While he blessed them, he

[y] Or *nations. Beginning from Jerusalem you are witnesses*

Jer. 31^{31-34}) and where God's favour to other nations besides Israel is recorded (e.g. Isa. 56^{7}). *beginning from Jerusalem* could also be a command, or could go with v. 48 (RSV margin).

48 The disciples, a community formed by Jesus to await God's decisive intervention, are now, like witnesses in a law court, to give their testimony to what has happened (cp. 21^{13}; Acts 1^{8}). This is possible because they have been eye-witnesses to the events (1^{1-4}; Acts 1^{22}).

49 *the promise*, or 'the promised gift': the Holy Spirit, promised by God in O.T. prophecy, by John the Baptist, and by Jesus (Joel 2^{28}; Luke 3^{16}, 12^{12}). *I send*, i.e. from God's presence, underlines the authority of the risen Jesus. He can do this (*a*) as the one who has initiated God's new era, and, therefore, brought into being the situation of Joel 2^{28}; (*b*) as the one in whom the Holy Spirit has found perfect expression (cp. 3^{16}), and who has now triumphed and so can pass the Holy Spirit to others; and (*c*) as the one whose special relationship to God, expressed in the words *my Father*, is now confirmed (see also Gal. 4^{2-6}; Eph. 1^{13}). *but stay in the city*: until God's appointed time. For *clothed* and *power* cp. Ps. 93^{1}; Isa. 51^{9}, 52^{1}. *from on high*: from God. In Acts 1 Luke describes how the disciples obeyed this command and remained inactive until the clear demonstration of God's power at the feast of Pentecost (Acts 2).

50–51 Is this parting of Jesus from his disciples a reference (*a*) to the ascension, in the sense of Acts 1^{9-10}, marking the end of the visible appearances of the risen Jesus, or (*b*) to a parting after a resurrection appearance? If 'and was carried up into heaven' (RSV margin) is part of the original text, then the reference is to (*a*); if it is omitted, as an early attempt to bring the incident into line with Acts 1^{9-11}, then (*b*) would be possible, but improbable, as *parted*, preceded by the

52 parted from them.[z] And they[a] returned to Jerusalem with
53 great joy, and were continually in the temple blessing God.

[z] Other ancient authorities add *and was carried up into heaven*
[a] Other ancient authorities add *worshipped him, and*

---

formal blessing of the disciples, suggests a final parting. The problem of the relation between the end of the Gospel and the beginning of Acts then arises, with two possibilities: (*a*) at the end of the Gospel Luke merely summarizes the closing stage of Jesus' earthly ministry, while in Acts 1 he recapitulates and expands his account of it; (*b*) Luke is placing two sources side by side without synchronizing them. *Bethany* has been associated with the state entry of Jesus into Jerusalem (19^{28}), and is now the scene of another regal triumph; again, just as Bethany is the starting-point for Jesus' entry into Jerusalem, his occupation of the temple and his teaching there, so now from the same village the disciples return to Jerusalem and make the temple their centre of praise.

52 At the end of the Gospel Christianity is represented by a small group of people in that politically and geographically unimportant place, Jerusalem; at the end of Acts, the new faith is firmly rooted in the capital of the Roman Empire. *great joy*, together with 'blessing God' (v. 53), brings the Gospel to a conclusion on a note that has been prevalent throughout. 'worshipped him, and' (RSV margin) is often regarded as a later addition to the text.

53 *in the temple*: the Gospel ends where it began (1^{5}). For the Christians' use of the temple see also Acts 2^{46}, 3^{1}, 5^{25}. Like their master, they put the temple to its proper use.

INDEX